MODERNIZING MINDS
IN EL SALVADOR

SERIES ADVISORY EDITOR:
Lyman L. Johnson,
University of North Carolina at Charlotte

Modernizing Minds in El Salvador

Education Reform and the Cold War, 1960–1980

HÉCTOR LINDO-FUENTES
ERIK CHING

UNIVERSITY OF NEW MEXICO PRESS

Albuquerque

Printed in the United States of America

17 16 15 14 13 12   1 2 3 4 5 6

LIBRARY OF CONGRESS CATALOGING-IN-PUBLICATION DATA

Lindo-Fuentes, Héctor, 1952–

Modernizing minds in El Salvador : education reform and
the Cold War, 1960–1980 / Héctor Lindo-Fuentes and Erik Ching.
    p. cm. — (Diálogos)
Includes bibliographical references and index.
ISBN 978-0-8263-5081-7 (pbk.: alk. paper)
ISBN 978-0-8263-5082-4 (electronic)

    1. Television in education—El Salvador.
    2. Educational change—El Salvador.
    3. Education and state—El Salvador—History.
    4. El Salvador—History—1944–1979.
    I. Ching, Erik Kristofer.
    II. Title.

LC6581.S2L56 2012
379.7284—dc23

                         2011042860

BOOK DESIGN
Composed in 10.25/13.5 Minion Pro Regular
Display type is Minion Pro

Contents

Illustrations
vii

Tables
viii

Preface
ix

Abbreviations
xiii

INTRODUCTION
1

CHAPTER 1
A Fight Within the Right:
Rivaling Visions of Modernization
29

CHAPTER 2
Modernizing Reform and Anticommunist Repression:
The First PCN Administration, 1961–1967
71

CHAPTER 3

"A Monitor Instead of a Teacher":
The Origins of the 1968 Education Reform and
How Television Became Its Centerpiece
103

CHAPTER 4

"A Feverish Laboratory": The Education Reform of 1968
137

CHAPTER 5

Modernization Projects and Authoritarian Practices in the 1970s
183

CHAPTER 6

"The Most Thoroughly Studied Educational
Technology Project in the World"
227

CONCLUSION
253

NOTES
271

BIBLIOGRAPHY
313

INDEX
333

Illustrations

～e

FIGURE 1. Celebrating the Revolution of 1948 in *Boletín del Ejército*, 1950   4

FIGURE 2. School, circa 1925   36

FIGURE 3. Celebrating the 1950 Constitution   49

FIGURE 4. Herblock editorial cartoon of the United States and Latin America, *Washington Post*, 1960   58

FIGURE 5. Editorial cartoon on rent control in *El Popular*, 1961   63

FIGURE 6. Anticommunist flier distributed by the Unión Democrática, 1960   65

FIGURE 7. Image from a story on the 1932 uprising, *El Diario de Hoy*, 1967   75

FIGURE 8. Herblock editorial cartoon of class inequity in Latin America, *Washington Post*, 1962   81

FIGURE 9. Organizational chart of the teachers' movement, 1964 or 1965   95

FIGURE 10. Newspaper image of teachers protesting the government's proposed retirement law, 1965   96

FIGURE 11. Salvadoran officials meeting with international aid experts, front page of *El Diario de Hoy*, 1961   106

FIGURE 12. Nando editorial cartoon on education administration, 1961   112

FIGURE 13. Image accompanying story about educational television in Japan and Italy, *UNESCO Courier*, 1964   128

FIGURE 14. Newspaper image of Béneke and his helicopter that he used to gain access to the offices of the Ministry of Education, 1968   144

FIGURE 15. Newspaper image of teachers marching during the
1968 ANDES strike   152

FIGURE 16. Newspaper image of ANDES leaders entering their
meeting with President Sánchez Hernández, 1968   155

FIGURE 17. President Sánchez Hernández, President Johnson,
and Minister Béneke during the inauguration of the
educational television studios, 1968   164

FIGURE 18. Illustration in seventh-grade textbook about the
Central American Common Market   176

FIGURE 19. Illustration in seventh-grade textbook comparing
traditional and modern life   178

FIGURE 20. Government advertisement portraying ANDES
leaders as being communists, 1971   206

FIGURE 21. President Molina's populist style, 1973   213

FIGURE 22. Foundations of former homes exposed by low water
levels of Lake Suchitlán, 2008   217

FIGURE 23. Newspaper image of National Guardsmen with
sugarcane workers, 1973   220

FIGURE 24. Television sets stacked in a trash heap outside a
former school, 2007   249

FIGURE 25. Mural from El Cenícero depicting the massacre of
Copapayo Viejo in 1983   255

Tables

TABLE 4.1. Main Elements of the 1968 Education Reform   160

TABLE 4.2. School Enrollment in 1967, Public and Private   162

TABLE 4.3. Middle School Enrollment, 1967–1971   169

TABLE 4.1. School Enrollment, 1967–1977   233

TABLE 4.2. Cost per Student, 1973   237

Preface

✦ OUR DECISION TO WORK TOGETHER ON THE PRESENT PROJECT GREW OUT
of the positive experience we had on a prior one, *Remembering a Massacre
in El Salvador*, also published by the University of New Mexico Press. When
El Salvador's Ministry of Education launched an education reform in the
1990s in conjunction with the World Bank, memories of and references to
past reforms arose. Naturally, the highly impactive and deeply controversial reform of 1968 became a reference point. The 1968 reform is sometimes
referred to in local settings as "the Béneke reform," after its architect, Minister
of Education Walter Béneke. For many years the 1968 reform was one of the
most talked about projects in the country. Throughout the late 1960s and into
the mid-1970s, it was in public discourse almost daily. One of its most heavily debated components was educational television, the plan to teach students
with lectures broadcast from a central location to television sets in classrooms throughout the country. Béneke envisioned that eventually almost the
entirety of the curriculum would be delivered to almost every student by television. But once the nation began descending into civil war in the late 1970s,
the education reform, as so many other things in El Salvador, took a back seat
in the public consciousness to more immediate, life-and-death issues. Indeed,
key players in the education reform became actively involved in the conflict,
and many of them lost their lives, including Béneke, who was assassinated by
guerrillas in 1980. By the time the war was over, the education reform was
rarely discussed outside of the confines of education circles.

Having been reminded of the 1968 reform, our curiosity as historians
was piqued. What had happened to the reform? Had it achieved its goals?
What was the legacy of such a dramatic manipulation of education practices,
however short-lived it might have been? Seeking answers to these questions,
we began mapping out a research agenda.

As with any study, our original agenda morphed and evolved in unexpected ways. We quickly learned that the 1968 reform was deeply enmeshed into El Salvador's domestic environment as well as the international setting of the Cold War and developmental aid. In pursuing those interconnecting storylines, we ran into multiple historiographic traditions and a plethora of new questions and lines of research.

We have incurred many debts, personal and financial, during the completion of this study. Our respective institutions, Fordham University and Furman University, have supported us in countless ways but specifically in the form of leaves and financial support for research. This project would be much weaker without our interviews. The interviewees are too numerous to mention individually (please see the bibliography), so we would like to acknowledge their collective generosity and graciousness in granting us time and access to their personal stories. A few interviewees merit special mention. The late Gilberto Aguilar Avilés, one of the key players in the Ministry of Education during the Sánchez Hernández administration, was very generous with his time and gave the invaluable perspective of an insider. We remember him fondly. Julio César Portillo not only granted us a lengthy interview but also provided us with a copy of his unpublished memoir. Special mention also needs to be made of Wilmer Erroa, who in addition to granting us an interview arranged additional meetings for us. More often than not it was the willingness of one interviewee to put us in contact with an acquaintance that led us to our next interview, so our research became dependent upon them in more ways than one. Meeting with each of them was the most rewarding aspect of the experience of the project, and for each of us it whetted our appetite for researching El Salvador's recent past.

Fellow academics in El Salvador have been supportive of us not only in this project but also throughout our careers of working on Salvadoran history. We would single out Carlos Gregorio López Bernal at the University of El Salvador and also Knut Walter, who has been a colleague, collaborator, and sage on things Salvadoran for too many years to count. Also Carlos Henríquez Consalvi, "Santiago," merits special mention. In addition to being a general supporter of our research, specifically he and his museum (the Museo de la Palabra y la Imagen—MUPI) in San Salvador acquired the collection of Adolfo Flores Cienfuegos during the late stage of this project. He immediately sought us out and generously shared the contents of that collection with us. Our research assistants in El Salvador, Alfredo Ramírez and Allan Martell, were invariably efficient, sending us copies and photographs of newspapers and magazines. In the United States our colleagues at conferences and on panels have stimulated our thoughts with incisive questions and apt suggestions. Michael Latham gave us useful suggestions for the section on modernization theory. John Hammond and Margaret Crahan commented on early versions of the project. The anonymous reviewers of the manuscript directed us to important scholarship.

For providing financial assistance to support research and/or writing, Lindo would like to thank specifically the deans of Fordham University who provided support in the form of a faculty fellowship sabbatical. Ching would like to thank specifically the Research and Professional Growth (RPG) Committee of Furman University, the Associated Colleges of the South and its Mellon Foundation–backed Faculty Renewal Program, and the Council of International Education Exchange's (CIEE) Fulbright Program.

This is the second book we have done for the Diálogos series of the University of New Mexico Press, and thus it is the second time we have had the opportunity to work with series editor Lyman Johnson. In both instances he proved to be a meticulous and insightful reader of our work. His diligence and insights improved both manuscripts more than we can describe here. The editor-in-chief at UNM Press, Clark Whitehorn, has been a continual supporter, and we thank him. We would also like to thank the anonymous peer reviewer who provided us with an encouraging review and directed our attention to additional historiographic materials. Professor emerita of English at Furman University Judy Bainbridge gave our manuscript one of its first reads and thus steered us away from some of our most egregious errors. We thank her for her time and analysis. Last but not least, we would like to thank Joy Margheim for a diligent and detailed copyedit that improved the manuscript in many ways.

The personnel of the libraries at our respective institutions deserve separate mention. We are convinced that the world is a better place thanks to the system of interlibrary loan. American librarians are the unsung heroes of the academic enterprise. In El Salvador we owe special thanks to the personnel of the Biblioteca del Museo Nacional David J. Guzman and of the Biblioteca "P. Florentino Idoate, S.J." at the Universidad Centroamericana "José Simeón Cañas." In Paris the personnel of the UNESCO Archive were extremely helpful, in particular Jens Boel, the archive director.

Finally, it goes without saying, but it must still be said, that we could never have done this without the support of friends and family. Ching would like to acknowledge the support of his spouse, Cathy Stevens, who bore many of the hidden costs that went into seeing this through to completion, especially after the arrival of Anders in 2008 and Halle in 2010.

Abbreviations

AGEUS Asociación General de Estudiantes Universitarios Salvadoreños (Association of University Students at the National University)

ANDES Asociación Nacional de Educadores Salvadoreños (National Association of Salvadoran Educators)

ANEP Asociación Nacional de la Empresa Privada (National Association of Private Enterprise)

ANSESAL Agencia Nacional de Seguridad de El Salvador (National Security Agency)

APNES Asociación de Profesores Normalistas de Secundaria (Association of Secondary School Teachers)

ARENA Alianza Republicana Nacionalista (Nationalist Republican Alliance)

ASI Asociación Salvadoreña de Industriales (Salvadoran Industrial Association)

BPR Bloque Popular Revolucionario (Revolutionary Popular Block)

CEL Comisión Ejecutiva Hidroeléctrica del Río Lempa (Hydroelectric Executive Committee of the Lempa River)

CETO Centre for Educational Television Overseas, UK

CGS Confederación General Salvadoreña (General Confederation of Salvadoran Unions)

CGTS Confederación General de Trabajadores Salvadoreños (General Confederation of Salvadoran Workers)

CIS Center for International Studies, MIT

CONAPLAN Consejo Nacional de Planificación (National Planning Council)

ECLA UN Economic Commission for Latin America

ERP Ejército Revolucionario del Pueblo (People's Revolutionary Army)

FAO Food and Agriculture Organization of the United Nations

FAPU Frente de Acción Popular Unificada (Unified Popular Action Front)

FARO Frente Agrario de la Región Oriental (Agrarian Front of the Eastern Region)

FECCAS Federación Cristiana de Campesinos Salvadoreños (Christian Federation of Salvadoran Peasants)

FESTIAVTCES Federación Sindical de Trabajadores de la Industria de Alimentos, Vestidos, y Similares de El Salvador (Federation of Workers in Food, Clothing, Textiles, and Related Industries)

FMLN Frente Farabundo Martí para la Liberación Nacional (Farabundo Martí National Liberation Front)

FMR Frente Magisterial Revolucionario (Teachers' Revolutionary Front)

FMS Federación Magisterial Salvadoreña (Salvadoran Teachers' Federation)

FPL Fuerzas Populares de Liberación Farabundo Martí (Farabundo Martí Popular Liberation Forces)

FUAR Frente Unido de Acción Revolucionaria (United Front for Revolutionary Action)

FUDI Frente Unido Democrático Independiente (Democratic Independent United Front)

FUSS Federación Unitaria Sindical de El Salvador (Unitary Federation of Salvadoran Unions)

ILO International Labor Organization

IMF International Monetary Fund

IMPRESS Instituto Magisterial de Prestaciones Sociales (Teachers' Institute for Social Welfare)

INA Instituto Nacional Agrario, Honduras (National Agrarian Institute)

IRI Index of Rural Instability

MAP Military Assistance Program, United States

MNR Movimiento Nacional Revolucionario (National Revolutionary Movement)

NHK Nippon Hōsō Kyōkai (Japanese Broadcasting Corporation)

OAS Organization of American States

ODECA Organización de Estados Centroamericanos (Organization of Central American States)

ORDEN Organización Democrática Nacionalista (Nationalist Democratic Organization)

OWI Office of War Information, United States

PAR Partido de Acción Renovadora (Party of Renovating Action)

PCN Partido de Conciliación Nacional (National Conciliation Party)

PCS Partido Comunista Salvadoreño (Salvadoran Communist Party)

PDC Partido Demócrata Cristiano (Christian Democratic Party)

PPS Partido Popular Salvadoreño (Salvadoran Popular Party)

PRI Partido Revolucionario Institucional, Mexico (Institutional Revolutionary Party)

PRUD Partido Revolucionario de Unificación Democrática (Revolutionary Party of Democratic Unification)

RN Resistencia Nacional (National Resistance)

ROCAP Regional Office for Central America and Panama, USAID

TVE Televisión Educativa (Educational Television)

UCA Universidad Centroamericana "José Simeón Cañas" (Central American University)

UCS Unión Comunal Salvadoreña (Communal Union of El Salvador)

UES Universidad Nacional de El Salvador (National University of El Salvador)

UMS Unión Magisterial Salvadoreña (Salvadoran Teachers' Union)
UNESCO United Nations Educational, Scientific, and Cultural Organization
UNO Unión Nacional Opositora (National Opposition Union)
UPI United Press International

USAID United States Agency for International Development
USIA United States Information Agency
USIS United States Information Service
USOM United States Operations Mission
WHO World Health Organization

ABBREVIATIONS IN THE NOTES AND BIBLIOGRAPHY

AGN Archivo General de la Nación, San Salvador, El Salvador
DOS-IAES United States Department of State, Records Relating to the Internal Affairs of El Salvador
IHNCA Instituto de Historia de Nicaragua y Centroamérica (Institute of Nicaragua and

Central American History), Managua, Nicaragua
MG Ministerio de Gobernación (Ministry of Interior)
MUPI Museo de la Palabra y la Imagen, San Salvador, El Salvador (Museum of Word and Image)
USNA United States National Archives, Washington, D.C.

Introduction

~~~

In a small, densely populated country, poor in natural resources, there is no possibility for economic development except through intense and rational improvement of its human capital.
—President Fidel Sánchez Hernández, 1971*

The question is what to do about the matter.
—Former U.S. ambassador to El Salvador
Thorsten Kalijarvi, 1962**

✢ PRESIDENT LYNDON JOHNSON HAD A LOT OF BAD DAYS IN 1968, BUT by all accounts July 7 was a welcome exception. He was on an official visit to El Salvador, where he had traveled to meet the presidents of the five member states of the Central American Common Market. On the morning of July 7, Johnson, together with Lady Bird and their daughter Luci Nugent, stepped into the presidential limousine and took off to the countryside. It was a pleasant, sunny Sunday. Johnson and his entourage visited a church, a market, and two schools. The approach of his long, black Lincoln Continental awed the locals, and by all accounts the U.S. president was greeted with enthusiasm. At lunchtime the first family picnicked with the Central American presidents at Los Chorros, a picturesque national park with lush vegetation, natural pools, and scenic waterfalls. Johnson spoke glowingly to the staff of the U.S. Embassy about the "smiles on the faces of the old women and the little boys and girls, the happiness and eagerness of expression on the faces" that greeted him along the way.[1]

The highlight of the day was a visit to the leafy campus of a teachers' training school, where Johnson inaugurated a U.S.-sponsored educational

1

television system. He told his audience, "Nothing we have discussed equals in importance—or in urgency—to the kind of work that you are doing here." He hailed the Salvadoran initiative as a model to be imitated; "you have already made the beginning to being the first nation in all the world with a complete educational television system. And some day we hope the United States can catch up with you."[2] After Johnson returned to Washington, D.C., he reiterated those sentiments to his cabinet members. He told them the "trip was well worth the weekend. Never—not even on the last night of a campaign, surrounded by my closest friends—have I experienced such a warm spirit of affection and hospitality." He went on to say that "the problems are many, and they are great . . . but there is no problem in Central America that money and resources cannot cure." He expressed his solution in the form of hope that "AID [United States Agency for International Development, USAID] and USIA [United States Information Agency] and the other agencies will follow up this effort, and help these Central American countries as they have helped other countries." But he concluded his summary of the trip with an ominous comment: "My most vivid impression is that there is so much to do—and so little time to do it." Perhaps that explains why Johnson's preparatory notes on the meeting include a proposal to put one of his highest-level foreign policy advisors on the task, the MIT economist and architect of modernization theory, W. W. Rostow.[3]

If July 7, 1968, was a good day for President Johnson, then it was a great day for his Salvadoran counterpart, President Fidel Sánchez Hernández. Playing host to the president of the United States and his four Central American counterparts provided Sánchez Hernández, barely a year into his administration, with a significant political boost. He had the opportunity to serve as a statesman and to see his pet project, educational television (Televisión Educativa—TVE), receive accolades. It must have been music to his ears to hear Johnson say that El Salvador set an example for the United States. By praising educational television, Johnson also celebrated the broader education reform that Sánchez Hernández had launched a few months earlier. The reform was generating plenty of controversy in El Salvador. Sánchez Hernández had staked both his legacy and his nation's future on it, so having the president of the United States come and focus on education was a public relations coup.

In this book we analyze modernization in El Salvador in the 1960s and 1970s with particular focus on the 1968 education reform and its core project, educational television. As Johnson's enthusiasm suggests, both Salvadoran and U.S. officials expected the reform and especially educational television to affect the nation well beyond the classroom. They intended for the newly designed education system to modernize the minds of Salvadoran youth and thereby propel the nation forward to industrialization and peaceful capitalist development. But as Johnson's trepidation suggests, both U.S. and Salvadoran officials believed that time was short, meaning that they interpreted failure as opening the door to opportunistic communists. At a most basic level, we study the 1968 education reform because it was a key event in recent Salvadoran history, on par with other modernization schemes, like land reform, yet it has received far less academic scrutiny. A central task in our study of education is to understand more thoroughly the origin and impact of modernization in El Salvador.

The 1968 education reform epitomized the modernizing ethos of a series of military-led governments that ruled El Salvador between 1961 and 1979 under the auspices of a new political party—the National Conciliation Party (PCN). The modernizing zeal of the PCN had its origins in the preceding era of military rule that began with a coup d'état in December 1948, the so-called Revolution of 1948. That coup brought to power a junta of three officers and two civilians who replaced President (and General) Salvador Castaneda Castro (1945–1948). The new leaders believed that Castaneda Castro continued the policies of the previous regime, the dictatorship of Gen. Maximiliano Hernández Martínez (1931–1944), and that those two administrations together had hindered El Salvador's march toward modern progress. In the words of the new leaders, Castaneda Castro's administration "continued a series of governments that for many years betrayed the will of the Salvadoran people, and once the people realized that those governments did not represent their interests nor allow them to realize their aspirations, they rejected them."[4] The "revolutionaries" saw themselves as a force for renewal, and they highlighted the generational distance between themselves and their predecessors by referring to themselves as the "military youth" (*juventud militar*). In their enthusiasm they compared themselves to the heroes of independence and spoke about the reformation of El Salvador. The nation, they claimed, ought to rest "on completely new foundations."[5]

As nationalists, the revolutionaries touted El Salvador's greatness and believed in its people's potential. As social reformers, however, they worried about the country's problems and looked to fix them. The main problem facing El Salvador, in their view, was that it was a small, densely populated nation with a monocrop economy built around coffee. Furthermore, they

FIGURE 1. An illustration in the *Boletín del Ejército* (Army bulletin) celebrating the Revolution of 1948 provides a masculine view of modernization. The figures stand on a map of El Salvador. An army soldier holds a torch that brings light to the country, while the wind wraps the Salvadoran flag around his body. A vigorous youth with a book under one arm and a working tool in the other looks to the horizon as if ready to march into the future. The figure lying on the ground represents the chained self that the youth has left behind or liberated with the help of the army. Doves with olive branches circle the figures. *Boletín del Ejército*, December 14, 1950, 1.

realized that the nation's coffee economy was dominated by a small number of rich, conservative families who owned the overwhelming majority of the nation's best land. The revolutionaries feared that unless they did something to restructure the economy, the rapidly growing population of rural poor would become a serious problem.

The revolutionaries drew upon new statistical evidence to support their views.[6] In 1950 a nationwide census showed that El Salvador had a population density of more than 250 people per square mile, making it second only to Haiti in the western hemisphere. The population was growing fast, at nearly 3 percent per year, and there were not many empty places to put them. No country in the western hemisphere was more deforested and heavily cultivated, except Haiti. The census also revealed the nation's stark inequities in wealth. The richest 8 percent of the population received more than half of the nation's annual income, while the poorest 60 percent received less than 20 percent of the national income.[7] With each passing year the divide between the haves and the have-nots increased. An agricultural census in 1961 showed that less than 1 percent of landowners controlled more than 50 percent of the nation's arable land and that almost 80 percent of landholders owned less than four acres each, far below the roughly ten acres necessary to sustain one family.[8]

Many Salvadorans shared the revolutionaries' opinion that the country needed to be modernized, but much debate ensued over how modernization was to occur and how far it should go. The revolutionaries were convinced that industrialization was necessary. They believed that a more modern industrial economy would dampen the semifeudal conditions of the countryside and squash support for radical alternatives. They were also convinced that the state had to lead the process of transformation because landed elites had little incentive to alter the status quo under their own volition.

When the new contingent of military leaders came to power in 1961 under the PCN, they confronted even more worrisome statistical trends than their "revolutionary" predecessors had faced.[9] In 1961 the share of rural families without any land stood at 12 percent. In one decade's time that figure rose to 29 percent, and by 1975 it hit 41 percent.[10] By 1980, 75 percent of rural Salvadorans lived in poverty, "without income sufficient to meet their basic needs," and more than half of rural residents lived in so-called extreme poverty, "without the income to pay for a minimum shopping-basket of food."[11]

The leaders of the PCN sought to improve the lot of Salvadorans. In doing so, they also wanted to defend the nation against communism and limit the influence of the Cuban Revolution. Their solution was to adopt an even more aggressive, muscular ethos of modernization than their "revolutionary" predecessors. From the perspective of the PCN leaders, the context of the heightening Cold War created an urgent need to do something to absorb landless labor, such as a land reform or the creation of manufacturing jobs. They feared social chaos would ensue if nothing were done to mitigate unemployment and economic disparity. And in the face of potential social chaos, PCN functionaries were more than willing to employ violence. The highly influential Jesuit scholar at San Salvador's Central American University (UCA), Father Ignacio Ellacuría, recognized these dichotomous qualities of the PCN. In discussing the government's response to the teachers' strike in 1971, he said the government exhibited a "hard handed tendency and intransigence, but also a tendency towards conciliatory compromise." [12]

The modernizing agenda of the Salvadoran military regime is generally acknowledged by scholars, but it gets lost in a metanarrative of civil war that has come to define conventional wisdom. According to this perspective, the causal variables in El Salvador's recent history are the conservative side of the military governments and their alliance with the landed elites. It highlights inequalities in land tenure, the negative impact of commercial agriculture, the increase in state repression, and a reactive popular mobilization. We agree that all those parts of the story are important and that they contributed greatly to the polarization of the 1960s and 1970s that culminated tragically in civil war (1980–1992). Yet the different administrations of the military regime were serious about changing the country and trying to avoid the looming catastrophe of societal meltdown. Their modernizing agenda was no mere sideshow, however poorly or well conceived it may have been. Each successive administration drew up ambitious plans and implemented them in one form or another. The 1968 education reform was one of the largest, most expensive, and most deeply impactive of all of the modernizing endeavors. Ultimately, our research into the education reform and the other modernizing programs of the 1960s and 1970s reveals a great irony. The military regime tried to use reforms to avoid revolution, but instead its reforms enflamed the opposition and precipitated societal collapse. [13]

The Ruling Bloc

A close examination of the 1968 education reform illustrates how the Salvadoran government interacted with economic elites in a concrete setting. Thus, it offers an opportunity to reexamine conventional wisdom on the alliance between the army and the oligarchy, or "the planter-army oligarchy," as *Time* put it in a 1959 article.[14] In the shorthand version of twentieth-century El Salvador, landed elites and the military formed an alliance in 1931 and ruled the country in concert for the next sixty years—actually, until the end of civil war in 1992, when the Peace Accords forced a restructuring of the state. According to most versions of the story, El Salvador's landowners surrendered government to the military as long as the ruling officers stuck to two basic principles: defend economic libertarianism and quell popular dissent.[15] The ideology of anticommunism held the system together, and anyone who veered from it was considered a threat and thus was expendable. The grandmother of an elite family explained the workings of the system to her grandson: "Don't forget. You were born rich and you'll die rich. You don't need to be in politics."[16]

For a small country that in the mid-nineteenth century looked every bit the case study of poverty and political instability, El Salvador had made impressive gains by the turn of the twentieth century. Its economy was growing rapidly. Coffee, which had been so much the engine of the economic turnaround, accounted for 90 percent of total exports by 1930 but receded in importance thereafter as the economy was diversified in response to government policies and market fluctuations.[17] By the time of the 1968 education reform, coffee accounted for 43.6 percent of exports. Its contribution to the economy was still large but was complemented by other agricultural commodities and manufactures.[18] Yet the oligarchy that had its origins in the golden age of coffee exports still had great power, in part because its members branched out into those other economic activities. An unequal distribution of income accompanied export-led growth throughout Latin America, but the problem was particularly acute in El Salvador.

El Salvador's elite landowning class credited itself for its country's prosperity. Its members portrayed themselves as civilizers who had brought economic rationality to the darkness of the Salvadoran countryside. They developed a rigid explanatory narrative around economic libertarianism to explain the country's turnaround and why they rightly controlled a disproportionate share of national wealth. The landowners claimed that they had created this wealth through their hard work and entrepreneurial spirit and thus they had a right to retain it. In their view, redistributive policies were inspired by communism and thus by definition were bad for the country. They said that one reason they had succeeded was because they had managed to keep government out of the economy and limit its focus to creating a safe environment for investment.[19]

The first officer to come to power during the modern era of military rule in El Salvador did so in a coup d'état in 1931 that overthrew the nation's lone democratically elected president, a social reformer named Arturo Araujo. The inaugural military president was Gen. Maximiliano Hernández Martínez, an appropriately stern, esoteric authoritarian. For the next fifty years, in one coup after another, military officers rotated in and out of office, some of them more congenial in personality than Hernández Martínez but all of them supposedly holding true to his values of authoritarianism and his close alliance with landed elites. In the descriptive words of historian Jeffrey Paige: "From the era of General Gerardo Barrios in the nineteenth century to the overthrow of President Arturo Araujo by General Maximiliano Hernández Martínez in the military coup of 9 December 1931, the coffee elite had ruled El Salvador almost without interruption. For the following sixty years, however, no member of the coffee elite occupied the Salvadoran presidency."[20] According to standard interpretations, the changing faces in government did not alter the continuity of rule. As one scholar puts it: "Martínez's regime forged an enduring alliance between the oligarchy and the military . . . this alliance agreed on the bottom line: the maintenance of the country's rigid class structure and its exclusionary political regime."[21]

Many different terms have been used to describe the military-elite alliance in El Salvador. One North American political scientist says that the state during that era can be defined in four mutually reinforcing ways: as an oligarchic-military alliance, as an arena of elite competition, as the product of class conflict, and as a counterinsurgency state.[22] Salvadoran historian Italo López Vallecillos calls the state "strongman conservatism" (*caciquismo conservador*), while another U.S. scholar, Enrique Baloyra, calls it "reactionary despotism." North American scholar Tommie Sue Montgomery says that the main purpose of the state was to maintain order, while sociologist Jeff Goodwin talks about institutional authoritarianism and elite backing for military rule. Political scientist Bill Stanley coined the term "Protection Racket State" to describe the landowner-military alliance.[23] In general these scholars portray the relationship between the economic elite and the army as a defining feature of the state.[24]

None of those scholars is so naïve as to assume the relationship to be friction free, and many of them recognize the modernizing aspects of the military regime. They observe that the landowner-military alliance was "riven by divergent interests" and that "the state is not a unitary actor but a collection of competing groups, institutions and factions."[25] But such concessions tend to be subsumed by the prevailing paradigm: "the military earned the concession to govern the country . . . in exchange for its willingness to use violence against the class enemies of the country's . . . elite."[26]

There are many good reasons to accept the standard narrative of the landowner-military alliance. Not the least is the degree of state-sponsored repression against the civilian population. After 1931 the Salvadoran state demonstrated a horrifying capacity to employ violence against its own people. The most explicit example was the 1932 Matanza, or massacre, when the state killed thousands of people throughout western El Salvador in response to a short-lived peasant uprising. Throughout the ensuing years the state used violence recurrently, whether through formal military units, informal paramilitaries, or secretive, so-called death squads. In Stanley's words, "In per capita terms, Salvadoran state terror was among the most severe in the hemisphere."[27]

Another reason to accept the standard narrative is the extent to which conservative politics have held sway in El Salvador. Whereas almost every country in Latin America has had at least one bona fide leftist or progressive government come to power, El Salvador has had virtually none. Until the 2009 victory of the Frente Farabundo Martí para Liberación Nacional (FMLN)—the former guerrilla army turned political party—El Salvador had been ruled by civilian elites or military officers who relied upon highly exclusive systems of rule. On the rare occasions when progressive challenges arose, such as in 1931, 1944, and 1960, conservatives closed ranks and beat them back. In short, El Salvador is a country where the right has ruled almost unabated, and the backbone of that system after 1931 would seem to have been an alliance between landowners and the military.

Among the scholars who question the prevailing approach is Salvadoran historian Jorge Cáceres Prendes. In his study of politics in the 1950s, Cáceres Prendes sees divergent opinions within both the military and the elites. He admits that a strong tendency of unifying conservatism existed, but so too did important divergences. Failure to appreciate them, Cáceres Prendes claims, has resulted in an overly deterministic understanding of El Salvador. He clarifies his approach in a description of elite views regarding investment options in the 1950s: "what existed in the early 1950's were less actual 'factions' than 'options' or 'tendencies' regarding capitalist investment and accumulation. Some capitalists, with or without strong roots in the traditional agriculture sector had already begun investing in manufactures years before, and there was already a certain degree of 'specialization by sectors' but also considerable 'mix,' so when the modernizing wave began hitting with increasing force in the 1950's all Salvadoran capitalists, were offered diverse investment options, and reacted to these (and to related government policy) in one way or another through time."[28] Cáceres Prendes sees a similar situation in the army, arguing that "it would be misleading to accept, without qualification, that the military as such acted in a coordinated manner as an institution in the actual conduction of the regime's policy." He similarly questions portrayals of the military as a pawn of landed elites: "The claim that the distinct social sector called 'the oligarchy' dominated the coalition ruling after the 1948 revolution (not even that it was 'a part of it') is misleading and in many cases simply wrong." Instead, the ruling officers had autonomous opinions that sometimes diverged from the conservative views of most elites. They "behaved with a 'logic of State,' promoting policy directly derived from the central lines of the government's reformist strategy." Rather than being totally deferential to elites, the officers and civilians who ran the state operated like any other political actor in any other political context; they measured the strengths and weaknesses of the relevant stakeholders and maneuvered accordingly in hopes of achieving their goals.[29]

Our research on the 1968 education reform and the corresponding environment of modernization suggests the merits of carrying Cáceres Prendes's views forward into the 1960s and 1970s. The main focus of our study is the reformist functionaries of the PCN governments. Most of them were civilians, and their various programs all sought to achieve a common goal— modernize the economy through diversification and industrialization. That objective inspired the 1968 education reform, whose architects, especially Walter Béneke, minister of education between 1967 and 1971, conceived of education as a component of economic development. They wanted to create a modern workforce that could staff the jobs in El Salvador's new economy. The same incentives spurred other PCN policymakers to consider tax and land reforms, to upgrade roads and communications, and to build the massive Cerrón Grande Dam to provide cheap, reliable electricity.

The conservative defenders of the status quo steadfastly opposed the core principles that inspired reform, especially the idea that the state needed to involve itself in the economy and direct national development. While landowners formed the cornerstone of this conservative view, they were joined by other sectors of society, including the traditional wing of the Catholic Church, whose members may not have liked laissez-faire capitalism but who were anticommunist and socially conservative. They also were joined by the conservative wing of the army, which tended to comprise older, senior officers. And they drew support from many poor people who shared their views of nationalism, anticommunism, or Catholicism or who benefited from the traditional system through participation in paramilitaries or networks of political patronage.

As the pace and scale of reform picked up in the 1960s and 1970s, the main media outlets decried the alleged communist orientation of all challenges to the establishment. One contribution of the present book is to explore the extent to which the notoriously anticommunist rhetoric of the conservative media in El Salvador grew out of opposition to the modernizing reforms of the military administrations after 1948 as well as the surge in mass-based organizational opposition.

Reformism drew support from throughout Salvadoran society. A small contingent came from elite families who believed that modernization mandated economic restructuring and state intervention. Their conservative brethren considered them to be traitors and opportunists.[30] Various groups within the military supported the reformist cause, especially younger officers, who often identified with humble people more than with elites.[31] Intellectuals, students, and the new liberationist wing of the Catholic Church were strong backers of reform, and they were joined by a host of people from throughout the working and middle classes. Together this amalgamation of Salvadorans advocated for change, some more radically than others.

The reformist impulse in El Salvador had domestic origins, growing out of citizens' longstanding debates over their nation and its future. It also came from external sources, from the newly emergent international development community in the 1950s and 1960s, with its ideological paradigm of modernization theory.

Modernization Theory, the Alliance for Progress, and Foreign Aid in the Cold War

Modernizing reforms were expensive and highly technical, and so it is no surprise that Salvadoran officials eagerly sought money and advice from outsiders. As soon as they came to power in 1948, the members of the "revolutionary" junta invited foreign experts to help them define the nation's problems and propose solutions. During their first year in power they approached the Public Administration Service—a nonprofit consulting agency based in Chicago—and the Pan American Union to help them devise solutions to the growing housing problem in San Salvador.[32] A few months later they sought advice from foreign experts on the census, agricultural projects, the construction of a new dam, and literacy programs. Over the next two decades, and especially after 1960, the presence of foreign advisors and foreign money became a common feature of government-led development initiatives. Most of the personnel and money came from the United States and arrived under the auspices of the Alliance for Progress—the massive foreign aid program launched by President John F. Kennedy in March 1961. Various other multilateral and bilateral agencies were involved as well, like the United Nations Education, Scientific, and Cultural Organization (UNESCO), the World Bank, the Internal Monetary Fund (IMF), the Inter-American Development Bank, and British and Japanese aid agencies.

The existence of development experts and the availability of foreign money to support development programs was a new phenomenon, reflecting dramatic changes in geopolitics. In the aftermath of World War II, politicians and analysts throughout the United States and Europe were trying to figure out how the newly emerging "Third World" nations of Africa, Asia, and Latin America fit into the Cold War order. Were these poor nations, many of which were just emerging from decades of European colonialism, potential sites of Soviet advance? Could they be guided toward capitalist development and thus serve as bulwarks against the spread of communism? The emergent development community answered these questions with new theories coming out of 1950s academe, primarily modernization theory.

Many different individual academics working in various disciplines at multiple institutions helped create modernization theory, but arguably the most influential was the MIT economist W. W. Rostow.[33] His book *The Stages of Economic Growth: A Non-Communist Manifesto*, published in 1960, articulated modernization theory in its most widely read and accessible form. At its most basic level, modernization theory purported that societies transitioned through stages, starting from backward traditionalism and ending in modern, "high consumption" capitalism. Rostow and his fellow modernization theorists believed that they had the prescription for how poor nations could reach that goal. But he warned that the process of transition was fraught with risks of communist incursion. Rostow considered communists to be opportunists who exploited the difficulties of the transition to promote their flawed vision of the future. His antidote was large amounts of foreign inputs—money and technical advice—to ease the transition and undermine popular support for communism. In addition, he advocated the use of armed force against communists if they made a move. The North American historian Bradley Simpson described this dynamic in an aptly titled study of U.S. policy in Indonesia in the 1960s, *Economists with Guns*.[34]

In the late 1950s and early 1960s modernization theory began to guide U.S. foreign policy. A main spark for that development, especially in regard to Latin America, was the Cuban Revolution in January 1959. In response to Castro's broad appeal, U.S. policymakers shifted course in their thinking about aid and its role in promoting U.S. interests. Whereas before they used aid sparingly in poor countries, now they saw it as a necessary way to counter the appeal of Castro and the revolutionaries. The election of John F. Kennedy in November 1960 pushed modernization theory to the forefront of foreign policy. Kennedy's announcement of the founding of the Alliance for Progress in March 1961 embodied the principles of modernization theory. The basic premise behind the Alliance was that billions of dollars in U.S. money in the form of aid to Latin American nations would promote capitalist modernization and counter the appeal of communism. Appropriately, Rostow became a high-level advisor to Kennedy, and the United Nations dubbed the 1960s the "decade of development." Rostow helped organize Johnson's trip to El Salvador in July 1968, and he wrote the president's post-trip talking points, showing his enduring impact on U.S. policy toward developing nations.

An early example of modernization theory as applied to El Salvador comes from former U.S. ambassador Thorsten Kalijarvi. In a brief book that he published in 1962 after he left his posting in El Salvador, he described the nations of Central America as classic examples of traditionalism that needed to be modernized. He said one of the region's main problems was its unequal distribution of wealth caused by exclusive land ownership. He even referred to Central America as "the last bastion of feudalism." His concern was that such conditions promoted the spread of communism. In assessing the situation, Kalijarvi posed the question that so many Salvadorans and international development experts would ask during the coming years: "The question is what to do about the matter." His answer looked like applied modernization theory—provide financial aid and technical assistance to ease the region's transition to modernity and thereby limit popular support for communism.[35]

Thus, early 1960s El Salvador was a convergence zone. At the same time that its reform-minded authoritarian leaders were looking for money and advice to support their modernizing programs, international development agencies, especially those based in the United States, were finding reasons to give them what they wanted. Among the many programs backed by the foreign development community in El Salvador in the 1960s and 1970s, few if any had a stronger backing than the 1968 education reform and its TVE component. When Johnson came to El Salvador in May 1968, the Alliance for Progress was in its final stages, but educational television was just beginning to be implemented, embodying the spirit of what Kennedy had envisioned earlier in the decade.

The Alliance for Progress was paradigmatic of the decade of development. There has been great debate about whether the Alliance was a success or a failure and whether the cause of either was due to design or execution. Admittedly, almost no one defines the Alliance as an unqualified success. After all, civil conflicts raged throughout Latin America in the 1970s and 1980s. Even the Alliance's defenders admit that its aspirations were unfulfilled, but they insist that the situation would have been worse without it, because at least it strengthened infrastructure and created planning bureaucracies.[36]

An early and lasting portrayal of the Alliance as failure came from Chilean president Eduardo Frei Montalva in an article for the journal *Foreign Affairs* in 1967. His title says it all—"The Alliance That Lost Its Way."[37] That title was later borrowed by Jerome Levinson and Juan de Onís for a study that remains a standard reference work on the topic.[38] As their shared title implies, Levinson and de Onís as well as Frei Montalva viewed the Alliance as good policy that was adulterated by Kennedy's successor, Lyndon Johnson, and especially by his assistant secretary of state for inter-American affairs Thomas Mann. The thrust of their argument is that the program had great potential and would have produced positive results if its bureaucratic eye had been fixed on democratization, development, and redistribution rather than anticommunism and political instability. As could be expected, the Nixon administration further eviscerated the program. According to political scientist Tony Smith, who shares the perspective of Levinson and de Onís and Frei Montalva, "The Nixon-Kissinger years, with their utter disregard for alliance-type goals in Latin America, paved the way for exactly the kinds of Communist insurgencies that triumphed in Nicaragua and have wrought havoc in El Salvador."[39]

More recent critiques take a harsher view and see the Alliance as congenitally doomed to failure. According to this perspective, the Alliance had two fundamental flaws. The first was its naïve modernization theory perspective that implied that the United States could go to Latin America and write over centuries of history, transform an entrenched political culture, and redistribute power.[40] The second flaw was the contradiction between the Realpolitik of U.S. Cold War foreign policy and the Alliance's stated goals of promoting democracy and development.[41]

The Alliance's potential for success was further undermined by opposition in the host countries, where both rightist and leftist political forces resisted it as a form of U.S. imperialism. Meanwhile, political pressure to limit spending on foreign aid was mounting in the United States.[42] In the end the amount of money devoted to the Alliance was much less than the amount originally pledged.[43] Furthermore, the Alliance's bureaucracy was plagued by infighting and other problems.[44] For example, some critics claimed that the Alliance favored American corporations over Latin American competitors and that its programs did not seriously address key issues such as population growth, terms of trade, or agrarian reform.[45] In the specific case of Central America, critics of the Alliance have mentioned that it strengthened local elites and authoritarian military regimes. The former learned how to take advantage of loans for industrial development and commercial agriculture while the latter received substantial support to increase their coercive and surveillance capabilities.[46]

We are not looking to overturn this strong and well-founded consensus that the Alliance was a failure. But our case study of an alleged Alliance success, El Salvador's 1968 education reform, sheds new light on the complex way the Alliance functioned in a host country. In the process of trying to better understand the 1968 reform, we have found it difficult to talk about development projects in isolation. Any one project, to say nothing of multiple overlapping projects, required the mobilization of disparate human, financial, and political resources. Thus, projects were bound to involve a wide array of actors at both the local and international level, all of whom came with their own way of doing things. As Alliance projects transitioned from the drawing board to real life, it was inevitable that they would deviate from the lofty ideals conjured up by Kennedy's skillful speechwriters. Moreover, once projects were implemented, they had consequences that neither planners nor scholars could have foreseen. Promoters of El Salvador's education reform saw it as an ideal Alliance project: it was a social program with economic implications; it was aimed at the majority of the population rather than at a narrow elite; it could help level the social playing field by making education more accessible; it was well funded; and it was not impaired by enormous bureaucratic obstacles.

The impact of the Alliance for Progress on a country like El Salvador must be understood in the context of the emergent development community in the 1950s and 1960s. Our analysis shows the extent to which Alliance projects interacted with and even depended upon diverse international agencies and bilateral donors. It can be argued that in Latin America the Alliance for Progress was simply the front edge of a much broader and more elusive concept of "developmentalism."[47] After all, the intellectual impetus behind capitalist development was modernization theory, which was just one particular, albeit dominant, version of development discourse. We investigate how modernization theory found its way into organizations like UNESCO and into the minds of legions of international development experts who went from country to country and from agency to agency imparting advice. In the case of El Salvador, one expert who played a particularly influential role was a professor of communications from Stanford University, Wilbur Schramm.

For any given development project to get underway, it had to rally diverse actors, including local modernizing elites whom some have come to call the "comprador" class, foreign aid agencies in industrialized countries, and various international organizations. President Johnson's visit to El Salvador in July 1968 highlighted the presence of all these players. Thus, El Salvador's education reform provides a distinct vantage point to see the diverse ways that modernization theory and developmentalism became hegemonic in a small Central American country in the 1960s and 1970s.

The functionaries who implemented the education reform and educational television received large amounts of money and technical advice from international development experts, mostly North Americans working through UN or U.S. agencies like UNESCO and USAID. The active and highly visible participation of this panoply of international advisors raises the question of how much of the project was a local initiative. To explore this question there is much to be learned from authors who see development as a historically situated discourse. In the past two decades sociologists and anthropologists have paid increasing attention to the "development community," with its origins in the 1950s and 1960s, which lorded over the design and implementation of large development projects in poor countries.[48] Arturo Escobar portrays its members as an unaccountable community that exercises enormous sway over poor countries by giving itself "the moral, professional, and legal authority to name [label] subjects and define strategies."[49] James Ferguson, in an influential study on development projects in Lesotho, focused on how international development professionals frame questions and construct narratives that make their services indispensable and their dictates unassailable.[50] In the case of Lesotho, Ferguson finds the experts pushing aside not only local actors but also on-the-ground realities that did not fit their preconceptions. For Ferguson the technocratic credentials of the development professionals and their scientific-sounding projects gloss over local power struggles that play a huge role in the success or failure of any given project. An important part of development experts' power is their ability to define projects as objectively valid and beyond politics.

Complementing the work of Escobar and Ferguson is another well-known work by James Scott, *Seeing Like a State*. Scott examines modernizing projects and their failures from a different vantage point. He is not concerned with development professionals from the first world coming to impart knowledge to their poor brethren in the developing world. Rather, he focuses on the modern state and its functionaries in a variety of national contexts, developed and developing, capitalist and socialist. He says that a particularly noxious brew emerged in nineteenth- and twentieth-century states. It combined high-modernist ideology, authoritarian politics, and a self-righteous belief in the infallibility of science. Armed with that mixture, government functionaries looked at their societies' problems from on high, "seeing like a state." They conceived of solutions in the form of massive infrastructure projects—huge dams and agricultural schemes, like Soviet collectivization, Tanzanian "villagization," and urban planning in metropolises like Paris, Brasilia, and Chicago. The architects of these projects saw themselves as enlightened technocrats who had the best interests of the population in mind, but who saw little need to solicit the population's opinion. Typically, the modernization schemes proved to be colossal failures, largely because they created or bolstered the same political enemies that the state set out to undermine in the first place.

Escobar, Ferguson, and Scott have in common a sense that the modernizing vision can be turned into specific projects that are backed by enormous power and are able to overwhelm local resistance. Local actors and citizens at the grassroots level, according to their perspectives, seem rather insignificant. They are local collaborators and facilitators of internationals, heirs to a "comprador" mentality, or in Scott's words, they comprise a "prostate civil society."[51]

We take cues from each of these authors, combine them, and add the findings of our study. We borrow Escobar's description of development as a discourse, Ferguson's study of development experts imparting self-serving knowledge, and Scott's description of modern state agents acting as social engineers. Our case study adds the dimension of local actors below the state level and the ways in which a large modernizing project, in this case an education reform, played out in the lived experience of real people, in this case students sitting in disparate classrooms throughout a small subtropical country in Central America. We look at the ways in which the reform's impact on students was interpreted by divergent political sectors and how and why they responded to it as they did. In the case of El Salvador, one response came from teachers, who opposed the reformers through well-coordinated, highly organized, and determined mass action.

The Cold War

It is an obvious statement, but it needs to be made: the 1968 education reform and the PCN's modernization program occurred during the Cold War. The simplicity of that statement hides more complicated questions. What did the Cold War mean to El Salvador? What determined conditions in El Salvador in the 1960s and 1970s more—the geopolitics of the superpower rivalry between the United States and the USSR or domestic traditions dating back decades, even centuries? These questions have taken center stage in debates about the history of the Cold War in Latin America. To the extent that our study engages a specific episode of modernizing reform in the context of the Cold War, we found ourselves drawn into the exchange.

At first blush it seems all too apparent that the superpower rivalry between the United States and the USSR profoundly affected El Salvador in the 1960s and 1970s. An emphasis on superpower rivalry forms the cornerstone of the traditional Cold War historiography from U.S. diplomatic (now known as "foreign relations") historians. Their analyses are centered on geopolitics and revolve around debates over the nature and strategies of policymakers in the United States and the USSR. When those scholars engage events in the global south—that is, in countries like El Salvador—they do so from a similar perspective, thereby limiting if not ignoring domestic actors and their distinct experiences. Complementary studies by Latin Americanist scholars tend to bring local actors in by situating geopolitical debates in specific local conditions. Nevertheless, many of them operate in a similar interpretive tradition, describing the left as romantic revolutionaries inspired by international comrades and the right as anticommunist allies of the United States.

The problem with these interpretations, according to a newer school of thought on Cold War Latin America, is that they tend to be "reductionist" and "disproportionately preoccupied with geopolitics and grand strategy." They subsume domestic conditions, local actors, and all their attenuating complexities to "master narratives from Olympian heights."[52] The critics of the traditional historiography call for a new trend, an interpretation of the "cold war from within," from the perspective of local grassroots players that highlights the importance of domestic variables. They agree that we cannot and should not ignore what the traditional historiography has shown us, that the geopolitics of the superpower rivalry framed certain domestic debates. In accordance with the traditional view, both rightist and leftist antagonists in Cold War Latin America reached outward to their respective allies on the international scene, either the United States or the USSR, and in turn, policymakers in those superpowers reached back in hopes of satisfying their foreign policy objectives.

More importantly, according to the new interpretive approach, both the right and the left in Latin America reached within, to local conditions and all the historical baggage that came with them. So, while the Latin American right allied with the United States and employed the discourse of stopping Soviet expansionism, it also operated within longstanding traditions of authoritarianism and "order and progress" that predated the Cold War and even predated the belief in socialism as a threat. Whatever they were doing during the Cold War in the name of anticommunism, conservatives did so to defend economic and political practices that had allowed them to rise to the fore during the preceding decades. Therefore, they were steadfastly opposed to anybody or any idea that threatened the status quo. To the extent that allying with the United States served their ends, they nurtured the alliance, and when allying with the United States no longer served them, they jettisoned it. The left did the same with its various international allegiances, be it Cuba, Nicaragua, Vietnam, China, or the Soviet Union. In his multi-archival, synthetic study of the Cold War in Latin America, historian Hal Brands summarized this new approach to the topic: "Latin America's Cold War was not a single conflict; it was a series of overlapping conflicts. It fused together long-running clashes over social, political and economic arrangements; the persistent tension between U.S. power and Latin American nationalism; the ideological ramifications of decolonization and the rise of the Third World; and the influence of the bipolar struggle for preeminence in the developing world."[53]

As a case study of a specific episode in a single country, our study fits
into this new interpretive framework of Cold War Latin America. We show
that Salvadorans of all political stripes conceptualized modernization through
decades of domestic experience rather than simply through a Cold War–
induced lens of superpower rivalry. The Salvadoran right rooted its interpretations of PCN modernization in ideas about liberalism dating back to the
nineteenth century. When the right put a face on "communism" in the latter
half of the twentieth century, they called up images from the past, especially
the 1932 uprising in western El Salvador. And even when the right began to split
into reformers and conservatives in the 1950s and 1960s, its members defended
their positions mostly with interpretations of their own nation's past.[54]

Similarly, the left rooted its interpretation of PCN modernization in the
history of popular demands for democracy and social justice dating back to
the 1930s, if not before. The Salvadoran left in the 1960s and 1970s was not an
agent of international communism, and its leaders were a varied group. Some
were inspired by Marxist theory, but many others came from a domestic tradition of challenging longstanding practices of economic and political exclusion
as exemplified by local thinkers like Alberto Masferrer.[55] Others found their
intellectual roots in the social doctrine of the Catholic Church. It was within
this complicated terrain of domestic debate and international geopolitics that
the PCN functionaries set out to overhaul El Salvador's schools.[56]

Origins of the Civil War

Given the worldwide attention generated by El Salvador's civil war, it is no
surprise that it has been studied by many scholars with divergent perspectives who are interested in revolutions and their origins.[57] This book does
not seek to settle the differences among the various schools of thought. Yet a
work on an important government project that provoked some of the most
significant popular street demonstrations of the 1970s inevitably has something to say about the road to civil war. Analyzing the 1968 education reform
helps resolve the apparent contradiction between a state that simultaneously
modernized and repressed, that presented itself as a defender of the majority
against an intractable reactionary elite and yet incited the a massive wave of
popular mobilization in the 1970s.

Readers familiar with theories of revolution will easily detect that our
work, to the extent that it says something about the origins of El Salvador's
civil war, is consistent with state-centered explanations of revolution such as

that provided by Goodwin. He recognizes that "revolutions are obviously complex historical processes that involve multifarious economic, social, cultural, organizational, social-psychological, and voluntarist factors," but he privileges the role of the state in his analysis of the cause of revolution. The main reason for doing so—and this is an insight that we find particularly relevant to our case—is that "certain state structures and practices actively form or 'construct' revolutionary movements as effectively as the best professional revolutionaries, by channeling and organizing political dissent along radical lines."[58]

Readers familiar with studies of pre–civil war El Salvador will realize that the state-centered approach is a departure from the norm. Most of the academic literature on El Salvador has tended to emphasize agrarian conflict, following the tradition of seminal works about peasant insurrections such as Eric Wolf's 1969 *Peasant Wars of the Twentieth Century* and Jeffrey Paige's 1978 *Agrarian Revolution.*[59] Operating in that tradition, authors such as Carlos Rafael Cabarrús and Robert Williams concentrate on changes in the agricultural economy and on social relations in the countryside to explain the antecedents to the Salvadoran civil war.[60] Even U.S.-sponsored scholarship geared toward policy making, like the work of Roy Prosterman, who helped designed the land reform in Vietnam in the 1960s, concentrates on the agricultural sector and rural class relations. One scholar refers to the focus on the agrarian economy as the "dominant paradigm."[61]

The contributors to this paradigm explain the outbreak of war in El Salvador as a product of the dramatic inequalities in land tenure, the rapid expansion of commercial agriculture at the expense of peasants, and the inevitable class conflict that ensued. The argument goes more or less along the following lines. By the 1960s and 1970s land and wealth had become heavily concentrated, the population was growing at a rapid pace, and the expansion of commercial agriculture was displacing the peasantry, replacing the production of foodstuffs, poisoning individuals and the soil with the heavy use of pesticides, and eroding the land. According to this interpretation, what ultimately mattered were material conditions. Marxist analysts saw rural despair as the inevitable crisis that would usher in socialism, whereas capitalist modernizers saw it as a clarion call for reform, believing that something had to be done to forestall radical militancy.[62] Either way, both schools of thought focused on material affairs.

The belief that conditions in the countryside had to be amended to avoid war is exemplified by Prosterman's Index of Rural Instability (IRI). The index measured the percentage of landless peasants relative to the total peasant population. Prosterman argued that a revolution was likely when the IRI was above 30 percent.[63] Even authors who concentrate on the formation of the radical opposition pay special attention to the countryside and the agrarian economy, albeit with distinct emphases. One variant says that the determinant variable was guerrilla leaders and their organizational activities in the 1960s and 1970s. Another opposes that notion of the guerrilla vanguard and instead stresses the autonomous role of peasants and their mass mobilization, especially its liberation theology variant.[64]

It would be foolish to downplay the importance of transformations in the countryside and the grievances of peasants and rural workers, as well as the role of the guerrilla vanguard in fomenting revolution. Yet other countries whose rural populations have suffered economic malaise due to dismal material conditions have not experienced revolution. Poverty was a powerful precondition, but it is not sufficient to explain the outbreak of social revolution. Goodwin notes that El Salvador's material conditions were not that much different than its neighbors Guatemala, Nicaragua, and Honduras, yet the four countries experienced divergent political outcomes. Nicaragua had a successful revolution, El Salvador's war ended in peace accords that effectively dismantled the military regime and allowed the political participation of the left but did not represent a revolutionary change, Guatemala's army and elites more or less defeated the insurgency, and Honduras did not experience any serious revolutionary movement. These different outcomes have led state-centered comparative scholars to argue that variables other than material conditions in the countryside must have been in play. Goodwin and others who share his view contend that a major explanatory variable is the state.[65]

In her study of the motivations behind peasants' response to the civil war in El Salvador, Elisabeth Wood concluded that material conditions alone were not sufficient to explain community members' decisions. The desire to have access to land, she found, "did not motivate insurgency."[66] She noted that some communities supported the guerrilla, others the government, and yet others remained neutral. For those who supported the insurgency, Wood says they were motivated by: (1) *participation*, inspired by the teachings of liberation theology that assigned value to participation as a way to realize the Kingdom of Heaven here on earth; (2) *defiance*, as the outcome of moral outrage over the repressive actions of the state; and (3) *pleasure in agency*, as the process of participating in the insurgency had the psychological rewards of self-determination, pride in taking their lives in their own hands, and enhanced self-esteem after being put down by the upper classes and the government for generations. But the main point here is to recognize that for those people who supported the guerrillas, "the delights of agency" had been denied them by a state that had opposed political freedoms and had constricted economic opportunities.[67]

Joaquín Chávez is another scholar of El Salvador's rural environs and their transition into fonts of insurgency who emphasizes the importance of the state to understanding the origins of the conflict in El Salvador. Chávez makes an important contribution with his research on the crucial role played by "popular intellectuals," grassroots organizers in both the countryside and poor suburban areas. He builds a strong case to prove that they were decisive to organizing the insurgency in El Salvador. But even though he focuses on those popular intellectuals, he also argues that a main causal variable of the insurgency in El Salvador was the actions of the state. In his words, "Although ideology certainly played a significant role in the mobilization of urban middle class insurgent intellectuals, my study shows that the radicalization of both urban and peasant intellectuals was centrally informed by the closing of political spaces, and mounting state repression in 1960s and 1970s. . . . My study shows that peasant leaders became insurgents as they articulated multiple self-defense strategies in response to the intensification of state repression against peasant communities in the 1970s."[68] With these words Chávez offers a revisionist interpretation of the origins of El Salvador's civil war, breaking with such scholars as Williams and Cabarrús. However, Chávez's traditional portrayal of the Salvadoran state as an alliance of landed elites and the military and the fact that he limits his focus on the state's role to actions of repression and terror stand in contrast to the arguments we advance in this book. He similarly limits the United States to being a blind-eye supporter and financial backer of the Salvadoran state's terroristic activities. While we agree that those aspects of the state and the U.S. government are important to understanding El Salvador's system of rule, we also believe that failure to appreciate the multiple story lines surrounding those players prevents a fuller understanding. For that reason we highlight divisions within the right; the military regime's modernizing agenda, highlighted by the 1968 education reform; and the U.S. backing of modernizing reforms.

Chávez's valuable new insights about popular intellectuals help us understand the dynamics of the urban movement. Wood's studies of the rural areas can also be applied to the urban setting, the most relevant context for the present study. The material conditions of teachers affected by the 1968 education reform did not guarantee that most of them would oppose the government and that many of them would join revolutionary organizations. Rather, such outcomes required distinct decisions by government functionaries and precise actions by the state that helped transform teachers from loyal servants to protestors and ultimately into militant revolutionaries. Goodwin makes this argument by applying his state-centered approach to El Salvador's civil war. He says that a crucial variable in the emergence of a revolutionary opposition was the actions of the ruling PCN regime during the 1960s and 1970s and the manner in which civil society experienced and interpreted those actions.[69] In his words, those people who become revolutionaries did so not "simply or even mainly as economically exploited classes, but also and more immediately as excluded and often violently repressed state subjects." Further arguing that the actions of the state were not simply extensions of economic structures, he claims that "the roots of revolutionary movements are found in the political context in which class relationships and economic institutions (among other factors) are embedded."[70]

Sociologist Paul Almeida opens a similar line of interpretation that we find useful. In explaining the emergence of the revolutionary upsurge in late 1970s El Salvador, he looks at the consequences of the PCN regime's decision to initiate a reformist opening in the mid-1960s. Almeida claims that the state's decision to open up the system in the mid-1960s was decisive in allowing the core oppositional movement to coalesce. Even though that movement was highly inchoate when the state then reversed course and began clamping down in 1972, it was too far along to simply wither away. Hence, Almeida's study is consistent with Goodwin's state-centered approach, showing that the Salvadoran state essentially created its own enemies. Regardless, Almeida demonstrates the explanatory causality of the state's fluctuations between populist modernization and authoritarian anticommunism.

The conclusions by Goodwin, Almeida, Chávez, and others are similar to what we found in our research.[71] The 1968 education reform reveals the coexistence of reformist and repressive impulses in the PCN, the verticality of state actions, the unwillingness or inability of state functionaries to listen to the grievances of important stakeholders, and the ways in which all of those dispositions fused together to promote the creation of a radicalized opposition. Most importantly, it shows how the Salvadoran state's distinct approach to modernizing reform served as a causal variable in the country's descent into war.

Organization of the Book

We have divided the book into six chapters that follow a roughly chronological pattern with some thematic framing. The first chapter sets the precedent for the modernizing reforms of the PCN by looking at debates within the political right over the meaning of modernization in the decades prior to 1960. Its goal is to show that El Salvador's economic elites and military rulers both viewed themselves as modernizers, but with differing definitions of modernity. Both groups considered themselves to be anticommunists and defenders of market-oriented capitalism. But the economic elites, especially the owners of coffee plantations, tended to adhere to a rigid economic libertarianism and a belief that government should refrain from any intervention in the economy that did not directly benefit capital. They and their various spokespersons, like newspaper owner Napoleón Viera Altamirano, defended that position with a rhetoric that grew stronger as calls for reform grew louder in the 1950s.

The voices making those calls for reform originated from diverse sources, including new political parties such as the Christian Democrats; moderate business leaders, most of them linked to industry; and various professional and academic groups, among others. The army also contained a reformist sector, usually among the younger officers. This amalgamation of reformers seldom held identical views about policymaking, but collectively they shared a general belief that the best way for El Salvador to progress was through state-led economic and social reform. A group of them, led by young, ambitious military officers, seized control of the state in 1948 and began to advance a reformist platform. The debates that emerged during the so-called revolutionary era of the 1950s laid the foundation for intensifying polarization in the 1960s and 1970s.

In the second chapter we focus on the first PCN administration (1961–1967) under Col. Julio Adalberto Rivera. Although he came to power in a coup that touted its conservative credentials and insisted that it was saving the nation from communism, Rivera and his fellow functionaries embodied the ruling strategy that defined military reformism, combining modernizing reforms with anticommunist repression. Under Rivera's watch, El Salvador experienced liberalization in politics, economics, and labor organizing. A key component of these reforms was the financial and technical support provided by international development experts, especially under the auspices of the Alliance for Progress. The chapter outlines the nature of that relationship as well as the ideological backdrop to U.S. aid in El Salvador, namely modernization theory. Finally, the chapter describes the emergence of one of the most important opposition sectors—teachers—whose new union, Asociación Nacional de Educadores Salvadoreños 21 de Junio (ANDES), would go on to become a major opponent of the PCN.

Chapter 3 sticks roughly to the same time period as chapter 2 but looks at preludes to the 1968 education reform. The chapter shows the interaction between the agents of modernization inside El Salvador and international foreign aid organizations in the field of education. Salvadoran modernizers prioritized education reform, and prominent members among them began pushing the idea of educational television. At the same time, international development agencies had developed a rationale for involving themselves in the affairs of countries like El Salvador, and they began to promote educational television. The activities of communications expert Wilbur Schramm and his embrace of educational television receive special attention. Schramm was major figure in defining the way communications theory should be applied to achieve modernization in poor countries like El Salvador. Therein, Schramm was at the center of the complex relationships and ideas that went into the making of development policy. He perceived television to be the latest and most useful tool of mass communication to effect development, and El Salvador and its education reform emerged as an ideal test case for using television in the classroom to achieve modernization.

Chapter 4 covers a narrower period, 1967 to 1971, when the second PCN president, Col. (later Gen.) Fidel Sánchez Hernández, and his new minister of education, the civilian Walter Béneke, oversaw the design and implementation of the 1968 education reform. The chapter describes the main elements of the reform and the manner in which it was implemented. It also analyzes the bubbling ferment among teachers. The growing opposition to the PCN regime by teachers culminated in a massive strike in 1968 that was triggered by conflicts over pensions and benefits. The government's antagonistic response to the teachers opened a breach between the government and civil society that would broaden in the early 1970s.

Chapter 5 picks up where chapter 4 leaves off, in 1971, and moves forward into the mid-1970s. Education remains a centerpiece, but the chapter broadens into the political context within which modernization was being debated. The chapter opens with descriptions of the education reform as experienced by students and teachers in the classroom. It progresses forward into the complex political context in which the education reform unfolded. As the government was introducing rapid changes in the educational system, the country went to war with Honduras in 1969 and the legislature started a divisive debate around land reform in 1970. These events set the stage for the second great conflict between teachers and the state, the 1971 strike. Like its predecessor in 1968, the 1971 strike was driven by bread-and-butter issues such as salaries, but the massive response by teachers had much to do with the generalized discontent over state-imposed reforms. By the time of the strike, the education reform had made clear its alienating impact on teacher's workload and their everyday experience. The 1971 strike had an additional ingredient, a political environment unsettled by broader conflicts over the definition and meaning of development in general. As the government responded with a similar belligerence to the striking teachers as it had in 1968, the gulf between it and the popular sectors grew even wider. Moreover, the land reform debate opened a gulf between the government and conservative landowners. The regime's decision to remain in power through massive electoral fraud in 1972 was an important turning point away from the liberalizing reforms of the early 1960s. The chapter describes that electoral fraud as well as another controversial PCN modernizing endeavor—the Cerrón Grande Dam project.

Finally, the last chapter looks at some crucial questions. Was the educational reform worth the trouble? Were PCN policymakers right in their belief that reforms would improve the quality of education and increase enrollment? Since U.S. foreign aid officials considered the Salvadoran reform as a "pilot project" for possible replication elsewhere, a small army of experts and academics sought answers to these questions. They made their assessments of El Salvador's education reform in the 1970s, as El Salvador descended into civil war. The chapter shows that their efforts to provide a technical answer to a technical question were far more complicated than appeared at first sight. The "anti-politics machine" assessed the performance of the reform in a highly politicized context. The chapter explains why varying onlookers— both national and international—interpreted the reform and educational television so differently; some saw them as profound successes, while others considered them dismal failures. The chapter contends that those alternative opinions originated in the onlooker's approach to modernization. Those who continued to subscribe to modernization theory and believe in its prospects for development viewed the Salvadoran case as a success story that should be replicated elsewhere. Those who were not enmeshed in modernization theory viewed the reform in the broader political and social context of El Salvador.

They questioned the merits of the Salvadoran government's version of modernizing development, pointed to the country's rapid deterioration, and said that not only was its education reform a failure but El Salvador also was a model to be avoided. Ironically, Schramm experienced an about-face and fell into this latter camp. In 1979 he critiqued the policies that he and other development agencies had implemented in the 1960s and 1970s. In his words, their goal had been to achieve "steady economic growth and a closing of the gap between the [poorer] 85 percent and the others," but instead they ended up with "disappointed governments and disillusioned people."[72]

CHAPTER 1

A Fight Within the Right
Rivaling Visions of Modernization

Our population is not ready for the exercise of free suffrage.
—José René Tobar, Armenia, El Salvador, 1968

We're the people who are building this country. It's the unions who
want to destroy it.
—Anonymous member of the Salvadoran elite, late 1980s

✣ IN 1961 THE CUBAN JOURNALIST CARLOS CASTAÑEDA DENOUNCED THE SAL-
vadoran landed elites and their historic alliance with the military in *El Popular*, a new weekly magazine in El Salvador. "The economic and political
life of El Salvador has always been controlled by powerful and influential
families. Feudal lords, owners of all the riches in the country, they make and
unmake presidents with the collaboration of ambitious military officers who
for a few coins serve as their personal police."[1] Publishing a criticism like
that in El Salvador in 1961 was uncommon, even dangerous, although not
unprecedented. A statement like that might appear in a broadside handed out
at a political demonstration, or in a fringe publication put out by the clandestine Communist Party, or perhaps in a journal produced by the University
of El Salvador, which witnessed a rapid rise in student activism. But none
of those published Castañeda's quote. What makes his quote remarkable is
the timing and location of its publication. It appeared in a weekly magazine published by the military junta that had come to power five months

prior in a coup d'état. The members of that junta boasted of their conservative, anticommunist credentials and accused the preceding government of
being riddled with leftists trying to hand the nation over to international
communism. This coup had been backed by both local business leaders and
the U.S. Embassy. And yet, shortly after they seized power, the junta leaders
founded *El Popular* and filled its pages with the kind of rhetoric contained
in Castañeda's article—criticisms of the so-called landed oligarchs and their
alliance with the army. Even the junta's supposed "communist" predecessors
had not made such direct attacks on El Salvador's traditional power holders.

The publication of Castañeda's article in *El Popular* reveals that the conservative ruling sector in El Salvador, comprising economic elites and the
army, was not as unified or coherent as initial observations might suggest.
Although its members shared a self-image as forward-looking leaders guiding the country toward modernity, they disagreed with one another over
the content and pace of change. Those among them who advocated reforms
believed that the state had to be proactive to prevent chaos and the rise of
communism. Their conservative counterparts argued that the role of the
state ought to be minimal, that the market operating unfettered by regu-
lation would bring prosperity, and that the response to challengers of the
status quo should be repression instead of accommodation. Divisions sharp-
ened in the 1960s and 1970s when reformers pushed their agenda.

The 1968 education reform emerged out of this intra-right debate. This
chapter sets the stage for that reform and other modernizing schemes of the
1960s and 1970s by looking at the evolution of those debates between 1870
and 1960. Ninety years is a long expanse to cover in one chapter, so we are
specific rather than comprehensive in our coverage. We focus on debates
within the right and also on the image that civilian and military rulers had of
themselves as modernizing agents for progressive change. Various scholars
have studied this ninety-year period in Salvadoran history. We draw upon
their work and also introduce new primary evidence.

Liberal Antecedents, 1871–1931

In a study from the late 1990s, political scientist Yvon Grenier describes the
self-image of El Salvador's economic elites: "The Salvadoran oligarchs, some
of whose forebears emigrated to the country in the second half of the nineteenth century, consider themselves pioneers of a sort, a truly national vanguard who developed the country single-handedly (without foreign help),

turning it into one of the most industrialized and economically successful countries in the region. According to their own self-image, the oligarchs did not take away from the people, and consequently are not obliged to give anything back through agrarian reform or other 'communist' (foreign) inspired, policies. According to the oligarchs, they created whatever resources the poor country has to go around."[2] Grenier captures the modernizing character that El Salvador's economic elites ascribed to themselves. They believed they were civilizing modernizers who brought economic rationality and enlightenment to the country and especially its rural areas. By the mid-twentieth century these elites would come to be known notoriously as the "fourteen families," a term that implies a small number of wealthy, intermarried families running the country. Research has proven that term to be technically incorrect, because the elite comprised about two hundred families, but it captures the essence of the story: El Salvador is a country where wealth and power have concentrated in a shockingly small number of hands.[3]

The roots of El Salvador's economic elite can be found in the late nineteenth century during the so-called liberal era. The year 1871 is commonly asserted as the consolidation of the liberal era in El Salvador, when liberal politicians deposed President Francisco Dueñas and brought an end to conservative rule. El Salvador's landowning sector was inchoate at the time. A handful of old families with origins in the Spanish colonial era owned large estates, but so too did Indian and peasant communities. The latter had received communal grants from the Spanish Crown during the colonial era or from conservatives in decades after independence. But regardless of who owned land in mid-nineteenth-century El Salvador, opportunities for wealth accumulation were modest. With the lone exception of indigo, El Salvador's agricultural commodities generated little wealth in depressed international markets. At the time of independence, El Salvador was a land of 250,000 people, most of whom were rural, poor, and indigenous. The capital city at the time was hardly more than a dirt-road village with fifteen thousand inhabitants. By 1871, little had changed.

El Salvador's economic fortunes took a turn for the better in the second half of the nineteenth century. Commercial activities along the Pacific coast of Central America increased due to westward expansion in the United States. Also, the second industrial revolution was getting underway in Europe and North America, and consumers in those lands were hungry for tropical products. Salvadoran liberals took it for granted that agriculture represented their nation's path to economic modernity. As one liberal

legislator put it, "agriculture is the most plentiful spring of life and the prosperity of the nation," and therefore "government had the necessary duty
of removing all the obstacles that opposed its [agriculture's] development."[4]
El Salvador's environmental conditions made it an ideal candidate to grow
coffee, and rising coffee prices gave land speculators and commercial agents
plenty of incentives to mobilize their country's productive resources toward
coffee cultivation.[5]

Seeking to dismantle what they saw as hindrances to economic growth,
liberals implemented a series of distinct and long-lasting economic reforms.[6]
The most influential reform was the privatization of communal lands in the
early 1880s. As in many other Latin American countries, liberal policymakers in El Salvador targeted communal landholding as a hindrance to economic modernization because they believed it kept land and labor hidden
from the beneficial effects of the marketplace. As the authors of the privatization legislation put it, communal land "nullified the benefits of property"
and encouraged "apathy and insensibility to improvements."[7] Not coincidentally, some of the nation's prime coffee-growing lands were communally
owned. Estimates of the amount of land affected by the privatization laws
range between 25 and 40 percent of Salvadoran territory.[8] Other reforms at
the time included centralizing state power, professionalizing the military,
and building infrastructure, much of which promoted the coffee economy.[9]
The emergent liberal elites pointed to the tangible byproducts of their policies—roads, ports, warehouses, a new National Palace, and an exhibition at
the Paris Exposition Universelle in 1889. They looked to nations like Belgium
to argue that a small country with a dense population could develop.

Following these reforms, coffee became the main crop that enriched the
Salvadoran elites. The land reforms of the early 1880s put potential coffee-
growing lands into the marketplace, and coffee steadily became the engine
of the Salvadoran economy. For reasons too numerous and complicated to
examine here, the benefits of the new economy went to a selective few rather
than a greater whole. El Salvador was not Costa Rica or Venezuela, where
coffee was grown by a large number of peasants and small farmers.[10] In El Salvador, coffee growing and coffee processing came to be controlled by a few
families, leaving large portions of the remaining rural population with no
option but to join the ranks of a swelling proletariat. The new coffee elite
consisted of old landed families like the Dueñases, Regalados, Guirolas, and
Escalóns, who intermarried with a handful of new immigrants from Europe
and North and South America, like the Hills, Dukes, and Alvarezes. While

we now know that the process of creating class inequity in El Salvador was complex and drawn out, the end result is indisputable: a small handful of intermarried families came to own and control most of the country's productive resources.[11]

As this new coffee-growing elite took shape, its members employed a highly partisan rhetoric of modernity, although they had to negotiate the complexities of liberalism—hardly a uniform concept with singular meaning. Liberalism's philosophical and intellectual traditions contained fluid and contradictory concepts. For example, did liberalism mean democracy, universal suffrage, equality, freedom of the press and association, and a bill of rights? Or did it mean small government, unregulated economic activity, opposition to taxes, and unmitigated exposure to the international marketplace? Should the government give priority to building infrastructure to promote export agriculture or to building schools for all children? Debates over these issues raged everywhere that liberals came to power, and El Salvador was no exception. But in the case of El Salvador, the prevailing variant of liberalism reflected the interests of the emergent agroexport sector, mainly coffee growers. They believed the young nation's economic prosperity depended on the state facilitating the rapid expansion of export agriculture.

The liberals employed a strong rhetoric of equality and liberty, even though they protected social hierarchy and limited political participation. In their writings and public statements, Salvadoran liberals portrayed themselves as a once-oppressed minority that had finally won its freedom from conservatives who drew inspiration from the Middle Ages rather than pursue a modernist future. Liberals referred to the political change in 1871 as "The Reform" or "The Revolution." One liberal editorialist even equated the idea of returning to the pre-liberal era as the equivalent of forcing a freed black to return to slavery.[12] In their writings and speeches, they appealed to natural rights, cited European philosophers of the Enlightenment and Romantic traditions such as Voltaire, Kant, Herder, and Guizot, and celebrated England and the United States as beacons of modernity for having blended economic development with political liberty.[13] They touted democracy, repeatedly defining their governments as a "democratic system," and celebrated one another's support for "high democratic goals."[14] They made the term "liberty" a guiding principle, as demonstrated by one liberal editorialist's claim in 1883 that "a nation becomes invincible when it links liberty to a celebration of knowledge and science."[15] Another editorialist defined civilization as "liberty, science, order and work."[16]

Ultimately liberals worked hard to limit the meaning of liberalism to laissez-faire economics. They defined liberty as the possession of private property and the freedom to pursue wealth in the marketplace. As one editorialist put it 1887, "liberty means having power over your person and belongings."[17] Another liberal leader, influenced by the famed Argentine liberal statesman Domingo Faustino Sarmiento, distinguished between "modern civilization" and a "primitive situation" and said that the former would be achieved only through "guarantees and protections of private property."[18]

Education provides a useful case study of the Salvadoran liberals' approach to modernization and government. As was typical elsewhere, El Salvador's liberals heralded public and popular education. A prominent liberal ideologue of the time, Francisco Galindo, stated in his *Cartilla del ciudadano* (Catechism of citizenship), which was first published in 1874 and became required reading in schools, that the liberal triumph marked the time to "start a campaign more glorious than that of Independence: the republican education of the masses."[19] Field Marshall Santiago González, president between 1871 and 1876, defined education as the instrument to "elevate men to the dignity of citizenship."[20] To that end, he claimed to have "dedicated the most careful attention to primary education, because it is at school where citizens ought to be formed."[21] The minister who oversaw education in 1872 defined it as "the indispensible foundation of all progress."[22]

The prevailing education model at the time liberals came to power was called "Education for Citizenship."[23] Its origins lay in the late colonial period, when the modernizing Bourbon monarchy proposed that education perform the role of Christianizing and civilizing the king's subjects.[24] The model established a core curriculum around religion, reading, writing, and a little math, and its pedagogy was that of rote memorization. In areas where the native population predominated, the schools were supposed to teach Spanish so that the inhabitants would learn "love for the conquering nation, banish idolatry, and civilize themselves for business and trade."[25] Despite the monarchy's centralizing tendencies, all schools were funded and administered at the local level, which led to highly erratic and mostly poor-quality teaching. After independence from Spain, Central America's new governing officials adopted the Spanish education model almost wholesale, albeit with the objective of creating citizens for the new federation (1821–1838) rather than subjects for the monarchy.[26] This education model was then embraced by the new Salvadoran leaders after the demise of the federation and the birth of the Salvadoran Republic.[27] In his cartilla, Galindo adhered to the basic dictates of

Education for Citizenship by defending the traditional curriculum and peda-gogy. Regardless, chronic warfare, political instability, and economic malaise ensured that education remained a distant priority throughout much of the nineteenth century.

The impact of the civic education exemplified by Galindo's cartilla was enhanced by the fact that it completely replaced religious education. After the enactment of the liberal 1880 Constitution that called for secular educa-tion, the government prohibited religious instruction in public schools. The bishop considered starting a system of parochial schools, but the authorities of the Catholic Church did not have the resources to carry out such a project. In the end, their only alternative was to "use their influence to encourage teachers in private schools to teach Christian doctrine correctly."[28]

The liberals' ideological approach to citizenship encouraged a highly exclusive approach to education. Once again, Galindo provided the expla-nation in his cartilla. In a question and answer format, he asked:

What is the people [*el pueblo*]?

It is a congregation of men that has as a goal the preservation and happiness of its members. It is governed by political institutions that originate from the congregation itself. In this sense, "the people" is the same as "the society," in contrast to the common meaning given to the word in which "people" means rabble [*populacho*]. Thus, the statement "the people are sovereign" is equivalent to this less danger-ous statement: "the society is sovereign."[29]

Galindo's phrasing is a bit obtuse, even for mid-nineteenth-century formal Spanish. But in essence he was distinguishing between those Salvadorans who should be included in "society," with all its accompanying benefits and responsibilities, and those who should be dismissed as part of the common "populacho." Arguments like Galindo's allowed policymakers to place a low priority on educational access. If the goal of education was to form citi-zens, then anyone who was not included in the citizenry, either formally or informally, need not receive an education. The liberal Constitution of 1871 had a fairly generous definition of citizenship for its time, denying it only to women, domestic servants, and men with character flaws—vice, idleness, begging, and so forth. The Constitution did not allow race or property to define one's citizenship. But the flexibility of Galindo's phras-ing along with prevailing Social Darwinist ideas made it easy to exclude

FIGURE 2. School, circa 1925, unidentified location. Photo provided courtesy of the
Museo de la Palabra y la Imagen (MUPI), San Salvador, El Salvador.

indigenous and poor people from "society" and lump them into the vulgar
"populacho."

A strong economic incentive also discouraged liberal policymakers from
supporting mass access to education. Landowners did not think national
progress would be served by interfering with the supply of labor in rural
areas by sending children to school.[30] "The education of the lower classes [in
El Salvador]," observed the North America traveler Dana Munro in the early
twentieth century, "has been purposely restricted to a few fundamentals,
because the authorities have desired to discourage the tendency, so harmful
in all parts of Central America, towards the adoption of the learned profes-
sions at the expense of agricultural pursuits."[31] By 1900 fewer than 5 percent
of school-age children attended primary school, and the few schools that did
exist offered dark, makeshift classrooms staffed by poorly trained teachers.[32]
Quality education remained an elite privilege available in private schools. In
rural areas with a heavy indigenous presence, the few schools that did exist
were oriented toward eradicating indigenous culture and language in favor of
a uniformly Spanish-speaking, ladino identity.[33]

While liberals deemphasized the importance of access to education, they placed high priority on centralizing education administration. They established so-called normal schools to train teachers in a more systematic manner. They passed a comprehensive education law in 1885 that, among other things, created the position of secretary of public instruction, which eventually led to the establishment of the Ministry of Education. The national state steadily usurped the funding and administration of schools from local officials. The 1885 law even extended compulsory education from primary school children to boys between the ages of seven and fifteen. Loopholes in the law and the utter lack of schools and teachers caused the compulsory rule to be ignored. Nonetheless, the law's existence revealed liberal policymakers' intent to increase the role of the national government in education oversight.[34]

Salvadoran liberals approached politics in the same manner as mass education. They used the language of democracy and presented the United States as a model, but their attitudes and practices opposed universal equality and mass empowerment. They centralized and controlled the electoral process. Galindo's distinction between *el pueblo* (the people) and *la sociedad* (society) once again provided the ideological rationale to promote exclusivity. Liberals were quick to point out that one person's liberty was another's tyranny, and they went to great lengths to confine the meanings of liberty and democracy and to control who qualified for inclusion in the nation. As far as they were concerned, the definition of liberty did not require popular suffrage or mass empowerment, even though they celebrated democracy and passed laws acknowledging every adult male's right to vote and his equality before the law, regardless of race or property. Liberal rhetoricians portrayed universal suffrage as leading inevitably to tyranny. As one spokesperson put it, "the masses are ignorant and susceptible to machinations by people of bad faith."[35] Based on this type of reasoning, Salvadoran liberals constructed a highly controlled political system in which a veneer of electoral democracy prevailed in the form of regular voting and high turnout on election day, but without freedom of choice.[36]

The emergent liberalism in El Salvador generated debate and dissention. The Catholic Church issued irate pastoral letters to resist secularization.[37] Local elites resisted the centralizing efforts of the national government. Peasants and indigenous communities struggled to preserve their autonomy by petitioning, resisting, and rebelling. Some economic modernizers balked at the way privatization created a few landed elites rather than a larger class of yeoman farmers. Some intellectuals and artists—fellow elites in many cases—accused liberal policymakers of ignoring Salvadoran culture in favor of foreign models, Anglo no less. They challenged the liberal paradigm through literature and art in a way that promoted Salvadoran national identity reminiscent of Uruguay's José Enrique Rodo, whose famed essay "Ariel" portrayed the United States and England as crassly materialistic and lacking in spiritualism.[38]

Regardless of debate and dissention, the version of liberalism that became dominant in El Salvador rested on the twin pillars of laissez-faire economics and authoritarian politics. The architects of this system were a small group of landowning families whose members believed they had created the nation's wealth by themselves, without foreign assistance, and by overcoming great obstacles. They also believed that the nation as a whole benefited when government stayed out of their affairs and concentrated instead on maintaining public order and disciplining anyone who questioned the status quo.

By the eve of the Great Depression, El Salvador was a monocrop economy, with 90 percent of export revenues deriving from coffee. The country had almost no industrial capacity and few prospects for industrialization in the absence of significant changes. The country's internal market was tiny, partly because wealth was so heavily concentrated in a few hands. Those who owned capital were willing to invest it anywhere they thought they could make money, but their profits from the status quo limited their willingness to consider new ventures.

The members of elite families came to accept the elite version of liberalism as orthodoxy, and by the latter half of the twentieth century they would morph such views into broader expressions of anticommunism and economic libertarianism. Naturally, elites would direct their ire at the rebellious masses and communists (both foreign and domestic). But they would also find their supposed allies, military officers in government, advocating different paths to modernity. Those officers began to link social stability to social reform and called for the state to play a stronger role in guiding the economy.

The First Era of Military Rule, 1931–1948: Setting the Stage

The period between 1931 and 1948 is generally and rightly seen as a conservative era in Salvadoran history. The prevailing liberal economic program was not seriously challenged, and social and political reforms were resisted by the government. In particular, this era was marked by the violent suppression of two reformist political movements, in 1931 and in 1944–1945. This first phase of military governance established the norms that would define military rule for the next fifty years, particularly the prospects for state-led modernization and the complex interplay of repression and reformism. It was during this first era that the complex structure of military rule emerged, a heterogeneous conglomeration of civilians and officers balancing constantly the competing interests of stakeholders in society.

The first serious effort to promote democracy amid the liberal paradigm occurred in the late 1920s. The nation's landed elites saw this experiment as a horrible failure, later presenting it as a cautionary tale about the perils of mass participation in politics. Pío Romero Bosque was the victor in the 1926 presidential election. Although he was not a member of the landed elite, he was a lifelong political functionary who had held high-ranking positions in government. He became president in the usual manner, in a noncompetitive election as the hand-chosen successor of the incumbent. Contrary to expectations, Romero broke with tradition and insisted that liberalism include genuine democratic practices.

Over the next four years, Romero worked diligently to apply the administrative and policing powers of the state to promote free elections. His efforts produced mixed results, but one clear success was the presidential election of January 1931, which was won by a landowner named Arturo Araujo who had been influenced by the Labor Party while he was a student in England. The relative freedom of the election and Araujo's victory emboldened Salvadorans who hoped for widespread reform, even radical change. But the economic crisis of the Great Depression dashed their hopes. With government revenues shrinking and criticism coming from all sides, Araujo's government fell in December 1931 to a military coup that placed Gen. Maximiliano Hernández Martínez in power.[39]

Martínez was a stern military man of humble origins with an authoritarian personality and an austere style.[40] His dedication to a variant of Theosophy, a religious philosophy rooted in mysticism, garnered him the nickname "el brujo" (witch or sorcerer). He dominated Salvadoran politics for almost thirteen years amid a one-party dictatorship. It is tempting to see Martínez's longevity as inevitable, but it was hardly so. Within just his first two months in office he faced economic catastrophe, diplomatic opposition from the United States, a peasant uprising in the western region, and disgruntled members of civil society who supported Araujo and his promised reforms. In later years he faced coup attempts and various political intrigues, particularly from within the officer corps, and the ever-rigid demands from landed elites.

One of Martínez's survival tactics was to employ Salvadoran nationalism against U.S. objections to the coup. Martínez responded to the United States' refusal to recognize his government with a nationalist rhetoric in which he criticized the United States for meddling in El Salvador's affairs. In a speech before the National Legislative Assembly in February 1932, he said, "it is not up to foreign governments to judge the legitimacy of personnel changes in a nation with which it has had relations. . . . [Doing so] represents an intrusion in the internal affairs of that nation, contrary to its sovereignty."[41] In adopting this nationalist strategy, Martínez capitalized on a wave of anti-imperialism that had been sweeping across the region, allowing him to capture support from groups that otherwise opposed him, like university students and social reformers.[42] When the United States finally relented and granted recognition in 1934, Martínez emerged as a sort of a regional anti-imperialist hero.[43] He demonstrated how effective nationalism could be in rallying domestic support against U.S.-based calls for change. This would not be the last time that an anticommunist military regime in El Salvador would use nationalism to resist U.S. pressure for reform.

In general, though, Martínez survived by employing a paradoxical blend of reform and repression that would typify military rule for the next five decades. In response to a massive peasant uprising in the western region in January 1932, Martínez unleashed a wave a terror unprecedented in modern Latin American history.[44] His overwhelming use of violence put an immediate end to rebellious activities and allowed him to construct a massive police state. In the succeeding years, Martínez created rural paramilitaries, built up a national network of spies and informants, and monitored and harassed all political rivals. He eventually did away with the fledgling democracy and built a dictatorship around a single political party, the Partido Pro-Patria (Party of the Fatherland).

These repressive traits were accompanied by a reformist current. Ironic as it may seem, Martínez introduced the idea that social reform in defense of poor people was necessary. He put a quick end to his military's reign of terror in the west and stated that his government had the responsibility to protect the nation's poor majority.[45] Martínez explained that the masses were not to blame for the uprising. Instead, their poverty and humility made them susceptible to communist agitators. Instead of holding the peasants solely responsible for their own poverty, as was standard in the dominant liberal paradigm, Martínez also held elites and the government responsible. In his address to the National Legislative Assembly immediately after the uprising, Martínez insisted that "it is up to the Government and the leading classes of society to unite before this urgent necessity . . . to resolve without delay the problems that exist between capital and labor. . . . In El Salvador there is only one justice, equal for everyone, poor and rich, knowledgeable and ignorant."[46] In various speeches and policy statements in the months and years that followed, Martínez and other high-ranking officials in his government defined the rural masses as an integral part of the nation, insisting that government and landowners had a responsibility to do more to improve their condition.

The centerpiece of the government's plan to help the poor and stifle communism was a social reform program known as Mejoramiento Social (Social Betterment). The program's projects included building low-cost homes for urban workers and acquiring agricultural properties to be sold to peasants at favorable rates. The achievements of Mejoramiento Social were modest, partly due to the state's financial limitations but also due to the limited willingness of the Martínez government to truly transform society. In the end, practical reforms were outweighed by the rhetoric surrounding them. For example, from its foundation until Martínez's fall in 1944, Mejoramiento Social built an average of twenty-six modest, wood-frame houses per year, at a time when the urban housing deficit was in the tens of thousands.[47] This suggests that Mejoramiento Social was more of a political marketing tool than a genuine effort to alleviate poverty. Nevertheless, the actions and rhetoric surrounding it generated some popular support. The clandestine Communist Party actually feared it would be unable to compete with Martínez for the hearts and minds of poor Salvadorans. According to one of its internal reports, "[Martínez] was trying to pose as champion of the masses, as a national government, a government of all classes. . . . Since he kept promising them things and making gestures, the tendency was for the masses to believe him."[48] Martínez's efforts to advocate for the poor and promote himself as a populist were hindered by his eccentric views and the often strange policies that emerged from them. In response to an epidemic, for example, he ordered the lampposts of the capital to be covered with cellophane paper in the belief that colored light would cure the suffering population.[49] Nevertheless, Martínez helped plant the idea in the mind of the citizenry that their government had an obligation to defend and protect them.

An episode that provides a revealing look into the Martínez government and its relationship with landowners is the campaign against plantation-owned stores in 1939.[50] It was a longstanding practice in El Salvador for large plantations to pay their workers in coupons (*fichas*) that could be redeemed only in stores located on the plantations and owned by the landowners. Opposition to this practice came from commercial-rights and labor-rights activists, who argued that the practice at once hindered capitalism, because landowners did not allow competitors onto their properties, and exploited laborers, because it forced them to spend their already meager earnings on overpriced goods in the plantations' stores.

In September 1939 the Martínez government took on landowners by ordering the closing of all plantation-owned stores and the payment of workers in legal currency rather than fichas. Officials in the government cited Article 55 of the Constitution, which barred monopolies over commerce. They also employed a flamboyant rhetoric that compared the plantation-owned stores to "the system of commissaries used in Soviet Russia; a system that we should not allow to be implanted on our soil owing to its unjust and unsuitable qualities."[51] One of the interest groups that stood to gain from the new policy was the Chamber of Small Commerce (Cámara de Comerciantes en Pequeño). Its members thanked the government for its courage in ordering the closing of the stores and "stimulating the good will of the masses in the countryside."[52]

Landowners seem to have been caught off guard by the government's action because immediately after the order was issued, many of them submitted desperate requests to the government asking that they be allowed to keep their stores open for a brief while in order to liquidate their merchandise. In most cases the government granted the request, but within two months the government reported that the system of plantation-owned stores had been dissolved and workers were being paid in cash.

The government's victory proved short-lived. Landowners launched a vigorous lobbying campaign, both in the public press and behind the scenes. The Coffee Growers' Association led the charge, with some of the nation's most well-known and powerful landowners taking a public lead in the opposition, such as Guirola from Santa Tecla, Alvarado from San Salvador, and Regalado from San Julián. Government documents also mention landowners' lobbying efforts through phone calls and personal conversations, although documentary records of these conversations do not exist. The lobbying went on for more than six months, through April 1940. The landowners pushed government officials relentlessly, insisting that the government was overstepping its bounds and that it was hurting workers by limiting their access to goods that were hard to come by in rural areas.

Starting in April 1940, the government surrendered to the pressure and quietly allowed the stores to reopen. Once it learned of the government's acquiescence, the Chamber of Small Commerce expressed its opposition in a letter to the government describing the decision as "causing a natural disgust among peasants who once again have to watch the fruits of their modest work return to the landowners' coffers."[53]

This episode of the plantation-owned stores reveals something not only about the Martínez government but also about the nature of relations between landowners and the military more broadly. First and foremost, the Martínez government surrendered to pressure from landowners and retracted a reformist policy that it considered beneficial to the nation as a whole. This episode would not be the last in which a military government retracted a reformist promise in the face of resolute landowner opposition—see the case of the failure of land reform in 1976. But at the same time, the campaign against the plantation-owned stores shows a military regime willing and able to take up the fight in the public arena of politics. Playing the conflict out in public like that carried many risks, such as raising the hopes of the masses only to see them downtrodden in the end and invoking the ire of landowners only to surrender to them. In the end, no one emerged victorious, because neither the rural laborers nor the government got what they wanted, and the landowners were riled up in their suspicion of government bureaucrats' willingness to intervene in their affairs. So while the ultimate conclusion to this particular story of the plantation-owned stores is one of government acquiescence to landowner power, the conflict was nonetheless real and public; it was neither an act, nor a sideshow, nor mere window dressing for some secret deal between military officials and landowners. Military officials in the government and landowners may have shared some things in common, but also they were independent stakeholders whose interests could diverge.

Education had a place in Martínez's reformist scheme, but, as with Mejoramiento Social, the achievements were modest. Throughout the 1930s, education was rarely mentioned, and no significant gains were made in improving quality or broadening access. The first major education reform came in 1940, late in the administration, and was implemented in a manner consistent with Martínez's governing strategy. The reform was conceived by a small coterie of government appointees without input from educators and was then imposed in a top-down manner in the name of modernization and progress. The objective of the reform was to bring pedagogical practices up to current international standards. A four-member coordinating commission conceived and implemented every aspect of the reform, rewriting the entire curriculum. Notably, they did not jettison the Education for Citizenship model, nor did they address the issue of educational access.[54] Years after the changes, an American observer described the mundane nature of a typical day in a high school classroom: "The teachers lecture, explain the assignment or the lesson, and then dictate a prepared summary or brief which the students enter into their notebooks. Class discussion of the materials studied is infrequent and student questions are extremely rare."[55] One of the commissioners later acknowledged that the commission's approach to reform ignored the socioeconomic needs of the country and focused instead on pedagogical matters.[56] However, that same individual claimed in a 1994 interview with a Salvadoran historian that Martínez had told him that the reform should be directed at the poor, because "the rich already have their schools."[57] The commission claimed its emphasis on pedagogical training was a major improvement over past practices. But in the absence of more impactive reforms, education continued to be a privilege, a pathway to power for a select few. It would be many years before an alternative approach to education would take hold. During the Martínez era, the percentage of children attending primary school hardly increased over the 1920s, with less than 30 percent of primary-school-age children receiving any form of education. Nonetheless, that figure was a vast improvement from the dismally low figures of the late nineteenth century.[58]

Martínez's economic policies followed a pattern similar to that of his education policies; he promoted change and created institutions that laid the foundations for altering the status quo, but ultimately things remained much as they were when he came to office. He placed a high priority on aiding export agriculture but was unwilling to alter land tenure. Thus, his agricultural policies supported the existing landowning elite. He wanted to modernize the economy, and to that end he increased the state's role in economic affairs. But he also worked in direct partnership with elites. For example, he founded the nation's first central bank, which created a monopoly over printing currency, but it was in the form of a partnership between the state and landowners. He founded the Salvadoran Coffee Company, a public-private partnership that was designed to promote coffee exports. He also established a mortgage bank to boost coffee production. The precise nature and intensity of the state's participation in the economy would be a matter of debate for many decades. Regardless, any policies that Martínez pursued reflected both his eccentricities and his Depression-era obsession with fiscal austerity.[59]

In exercising this paradoxical blend of hard-line repression with evocation of social reform and economic modernization, Martínez foreshadowed internal debates within the Salvadoran right that would proceed for the next fifty years. Members of the army, many of whom were of humble social origin, saw themselves as reformers who sided more with workers than with landed elites. They claimed that the army was best equipped to soften the rough edges of capitalism by addressing social concerns because soldiers better understood the day-to-day reality of most Salvadorans. Even when these portrayals were nothing more than expedient attempts by individuals to gain power and were swiftly neutered by angry landowners, they kept the idea of social reform alive and raised expectations about the government's responsibility to its citizenry. By the 1940s the ideas of the British economist John Maynard Keynes made it acceptable for the state to intervene in the economy, and the leaders of the Salvadoran military regime embraced those ideas. Landowners, in contrast, tended to be more inflexible, opposing reform and seeing the path to progress in a more rigid economic liberalism that did not include government action to help the poor (the majority of the population). The U.S. chargé opined in 1934 that some landowners had grown suspicious of Martínez because "[he] has been too solicitous for the welfare of the lower classes."[60]

Martínez stayed in power amid his eccentricities, authoritarianism, and flashes of populism, but the powerful elites tolerated him only so long as he maintained stability and quickly suppressed mass movements. His ability to provide those services eroded when he tried to stay in power too long as the world changed around him. In 1944 he attempted to amend the Constitution for the second time to allow himself to remain in office for a fourth term. At this time the economy had recovered, Allied forces were advancing in World War II, and pro-democracy rhetoric was pervasive. Many dictatorial regimes in Latin America were falling amid a regional surge of democratization.[61] Martínez's attempt to stay in office generated widespread opposition, particularly among the middle class, urban reformers, and some military officers who wanted El Salvador to take full advantage of the economic opportunities offered by international markets. Even some conservative elites worried that Martínez was risking national progress for personal power. While they cared little about his authoritarian politics, they placed a high priority on order, and Martínez's attempt to stay in power was causing instability.[62]

Martínez tried to rally popular support at the last minute by implementing some populist programs. Reformers were too savvy to be fooled, and

conservatives only grew angrier. In the end Martínez faced a broad oppositional wave that included a coup attempt by some of his own officers in
March 1944. He held off the inevitable for a few months by crushing the coup
and executing more than one dozen officers who led it. By July the opposition had become widespread, and his government collapsed. An elite business leader offered his view of what happened: "The downfall of Martínez
was something brought about by the people. The clerks in the stores and
other *empleados* quit their jobs. Stores closed down. The factory workers quit
their jobs, and finally the situation got to be such that Martínez could no
longer stay in power." [63] The discourse of the victors was distinctly modernist
sounding. They defined the Martínez era as archaic and backward and called
for the creation of a new government that would modernize El Salvador.
They made martyrs out of the officers executed after the March coup. [64]

The junta that took power after Martínez's departure promised free and
fair elections. The candidate that emerged as the frontrunner was Dr. Arturo
Romero, a civilian social reformer whose vision for change was seen as too
radical by the conservative right. [65] A reactionary coup led by Martínez's
chief of police, Osmín Aguirre y Salinas, ended the electoral experiment.
Coup leaders sent Romero into exile and placed Aguirre in power as interim
president. Some of Romero's supporters, mostly idealistic university students, tried to take up arms against the usurpers, but the army discovered
their hideout in Santa Ana and massacred them, creating yet another coterie
of martyrs. Just as in 1931–1932, a progressive civilian movement that threatened the reigning liberalism was suppressed. Eventually Martínez's former
minister of government, Gen. Salvador Castaneda Castro, became president
through the traditional mechanism of a noncompetitive election. Castaneda
stayed in power until 1948, when he was overthrown by another military
coup. Its leaders were more reformist in orientation, and their regime rein-
vigorated the debate over modernization. [66]

The Second Phase of Military Rule, 1948–1960:
The Initial Steps Toward Modernization and Foreign Advice

After 1948 debates within ruling groups over the meaning of modernity, liberalism, and nationalism intensified, and education assumed a more prominent place in the dialogue. The leaders of the 1948 coup were a coterie of
young, ambitious military officers and a handful of allied civilians who identified themselves as modernizing reformers. They called their movement a

revolution and cited as precedent the overthrow of Martínez in 1944.[67] They drew inspiration from modernizing reforms in neighboring countries, including the Mexican Revolution, Guatemala after 1945, and Costa Rica after 1948. In an interview later in life, President José María Lemus, the second of the "revolutionary" presidents (1956–1960), told a Salvadoran historian that he and other members of the new leadership drew inspiration from Guatemala and Costa Rica. But he also said they saw cautionary tales of reformism that had gone too far, especially in Costa Rica, where that nation's new leaders disbanded the army.[68] Lemus and the other "revolutionaries" wanted reforms within safe limits.

The new leaders ruled as a junta for two years until they formed a political party, the Revolutionary Party of Democratic Unification (PRUD). They then oversaw the election of one of their own, Col. Oscar Osorio, as president in 1950. Six years later they arranged for Lemus, who had been Osorio's minister of the interior, to be elected as his successor. In 1960 Lemus was overthrown in yet another coup that brought the "revolutionary" era to an end and began the transition to the next phase of military rule under the National Conciliation Party (PCN).[69]

Osorio had lived in semi-exile as a diplomat in Mexico and was inspired by its government's combination of populism and strong central authority. He witnessed firsthand the use of revolutionary rhetoric to promote the institutionalization of power, and he wanted to replicate it in El Salvador. He surrounded himself with revolutionary symbols, including a prominent monument in San Salvador that bore a strong resemblance to the imagery of the Mexican muralists, and organized yearly commemorations of the 1948 Revolution.[70] The reformist agenda of the 1948 junta was well received by some people, including labor leaders. As one of them put it in 1949, "the new regime initiated a real change of attitude with regard to the unions. As a result, a number of trade unions increased."[71]

The attempt by Osorio and his fellow revolutionaries to copy the Mexican model revealed the two nation's great differences. Beyond the obvious examples of geographic size and population, Mexico's government was headed by a political party (the Institutional Revolutionary Party, PRI) that emerged directly out of the Mexican Revolution, a massive social upheaval that targeted the old liberal order. In contrast, El Salvador's landowning elites had never faced a comparable challenge. And so regardless of what Osorio or other reformers in El Salvador might have wanted to do, they had to negotiate with the powerful landed elites.[72]

Nonetheless, Osorio and the other PRUD leaders believed that El Salvador faced long-term problems if the existing liberal economic order remained unchanged. In particular, they believed the country needed to diversify its economy through industrialization. They reasoned that most of the landowning elites did not share their view, so they would have to take the initiative themselves and use the power of the state to effect change. Beyond the obvious problem of inciting a conservative backlash, Osorio and the other revolutionary leaders had to face the fact that the state lacked money and had limited constitutional powers. To help resolve these problems they first raised taxes on coffee exports, a very risky act. The price of coffee had been rising rapidly since 1945, and the new leaders reasoned that the state should reap some of the windfall profits. They also wrote a new Constitution that gave the state the legal right to intervene in the economy. The new charter stated that the economic system had to "respond essentially to principles of social justice that tend to secure, for all the inhabitants of the country, an existence worthy of a human being."[73] It even redefined private property as having to serve a social function or be subject to expropriation.

In hopes of buffering conservative reactions, the new leaders invited members of rich families to join their government. Immediately after the 1948 coup, for example, leadership of the Ministry of Agriculture went to Enrique Alvarez, the patriarch of a landowning family who had made its money in coffee and cattle. After Osorio's election in 1950, he brought into his cabinet three members of well-known elite families: Roberto Canessa in foreign affairs, Roberto Quiñonez in agriculture, and Jorge Sol Castellanos in economy.

Such overtures, however, did little to alleviate conservative elites' concerns. Alvarez remained a stalwart conservative and had a falling out with the new leaders only one year after his appointment. Supposedly he financed a coup attempt against them in 1950. Other elites considered their counterparts who continued to work with the PRUD government as traitors. According to one report from of the U.S. Embassy, conservative landowners took particular offense at the presence of Sol Castellanos in Osorio's cabinet, because they considered him to be a "leftist-minded power grabber."[74]

As for the PRUD leaders' economic policies, they supported the creation of a Central American common market to increase the market for Salvadoran goods. They also embarked upon infrastructural upgrades, included the building of the coastal highway and the Fifth of November Dam on the Lempa River to provide cheap electricity. At the inauguration of the dam in 1954, Osorio and other government leaders displayed their

El Estado tiene la obligación de asegurar a los habitantes de El Salvador el goce de la libertad, y de velar por que sea una realidad la justicia social.— (Art. 2).

FIGURE 3. In 1952, the "revolutionary" government under President Osorio celebrated the 1950 Constitution and its reformist elements. The caption under the image reads, "The State has the duty to make sure that all Salvadoran citizens enjoy freedom and that social justice is a reality." González Ruiz, *El Salvador de hoy* 1952, 129.

self-conceptualization as modernizing reformers, claiming the dam and its cheap electricity would push El Salvador out of "backwardness" and into "modern times" by promoting industrialization and reducing reliance on agricultural exports.[75]

PRUD officials also relied on foreign development consultants. In 1952 the government welcomed a United Nations technical assistance team that included University of Chicago economist Bert Hoselitz, a specialist in the newly emerging field of development economics. According to Hoselitz, if El Salvador wanted to modernize and diversify its economy, then its leaders had to use state power to enact sweeping reforms in a variety of areas, including land, taxation, banking, and customs. He said El Salvador's landowning capitalists did not have sufficient incentive to do it through the marketplace "because the high risk factors assigned to new investment [made] the expected net rate of return rather low." Thus, he continued, "Governmental sponsoring of industrial development is needed." He reasoned that one of El Salvador's problems was its small internal market, and his solution, which was anathema to landed elites, was to bring about "a certain redistribution of domestic income, and especially a general elevation of the real income of the lowest income layers of the population." Hoeslitz first provided his findings to the government in a confidential report in 1952 and later published them in a book. In a later interview, former president Lemus referred to that book as "our Bible for economic modernization."[76]

Under the influence of advisors like Hoselitz, PRUD leaders more intensely embraced the image of themselves as modernizing state managers using up-to-date knowledge to improve El Salvador. Unfortunately, change cost money, and the modest tax increase on coffee hardly sufficed. Foreign loans were available for certain kinds of projects, and indeed the revolutionaries took out six loans with international banks in amounts greater than US$1 million, with the two largest in excess of US$10 million—for the Fifth of November Dam and the coastal highway.[77] But loans had to be paid back, and interest rates were not favorable. Outright grants-in-aid from the United States did not yet exist in the 1950s. For those, Salvadoran leaders would have to wait for a massive shift in U.S. policy regarding foreign aid, which would happen after the Cuban Revolution in 1959. Ultimately, any willingness that PRUD leaders had to enact widespread modernizing change confronted the hard reality of limited practical ability.

Education assumed a more prominent place in the modernizing agenda of the PRUD than it had during the preceding Martínez era. PRUD leaders recognized, partly due to recommendations from foreign consultants like Hoselitz, that El Salvador's most abundant and precious commodity was its people. As Hoselitz put it, "The major resource of El Salvador . . . is its population, and . . . any programme of industrial development, if it is to be economically sound, must be based on that." Capital investment would be to no avail, Hoselitz reasoned, "if there are not present men who can operate the new machines."[78] Still, at that time PRUD leaders tended to define education in terms of social justice rather than as a mechanism to create skilled labor for industrialization. The latter kind of reconsideration of the goal of education would have to wait until the 1960s. Still, they addressed the limitation of the education system to an unprecedented degree.

They included articles in the new Constitution of 1950 stating that every citizen should help fight illiteracy, which was estimated officially to affect 40–50 percent of the population, although the rate was probably much higher. As a result, the Ministry of Culture established a new unit to attack illiteracy. To deal with the scarcity of teachers, the PRUD government founded new teachers' schools, including the Escuela Normal Superior, to train primary- and secondary-school teachers. It also founded a pair of teacher training schools specifically for rural teachers.

Wanting to emulate programs that Osorio had seen in Mexico, his government built "revolution style" schools in urban and rural areas and called for the creation of cultural brigades to support the literacy programs. The literacy campaign in rural areas was supposed to be complemented by workshops to teach crafts and domestic chores, "to improve the conditions in rural households," as President Osorio said in a speech. But the public pronouncements were more grandiose than the achievements; in fact, only two cultural brigades ever functioned.[79]

PRUD leaders wrapped all of their policies in a strongly reformist rhetoric, nowhere more evident than in a new weekly periodical, *Boletín del Ejército* (Army bulletin), launched in January 1949. In the pages of the *Boletín*, the "revolutionary" leaders heralded democracy, workers' rights, and the need for harmonious relations between capital and labor. They promoted a socially inclusive nationalism that opposed Galindo's classically liberal definition of the pueblo back in 1874. Instead of the pueblo being "rabble," the leaders of the 1948 coup defined them as *"civilidad"* (civility) and as "all the men who reside in the national territory without any distinctions between them."[80] They said that civilidad applied especially to peasants and "the working class." They described the army as being "of the people, by the people and for the people" and defined the army as the people's "armed wing" rather than the praetorian guard of the elite.[81] Repeatedly, the new leaders appealed to workers, both urban and rural, telling them that the new government supported them and therefore they should support it.[82] Osorio's influential minister of the economy, Sol Castellanos, later wrote that the army became conscious that its interests "were different from those of the oligarchy" during this period.[83]

As further evidence of the new leaders' reformist orientation, they minimized their anticommunist rhetoric, especially during their first three years in power, and instead focused their criticism on "reactionary" elites. They defined such elites as enemies of modernity, as people who opposed social reform and wanted to keep El Salvador a backward place where a tiny minority controlled the nation's resources. The coup leaders avoided implicating the wealthy as a class and instead said that bad individuals were the problem. The *Boletín* defined reactionaries as those who "do not comply with labor laws and do not see capital as serving a social function."[84] President Osorio further clarified these views in a speech to the nation in 1951 in which he accused individuals of not wanting to join "modern times."[85] The *Boletín* even used nationalism against them by accusing them of being "anti-Salvadoran."[86] When the new leaders began to emit a more traditional anticommunist rhetoric after 1951, they employed the same explanation for the rise of communism that Martínez had used to explain the peasant uprising back in 1932. They insisted that exploitative "ricos" (wealthy people) caused problems because their discriminatory policies made workers susceptible to communists' promises.[87]

Notwithstanding noteworthy achievements in the arena of social policy, the accomplishments of the PRUD administrations hardly matched the enormity of the nation's problems. Just as with Martínez, the revolutionaries' rhetoric outpaced the reality of their reforms. They created the Procuraduría de Pobres (Advocate for the Poor), but the plight of the poor was barely relieved. They tackled the housing problem, but their highly publicized projects were grossly inadequate and reached only the middle sectors. They introduced social security, but the program was made available only to a few urban workers. They identified illiteracy as a serious problem, but their efforts hardly improved literacy statistics. They celebrated democracy but continued to control elections. They claimed to be empowering the citizenry but centralized control and suppressed dissent. They also accused rich landowners of abusing workers and monopolizing the country's productive resources, but they opposed land reform and the organization of rural labor.[88]

Ultimately, the PRUD stayed true to its authoritarian roots. In 1951 Osorio and the PRUD pushed through the Ley de Defensa del Orden Democrático y Constitucional (Law for the Defense of a Democratic and Constitutional Order), which allowed them to crack down on anyone who committed the vague crime of supporting "doctrines contrary to democracy."[89] The regime used this as pretext to suppress any signs of independent labor organizing and political radicalism.

In the final analysis, the "revolution" had clear limits. Sol Castellanos later described the regime's boundaries: "they [the leaders after 1948] could carry out some changes within parameters, such as not touching the interests of the oligarchy."[90] In the words of historian Jorge Cáceres Prendes: "The regime established after the 1948 coup resembled other 'populist' experiments existing in Latin America from the late 30's onwards. As in other variants of 'populism,' the Salvadorans set up a formulae of combining a strong military presence—most visible in the selection of the President—with a 'Ruling Party'—the unquestioned winner of every election, by whatever means—led by middle class civilian professionals, especially those linked to the government, and finally a mobilized population—coopted through clientelism, nationalistic rhetoric and the lure of social reforms."[91] Nevertheless, the revolutionaries of 1948–1960 framed the battle lines for intra-right debates for decades to come. Their level of reformist rhetoric was unprecedented. They created the legal foundation for the state to intervene in the economy in ways that were contrary to liberal fundamentalists. Even if they did not use those powers, landowning elites worried that future governments would be willing to do so.

The Conservative Voice Emerges:
Napoleón Viera Altamirano and *El Diario de Hoy*

As the populism of the revolutionaries persisted, the intra-right debate assumed a more visible and public character. Conservatives used the press to articulate their positions, if not in direct opposition to PRUD officials, then at least in favor of contrarian principles.[92] Conservatives channeled their thinking mainly through daily newspapers, particularly *El Diario de Hoy*. Although *El Diario de Hoy* was not the only outlet for conservative thought, it was the most influential and articulate. We analyze it in some detail because it epitomized the thinking of a very influential group within the economic elite.

El Diario de Hoy was founded in 1936 by Napoleón Viera Altamirano (1893–1977), one of El Salvador's more renowned and iconoclastic men of letters. A deeply committed defender of economic liberalism and an admirer of Argentina's canonical liberal Domingo Faustino Sarmiento, Viera Altamirano was devoted to economic growth but believed growth could occur only when owners of capital were not obstructed by either the state or organized workers.[93] Viera Altamirano was joined in expressing this newly vocal conservatism by other writers of the day, including Ricardo Fuentes Castellanos, Jorge Lardé y Larín, José Antonio Rodríguez Porth, and Ricardo Dueñas Van Severén, among many others. Almost none of them belonged to the Salvadoran oligarchy. A few were doctors or lawyers, and some held government posts, such as Lardé y Larín, who made his living as the dependable in-house historian for the military. Most of them lived modest lives as writers, editorialists, and paid propagandists. Together, starting in the 1950s, this conglomeration of intellectuals projected into the public arena a daily dose of consistent conservative commentary on any given topic. The pages of *El Diario de Hoy* provided a home for their writings, and none of them was more prolific than Viera Altamirano, who reportedly worked from morning to night, writing constantly.[94]

Consistent with his admiration for Sarmiento, Viera Altamirano moved comfortably between liberalism and nationalism, embracing both concepts but drawing upon them selectively. One of Altamirano's unrelenting positions was hostility to government spending on social programs or any state intervention in the economy to benefit labor. The editorial pages of *El Diario de Hoy* insisted that El Salvador's export crops were subject to market forces and workers' wages should be too.[95] In his view the poor would benefit from economic growth, and everything that impeded growth, such as minimum wage laws, was bad for everyone.

The government's announcement about building the Fifth of November Dam in 1949 provided Viera Altamirano with an opportunity to express his typical form of nationalism. He strongly favored building the dam as a source of cheap power and therefore as a spur to economic growth, insisting that the rewards from the dam would benefit all Salvadorans, rich and poor alike. But he lamented the government's reliance on foreign technical experts, insisting that Salvadorans could have designed and built the dam themselves.[96] He also opposed the millions of dollars in foreign loans that the government took out to finance the dam's construction.[97]

When it came to the issue of international affairs, Viera Altamirano and *El Diario de Hoy* applied an opportunistic nationalism. Steadfastly anticommunist, *El Diario de Hoy* and Viera Altamirano naturally sided with the United States in the Cold War and celebrated the United States as a beacon of liberalism and modernity, just as Sarmiento had done a century earlier. But *El Diario de Hoy* strongly opposed foreigners, especially North Americans, coming to El Salvador and telling Salvadorans what to do. In one editorial,

Viera Altamirano wrote that "we [Salvadorans] want to avoid being targeted by international philanthropists who come down here and feed us, as if we were incipient communities of the dessert or forest."[98] Particularly irksome to Viera Altamirano were North Americans or Europeans who described El Salvador as a poor, underdeveloped, or backward nation, even though he used exactly the same language in his own descriptions of the country. For example, he frequently said that El Salvador needed to escape its "colonial backwardness" and diversify its economy by industrializing. But when foreigners made the same arguments, Viera Altamirano took it as an insult.[99]

Viera Altamirano's nationalism could contradict his commitment to economic liberalism. He called for the state to use tariffs to protect Salvadoran capitalists, such as those who had invested in the fledgling cotton and milk industries.[100] No sooner had he advocated for their protection than he supported a free-trade deal with Guatemala because he believed Salvadoran capitalists would benefit from expanded markets.[101] He justified such apparent contradictions by adhering to the logic that any and all state policies should be designed to favor Salvadoran capital.[102]

He promoted industrialization in principle as a good thing for the future of El Salvador but remained steadfast in his belief that any such transformation had to be achieved through market mechanisms by entrepreneurial capitalists without state intervention. To this end, he promoted the creation of a Central American common market and other, more ambitious economic integration schemes. By growing the size of the overall market and then allowing capitalists throughout the region to pursue profit, economic transformation would take care of itself, he believed.[103]

In the late 1940s and early 1950s, the conservative right did not have reason to be too opposed to the leaders who had taken power in 1948. Those leaders had not done much to turn their populist rhetoric into widespread reforms. Nonetheless, some of their policies and the degree of their rhetoric generated concern, and the pages of *El Diario de Hoy* began to stake out an ideological difference with PRUD leaders. The conservative response to the PRUD's reformist impulses boiled down to a simple mantra: Salvadoran capitalists had the right to define modernization on their own terms, in the absence of foreign advisors and interventionist state managers. In the 1950s PRUD governments were able to advance their agendas without much resistance thanks to the flow of cash entering state coffers when coffee prices and exports were at unprecedented highs. But things would change in the 1960s.

Tensions Deepen Within the Right, 1960–1961

A combination of domestic and international events between 1959 and 1961 raised the stakes of intra-right debates over modernization. On the international front, the Cuban Revolution in January 1959 brought the Cold War home to Latin America in a shocking manner.[104] The following year John F. Kennedy was elected president of the United States, and shortly after his inauguration he announced the creation of the Alliance for Progress, a massive foreign aid program designed to promote economic development in Latin America and counter the appeal of the Cuban Revolution. The ideology behind the Alliance was rooted in modernization theory. Alliance architects argued that Latin America was trapped in a semifeudal state of backwardness and thus remained susceptible to communist incursion. They reasoned that a short-term, massive infusion of foreign aid combined with technical advice and social reforms could push the region safely toward development and capitalist modernization.[105]

Events like the Cuban Revolution and the launching of the Alliance for Progress brought into sharp focus alternative views of modernity. Reformers in El Salvador hoped for an infusion of money, technical expertise, and military supplies, all in the name of modernization and anticommunism. Conservatives remained skeptical of reform. Some of them saw the need for change, but they exhibited diverse opinions about how much change was necessary. Many clung to the belief that no change would be best.

A consistent view of the conservatives was opposition to meddling outsiders, be they socialists or capitalists. Members of the conservative landowning and business sector welcomed allies in their battle against communism, but they opposed outsiders targeting El Salvador for reform. In fact, as much as they hated communists, they held special antipathy for modernizing North American capitalists who believed that Salvadoran landowners were a source of backwardness. El Salvador's landowners adamantly opposed land reform and considered anyone who supported it to be a communist, even if that person was a North American capitalist or an anticommunist military officer in El Salvador.

Events inside El Salvador also intensified debates within the right. El Salvador's economy took a turn for the worse in the latter half of the 1950s, forcing President Lemus to retract many of his promises for reform. In response, a civilian-based opposition movement percolated in 1958, demanding that the government maintain its commitment to reform.

One solution that Lemus pursued in hopes of alleviating the crisis was to solicit funding from foreign sources, especially the United States. At that time the politics of foreign aid in the United States were still not geared toward providing large sums of money to countries like El Salvador in the name of national development and anticommunism. In 1958 Lemus welcomed an official visit from Milton Eisenhower, brother of the U.S. president. In his later description of the trip, Eisenhower expressed concern about the depressed conditions he saw in El Salvador, but he did not even mention the issue of communism.[106] The U.S. Embassy in El Salvador offered a similar assessment in its reports to Washington, saying that El Salvador had significant development needs but that its Communist Party was small, ineffective, and unable to count on more than six hundred sympathizers.[107] Nothing in the form of substantive financial aid resulted from Eisenhower's visit, and Washington even balked at supporting El Salvador's bid to purchase U.S. armaments under the favorable terms of its Military Assistance Program (MAP).[108] All of that would change after Castro's rise to power in Cuba in January 1959.

In the wake the Cuban Revolution, the Eisenhower administration changed course and identified foreign aid as one mechanism to enhance the image of the United States and hinder the spread of communism. Suddenly a president like Lemus became a high priority for U.S. foreign policy. Instead of being a head of state in a poor country begging for money, as he was seen during Milton Eisenhower's visit, Lemus was transformed into a reformer defending the Western Hemisphere against communism. This shift in perception was evident during Lemus's official visit to the United States in March 1959, less than three months after Castro's victory. He received a ticker-tape parade in New York City and addressed a joint session of Congress in Washington, D.C. He told Congress of the need for economic development and the threat of communism in the Western Hemisphere. He encouraged Congress to "not hold any illusions as to the magnitude of the danger."[109]

A direct outcome of Lemus's visit was a positive response from U.S. policymakers to his request for aid. The United States had devoted funds to the Act of Bogota, a program of social improvement and economic development drafted by U.S. and Latin American representatives at a meeting of the Organization of American States (OAS) in September 1960. In October 1960 the U.S. ambassador to El Salvador, Thorsten Kalijarvi, was getting ready to disburse aid to the Lemus administration. Kalijarvi said that El Salvador could be a good showcase for how a massive foreign aid program could

"Oh, It Was Nice Meeting Him — But I Just Don't Understand That North American Manana Attitude"

FIGURE 4. Editorial cartoonist Herblock (Herbert Block) captured the United States' dismissive attitude toward Latin American aid programs in this 1960 drawing in the *Washington Post*. U.S. policymakers would change their views as the Cuban Revolution consolidated. *Washington Post*, March 6, 1960. Reproduced with permission of the Herb Block Foundation.

promote development and stop communism: "El Salvador could at a minimum be a successful example of an all-out attack on national development problems in the troubled Caribbean area."[110]

But the promise of aid was not enough to save Lemus. What began as small demonstrations and marches in 1958 turned into larger protests that initiated a downward spiral of popular protest and reactive state violence. A decisive event occurred in early September 1960 when government troops attacked a demonstration of university students, killing at least one person and wounding many others.[111] A prominent victim of government repression was Roberto Canessa, member of a prominent family and the former minister of foreign affairs under President Osorio. He was arrested and beaten so badly while in detention that he died of his injuries four months after his release. The night after Canessa's arrest a contingent of leading political figures, many of them belonging to wealthy families who had supported PRUD reformism, went to Lemus to encourage him to scale back the repression. Reports from the meeting claim that the delegation could not break Lemus of an obsessive belief that his regime was being attacked by an international communist conspiracy.[112] On October 26, 1960, Lemus was overthrown in a coup led by a group of reformist officers and civilians.[113]

The leaders of the coup insisted that Lemus had abandoned the spirit of reform, and they promised to reinvigorate it. They opened up the political system and allowed any political organization, other than communists, to organize freely. In response, various reformist-oriented political parties emerged, including the Christian Democratic Party (PDC). In its inaugural manifesto in November 1960, the PDC set out eighteen guiding principles, some of which took reformist rhetoric to a new level: "Justice to us is a reformation of the social structures of the country to permit all to receive their corresponding share in the national income and, above all, to lead us to the redemption of the peasantry."[114] Statements like that sent shudders down the spines of El Salvador's conservative landholders, and it would not be long before the conservative press would begin lobbing accusations of communism against the Christian Democrats and any other supporters of social reform.

In addition to opening up the political system to groups like the PDC, the reformist junta stressed the importance of education and prioritized access to education. They also took a favorable stance toward teachers who sought to form an independent labor organization, even though they were state employees and traditionally subservient to the Ministry of Education.

The junta did not survive very long, but its reformist stance toward education had long-term implications for education policy.[115]

Just as in 1944, a conservative countercoup struck back against the reformist tide. In late January 1961 a group of officers and civilians ousted the reformers, accusing them of being communists and promising to return the system to its original, conservative foundation. The coup brought to power the individuals who would go on to form the National Conciliation Party (PCN) and oversee the election of Col. Julio Rivera in 1962, Col. (later Gen.) Fidel Sánchez Hernández in 1967, Col. Arturo Armando Molina in 1972, and Gen. Carlos Humberto Romero in 1977. In fact, Rivera was a leader of the 1961 coup and a member of the first governing junta, the Directorio Cívico Militar (the Directorate).

The U.S. Embassy supported the January coup and insisted that it had saved the nation from communism.[116] One embassy report claimed that "communism and its local agents played an important role... for a three-month period (October 26, 1960–January 25, 1961) [and] rapidly infiltrated key Government positions and launched a drive to organize the local peasantry."[117] This assessment of the predominance of communists was not supported by the facts.[118] Regardless, the embassy had broken off all discussion of aid with the coup plotters in October, and now with the conservative countercoup in January, embassy officials anxiously reopened dialogue about aid disbursement.

The embassy was concerned about the January coup's prospects for survival. Embassy officials surmised correctly that the coup plotters did not enjoy widespread popular support and that they needed to do something to generate broader appeal. In a precursor to what would become a typical Alliance for Progress response to such situations, embassy officials believed that the solution lay in a program of social reform backed by a large infusion of U.S. funding and technical advice. According to the embassy's assessment, "A strongly anti-communist regime has just come to power in El Salvador, which is friendly to the United States. It is in our interest to see that this regime survives. Unfortunately for its survival strength, the new Government has not as yet a broad basis of popular support, and is looked upon by elements as having a rightist and military coloration. It is therefore very much in the U.S. interest to have this Government undertake economic and social reform ... [which] is long overdue in El Salvador."[119]

The members of the Directorate shared the U.S. Embassy's opinion and soon adopted a strategy of advocating modernizing reforms amid rhetoric of anticommunist populism. They also established a close relationship with the United States in hopes of receiving money and technical expertise. The Directorate lost no time in sending the right signals to Washington to encourage the influx of aid. In February 1961 all active-duty military officers signed a document stating their "pledge to carry out sweeping reforms inspired by the Act of Bogota."[120] A few days after the signing of the pledge, the embassy, together with the U.S. Information Service (USIS) and the U.S. Operations Mission (USOM), a unit for economic assistance, drafted a joint cable outlining a comprehensive aid program for El Salvador under the Act of Bogota.[121]

Whether or not they were aware of this particular document, Salvadoran authorities knew quite well that the Kennedy administration was eager to dole out financial aid in the name of anticommunism. President Kennedy had announced the Alliance for Progress in March 1961, and in June the Salvadoran ambassador to Washington paid a call to the State Department and "suggested that the US consider using El Salvador as a model for carrying out the President's Alliance for Progress."[122]

The Directorate's strategy proved highly polarizing. U.S. diplomatic officials and international development experts welcomed it, as did economic modernizers in El Salvador. But conservative business leaders and landed elites opposed it. So too, for the most part, did the political left. Even if some members of the left believed in the need for reform, they viewed the United States with suspicion and had supported the reformers in October 1960, so they considered the leaders who came to power in the January 1961 coup to be reactionary usurpers. Balancing these competing interests would preoccupy the leaders of the Directorate from the moment they took power.

True to their strategy, the leaders of the Directorate picked up the standard of social reform and tried to portray themselves as standing between the leftism of their predecessors and conservatives on the right. They promised sweeping reforms in such areas as taxation, health, education, housing, and labor.[123] They situated these promises in highly populist rhetoric designed to generate popular support. That rhetoric was disseminated in various formats, but one of the most influential was the weekly magazine *El Popular* (The Popular, or The Popular Voice). Officially it was an independent magazine, but most everyone, including staffers in the U.S. Embassy, understood it to be a government mouthpiece.[124] It most likely received government subsidies and had a circulation of between five thousand and ten thousand copies per week. The pages of *El Popular* called for social reform and touted the leaders of the Directorate as the defenders of the common

Salvadoran. Each issue included sympathetic photographs of poor people or dramatic portrayals of poor Salvadorans trying to survive.

The editors recurrently criticized El Salvador's landed elites, referring to them by their notorious moniker, "the fourteen families," and accusing them of being selfish oligarchs who put their interests ahead of the nation's.[125] They described the conduct of "our millionaires" as "suicidal," saying that their actions "provoke the ire of the gods and call upon us the enemy hosts who will ruin our land."[126] On various occasions, the editors told their readers that their support for reform and their barbs against the wealthy led conservatives to accuse them of inciting class warfare. The editors proclaimed loudly in bold headlines that "We Want to Avoid Class Struggle" and referred to their conservative detractors as "reactionary elites." They claimed not to oppose the rich people as an entire class but rather to oppose "those private persons and institutions that have established an economic dictatorship over the rest of the Nation."[127] The editors informed their readers constantly about conservatives' criticisms of them in an effort to boost their populist image and prove that the new leaders in the Directorate were not pawns of the landed elites.

A recurrent theme throughout the pages of El Popular was an insistence on the need for a strong, interventionist state to enact reforms. As just one example, the editors of El Popular pointed to the looming crisis in the countryside that resulted from a high concentration of land ownership and a high birthrate among the rural poor. The editors argued that something had to be done to avoid the crisis, but landowners were unwilling to take the necessary steps. They said that landowners were unwilling to adjust land tenure, nor were they willing to promote such policies as birth control because "the byproduct of a high birth rate is the low cost for manual labor." The editors then spoke to landowners directly, asking them: "Wouldn't it be better to open ones' eyes to the present reality and promote a series of economic and social reforms that would allow the great majority of the rural population to live a decent and dignified life?" The editors pitched this to elites as self-preservation, saying that failure to do something would cause greater misery in the rural areas, leaving the growing population of hungry, desperate people with no other option than to "turn to thoughts of assaulting landowners."[128]

It is no surprise that the rhetoric in El Popular drew the ire of conservative landowners and business leaders. Even the U.S. Embassy felt that El Popular had gone too far, and U.S. officials advised the new leaders to tone down their rhetoric.

El "rebajón" fué propicio
y la idea, formidable.
Pero el mayor beneficio,
aunque de él no se hable,
¡es que a la gente "honorable"
por fin se le vió el "oficio"!...

Integran la oscura lista
del taimado "mesonero",
un "esdrújulo" dentista,
un señor cafetalero,
y —me olvidaba— primero
¡hasta un editorialista!...

FIGURE 5. Editorial drawing that appeared in the magazine *El Popular* in 1961. It
promotes the new Directorio government's proposal to enforce rent reductions and
thereby defend poor renters from rich (portrayed as portly) landlords. *El Popular*,
June 27, 1961, 4, in DOS-IAES, 1960–1963, 716.00/7–1061, Sowash, U.S. Embassy,
San Salvador, to U.S. Department of State, Washington, D.C., July 10, 1961.

The articles and editorials [in *El Popular*] attack this "counter-revolutionary" [elite] class with an air of near hysteria better befitting the press of Cuba today than that of the relatively free local press. This line of El Popular has deepened the apprehension of the wealthy classes here, who are already deeply upset by the effects on their interests of the reform measures enacted by the Directorate.... One wonders too whether the Directorate, having unloosed such dissolvent forces in Salvadoran society, may not in time find itself a prisoner of its own propaganda and be forced by such forces into measures at variance with economic and political good sense.[129]

According to embassy reports, *El Popular* exacerbated tensions between the Directorate and El Salvador's landowners and business leaders. Just as the Directorate was launching *El Popular* in April 1961, its two conservative civilians resigned. They were José Antonio Rodríguez Porth and José Francisco Valiente. When he explained his reasons for resigning later that year, Rodríguez Porth cited the Directorate's hostility to business, its enthusiasm for unnecessary social reforms, and its willingness to ally with the United States.[130] Over the next four months no contact occurred between the Directorate and business leaders. The U.S. Embassy saw this as a bad sign, an indication of a potentially destabilizing rift, and so it encouraged both sides to meet. They did so in late July 1961. Reports of the meeting provided secretly to the U.S. Embassy say that dialogue occurred but differing views about social reform and economic planning were apparent.[131] One concession by the Directorate was to stop publishing *El Popular*.

Shortly after the meeting, two new, shadowy, pro-business organizations appeared and began criticizing the Directorate. Calling themselves the Comisión de Defensa de la Economía Nacional (Commission for the Defense of the National Economy) and the Comité de Información Cívica (Committee of Civic Information), they bought advertising space in main daily newspapers to rally opposition to the Directorate's plans for social reform. One of their advertisements in October 1961 accused the Directorate of going too far with reforms and even made veiled calls for another coup by encouraging "the Armed Forces to fulfill its historic responsibility."[132]

The appearance of the Comisión and the Comité represented a significant development in the debates over modernization and government policymaking. There had been other private, pro-business organizations that defended free-market policies, such as the Coffee Growers Association. But they had found governments to be favorably inclined toward them, and their

A: OREÑO DEFENDED A LA PATRIA
IMPERIALISMO SUVIETICO

PUEBLO SALVADOREÑO

CAMPAÑA DE LA UNION DEMOCRATICA SALVADOREÑA

FIGURE 6. Anticommunist flier distributed by the Unión Democrática, 1960. These kinds of extragovernmental anticommunist efforts would become steadily more common throughout the 1960s. In this example, El Salvador is portrayed as a machete-wielding peasant, demonstrating the organization's attempt to draw upon anticommunism within the ranks of El Salvador's poor sectors. DOS-IAES, 1960–1963, 716.001/2–761, Sowash, U.S. Embassy, San Salvador, to U.S. Department of State, Washington, D.C., February 7, 1961.

memberships were publicly known.[133] The Comisión and the Comité were different. They were anonymous organizations battling against a perceived leftist threat to the nation. Both the Comisión and the Comité accused the regime of being too reformist and surrendering national autonomy to foreigners. Such anonymous voices would become more commonplace in coming years, especially as calls for land reform increased.

Even though conservatives accused the Directorate of drifting toward radicalism, many on the left, such as the organization of university students, opposed the Directorate and considered its populism to be a demagogic cover-up for defending the oligarchy and U.S. imperialism.[134] Within the clandestine Communist Party an intense debate emerged as to the appropriate response to the coup. Younger radicals within the party drew inspiration from Cuba and said the time to go on the offensive had arrived. Traditional party leaders opposed them, saying that conditions in the country did not justify militant action and instead the party should continue to focus on its traditional strengths of organizing workers and forming electoral coalitions. After much debate, the traditionalists relented and allowed the radicals to form a militant wing, which came to be called the United Front for Revolutionary Action (FUAR). In March 1961 the FUAR issued a manifesto to the general populace calling for the revolutionary overthrow of the Directorate.[135] In reality, the Communist Party was small and the FUAR lacked the capacity to launch military assaults. Both the U.S. Embassy and the CIA, which were prone to seeing communist conspirators, described the communist movement in El Salvador in the early 1960s as small and incapable of garnering widespread support. The embassy reported in 1962 that "guerrilla warfare in rural areas does not now seem to pose a real threat."[136] The FUAR lasted only two years before it was dismantled, and within that time it had done almost nothing to carry out its call for revolution.[137]

The nuances of these intra-left debates mattered little to Viera Altamirano and other conservatives. From their vantage point, international communists were trying to spread revolution to El Salvador and domestic communists were calling for the overthrow of the state. Whereas one decade earlier the pages of *El Diario de Hoy* had offered only occasional references to communism, now they included frequent descriptions of the threat of communism to El Salvador. The basic premise was that communism and social reform, which were portrayed as one and the same, were on the rise and needed to be stopped. In response to a rumor in April 1961 that the Directorate was considering a program of bank nationalization, Viera Altamirano and *El Diario de Hoy* pulled no punches, immediately suggesting that the Directorate was falling prey to Communist propaganda. "The subtle propaganda of international communism has been on the rise in El Salvador, with increasing sophistication, diffusing nefarious tendencies against our republican and democratic institutions, pushing the State to increase its presence in areas that it does not belong at the cost of greater inefficiency."[138]

Viera Altamirano was particularly opposed to the bureaucracies that accompanied such programs. In his opinion, state bureaucracies consumed financial resources better utilized by the private sector. Bureaucracies also required the existence of managers, whom Viera Altamirano believed invariably enriched themselves at public expense. It was on these same grounds that he opposed land reform and the Act of Bogota.[139] But his more fundamental reason for opposing reform, especially land reform, was that it "takes away earnings from those people who rightfully earned it."[140] This appeal to the idea of wealth remaining rightfully with the people who created it would emerge as the most basic and fundamental line of rhetorical defense for the conservative right. They would use it to oppose land reform and any other policy that they could portray as being redistributive. To the defenders of such a view, it mattered little that the tax burden of rich families in El Salvador was far smaller than in the United States and one of lowest in all of Latin America, if they even bothered to pay them.

Viera Altamirano claimed that El Salvador's problems would be solved by the unfettered action of free markets rather than social reform. "We should transform our people with a maximalist liberal economy," he wrote in April 1961.[141] He believed that individualism was an inherent trait of Salvadorans, and it would serve them well in their battle against communism and social reform.[142] But he kept pushing for state intervention to protect domestic capital. He continued to support the fledging cotton industry, insisting that the government provide cotton growers with long-term, low-interest loans.[143] Workers did not fare as well in Viera Altamirano's demands. He opposed any state protections for labor and viewed such policies as minimum wage and the forty-hour work week as increasing the cost of production. A wiser strategy was to establish a maximum wage for labor, which would lower production costs and encourage economic growth. "We must have maximum salaries," he wrote, "not the demagogic mystification of minimal salaries."[144] An editorial by Trinidad Romero sounded a similar tone. He admitted that the rural poor were suffering but insisted that landowning elites were best positioned to help, because they knew the rural poor and therefore would be more effective in providing aid than the government.[145] One justification used to oppose social programs for the poor was to discredit arguments that "attribute poverty to injustice." Viera Altamirano claimed that inequality was a natural state of existence and the "hierarchical order [is] part of the Natural order." Thus, any attempts to reverse inequality and hierarchy were contrary to nature.[146]

Editorialists like Viera Altamirano and Romero claimed that improving the lives of working people was important to them. They feared that disgruntled poor people would become susceptible to communism and "threaten the social order."[147] Viera Altamirano wrote about the miserable conditions of the rural poor and called for their improvement.[148] But in his view the only way to do so was through economic growth, and growth came only when the market functioned freely.

Just like government officials and their nineteenth-century predecessors, Viera Altamirano saw himself as trying to create a more modern and progressive country. He called for economic diversification and industrialization because it would allow El Salvador to "escape the confines of the colonial economy."[149] He celebrated the "modern world" and "modern society" against "primitiveness" and El Salvador's "pastoral" economy.[150] But he continued to direct nationalist critiques against foreigners who said the same thing. He chastised a *New York Times* reporter for describing Latin American nations as poor and in need of social reform. He entitled his editorial response "Once Again the Ignorant Reformer" and accused the reporter of lacking an understanding of local realities or having any idea how to turn his grandiose ideas into viable policies.[151]

Viera Altamirano extended a similar disregard to Kennedy and his aid programs. He opposed a food aid program called Food for Peace as an insulting handout.[152] He noted that there were poor people in the United States too, so perhaps the food aid should be sent to them instead. He also used the editorial as an opportunity to downplay the severity of hunger in El Salvador and the need for massive reforms to rectify it. He said that malnourishment was the problem, not hunger, and the difference is that hunger is caused by poverty, whereas malnourishment derives from people's ignorance about nutrition. Obviously, then, the solution was simply to enlighten poor people about nutrition rather than incite economic change. He also insisted that El Salvador did not need assistance from the United States to battle communism. Rather, Salvadorans had to battle communism themselves, for only they knew best how to handle their local affairs. He said Kennedy was a fine president until he called for land reform, and then he became just another ignorant North American calling for the demise of the Salvadoran entrepreneurial sector.[153]

At times Viera Altamirano's nationalistic writings against foreign intervention sounded surprisingly similar to the anti-imperialism of the leftists he so despised. He wrote in 1961 that "the foreign investor will come and will try to appropriate everything. . . . We must resist, but intelligently."[154] But true to his Sarmiento roots, Viera Altamirano did not harbor a xenophobic opposition toward North Americans and Europeans. As long as they kept their opinions to themselves, he welcomed them and their investment capital to his country. In fact, he even said that Latin America needed North American and European immigrants if it wanted to progress: "Now more than ever, [Latin America] needs the capital and people of Europe."[155]

Ricardo Valdivieso Oriani is a wealthy Salvadoran who was born in 1941. His story is not typical of a Salvadoran "oligarch." Most of the families who comprise the notorious oligarchy made their fortune around the turn of the twentieth century and then left money and businesses to successive generations. Valdivieso's family acquired land in the early twentieth century but due to peculiar circumstances did not build a financial empire, and so by the time Valdivieso was weighing his options as a young adult in the 1950s, he had few prospects. He actually enlisted in the U.S. military and served in Germany.

When Valdivieso returned to El Salvador following his military service, he decided to pursue a career in farming, and so he took up the challenge of making his family's land profitable. Within a few years he became a successful and wealthy coffee grower, and in the process he developed strongly conservative political views. Amid El Salvador's polarization in the 1970s, he became active in conservative political circles, and eventually he emerged as a founding member of the Nationalist Republican Alliance (ARENA) party and a close associate of its patriarch, Roberto D'Aubuisson. Not surprisingly, Valdivieso was an aggressive anticommunist hawk during the civil war. A few years after the war ended, he penned his memoir, in which he described ARENA as "not a party, but a pathway to civilization." Valdivieso also used his memoir to present his philosophical ethos and ideological views.[156]

In that memoir Valdivieso revealed his staunch anticommunism and his unbridled belief in the merits of economic libertarianism. He provided a history of El Salvador and told his own life story to support his views, believing that he, like most other rich Salvadorans, was a self-made man who had created wealth through hard work. He summarized his views in a celebration of El Salvador as a land of opportunity: "El Salvador was a place where a person could make an excellent future for himself, especially if he was young and willing to work hard."[157]

A close read of Valdivieso's text reveals that his life story contradicts his claim that a fortune was available to anyone in El Salvador willing to work hard. He fails to acknowledge the tremendous advantages he had when he launched his farming enterprise—land, connections, family reputation, education, and access to credit, among many others. Regardless, Valdivieso's memoir provides a window into the thinking of a conservative, wealthy, politically active Salvadoran. It reveals that he fully embraced the concepts of modernization and progress but simply had specific definitions of those terms—economic libertarianism, small government, and militant anticommunism. Not surprisingly, Valdivieso had nothing positive to say about the social reformers of the PRUD in the 1950s, and especially the 1950 Constitution that gave the state the legal right to expropriate private property: "This seems incredible at first glance, that a legislative body in a sovereign and free state would allow itself to do something so low and traitorous."[158]

Valdivieso's memoir reveals the longstanding debate within El Salvador's ruling circles about how best to modernize the country. That debate began to simmer after the "revolutionaries" took power in 1948, and it rose to unprecedented levels during a brief and tumultuous period in 1960 and 1961. At the core of the debate lay issues about the role of the state in the economy and the desirability of policies to achieve economic diversification, poverty alleviation, and political liberalization. From the perspective of conservatives, foreboding signs abounded. They saw communists and meddlesome development experts on the march. Every administration after 1948, even though they were headed by anticommunist military officers, advocated an interventionist state and social reform. Conservatives believed that their traditional monopoly over the meaning of modernity was in jeopardy. They responded with free-market, anticommunist rhetoric. As we are about to see, the debates would intensify in the late 1960s and 1970s, and so too would the bellicosity of conservative rhetoric.

CHAPTER 2

Modernizing Reform and Anticommunist Repression
The First PCN Administration, 1961–1967

We will fight against communism with the weapon of socioeconomic reform.
—President Julio Rivera, inaugural message, 1962*

✦ THE MODERNIZING VISION INTRODUCED BY THE REVOLUTION OF 1948 TOOK
on a new and more urgent dimension after the success of the Cuban Revolution
in 1959. In June 1966, toward the end of his time in office, President Julio
Rivera delivered a speech that encapsulated his strategy of rule during that
important era in Salvadoran history—combining modernizing reform with
social order and anticommunism.[1] The occasion for the speech was the
annual meeting of the Council of Central American Defense (Consejo de
Defensa Centroamericano), a meeting of Central American governments to
discuss regional security issues. The meeting happened to be in San Salvador
that year, and Rivera delivered the inaugural address. He opened his speech
with a standard anticommunist description of the threat posed by Soviet and
Chinese communists. He insisted that the region's armies were the first line
of defense. "Personally, I am of the opinion," he said, "that it is the task of
our Armed Forces to guard the domestic front, to impede the actions of local
communists favored by the [international] communist bloc." But like both
President Martínez back in 1932 and the "revolutionary" leaders of the PRUD
between 1948 and 1960, Rivera stressed the causal relationship between

poverty and communism. He insisted that social reforms must accompany armed defense: "It is useless to think we can defend against communist subversion amid popular dissatisfaction with politics . . . and society."[2] He said the army was best situated to perform the task of reform because soldiers understand the plight of the poor. Rivera went on to hail the Alliance for Progress as a cornerstone of the defense against communism, saying it disproved leftists' arguments that the United States wanted to exploit poor nations by preventing their industrialization. Rivera concluded his speech with an appeal to democracy, but with the caveat that "order" must prevail: "I am certain that all of us would condition our support for . . . [democracy], or better said our ideals, to the need for political, social and economic order."[3]

Rivera had been among the coterie of officers and civilians who seized control of the state in January 1961, creating a political machine that remained in power until the eve of civil war in 1979. During his time as the main leader in El Salvador, between 1961 and 1967, Rivera cracked down on the left, wooed the masses with reforms, tried to placate the conservative right, and established a close relationship with the United States and international development agencies. He and his fellow leaders portrayed themselves as conciliators who balanced the competing demands of left and right. The name of their new political party, the National Conciliation Party, reflected their self-conceptualization. They gave the highest priority to modernizing the economy but also advanced social and political reforms.

Rivera's projects were a continuation of the agenda of Osorio and the PRUD, but they were possible thanks to U.S. foreign aid channeled through the Alliance for Progress. The president turned out to be ideally situated to combine the spirit of the 1948 Revolution and the Alliance for Progress. His reformist impulses did not escape detractors, though some thought he was doing too much, others that he was doing too little. In the words of the former secretary general of his cabinet and his later biographer, Carlos Armando Domínguez, "The left accused him of being a servant of oligarchic interests and the right accused him of socializing society, calling him a socialist, even a communist."[4]

In fact, Rivera's reformist impulse was more than mere window dressing. He may have stopped short of full democratization and he remained steadfastly opposed to collective action in rural areas, but he oversaw the opening of the political system and the relaxation of rules regarding labor organization in the cities. The wave of liberalization during his tenure provided the opportunity for the creation of one of the most important urban movements in recent Salvadoran history, teachers and their new union, ANDES 21 de Junio.

The first two sections of this chapter describe Rivera's reforms and their main source of funding, the Alliance for Progress. The next two sections are devoted to the response to the government's reformist policies by both conservatives and progressives. Finally, the last two sections focus on teachers and how they worked within the reformist opening to organize a powerful civic movement.

Reform and Repression under Rivera

Barely forty-one years old when he assumed office, Julio Rivera set the tone for his modernizing reforms by presenting himself as a gregarious modern man of the people who enjoyed riding his Harley Davidson motorcycle on country roads. He was friendly with the American ambassador and kept a certain distance from the nation's landed elite. He was a committed anticommunist and a doer. His political pedigree also set him up to play the role of a modernizing reformer. As a young officer he had joined the failed coup against President Martínez in April 1944, and he went into exile to avoid the fate of more than a dozen officers that Martínez executed in the aftermath. Those officers became martyrs to the cause of modernization, and Rivera drew upon that tradition of forward-looking, energetic change. For all those reasons, he was a model Alliance for Progress–type leader.[5]

The Rivera administration developed a close relationship with the United States under the auspices of the Alliance for Progress. During the 1960s, El Salvador received more than $100 million in nonmilitary aid from the United States, and many millions more came separately from the World Bank, the Inter-American Development Bank, and other bilateral foreign aid organizations. El Salvador's share of Alliance aid may have been a miniscule portion of the $20 billion that Kennedy pledged to the program, but those millions represented a significant boon to El Salvador's capital investment and operating budgets. The money financed programs that the PCN could never have considered otherwise, including but not limited to school construction, food distribution, housing, and telecommunications upgrades. In the early years of the Alliance, many social projects received support, but ironically, the bulk of the aid (about 80 percent) went toward commercial agriculture, industry, and road building, therein bolstering the existing elite.[6] That may not have been exactly what President Kennedy had in mind in his "inevitable revolutions" speech.

Nevertheless, much of the PCN's modernizing zeal was designed to bring the Salvadoran economy in line with that of other capitalist countries. The nationalization of the Central Bank in 1961, which until that time had been partly owned by the Coffee Growers' Association, put control of the money supply in the hands of the state, a standard feature in modern capitalist nations. Likewise, a proposed tax reform in 1962 sought to increase tax revenues by shifting the burden slightly to the wealthiest people, who until then paid shockingly low taxes, even by regional standards.[7] El Salvador's participation in the Central American Common Market between 1960 and 1969 increased the market for its incipient manufacturing sector, thereby promoting economic diversification. Education reform, which Rivera promoted and his successor, Fidel Sánchez Hernández, embraced even more, was seen as a way to grow the economy by creating well-trained, productive workers.

Along with its economic reforms, the PCN also experimented with a variety of social and political reforms, which included opening up the political system to competitors. In the aftermath of the coup in January 1961, the nascent PCN monopolized the first two elections. It won all fifty-four seats in the Legislative Assembly in December 1961, and Rivera ran unopposed in the presidential election in April 1962. The Christian Democrats called the elections a farce and thereby helped create a lingering crisis of legitimacy around the PCN's reformist endeavors.[8] The Rivera administration responded the following year by amending the electoral laws to allow for proportional representation in the assembly.[9] The new policy meant that opposition parties, with the exception of the still-illegal Communist Party, could put forth candidates in both assembly and mayoral races, and some of them would be almost guaranteed representation in the assembly. Admittedly, the PCN subjected anyone who dared challenge its dominance to relentless attack, but various opposition parties persevered, particularly the Christian Democrats. They won fifteen seats in the 1964 assembly as well as a number of mayor's offices, including the capital city of San Salvador. In contrast with the past, opposition parties became very visible, bringing an unprecedented level of debate to the legislature and providing opposition mayors a platform to court popular support.

When it came time for the 1967 presidential election, Rivera and the PCN stayed true to the spirit of political reform and allowed multiple parties to put forth candidates. The PCN did not have to resort to the same fraud as in 1962 to retain power, mainly because the opposition divided into three different parties. Still, the PCN and its allies intimidated and harassed

FIGURE 7. During the 1967 presidential campaign, conservative groups sought to revive fears of communism by retelling the story of the 1932 uprising that led to the mass murder of thousands of peasants accused of being communists. This page from the newspaper *El Diario de Hoy* contains an image of the activist and supposed instigator Farabundo Martí. *El Diario de Hoy*, January 20, 1967, 36.

its opponents. One of its tactics was to run a multipart exposé of the 1932 uprising in the weeks leading up to the election, allowing readers to make the obvious connection between the "leftist" candidates running against the PCN and the "communist" rebels three decades earlier.[10] In the end, Rivera's chosen successor, Sánchez Hernández, won with a slight majority over all other parties combined and avoided a runoff. Nevertheless, the opposition persisted and continued to win assembly seats and mayor's offices, with the Christian Democrats playing the role of lead opposition. The strength of the opposition in the Legislative Assembly was such that at one point in 1969 President Sánchez Hernández lost his grip on it due to the independent stance of only a handful of PCN deputies.

Looking back on this era in his memoir more than four decades later, Julio Adolfo Rey Prendes, a founding member of the Christian Democratic Party, celebrated the political reforms and praised Rivera for supporting them: "Upon closing this episode in our history [the presidential election of 1967] it must be recognized that those of us who struggled for the democratization of the country felt optimistic. The system of proportional representation in the Legislative Assembly had opened the doors of governance to us and allowed us to impact national politics. . . . It is appropriate to acknowledge the role of Colonel Julio Adalberto Rivera, President of the Republic, for supporting this advance in democracy."[11] While aware of the system's imperfections, Rey Prendes recognized the uniqueness of the moment, especially in the context of El Salvador's long history of dictatorship. Even a member of the communist party at the time, Arnoldo Vaquerano, spoke highly of the Rivera era and described it as a "genuine opening." He described Rivera as a "man of the people" who "spoke in common vernacular, went out amongst the population with limited security, such as to neighborhood dances [*bailes populares*], and rode around on his motorcycle."[12]

The CIA had a similarly positive assessment of Rivera, seeing him as precisely the kind of leader El Salvador needed, a pragmatic anticommunist military man who could promote necessary reforms without alienating the conservative landowners. "One of the more encouraging signs has been the success of the Rivera government in securing the cooperation of the economic upper class in promoting economic and social reform. On the whole the present government has been more energetic in attacking the problems which have given Communism its influence than any of the previous governments. Rivera seems to enjoy enough support to finish out his term and, hopefully, to effect an orderly transfer of power in 1967."[13]

The PCN employed the same kind of dichotomous reform/repression strategy when it came to labor organizing. Along with the political reforms that began in 1963, it passed various labor laws that legalized unions and strikes. The PCN had already established a close relationship with the moderate labor union, the General Confederation of Salvadoran Unions (CGS). According to reports from the U.S. Embassy, PCN leaders gained the union's support with classic patronage, giving its leaders positions in the government in exchange for their efforts to secure the support of the union's rank and file.[14] But the new labor laws also granted recognition to unions that were oppositional to the government, even those believed to be affiliated with the clandestine Communist Party. A main beneficiary was the Unitary Federation of Salvadoran Unions (FUSS), which had emerged out of the semi-clandestine General Confederation of Salvadoran Workers (CGTS).[15] The FUSS gained legal recognition as a union in 1965 and grew steadily in membership and influence. It played a lead role in a wave of labor mobilizations and strikes that erupted in 1967. One of the PCN's concessions to those strikes was to raise the minimum wage of industrial workers, despite strong opposition from the business sector.[16] Another beneficiary of the PCN's labor legislation was public employees, various sectors of which were allowed to form unions for the first time. One of those new unions was the teachers' union, ANDES 21 de Junio, which went on to become a major nemesis of the PCN, especially during two massive strikes in 1968 and 1971.

The PCN did not extend its olive branch to rural workers, demonstrating its inability or unwillingness to intrude upon the arena most sacred to landed elites. Even though rural workers desperately needed protective legislation, the government banned rural organizing. Throughout the 1960s, the gap between the minimum wage paid to agricultural workers and to industrial workers increased substantially.[17] The PCN's most consequential policy to suppress labor mobilization in rural areas was to create a massive paramilitary organization in the rural areas called the Nationalist Democratic Organization (ORDEN) in 1963. The notorious head of the National Guard, Gen. José Alberto "Chele" Medrano, was put in charge. A hero to some, "father of the death squads" to others, Medrano described ORDEN as sixty thousand patriotic peasants serving as citizen defenders against communist subversion.[18] ORDEN occasionally bought advertising space in local newspapers to present itself as an innocuous organization dedicated to peace and anticommunism.[19] Similarly, PCN modernizers portrayed ORDEN as an extension of their reformist agenda. One pro-PCN editorialist in *La Prensa Gráfica* even threatened landowners with a veiled reference to ORDEN, saying that the existence of paramilitary organization should remind landowners to treat their workers well and pay fair wages.[20] Waldo Chávez Velasco, one of the PCN's chief strategists and propagandists, described the members of ORDEN as "humble, disciplined and serious people."[21]

Some members of ORDEN may have embodied those innocuous qualities of conservative peasants who felt that communism threatened the proper order of society. But as a whole, ORDEN was a ruthless paramilitary apparatus that operated in direct coordination with the military high command and especially its intelligence wing, the National Security Agency (ANSESAL). ORDEN employed violence and intimidation to thwart the organization of any opposition, especially in the rural areas. In addition to suspected leftists, ORDEN targeted political parties, such as the Christian Democrats, and members of the growing Christian Base Communities.[22] In his memoir, Chávez Velasco said he worked closely with ORDEN during PCN electoral campaigns.[23]

The U.S. provided both training and funding for ORDEN. U.S. military advisors in El Salvador provided on-the-ground training, and various Salvadoran officers, including Medrano and others affiliated with ORDEN, received training either in the School of the Americas in the Panama Canal Zone or at military bases in the United States. In explaining why the United States supported such a repressive military sector, the U.S. ambassador to El Salvador during the Kennedy years, Murat Williams, recalled in a 1980 editorial that "there was a time when the republic [of El Salvador] made great social progress, back in the early 1960s, but fearful of Castroism we began to build up the security forces."[24] Together the United States and the PCN followed a paradoxical approach to development. They implemented reforms that were supposed to improve the lives of common citizens, but they built up the machinery of repression that beat down those same citizens when they voiced their opinions or organized.[25]

In the 1950s the governments of Osorio and Lemus muted their repressive side with reforms financed by high coffee prices. Rivera's strategy was not markedly different, but the resources available to him were significantly higher as a result of U.S. aid. The Alliance for Progress also combined reformism and anticommunism, and therefore it reinforced policies already present in the Salvadoran military regime. The leaders of those military governments drew upon the liberal tradition of "Order and Progress" from the nineteenth century as well as from the modernizing tendencies of the early twentieth century, including such events as the overthrow of the Martínez dictatorship (1931–1944). By comparison, the Alliance's blend of reformism and anticommunism was based on a new and elaborate theoretical construct: modernization theory.

Modernization Theory and U.S. Aid to El Salvador in the 1960s

In both design and execution, U.S. policy toward El Salvador was heavily influenced by modernization theory, a social scientific theory that emerged from American academe in the 1950s.[26] Many different individual academics working in a variety of disciplines contributed to its formation, but the Center for International Studies (CIS) at MIT was most responsible for its conceptualization and dissemination. MIT founded CIS in 1952 in conjunction with the U.S. State Department. According to historian Nils Gilman, "the very creation of CIS was the result of a top secret anti-Communist propaganda project conducted at the Massachusetts Institute of Technology in the fall of 1950."[27] The goal was to assemble a team of interdisciplinary scholars to propose policies for fighting the Cold War.

One of the byproducts of CIS's endeavors was modernization theory. The economist W. W. Rostow, a founding member of CIS, is generally recognized for playing a lead role in articulating the theory, especially in his widely read 1960 book, *The Stages of Economic Growth: A Non-Communist Manifesto.* Rostow went on to hold high-ranking positions in the Kennedy and Johnson administrations, giving him the rare opportunity to turn his own intellectual concepts into public policy.[28]

In a nutshell, modernization theory proposed to explain societal development over time. Rostow and the other architects of modernization theory believed that only a few societies had progressed into advanced capitalism, while the rest remained stuck in primitive traditionalism. They claimed that their theories explained why and how this situation had transpired. By extension, their theory allowed them to design policies that could accelerate the development of "traditional" societies and simultaneously diminish their inhabitants' vulnerability to the dangers of communism.

According to Rostow, traditional societies were economically stagnant and had a ceiling on productivity. Their main economic activity was agriculture, and their politics were hierarchical and rigid, granting little or no social mobility. The people in a traditional society lived by pre-Newtonian rules, and they were "unmoved by man's new capability for regularly manipulating his environment to his economic advantage."[29] More sociological variations of modernization theory, such as those developed by Daniel Lerner, emphasized the institutions and values of traditional peoples. According to him, traditional societies had authoritarian institutions and their people valued loyalty, obedience, and inertia. Individuals lacked curiosity and initiative, and they rarely ventured out of their small environment. For sustained economic growth to occur, traditional societies had to be reoriented toward wealth maximization, which required "nothing else than the ultimate reshaping of all social values." Lerner defined modernization as a "process of social change in which development is the economic component."[30] In a country like El Salvador, modernization theorists considered the forces of tradition to reside both in the poor masses, who lacked a modern education, and in landed elites, who, like feudal barons, hoarded wealth and employed a retrograde ideological outlook to justify the status quo.

Under certain conditions, traditional societies would move to the second developmental stage, a transitional period in which the "preconditions for take-off" emerged. Once a society entered the transition, the next period was "the great watershed in the life of modern societies," the "take-off." In this all-important stage "the forces making for economic progress, which yielded limited bursts and enclaves of modern activity, expand and come to dominate society."[31] Lerner claimed that at this moment cultural values would change to promote self-sustained growth. Individuals would aspire to better themselves, and they would engage in teamwork and participate in their polities. In the fourth stage, the "Drive to Maturity," a prolonged period of self-sustained growth occurred, in which modern technology spread to all economic activities. Those endeavors finally culminated in the "Age of Mass Consumption," that is, development.

Rostow believed that the most delicate moment in a society's ascent to high consumption was the transitional precondition for takeoff. That was when the struggle between traditional and modern forces was most intense, and thus it was when society was most vulnerable to a rival version of modernity, namely communism. To Rostow, communism was "a disease of the transition," when "the seizure of power by Communist conspiracy is easiest."[32] And because Rostow believed that communism was the greatest threat to achieving modernization, he was willing to support nondemocratic and authoritarian governments in transitional societies as a necessary evil. As he put it, "a centralized dictatorship may supply an essential technical precondition for take-off and a sustained drive to maturity."[33] Other architects of modernization theory concurred, such as the social scientist Ithiel de Sola Pool. He said, "to the extent that a society is backward its potential contribution to support America is small and its susceptibility to Communism large."[34] This Cold War line of thinking became particularly compelling after the Cuban Revolution in 1959. "Those who make peaceful revolution impossible," said John F. Kennedy, alluding to the changes necessary to obliterate traditional forces, "will make violent revolution inevitable," meaning a communist-inspired upheaval.[35]

Adherents of modernization theory reasoned that traditional societies did not have to reinvent the wheel; they had the models of developed countries to follow. The latter were, after all, in Lerner's words, a "picture of their own future." But because of the threat of communist conspiracy, societies experiencing the transition needed to be closely monitored and probably assisted with money and weaponry. Modernization theorists perceived of foreign aid as an important component of Cold War foreign policy, serving as a protective barrier against communism. Without aid from the West, poor societies in transition would be more vulnerable to communists'

FIGURE 8. Herblock captured the ethos of modernization theory in this depiction of class inequity in Latin America. The two onlookers, either businessmen or aid experts, presumably from the United States, offer commentary. *Washington Post*, February 11, 1962. Reproduced with permission of the Herb Block Foundation.

machinations and even less likely to transition to capitalist modernity at all. And so technical advice, financial assistance, and military support were all necessary and mutually reinforcing. A precious weapon in the modernizers' arsenal was mass media. Communications experts working under the umbrella of modernization theory, like Wilbur Schramm, conceived of print, film, television, and radio as assisting societies through their transition.[36] In the case of El Salvador, educational television exemplified communications experts' belief in the power of mass media to modernize society.

The fact that modernization theory became paradigmatic within the international development community was not by chance. The public diplomacy apparatus of the U.S. government actively promoted it to local policymakers who were going to serve as their allies during implementation. In Latin America the journal *Facetas* (also published in English and Portuguese under the title *Dialogue*) was one of the instruments to explain modernization theory to local officials. *Facetas* was self-described as a "quarterly journal of opinion and analysis on subjects of current intellectual and cultural interest in the United States." U.S. embassies distributed it to a comprehensive list of government officials, politicians, opinion makers, and intellectuals. It included articles by leading U.S. academics and policymakers that had originally appeared in English in major U.S. academic journals. The USIA selected the articles and translated them into Spanish. Margaret Mead, Arthur Schlesinger Jr., Seymour Martin Lipset, John Kenneth Galbraith, and Irving Kristol were just a few of the well-known authors whose writings appeared in *Facetas*. The contents of *Facetas* leaned toward socioeconomic matters, with a heavy emphasis on development issues. The article titles alone reveal that modernization theory had a strong presence in the journal's content: "The Impulse for Modernization," "Development, Productivity and Talent," and "Three Models of Nations in Development," for example.[37]

Facetas was not the only publication that spread development paradigms to an international audience. Various development agencies within the United Nations began distributing publications to publicize their innovations and best practices. In the field of education the best example is the *UNESCO Courier*. It is a monthly publication established in 1947, and like *Facetas*, during the 1960s it published articles on development that followed a modernization-theory paradigm. Salvadoran policymakers not only received copies of the *Courier, Facetas*, and similar publications, but they were also exposed to the influence of the development community through frequent ministerial meetings organized under the auspices of UN agencies and the Alliance for Progress. These meetings were held in various locations throughout Latin America with the purpose of assembling ministers from every Latin American country to discuss development in both theory and practice. Along with exposing attendees to new ideas, the meetings socialized them in a common language of development.

The practical side of modernization programs was a heavy emphasis on planning. In fact, *planning* became the buzzword of development in the

1960s, even though it carried with it the stigma of the centrally planned economies. But a belief in the need for planning emerged from projects like the Tennessee Valley Authority and the Marshall Plan, which showed U.S. policymakers the importance of planning to accomplish development goals. Since modernization theorists considered industrialized countries to be the example for poor countries to follow, it was only natural that planning would be necessary to determine the proper course of action. Any country that wanted development aid in the 1960s had to prove that it had a well-conceived plan, and aid disbursement under the Alliance for Progress required recipient nations to create planning units within their governments to coordinate projects.

It is clear that Salvadoran officials understood the priority given to planning by U.S. officials. The issue of planning assumed center stage during a meeting at the U.S. Embassy in January 1962 between leaders in the Salvadoran government and high-level U.S. diplomatic officers. The goal of the meeting was to discuss aid disbursement under the Alliance for Progress. In his notes of the meeting, U.S. Ambassador Murat Williams reported that Julio Rivera raised the issue of planning, saying that the Salvadoran ambassador to the United States (Francisco Lima) had "fully briefed [him] on the necessity of the Government's producing a long-range plan and assigning priorities to separate projects." Rivera went on to say that "El Salvador did not have a sufficient number of persons with the required competence to carry out this work unaided," and thus it would have to rely upon "the services of foreign technicians."[38]

Shortly thereafter provisional president Eusebio Cordón created a new planning unit called the National Planning Council (CONAPLAN). In his final speech as president, Cordón said that CONAPLAN was created "to take maximum advantage of the collaboration offered under the program of the Alliance for Progress."[39] The importance of planning for development was again emphasized by Teodoro Moscoso, regional program coordinator for the Alliance for Progress, during his June 1962 visit to El Salvador. He congratulated El Salvador's leaders on their efforts in planning: "I am deeply impressed by the vigor and seriousness of purpose that the Salvadoran government has demonstrated in carrying out the urgent work of planning for El Salvador's social and economic development."[40] Moscoso's words may sound like bland rhetoric from a development technician, but in 1962 El Salvador his words and everything he embodied ruffled the feathers of powerful people.

Conservatives Respond to PCN Reforms and
Its Relationship with the United States

In the previous chapter we caught a glimpse of the conservative right's mixed response to the PCN and its relationship with the United States. On the one hand, its members celebrated the United States as the defender of capitalism, and they welcomed U.S. assistance in battling communism. As one of the secretive right-wing propaganda organizations would later put it, "We are not enemies of the people of the United States . . . we hold them in the highest respect and admiration."[41] On the other hand, conservatives opposed U.S. meddling in their affairs, and in particular they hated one basic premise behind U.S. development aid—that El Salvador's landowning elites were traditional and therefore the main obstacle to modernization. As Viera Altamirano put it in one of his editorials, "We are seeing emerge absurd views from this extremist line, like the country is ruled by an oligarchy that retains its control of land through feudal and semifeudal systems."[42]

In 1960, before planning discussions had even begun, a vocal conservatism emerged in response to the creation of the Act of Bogota, the precursor to the Alliance for Progress. The act's call for land reform inflamed conservative passions in El Salvador, particularly since it coincided with the reformist coup of October 1960. Over the succeeding months, *El Diario de Hoy* frequently criticized the Act of Bogota and its "socialist-like" call for state intervention: "Once the state intervenes in everything, socialism arises, converting the country into concentration camps of regimented lives. . . . The propaganda against the liberal economy is socialism's trick to create a totalitarian State."[43]

The supposed rescue by the "conservative" coup in January 1961 proved illusionary, as the new Directorate promoted modernizing reforms and a close relationship with the United States amid a populist rhetoric. Making matters worse, shortly after the Directorate came to power, Kennedy unveiled the Alliance for Progress. All of a sudden "development" was the new paradigm, and terms such as *modernization, reform, foreign technicians*, and *international aid* made daily appearances in the parlance of politics and journalism. The mere mention of those words antagonized conservatives, as did the recurrent photos in morning newspapers of North American and European development experts sitting around tables with PCN functionaries discussing development projects.[44] A decades-long battle within the ruling sectors over development, modernization, and U.S. aid was taking shape.

Moscoso's visit in June 1962 served as a lightning rod for conservatives. The Comisión de Defensa de la Economía Nacional, one of the new, shadowy, right-wing propaganda organizations, took out advertising space to oppose Moscoso's presence in El Salvador. It said the Alliance would allow foreigners to mandate social reforms and harm El Salvador's economy by weakening capitalists' freedom.[45] Moscoso tried to stave off these criticisms by delivering a speech before the Association of Industrialists. His speech emphasized the pro-business, pro-market nature of the Alliance. He countered right-wing allegations that planning and development were socialist by asking, "What well administered private business does not plan annually and for the long-term? . . . Surely you want your government to plan for the future as well."[46]

As Alliance aid increased and U.S. involvement in El Salvador's domestic affairs deepened throughout the 1960s, the skepticism of the conservative right grew. Conservative spokespersons developed a rhetorical strategy of repeating constantly a few buzzwords to describe their reformist adversaries, such as *socialists, the international mafia, developmentalists*, and *thirdworldists*, among others.[47] They used these words so often that the sheer repetition of their accusations, as well as their skill in linking them to broader values of nationalism and individualism, became difficult to counter. According to one conservative editorialist, Juan Vásquez, the Alliance promoted wealth redistribution, thus proving its "socialists proposals." He went on to say that "in the United States, the leftist infiltration continues in the Democratic administration, principally in the State Department."[48] Fuentes Castellanos said that Kennedy was "imbued with a strong dose of socialism" and that the Alliance was a "variant of international socialism."[49] Viera Altamirano repeatedly denounced Alliance-based reforms as "one step backwards in matters of liberty and economic growth, and one step forward toward socialist servitude."[50]

Conservatives rarely referred to modernization theory by name, but they were well aware of the Ivy League origins of its architects. In the words of Viera Altamirano, "economists and activists of the international conspiracy, trained in Harvard, Yale or MIT . . . come here pushing social reforms . . . and advancing the State towards socialization."[51] He added in another editorial that the main economics programs in U.S. universities have become "centers for teaching about socialism and political agitation," where students leave "confused about the most basic facts . . . of free enterprise."[52]

More anonymous pro-business organizations appeared on the scene in the late 1960s, joining their predecessors from earlier in the decade. One such organization was the Comité Pro-Defensa de la Dignidad Nacional (Committee in Defense of National Dignity). In a typical example of its rhetorical attack on the PCN and its collaboration with international development programs, the committee declared its intention to "unmask the enormous conspiracy of this group of nationals and internationals" and to resist the "North American technicians . . . who come to our land to legislate in mysterious ways or in secretive meetings with a small number of people chosen by the mafia."[53]

Appeals to nationalism and anti-imperialism remained a consistent part of conservatives' critique. Fuentes Castellanos framed his opposition to Kennedy and the Alliance with such a strong rhetoric of anti-imperialism that his argument was almost indistinguishable from that of his leftist adversaries. In one of his longer expositions, he said there were two great poles of international imperialism, "Moscow and Washington." He then proceeded to defend Salvadoran autonomy with an extended history of U.S. imperialism in Latin America, starting with Teddy Roosevelt's "Big Stick" and ending with the Alliance for Progress.[54] Viera Altamirano echoed Fuentes Castellanos by claiming that international development agencies and backers of the Alliance for Progress wanted to create "global hegemony" under the guise of "protecting" smaller nations and promising them that they could become "equal to the largest and most powerful [countries] in the world."[55] He employed this type of anti-imperialist framework to oppose an Alliance program to create a savings bank for workers, the Banco Obrero. He said that the program was being forced on El Salvador and that rejecting it would result in "no more loans for us. In this way, we are converted into true puppets—dolls that foreign hands make dance, jump and kneel."[56]

In the latter half of the 1960s the National Association of Private Enterprise (ANEP) joined the fray. ANEP comprised representatives from almost every important business concern. Until that time it had remained on the sidelines, lobbying from behind the scenes and exerting its influence quietly. But suddenly it took a public stance by publishing broadsides in daily newspapers, especially during the wave of strikes and labor demonstrations in 1967 and 1968. In one of those broadsides, it called upon the PCN to protect free enterprise by "maintaining the guarantees necessary for the functioning of business, such as the freedom to work for the immense majority of the nation's workforce, who want to work in a climate of harmony and peace." The fact that ANEP felt the need to publicly make demands upon the PCN regime should have been a warning sign to government officials.

So too should have been the decision by the notoriously autonomous Coffee Growers' Association to join ANEP in 1973, signaling a unification of the traditional business elite in apparent opposition to the government's modernizing reforms. This process of unification was precursor to the all-out, no-holds-barred confrontation between ANEP and the government over land reform in 1976.[57]

Throughout the 1960s the PCN and its supporters defended themselves against such attacks from the conservative right in editorials, broadsides, and speeches. They relied upon a twofold defense, describing the benefits of modernization, social reform, and foreign technicians while referring to their conservative opponents as out-of-touch, self-serving reactionaries. One of the PCN's main propaganda voices, José Luis Salcedo, editorialized in 1966 that the right wing's use of the term *socialist* was based on "a vague, sentimental, fanciful and unscientific conceptualization of socialism." He said that the people accusing the PCN and the United States of being socialists were the "most reactionary, retrograde and passionate of the decrepit and unproductive rural oligarchs."[58]

The PCN also directed its attack against individual right-wing spokespersons in hopes of discrediting them. One such effort targeted José Antonio Rodríguez Porth, an influential lawyer with a long history of political involvement dating back to the 1940s. He had been an original member of the Directorate after the coup in January 1961 but had resigned along with José Francisco Valiente just three months after the coup. He accused the other Directorate leaders of being too reformist and too willing to collaborate with U.S. development agencies. As he later described it, he opposed "the influx of foreign technicians with their prefabricated solutions and our Government surrendering to them and what they dispense."[59] Rodríguez Porth remained a critic of the PCN throughout the 1960s, but in a 1968 editorial he pushed the new PCN president, Sánchez Hernández, too far. In that editorial Rodríguez Porth challenged a proposed economic reform with a not-so-veiled threat from "we the taxpayers who provide funds to the State."[60]

PCN leaders responded to his threat by turning their propaganda wing loose on him. Again, Salcedo did the dirty work. The week after Rodríguez Porth criticized Sánchez Hernández, Salcedo attacked him in a pair of broadsides in one of the daily papers. Salcedo questioned Rodríguez Porth's motives for resigning from the Directorate back in 1961 and intimated that he had been involved in political intrigues against the government. In an ironic argumentative twist, he even accused Rodríguez Porth of "forming a tactical alliance with communists" and of masking his critique of Sánchez Hernández in "clothing borrowed from communists." For good measure he also threw in a critique of Viera Altamirano, saying that the outspoken conservative editorialist defended "recalcitrant capitalists who don't want to pay their fair share in taxes."[61]

Progressives and the Left Respond to the PCN's Reforms and Its Relationship with the United States

Just like the conservative right, leftists and progressives had a strong but mixed reaction to the Alliance for Progress and the PCN's close relationship with the United States. These left-leaning views originated from various sources, including the new opposition political parties, labor unions, the clandestine Communist Party, the liberationist wing of the Catholic Church, progressive academics at the public National University of El Salvador (UES) and the new private, Jesuit-run Central American University (UCA), and from many other organizations and individuals. Generally speaking, this conglomeration of leftist and progressive voices viewed U.S. involvement in their country through the local discourse of imperialism. They tended to believe that the first concern of U.S. policymakers was improving the United States, not El Salvador. Therefore, they questioned the motives of Salvadoran officials who nurtured close relations with the United States. They looked suspiciously at programs originating from the United States, assuming that their benefits would go to North American capitalists and a select few Salvadorans rather than the greater whole of the Salvadoran population. One expression of this view came from the FUAR, the short-lived militant wing of the Communist Party in the early 1960s. Its May 1962 platform described the Alliance for Progress succinctly as a "new form of Yankee imperialism."[62] Even though the FUAR was one of the more doctrinaire voices on the left, its comment captured the general belief of many left-leaning opponents of the PCN.

Concerns over the imperialist motives behind U.S. aid transitioned easily into a broader criticism of the definition of development adhered to by the United States and the PCN. Spokespersons at the UCA provided a succinct critique, asking, "Is the development of these countries [developed nations, like the United States] a normative model? Should development represent our ideal? We do not reject development, what we reject is just any development."[63] The left-leaning academician Rafael Menjívar was even more targeted in his criticism, saying that the Alliance for Progress, embodied in the

Declaration of Punta del Este in 1961, called for structural change but in fact "has produced, for political reasons, no change in the structures of Latin American countries, least of all this one [El Salvador]." He went on to say that notwithstanding pretensions to contrary, development continued to be defined in singular terms of capital investment, and thereby it remained true to the wishes of a "strong minority sector" of society, namely landed elites and business leaders.[64]

However, some leftists and progressives adopted a more moderate, even positive stance toward the Alliance and U.S. development aid. They reasoned that material aid was desperately needed by the nation's poorest people, and therefore they welcomed it, regardless of its origins. Interviews with left-leaning Salvadorans who distributed Alliance for Progress aid around the town of Suchitoto in the early 1960s illustrate this perspective. One interviewee, Rutilio Melgar, was the mayor of Suchitoto at the time, but he belonged to the political opposition. He distributed food and medical supplies to poor peasants in conjunction with Father Eduardo Alas, a young Catholic priest recently out of seminary who would go on to be an important source of liberation theology in the region. Melgar described the rural poor who came in search of aid as "humble, decent people" who had "desperate needs." Even though he was no fan of the United States and opposed U.S. support for the PCN and its militarist wing, he admitted that U.S. aid "eased their [peasants'] suffering a bit." He was later targeted for death by paramilitaries and had to flee Suchitoto for his life.[65] Another left-leaning interviewee distributed Alliance-based educational materials to rural schools around Suchitoto. Trained as a teacher and also belonging to the political opposition, he spoke of the deep void in teaching aids among rural schools and the help that U.S. aid represented.[66]

The presence of a left-leaning teacher activist in Suchitoto was no surprise, nor was the Alliance for Progress's involvement in an education-related project. Both were common features of the political landscape in El Salvador in the 1960s and early 1970s. But teachers had not always been predictable supporters of progressive causes.

Teachers Take the Lead

Teachers were one of the most important and most unexpected sectors to emerge as part of the left-leaning opposition to the PCN. In the first half of the 1960s teachers developed a collective consciousness and began questioning their traditional position in the military's system of rule. "Teachers began to lift up their heads," as one political activist of the day put it in his memoir.[67] Teachers had long been loyal clients of the state. The official discourse during the Osorio administration portrayed them as working in tandem with the army. This idea was clearly articulated in an act that teachers organized in 1954 to honor the army. During the ceremony the deputy minister of culture exalted "the union that ought to exist between the teaching profession and the army as progressive forces for the betterment of the fatherland."[68] But suddenly, in the early 1960s, teachers began to transform themselves into a powerful opposition movement ready to challenge the PCN on issues relating to education and teachers' working conditions. How that rupture occurred has received little attention from scholars, partly because sources have been few and far between.[69] Interviews with former teachers help fill this gap, particularly a series of interviews with Arnoldo Vaquerano, a prominent figure in the teachers' movement from its earliest stages. Also valuable is a small but robust archival collection donated to San Salvador's Museum of Word and Image by a former teacher activist, Adolfo Flores Cienfuegos.[70]

Vaquerano explained that the transformation of teachers from loyal clients of the PRUD and PCN to independent-minded opponents began with the civic mobilization against President Lemus between 1958 and 1960.[71] The anti-Lemus campaign provided the first opportunity for teachers to develop an independent consciousness and mobilize against their employer, the national government. In October 1958 a group of young, activist teachers in San Salvador founded the Teachers' Revolutionary Front (FMR) and joined the small civil movement against Lemus. The number of teachers involved in the FMR was small, perhaps a few dozen at most. But those who participated found the experience transformative. Most of the eventual leaders of ANDES were among those who joined, including Vaquerano, Mario Medrano, Carmen Hill de Minero, and José Mario López. Most of these initial activists had graduated from either the UES or one of the two main teacher preparatory schools, the Normal Masferrer for men and the Normal España for women. The two normals offered a high-quality education, often delivered by foreign teachers who brought new ideas and promoted open-mindedness.

The FMR operated in the open, and its members handed out leaflets and participated in marches and street demonstrations against Lemus. It made no specific demands on behalf of teachers, and it claimed no specific ideological perspective, despite the *revolucionario* in its name. Admittedly, one of its members, Arnoldo Vaquerano, joined the Communist Party the same year that the FMR was formed, but his affiliation was secret and almost no other teachers were among the communists' ranks at the time.[72]

When Lemus was ousted in October 1960, this small band of organized teachers found themselves with an unprecedented opportunity to advance the cause of teachers and education. The new ruling junta included Dr. Fabio Castillo, a well-known academic who oversaw the appointment of Dr. Marina de Quesada as vice minister of education.[73] She was similarly sympathetic toward teachers. During the junta's rule, the teachers in the FMR expanded their organization beyond San Salvador and founded a new teachers' organization, the Salvadoran Teachers' Federation (FMS). Its goal was to raise awareness among teachers about the problems of inadequate salaries and limited benefits and to channel those issues into a collective movement.

Even amid the ambient of reform represented by the new junta, members of the FMS found recruiting teachers difficult. Most teachers remained "oficialistas" or "gobiernistas"—loyal clients of the PRUD and later of the PCN.[74] They had little or no interest in politics and did not want to break their traditional bond with the state. Teachers joined the official party to secure jobs. During presidential campaigns they were expected to become part of the official Teachers Fronts (Frentes Magisteriales).[75] Salvador Acosta in Suchitoto, who had worked as a teacher between 1956 and 1967, said during an interview in 2005 that many teachers remained loyal to the government at the time because of their paycheck. They did not want to threaten their modest but dependable income by challenging the state.[76] The fall of the reformist junta in the coup of January 1961 brought teacher organizing to a sudden halt. The new junta—the Directorate—cracked down on the civic organizations that had arisen in the previous four months. All the leaders of the FMS went into exile—Vaquerano in Guatemala, José Mario López in Nicaragua, and the others elsewhere. The departure of the FMS leadership left the organization vulnerable to reincorporation into a traditional patron-client relationship with the state. Following the example set by their PRUD predecessors in the 1950s, the new PCN leaders made public appeals to teachers as the cornerstone of the nation and the backbone of the administration. In one published appeal, the PCN told teachers that "now more than ever the Fatherland needs your effective support to achieve social justice for national conciliation."[77] After the exile of its former leaders, the new, pliant leadership of the FMS responded to such appeals with declarations of support for the PCN and for Julio Rivera's candidacy for the 1962 presidency. In a broadside setting out its position, the FMS presented itself as representing the interests of the common person, saying that teachers "have palpable experience with the misery . . . of the lives of the workers in the countryside and the city." It then praised the PCN for its commitment to social justice and anticommunism and explained that a PCN victory would produce "better living conditions of our people while preventing . . . communist infiltration."[78]

Despite the brevity of its rule, the reformist junta (October 1960–January 1961) represented a decisive moment in teacher organization. Within that window of opportunity, a core group of dedicated, young teacher activists laid the cornerstone for teacher mobilization.[79] After Rivera won the uncontested election for president in April 1962, the exiled teachers were allowed to return. True to form, they reinitiated their organizational activities in hopes of creating a nationwide teacher organization to pressure the government on education and working conditions. They abandoned the compromised FMS and formed two new organizations, divided along gender lines, just like the teacher training schools. The new women's organization was the Association of Secondary School Teachers (APNES), founded by Mélida Anaya Montes. She rapidly emerged as one of the most important political activists in El Salvador in the 1960s and 1970s. The men's organization was the Salvadoran Teachers' Union (UMS), founded by José Mario López, who also would go on to be a major activist and leader. The Rivera government seemed to recognize the threat posed by these new organizations, because it quickly created a counter organization, the Solidaridad de Maestras (Teachers' Solidarity).[80]

Teacher organizations grew slowly but steadily over the next three years. Low pay and limited access to social services brought teachers together and fostered a collective consciousness. Dynamic leaders such as Anaya and López generated enthusiasm among the rank and file and boosted the nascent organizations' appeal. They traveled to every corner of the country organizing teachers' assemblies to promote the idea of a new union to defend their interests.[81] Interviews with former teachers reveal widespread respect for the two leaders, who were described as especially intelligent, dynamic people with seemingly unlimited energy for organizing. Julio Flores remembers his surprise when López showed up at a teachers' meeting in his remote hamlet outside Lourdes. He also praised Anaya's ability to connect with common people and her unflagging commitment to open discussion within the organization, which stood in stark contrast to the top-down, authoritarian manner of the PCN and the Ministry of Education.[82]

Being a teacher organizer in the early 1960s was hard work. Money for organizing was almost nonexistent, teachers throughout the country were in a state of disorganization, and time was at a premium. Organizers worked full-time jobs as teachers throughout the week, "leaving only nights and Sundays for [organizational] work," as Anaya put it in a speech to fellow teachers in 1965. She went on in that speech to say that "our struggle has not been easy . . . we have experienced many failures, being unaccustomed as we are to fighting." But she insisted that "we have made steady strides because of our good will and our decision to improve conditions for teachers."[83]

One factor that promoted teacher organizing was teachers' steady realization of their subservient position in the system of military rule. Even though the leaders of the PRUD and the PCN understood the importance of teachers to their political survival and made strong appeals to them as the bedrock of the public sector, their relationship with teachers was that of patron-client rather than partners. The leaders of the ruling parties expected teachers to do as they were told and accept a position inferior to local military commanders, mayors, and leaders of the rural patrols.[84] Teachers like Julio Flores's father, who considered themselves educated and capable, found the relationship aggravating. But few outlets existed for them to channel their frustration. Staring in the early 1960s, however, he and other teachers like him found strength in the nascent teachers' organizations and the new political parties, especially the Christian Democratic Party after its founding in 1960. When given the opportunity to break ties with their traditional patron and join these new oppositional sectors, many teachers did so, including Flores's father.[85]

Former teacher Julio Alberto Gómez expressed a similar view when interviewed. He said teachers' jobs were more or less at the mercy of local military commanders. As one example, he recalls an incident when he was working as a fifth-grade teacher in an all-girls school in Ayuxtepeque in the late 1960s and the local commander of Cojutepeque falsely accused a female teacher of being a prostitute so he could force her removal.[86]

Another former teacher, Julio César Portillo, described education administrators, who served directly at the behest of the ruling party, as corrupt bureaucrats. They acted with a sense of arrogant entitlement, even hiring female teachers based solely on their looks. Portillo went on to say that "government officials had an attitude of considering teachers to be the loyal followers of the officialdom. . . . All of this created a strong feeling of resentment . . .

and supported the idea of breaking free of this cruel paternalism."[87] This sentiment was reiterated by Salvador Sánchez Cerén, who was a young teacher in the early 1960s and went on to serve as the ranking commander of the Farabundo Martí Popular Liberation Forces (FPL) in the 1980s and eventually as vice president after the FMLN victory in 2009. In his memoir, he describes the motives that pushed teachers to begin mobilizing against the state in 1963 as "combating the abusive politics and irresponsibility of the Ministry of Education and denouncing the conduct of the directors and supervisors who acted contrary to the rights of teachers."[88] No membership statistics exist for this stage of teacher organization, but by all accounts these nascent organizations represented a small fraction of teachers. Nevertheless, a core group of dedicated organizers within the ranks of the teaching profession made the most of the window of opportunity provided by the Rivera administration's reforms, and as a consequence the regime began to lose its ability to control teachers.

The Founding of ANDES

By late 1964 the leaders of the nascent teachers' organizations had made steady progress in getting their message out to the nation's teachers. They experienced their greatest organizational success in the central and western areas of the country, partly due to close geographic proximity to the capital and partly due to the personal contacts of those teachers who happened to join the organizational effort early. Success was more limited in the eastern region, but that was about to change as teacher organization and mobilization increased rapidly.[89]

A new pension law put forward by the Rivera government in 1964 provided the spark that took teacher organizing to a new level. The law, called the Sistema Nacional de Retiros (National Retirement System), was put before the Legislative Assembly in 1964 and approved in early 1965. It was a comprehensive overhaul of the pension and benefit program for all public employees, including teachers. Military personnel were not included in the new law because they operated under their own pension system. The new law granted pensions to public employees who had worked for forty years and paid 5 percent of their annual salary into the system. The government considered the law a social benefit and touted it as evidence of its commitment to reform. Teachers interpreted it quite differently.[90]

Many teachers believed that forty years of service was too long and a 5 percent contribution was too much. Furthermore, under the prior law they

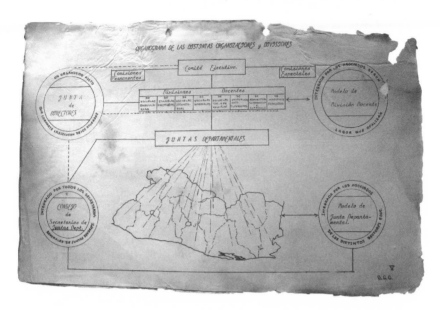

FIGURE 9. An organizational chart of the teachers' movement, 1964 or 1965. Flores Cienfuegos collection, caja #1, folder "Comité Pro-Ley de Protección Social 1964," MUPI.

received 100 percent of their salary upon retirement, whereas the new law awarded them only 80 percent unless they paid an additional premium. The leaders of the teacher organizations made the pension law the focus of mobilization. As Vaquerano recalls, "the law allowed us to mobilize; it was the banner of struggle that led to the formation of ANDES." Vaquerano, Anaya, López, and the other leaders of the teachers' movement created a new umbrella organization, the Comité pro Defensa del Maestro (Teachers Defense Committee), that united women's and men's organizations into a common front. The comité drafted an alternative law, the Ley de Protección Social Para el Magisterio Nacional (Social Protection Law for National Teachers), a highly sophisticated, technical document that exempted teachers from the government's new law and laid out an alternative benefit program.

The leaders of the teachers' movement introduced the Social Protection Law to the Legislative Assembly in September 1964 and quickly organized teachers to pressure the assembly to accept it. They organized a general assembly of teachers on September 13 at one of the teacher training schools. It included representatives from forty-five schools around the country and from different associations, including, of course, APNES and UMS. About six hundred teachers attended.[91]

FIGURE 10.   A newspaper image of teachers gathering in the National Gymnasium
in February 1965 to protest the government's proposed retirement law.
El Diario de Hoy, February 8, 1965, in Flores Cienfuegos collection,
caja #3, folder "Recortes de periódicos," MUPI.

The main resolution called for support of the Social Protection Law.[92] The committee that organized the general assembly included Anaya and López. The next
step was to get the newspapers to cover the story. The leaders were very successful at achieving that goal. Throughout the rest of the month they got newspapers
to publish photographs and statements of support from teachers throughout
the country.[93]

To keep the issue alive, leaders organized departmental committees and
instructed them to "develop to the greatest extent the campaign prior to the
approval of the law." They instructed teachers on how they could support
the cause: "Reproduce every bulletin issued by [the] National Coordinating
Committee. . . . Organize as soon as possible the teacher delegations that
will be present at the National Legislative Assembly during the discussion of
the project. . . . Reproduce articles in favor of the campaign published by the
national press."[94] This style of relentless and highly effective organizational
activity characterized the teachers' movement from the outset. The steady
alienation of teachers by government intransigence would be crucial for the

success of the movement, but it took effective organizing for the emerging teachers' leadership to be able to profit from it.

The comité organized another national gathering of teachers in February 1965 to discuss the situation and plan future action. Out of that meeting came the decision to request that President Rivera exempt teachers from the new law and accept their alternative. The government rejected that proposal, which prompted the comité to organize a mass march to press its demands. The comité's leaders selected May 3, 1965, but an earthquake struck the capital that morning, forcing the postponement of the march to June 21, the day before the annual Día del Maestro (Day of the Teacher) holiday.[95] On that day, teachers poured into San Salvador from throughout the country and gathered in Cuscatlán Park. The march started mid-morning and proceeded to the center of town, passing in front of the National Palace, which housed the main offices of government. The plan was to end up at the president's official residence (the Casa Presidencial), where representatives would ask Rivera to reconsider the government's position.

Organizers insisted that the march be carried out in a professional and orderly manner, fitting of the teaching profession and consistent with the reasonable nature of their demands. They divided the marchers into two groups, women in front and men behind, and only three banners were present—the national flag and two large placards—one in front of the women and another in front of the men. Marchers walked in orderly, rank-and-file lines, and they were provided with strict instructions by organizers to "conduct themselves in an ordered and well composed manner during the march." They were told specifically "not to attack the government, its institutions or its personnel" and to be "absolutely apolitical." The goal of the march was highly specific, "a peaceful demonstration of teacher unity reaffirming our position in regard to the new National Retirement System."[96] As many as ten thousand of the total of fourteen thousand teachers throughout the country participated. They were joined by people who sympathized with them or had their own reason to oppose the pension law, so the total number of marchers probably exceeded fifteen thousand. Whether or not these numbers are exactly accurate, the fact remains that the march was enormous and marked a momentous occasion in the history of labor organizing and collective action in El Salvador. Traveling to San Salvador, especially from the far reaches of the country, was expensive and time consuming, so achieving such a high level of participation was testament to the diligent and competent organizational efforts during the preceding months and years.

The marchers arrived at the Presidential House (Casa Presidencial) at midday. Leaders of the comité demanded that the president meet them to discuss the pension law. Rivera received them in the meeting room of the Presidential House. One of the teachers present at the meeting claimed that Rivera acceded to their demands and agreed to exempt teachers from the law and consider their alternative proposal.[97]

The leaders of the teachers' organization considered it a great victory to have gained the president's promise as a result of mass organizing and collective action. According to Vaquerano the idea of forming a new, nationwide teachers' union emerged from the march. Shortly thereafter, six of the young leaders, including Vaquerano, Anaya, and López, founded ANDES 21 de Junio and began soliciting membership from teachers throughout the country.[98]

The rise of Christian Democracy and teacher organizing mutually reinforced one another.[99] The PDC supported the teachers, and many teachers in turn joined the ranks of the Christian Democrats. Former teachers uniformly remember the close relationship that existed between the PDC and teachers. Julio Flores says that his father joined the PDC when he broke with the PCN and then encouraged him to join the PDC youth league. Arnoldo Vaquerano says that teacher support for the PDC was widespread and growing when ANDES was founded in 1965. In Suchitoto, Salvador Acosta and his son both emphasized the close ties between the PDC and teachers. Acosta *hijo* said that teacher support for the Christian Democrats remained strong even after a fraudulent election in 1972 deprived the PDC of the presidency. It waned only when state repression intensified in 1974 and 1975, which pushed some teachers to abandon the centrist PDC in favor of more militant organizations. Vaquerano seconded Acosta's recollections by pointing out the miniscule number of teachers in the Communist Party in 1965 (only eight of them). Just as the teachers had been so successful in sustaining the PRUD and the PCN throughout the 1950s and early 1960s, their support for the Christian Democrats was an important component of that party's rapid ascent.[100]

Even though the Rivera administration passed an electoral reform law that introduced proportional representation in the legislature and tolerated some electoral competitiveness, including the loss of the San Salvador mayor's office, the PCN waged a relentless battle against competitors. The Christian Democrats received the brunt of the attacks. PCN spokespersons accused the Christian Democrats of being communists and serving as a front for subversion by Moscow, and occasionally they even called them "fascists."[101] The PCN's tactics against the PDC did not stop at slogans, propaganda, and electioneering but soon progressed to violence and the use of paramilitary intimidation. Julio Flores recalls the fear he felt as a young boy when his father broke ties with the PCN and began working for the Christian Democrats. The cordial relationship between his father and local military commanders and PCN officials disappeared, and he recalls having serious discussions with his father about politics when he was in primary school. Flores hijo learned that anyone belonging to the PDC or ANDES, and especially a leader like his father, received death threats and was subjected to intimidations by ORDEN.[102]

ORDEN's existence in a rural community like Flores's was no secret. Everyone knew who was involved, and so when intimidation began, it was quite personal. Flores recalls verbal threats, slogans being painted on the walls of teachers' homes, and then, one night when he was thirteen years old, having his house pelted with stones in the middle of the night. Flores's experience highlights the classic paradox of military rule, the overtures of reform running up against the reality of repression. It was no different than President Rivera meeting the teachers during the march on the Presidential House in 1965 and accepting their demands, while in the countryside local PCN officials and ORDEN paramilitaries threatened and intimidated anyone associated with an opposition organization.[103]

Despite Rivera's promises during the June march, the government balked at exempting teachers from the new pension law and considering their alternative. Government leaders promised that they were considering the teachers' proposal, but as the months passed without action, teachers grew impatient and became convinced that the government would have to be pressured once again. ANDES placed the pension issue at the center of its organizational efforts. It held its first national congress in December 1965 in San Salvador, where in the words of Anaya, ANDES's goals included "organizing teachers into [a] single National Association . . . [and] gaining the exclusion of teachers from the National Retirement System, which the President of the Republic had promised us at the June 21st march, organized by our [National] Committee, standing shoulder to shoulder with the Departmental Committees and Sub-Committees."[104]

A pro-government editorialist, Carlos Samayoa Martínez, explained the reasons for resisting the teachers' demands. He said that the teachers' requests were "impractical and economically inconvenient." He chastised teachers for seeing themselves as better than other public sector employees, and he defended the existing pension system as being sound and just and, "despite its deficiencies, providing a great service to the Salvadoran worker." He concluded by saying that "our country cannot afford the luxury of duplicating its institutions, and it is necessary to maintain a realistic perspective."[105]

Teachers responded to such criticisms with appeals to the special demands of the teaching profession and descriptions of the pivotal role played by education in national development. In the words of a delegation of teachers from San Miguel at the first ANDES Congress in 1965, "the teaching profession constitutes the most important factor in national progress." Therefore, "the Government must accept that the destiny and survival of the Salvadoran people and its public institutions, depends on the moral, civic, intellectual, technical and spiritual nurturing provided by teachers."[106] The delegates insisted that teachers deserved more compensation and benefits, as appropriate for their profession. The leaders of the Teachers Defense Committee had expressed those same sentiments the previous year in a public message to teachers, saying that "despite the important mission fulfilled by teachers, we lack basic social services." They went on to shame the government by saying that El Salvador was falling behind other countries, where "such benefits have already been provided, such that El Salvador was one of the painful examples in the Americas where teachers' rights are not recognized."[107]

The government's ongoing failure to address the teachers' requests caused the union's ranks to swell throughout 1966 and 1967. By the end of Rivera's time in office the union claimed to have nearly four thousand active members and the support of most of the remaining ten thousand teachers. ANDES leaders used that emergent weight of membership to pressure the government. Throughout much of 1967, the union launched localized collective actions to pressure the government to listen to its demands on pensions and working conditions. On an almost weekly basis, teachers in municipalities throughout the country published broadsides in the main daily newspapers expressing their support for ANDES, and the union organized regular marches in the larger cities to press their demands.[108]

In early 1967, shortly before Rivera was to turn the presidency over to his former minister of the interior, Sánchez Hernández, ANDES put its growing organizational power behind a new demand for improved benefits. Its leaders presented Rivera's Ministry of the Interior and the Legislative Assembly with a new pension plan known as the Instituto Magisterial de Prestaciones Sociales (Teachers' Institute for Social Welfare—IMPRESS). It outlined a series of benefits that ANDES believed the state should provide teachers, including access to health care comparable to telecommunications employees, who had their own hospital. IMPRESS also laid out regulations for pensions and various other social services. Although low pay loomed as an issue, IMPRESS did not address salaries. During the months of May and June teachers organized demonstrations throughout the country to put pressure on the government to give legal status to ANDES and to accept IMPRESS.

Rivera's term was coming to an end, and the IMPRESS project was left pending. However, exactly two years after the initial demonstration, on June 21, 1967, Rivera signed the bylaws of the new teachers' union.[109] One week later Rivera handed over the reins of office to his successor, Sánchez Hernández, the "education" candidate, who had promised to make educational reform a priority during his presidency. After he appointed Walter Béneke as minister of education, they unveiled the outlines of a massive education reform. Relations between teachers and the state were about to change considerably, as the new leaders pushed aside IMPRESS in favor of a more comprehensive reorganization of teachers' roles.

At first blush, the pursuit of modernity would seem noncontroversial. After all, who does not want to be modern? Even in El Salvador in the 1960s, a strong consensus existed about the desire, even urgency, to modernize. But that same consensus produced acrimonious debate over the meaning of modernity. Did modernization mean land reform, a strong central state, a progressive income tax, and a close relationship with international development agencies? Did it mean freeing up the owners of capital to unleash their entrepreneurial spirit and let market forces allocate resources, à la Adam Smith? Did it mean repressing challenges to the system harshly and without quarter? Or did it mean scratching the entire system in a revolution? Obviously, these were not trivial matters.

The Alliance for Progress and the PCN's modernization programs created a complex and unpredictable political environment. Both leftists and conservative rightists responded to the Alliance and the PCN's relationship with the United States paradoxically, with a mixture of both support and opposition. The conservative right welcomed the United States as an ally in the fight against communism, but it wanted U.S. policymakers, and especially its development agents, to stay out of elite Salvadorans' affairs. The left opposed U.S. backing of the Salvadoran military and considered the United States to be a self-interested imperialist power, but some of its members saw the benefits of U.S. aid and supported the kinds of reforms being proposed by U.S. development experts. The terms *communism, imperialism, nationalism*, and *modernization* were employed commonly by all parties in these debates, but in different ways with different meanings to achieve alternative ends. Even in hindsight, it is bewildering to see the manner in which these debates played themselves out, such as conservative spokespersons deftly utilizing anti-imperialist rhetoric, and PCN functionaries accusing a conservative representative of the business sector of being affiliated with communists.

Out of this fluid terrain emerged one of the most important oppositional sectors in recent Salvadoran history, the teachers and their new union, ANDES 21 de Junio. Our analysis of the emergence of the teachers' union and teacher collectivization concurs strongly with the analysis of sociologist Paul Almeida. He claims that the reformist opening under Rivera represented a decisive moment in creating a long-lasting opposition movement. Along with other labor organizations (to be discussed in chapter 4), the Rivera reforms created a space that allowed dedicated and capable teacher organizers to plant the seeds of organization. Teachers represented such an important sector because they were the largest single group of public employees, they held moral authority in society, and they had been traditional clients of the state. But suddenly teachers began acting autonomously and organizing against their patron. As per Almeida's formulation, what was a seed of organization in the first half of the 1960s grew into a stubbornly resilient plant in the late 1960s. Teachers would find their organizational capacities put to the test by the 1968 education reform, sponsored by the new "education" president, Sánchez Hernández. Not only would they challenge the reform's impact on the teaching profession, but they also would challenge its very definition of modernity. When the PCN eventually reversed course on reform and began to clamp down on organizations like ANDES, it would be too late. Teachers would be fully mobilized, and as state repression intensified, many teachers would radicalize instead of capitulate.

CHAPTER 3

"A Monitor Instead of a Teacher"
The Origins of the 1968 Education Reform and How Television Became Its Centerpiece

In Utopia every classroom in every school would be equipped with a television receiver.

—Charles Siepmann, 1952*

It is only with a restructuring of our agrarian system and a revolutionary process of humanizing wealth that El Salvador will be able to overcome its population pressures.

—*El Popular*, 1961**

⁜ IN 1973 AN EDUCATION RESEARCHER IN EL SALVADOR DESCRIBED A typical day in the life of a junior high school student. The student's favorite time of the day was when the tallest kid in class stood up and turned on the TV monitor that was installed on a podium. The flickering, grayish light of the tube gave way to the grainy image of a teacher giving a lesson. The program was broadcast from a distant location in the country, but the student embraced it as something near and dear. "I like this class," says the narrative of the fictional student, "I think the subject is interesting and I like the 'telemaestro.'" One of the virtues of the televised class, according to the researcher, was the quality of the teleteacher, who explained things very clearly. The televised class was also entertaining: "The TV music really livens me up in the morning. I don't know the title of this song, but I think it's from the United States," comments the student. Overall, the class, which discussed the native peoples of El Salvador, was informative and entertaining.

But all good things must come to an end: "Mr. Soto, our telemaestro, is wav-
ing goodbye. I'm embarrassed to wave back, but other students are doing it.
So why can't I? It's getting noisy with all the feet stomping to the music."[1]
By 1973 this was supposed to be the typical day in school for every junior
high school student in El Salvador. Even though the researcher embellished
the students' engagement with their education, the fact remains that most
junior high school students received large portions of their daily education
by television. The Salvadoran government had plans to extend the program
to every level of education. How could this have come to be?

The use of educational television in El Salvador was part of a massive
education reform that began in 1968. The reform was no minor upgrading
of textbooks or a mere tinkering with curricula. It was a deep and comprehensive overhaul of the nation's public school system, particularly at middle
and high school levels. It was ambitious and well funded, and policymakers
conceived it as transforming El Salvador into a modern, urban, industrializing nation. The most comprehensive account of the education reform identified twelve main components: a reorganization of the Ministry of Education,
extensive teacher training, curriculum revision, development of new teachers'
guides and student workbooks, improvement of school supervision to provide
"advice" instead of inspections, development of a wider diversity of technical
training programs in grades ten through twelve, extensive building of new
schoolrooms, elimination of tuition in grades seven, eight, and nine, the use
of double sessions and reduced contact hours to teach more pupils in existing facilities, a law regulating teachers' hours and pay scales, a new student
evaluation system incorporating changes in promotion and grading policies,
and the installation of a national instructional television system for grades
seven through nine.[2] As we will discuss in the next chapter, these components
were not conceived together as part of a concerted planning effort. Rather,
the reform was carried out in a rather hodgepodge manner, with each step
being conceptualized as the process went along. But television was there from
the inception. In the words of one report: "The present educational reform in
El Salvador was first conceived as little more than the placing of a television
receiver in each classroom. As plans developed, however, and as the full implications of the introduction of new technology became clear, it was seen that
television was not only an innovation important in its own right, but also a
catalyst of change that would affect every aspect of education in El Salvador."[3]

Televisión Educativa (TVE) emerged as the driving force behind the
entire reform. Not only did it receive the bulk of the reform's financial,

human, and political resources, but it also determined how and when other elements of the reform were implemented. For most Salvadorans, TVE became the face of the education reform. When parents were surveyed in 1970 about the government's new policies in education, almost all of them mentioned educational television alone. Since roughly thirty of the forty international consultants who worked in El Salvador on the education reform devoted themselves exclusively to educational television, this was a predictable outcome.[4] Educational television consumed half of the total reform budget from 1966 to 1970.[5] International donors provided most of the funding for television, including US$11 million in grants and loans from the United States, US$5 million from the World Bank, and another US$2 million from bilateral aid. Overall, one source estimates that the project received US$14 million from non-U.S. donors.[6] Thus, educational television rapidly emerged as a major component of the Alliance for Progress in El Salvador.

The present chapter discusses the background to the 1968 education reform, the increasing role of foreign aid and foreign experts in shaping the reform's agenda, the role of communications expert Wilbur Schramm in advocating the use of television to promote development, UNESCO's embrace of Schramm's ideas, and its promotion of educational television in developing countries like El Salvador.

The Salvadoran Project and the Advice of Foreign Experts

Since the nineteenth century, governing officials in El Salvador's liberal-oriented administrations spoke regularly about the educational needs of their citizens. Even Gen. Maximiliano Hernández Martínez, who had presided over a stagnant educational system during his tenure in office (1931–1944), spoke of the importance of education and sponsored an education reform in 1940. Not until after World War II, however, did Salvadoran leaders devote increased attention and funding to education. The direct antecedents of the 1968 education reform took shape after the fall of Martínez in 1944, during the consolidation of the modernizing military regime after 1948. Governing officials who had seen education primarily as a way to "form citizens" began discussing the role of education in promoting economic development, and particularly as a way to create the educated labor force necessary for industrialization. The 1956 regulations for high school education listed "economic efficiency" as one of the "fundamental problems" around which high school education should define its objectives, although it was a lower priority than

67 MILLONES DE COLONES PARA TELECOMUNICACIONES.

FIGURE 11. A front-page image from *El Diario de Hoy* showing Salvadoran government officials meeting with international aid experts to discuss financing and design
of a telecommunications upgrade. It was images like this, of the sudden and seemingly
ubiquitous presence of international aid experts, that promoted conflict between the
new Directorio government and conservatives. *El Diario de Hoy*, March 21, 1961, 1.

"conservation of health," "family life," and "citizenship."[7] The explicit link
between education and the economy was made in the early 1960s, when technocratic officials in the National Conciliation (PCN) governments (1962–1979)
found themselves spurred on by international development experts and the
Alliance for Progress.

The first months of 1962 were a period of intense political activity in El
Salvador. The PCN was founded, a new constitution was written, a provisional
president was selected to replace the Directorio Cívico Militar (Directorate),
and presidential elections were held in April. Col. Julio Rivera won the uncontested election and was inaugurated on July 1, 1962. The legitimacy of the
Rivera administration was in question from its inception, as had been the level
of popular support for the coup of January 1961. *La Prensa Gráfica*, the newspaper with the largest circulation in the country, questioned the meaning of
an election in which only 25 percent of voters had gone to the polls.[8] At the

same time, the issue of educational quality and past governments' poor record on improving education emerged as topics of public debate. In the months preceding Rivera's inauguration, newspapers published almost daily references to the problems of public education.[9] Even the unofficial publication of the Directorate, *El Popular*, printed frequent articles about the dire state of Salvadoran schools. One article demanded government action on the matter: "The State ought to use energy and vision to plan a comprehensive solution to the problems of public education."[10] The Catholic Church also acknowledged the problem and responded with the foundation in 1961 of a radio school (*escuela radiofónica*) to help combat rural illiteracy.[11]

Most of the newspaper debate about education focused on flaws in the current system rather than possible solutions. One notable exception was a series of articles published in April 1961 about Japan's education system. The author of the articles was Walter Béneke, then serving as the Salvadoran consul general in Tokyo, who had become an enthusiast of the Japanese education system. As a result he worked tirelessly through public and private channels to encourage Salvadoran authorities to attempt to implement a version of the Japanese system in El Salvador. Béneke believed the Japanese system illustrated how education could help industrialize an agricultural economy by creating an abundant skilled labor force. In his articles Béneke claimed that the comparison was particularly apt for El Salvador because both nations were geographically small, had limited natural resources, and had high population densities.[12] He found that the most important characteristic of the Japanese system was its emphasis on technical education and concluded that "the problem of technical education in general and industrial education in particular is, thus, the most important of all that we have for our economic development." Béneke argued that high school was the critical level, and he advocated for El Salvador reorienting secondary education toward technical instruction.[13] As an example of the new direction that El Salvador should follow, he referred to the opening of a new school in San Salvador, the Instituto de Educación Técnica (Institute of Technical Education), created with support from the Japanese government. Eventually Japan would donate equipment to the school and also give scholarships for seven teachers to travel to Japan to receive technical training.[14]

Béneke was not a lone voice in the wilderness. Key policymakers in the Directorate shared his views. Even before Rivera's inauguration in 1962, officials in the government of provisional president Eusebio Cordón (1961–1962), who had been appointed by the Constitutional Assembly to replace the Directorate while presidential elections were organized, had mentioned publicly the possibility of launching an education reform.[15] A heavily publicized international conference in Chile in March 1962 helped push education to the top of government's priorities. The conference was hosted by UNESCO in conjunction with a series of other development organizations. Ministers of education, economy, planning, and treasury from throughout Latin America had been invited, and the main topic of discussion was the relationship between education and development.[16]

It was shortly after the UNESCO conference that provisional president Cordón created the planning unit, CONAPLAN, to coordinate development activities and, as he put it in his final speech as president, "to take maximum advantage of the collaboration offered under the program of the Alliance for Progress."[17] Thereafter, CONAPLAN would prove instrumental in promoting education as a central aspect of the nation's drive to industrialize. The Cordón government had also signed an Alliance for Progress agreement with the United States to finance educational improvements with loans.[18]

For all these reasons, it is no surprise that incoming president Rivera made education a focal point of his new government's platform. He and other governing officials may or may not have had an intrinsic interest in educational quality, but they realized that the topic of education provided them an opportunity to boost their legitimacy. In his inaugural address, Rivera presented education as a way for El Salvador to both industrialize and defeat communism, a winning combination in 1960s El Salvador. He labeled communism the "greatest danger" facing the country and said that one strategy his government would use to meet that threat was socioeconomic reform, including education reform, and well-planned development projects, all in the spirit of the Alliance for Progress, which he embraced "without prejudice or reserve."[19]

During Rivera's five years in office (1962–1967), governing officials came to believe that far-reaching education reform was necessary, and indeed they put in place many of the building blocks that made the 1968 education reform possible. Rivera launched three major initiatives in the field of education in his first year: a literacy campaign, an ambitious school building program with Alliance for Progress funds, and the promotion of technical education. The first two items were a continuation of policies from the 1950s. The third item—promoting technical education—represented a directional shift that Rivera duly noted in his first report to the Legislative Assembly. He called for a "radical and urgent change" in education to reorient it toward the development of skilled workers and technicians. Following Béneke's 1961 suggestions, Rivera described secondary school as the key level, when students were ready to "easily assimilate the exact knowledge of new and numerous disciplines in the fields of mechanics, construction, industrial technology, telecommunications."[20] Admittedly, the actual amount of change in high schools during the Rivera years was limited. Expenditure in technical schools increased only from 4.38 percent of the 1960 high school education budget to 5.81 percent in 1965, hardly a radical change, but a reorientation in thinking about education as a tool of economic development was underway.

The charter of the Alliance for Progress encouraged governments to prepare planning documents, and in response, the Rivera administration issued a five-year plan for the period 1965–1969. The section on education provided a clarified expression of the Rivera administration's view of the relationship between education and industrialization. The plan highlighted the need for a better-educated workforce to promote industrialization. It stressed the need for agricultural entrepreneurs who could command modern techniques. It also ranked the various problems of the educational system. School absenteeism was listed first, followed by high dropout rates, poor school achievement, bad teaching, inadequate curricula, and the negative impact of low teacher salaries.[21]

As solutions to these problems, the five-year plan set out a series of lofty goals and called for aggressive policies to achieve them. Some of the goals included immediate universal enrollment for students at the primary level and a similar degree of enrollment at the junior high school level in the near future. To achieve its goals, the plan called for such policies as building classrooms, increasing the number of teachers, and reforming the system of teacher training. One noteworthy aspect of the plan is that it presumed continuity with the succeeding administration. Rivera's presidential term ended in 1967, yet the five-year plan was supposed to be implemented between 1965 and 1969.

The five-year plan did not mention educational television, but the government had already considered the possibilities of this new technology. Walter Béneke was a key player in bringing the prospects of educational television before his Salvadoran cohorts. Predictably, he encouraged officials in the Rivera administration to imitate the Japanese model, in which televisions were used in schools. His tenure in Japan in the early 1960s had coincided with the rapid expansion of educational television there; it increased from 2 educational broadcasting stations in 1959 to 238 in 1964.[22] The international development community considered the Japanese system to be "the best developed school broadcasting system in the world."[23] Japan and El Salvador had in common a highly centralized education administration, exemplified by the strong role of the Ministry of Education in policing curriculum, to the point that in both countries the ministry reserved the right to approve the use of each and every textbook. The Japanese system may have "fostered among the teachers a servile attitude and killed initiative," as one international education researcher claimed, but its homogeneity and centralization made it ideal for centrally broadcast school lessons.[24]

In contrast to what would transpire in El Salvador, the Japanese had developed their project amid a thorough discussion of the potential repercussions for pedagogy. They decided that televised lessons should be a tool to "aid the instructor in his pedagogic approach through the presentation of richer material and by introducing new methods." They never intended television as a substitute for classroom teachers.[25] Moreover, they concentrated the use of television in kindergarten and primary school, rather than middle school, which is the level at which El Salvador would implement it.[26] Regardless of these differences, Béneke wanted his country to emulate the Japanese Broadcasting Corporation (Nippon Hōsō Kyōkai, or NHK).

The idea of using technology to improve education was becoming widely popular in international circles by 1961, thanks partly to relentless promotion by international development organizations. Even the editorialist of *El Diario de Hoy*, a paper that tended to reject all suggestions from international development experts, wrote approvingly of UNESCO's idea to put mass media at the service of education, saying that "mass media multiplies the reach of educators."[27] At some point in 1961 Béneke, during one of his periodic visits from Japan, mentioned to El Salvador's minister of education the possibility of using television to reform the education system. After that initial conversation, Béneke lobbied midlevel officers at the ministry to keep the idea alive.[28] His efforts quickly bore fruit. At UNESCO's thirteenth general conference in 1963, Rivera's minister of education, Professor Ernesto Revelo Borja, solicited the organization's help for a television project.[29] The subsequent collaboration between UNESCO and El Salvador started modestly, with the creation of two scholarships to study instructional television.[30] At the same time, Béneke, who had since been made ambassador to Japan, obtained Japanese financial support to conduct a feasibility study for the use of educational television. The Salvadoran government responded by appointing a commission to study the possibility of implementing a comprehensive television project. The commission included representatives of CONAPLAN, the Ministry of Education, and a businessman involved in broadcasting.[31] Ambassador Béneke traveled back to El Salvador to join the commission in late 1963. The composition of the commission, with the incorporation of a representative of the business community, typified the PCN's governing style. It conceived of its decision-making process as being driven by purely technical concerns and in full agreement with the *empresa privada* (the private sector), an oft-repeated term that was basically a euphemism for economic elites.

In 1964 Guillermo Borja Nathan, the executive secretary of CONAPLAN, delineated the government's rationale for educational television in a letter to the World Bank:

> Education, at the high school and university levels, is particularly important for accelerated economic growth. It is estimated that during the next five years it will be necessary to create at least 30,000 new jobs each year. Most of these jobs will be in the commercial, industrial and service sectors, and many of them will need training at the secondary or vocational school levels. . . . Education by television could play an important role in all these levels. Particularly where school enrollments are small, the use of a monitor instead of a teacher could make it possible that high quality teaching would be available in places where it would not be otherwise available. Supervision would be left in the hands of moderately trained teachers. The advantages of this system could be significant for secondary and vocational education in the rural areas of the country.[32]

Amazingly, the Ministry of Education had no knowledge of this letter. When a UNESCO representative in El Salvador visited the minister of education to inquire about the details of the television project, the minister had no idea what he was talking about.[33]

This episode at first glance might seem an innocuous lapse in communication between government officials, but in fact it reveals the high stakes of linking education to development. In concrete ways the power and influence of traditional education authorities was being usurped by development experts and economists. Business leaders also were assuming a more central role in shaping education policy, even in designing curricula.[34] The traditional education authorities had close ties to teachers, and they were sensitive to teachers' concerns; in fact, many of them began their careers as

FIGURE 12. The renowned Salvadoran editorial cartoonist Nando, in this 1961 drawing, captured the strong sentiment among teachers that the administration of education should be done by teachers. The image is referring to the new subsecretary of education, a teacher who fits the position like a ring on a finger and who is supported by teachers, looking on in the background. The Sánchez-Hernández administration risked losing teacher support as it moved education administration over to economists and technocrats. *El Diario de Hoy,* April 20, 1961, 6.

teachers. As their influence diminished, teachers lost a voice in government, a change that would have serious consequences for teacher-state relations in the near future.

A UNESCO mission that came to El Salvador at the end of 1964 highlighted the firm belief among international development experts that El Salvador's success depended upon vigorous action by government leaders to transform the economy through educational reform. The mission produced a confidential report that was given to the Salvadoran government by the director general of UNESCO, who emphasized its importance by saying that it contained "the conclusions reached by the UNESCO secretariat."[35] The report highlighted the already serious problem of underemployment in rural areas and stated that it would get worse as improvements in agricultural techniques reduced the need for labor. The solution, it claimed, was to train laborers to work in industry and the service sector and then create jobs to absorb displaced rural workers. The report said that the current education system was ill equipped to handle the transformation, and thus significant changes were necessary. Among other things, Salvadoran officials needed to focus their attention on technical training at the high school level and revamp the curriculum to "encourage the idea that the use of apparatus, tools and machinery is a means of earning a living fit for an educated person. In this way many of the pupils, including some of the ablest, might be predisposed to pursue scientific and industrial studies as an alternative to the traditional courses."[36] Finally, the report recommended the creation of a system of educational television.

Rivera had budgeted more than 2 million colones to TVE for the period 1965–1969.[37] But implementing the new policy within the existing education bureaucracy was slow. To speed things up, in 1967 the Rivera government proposed the creation of the Instituto de Educación por TV (Institute for Educational Television), an autonomous organization within the government that would oversee the establishment of educational television. Creating that new layer of bureaucracy, however, required approval from the Legislative Assembly. Normally gaining such approval was not a challenge, but by 1967 Salvadoran politics had changed with the rise of opposition parties thanks to proportional representation.

The proposal to create the institute resulted in an unexpected debate in the assembly that lasted for weeks. Columnists in conservative newspapers, frequent critics of the Alliance for Progress, questioned the television project, its costs, and its heavy reliance on foreign money and technicians. One op-ed piece took issue with the administration's assertion that the use of television in education was going to save 44 million colones: "Since that figure is similar to the total investment of the State in the operation of the educational system, the statement of the madam Head of the Department of Educational Television would have to be interpreted as meaning that the new service would leave unemployed all the teachers in the country as being unnecessary and superfluous."[38] Another columnist made the point that "a television monitor will never be able to replace teachers."[39] This theme was explored more deeply by an article that argued that the best education takes place when students perform science experiments by themselves instead of watching them on television and when they have a teacher in front of them answering questions and providing clarifications.[40] Another commentator concluded, "Psychology and pedagogy tell us about the value of the direct lesson with the teacher in front of the class. This will not be achieved with televised education."[41] The proposal to create the institute faced such serious resistance that the assembly eventually voted it down.[42]

The failure of the institute had PCN leaders concerned about their ability to advance education reform according to their own dictates, especially in the midst of transitioning to the new administration of Fidel Sánchez Hernández. In hopes of dampening criticisms, Rivera looked to smooth relations with one of the government's antagonists, teachers. They had grown increasingly angry with the government over a proposed retirement law that would affect their benefits. Two days after the assembly rejected the institute, Rivera signed the charter of ANDES 21 de Junio, the teachers' union, thus giving it legal standing.

The reformist agenda of the Rivera administration between 1962 and 1967 accelerated after the inauguration of President Sánchez Hernández in July 1967. Sánchez Hernández selected as his minister of education the enthusiast for Japanese TV education Walter Béneke. Béneke lost no time in taking the steps necessary to advance his ambitious agenda for reform, which was predictably focused on educational television. UNESCO advisors at the Ministry of Education helped prepare the necessary documentation to solicit a loan from the World Bank and additional support from USAID. Béneke's efforts in late 1967 and early 1968 created the blueprint for an education reform that would be announced a few months later. Béneke worked in close conjunction with Román Mayorga Quirós, an engineer who headed the social sector division of CONAPLAN. According to an interview with a government official in 1979 by a team of international education researchers, "Béneke was an incredible doer, but he had to be understood. Mayorga put his ideas in order, criticized them, softened them, gave them a rationale or budgeting justification. . . . This structured what the Minister wanted to get done."[43] One of the foreign advisors who was present for many of the discussions during this period described the strong presence of Minister Béneke in all the formulations relating to education reform: "It would not be accurate to assume, and the reader should not do so, that the [UNESCO] planning mission exercised a real influence on the structure of the document that emerged from this effort. The most determinant person to determine the shape of the result was the Minister of Education whose ideas about secondary education seemed to reflect his relation with other Latin American Ministers of Education as well as his own ideas."[44]

Thus, by 1968 key authorities in the Salvadoran government had embraced the idea that a massive education reform needed to be undertaken and the use of educational television should be one of its main components. Early support from UNESCO helped turn the simple and original idea of using "a monitor instead of a teacher" into a concrete project that made television a key tool to promote economic development. Under influential leadership from Béneke, dating all the way back to his time as a diplomat in Japan during the Rivera years, the government was prepared for an aggressive era of implementation during the Sánchez Hernández presidency.

Foreign Aid

Access to large amounts of foreign aid helped propel the Salvadoran government's ambitious plans for reforming education in the 1960s. The concept of using foreign money to finance development programs was relatively new.[45] All of the international organizations that would provide funding and guidance for development in El Salvador were created during or after World War II. UNESCO and the World Bank were founded in the mid-1940s, and Truman's Point Four Program in 1950. USAID, in turn, replaced the Point Four Program in 1961, and the Inter-American Development Bank preceded it by only two years. For their part, Latin Americans had demonstrated a willingness to incorporate foreign ideas about education. The English educator Joseph Lancaster had significantly influenced education policy throughout Latin American in the immediate years after independence from Spain.[46] But like their international counterparts, Latin American nations were also new to the idea of foreign aid being used to promote development in "third world" nations in the midst of the Cold War.

UNESCO

UNESCO's technical assistance to El Salvador started on a small scale in 1951. In 1950 the Salvadoran representative to UNESCO wrote an exploratory letter to the secretary general saying that his government would welcome assistance, "preferably in the fields of literacy, not only for the highly beneficial effect of this on the cultural level of El Salvador, but also for the consequences it would have on its economy, which in many aspects is entering a period of great evolutionary importance."[47] After this initial solicitation, Salvadoran authorities followed up with a more comprehensive program to develop the San Andrés Valley in western El Salvador. It was to involve UNESCO and various other UN and U.S. agencies, such as the International Labor Organization (ILO), the Food and Agricultural Organization (FAO), and the World Health Organization (WHO).[48] The project was in response to a WHO initiative that called for "integrated area demonstration projects in the Western Hemisphere." The Salvadoran plan received international attention, including mention in a *New York Times* editorial, that said the initiative would "make the lives of those 100,000 persons [living in the area] happier, richer and more fruitful."[49]

Along with the San Andrés proposal, the Salvadoran government approached UNESCO in 1951 to request technical assistance for all educational levels.[50] That request resulted in three education consultants coming to El Salvador. Their report and the successive documents written by UNESCO experts then influenced Salvadoran decision makers.[51] The first team of experts in 1951 defined the educational problems of the country as a lack of skilled labor to sustain industrial growth: "Many previously discussed expert reports refer to the fact that trained personnel is lacking and that the low education standard in the country has a retarding effect on economic and industrial progress. Particularly in the report on industry it was noted that efficiency was low and that without better education and additional training the workers cannot be expected to produce more efficiently."[52] As that message was repeated in one report after another, year after year, the cumulative impact influenced greatly the thinking of Salvadoran officials.

U.S. Aid

The overall amount of U.S. nonmilitary funding to El Salvador throughout the 1950s was modest, less than $1 million per year. After 1960, under the auspices of the Act of Bogota and the Alliance for Progress, in the aftermath of the Cuban Revolution, the amount of annual aid to El Salvador increased between tenfold and twentyfold. The anticommunist impulses behind the aid were clearly evident in discussions over the first aid package that had been arranged in February 1961. A portion of that package was devoted to education and literacy programs. U.S. officials made clear that anticommunism was their top priority, worrying that the proposed literacy program could aid communists' propaganda efforts. Literate rural peoples could read their printed propaganda, after all: "A literacy campaign could represent one of the target points for communist influences in the Government. By the same token, it represents a point where U.S. aid could be made effective: not only in supplying anti-communist literature and pamphlets, but also in supplying soundly conceived educational materials apart from political orientation." That same anticommunist impulse supported the idea of developing new school textbooks in hopes of filling the "intellectual and even emotional void in the urban and rural schools which now can only too easily be filled by literature supplied from leftist sources." When it came to buying books for libraries, U.S. aid officials wanted to make sure that the topics of the new books "get directly to the area of educational and spiritual response in which the Communists can make their greatest inroads." Similarly, money for the university library needed to "help to create a University atmosphere conducive to study, thus tending to diminish the interest of the students in outside political activities."[53]

In the early years of the Alliance for Progress, El Salvador received support for a variety of education improvement programs, including school construction and the writing of new textbooks.[54] In theory, U.S. aid for educational programs should have decreased toward the end of the 1960s, when Congress began cutting funding for the Alliance for Progress. Ironically, it was at that moment that U.S. aid to El Salvador increased rapidly to support the 1968 education reform and its television component. Ultimately the United States would give more than US$11 million for educational television, making it the most prominent USAID project in the country.

The Alliance for Progress was very visible throughout El Salvador. The Alliance's logo was prominently displayed on every bag of donated food, on road signs alongside newly constructed roads, in every new textbook, and on the side of every new school building. This propaganda produced resentment in some people, but for others it provided a ray of hope. A U.S. Embassy staff member reported in 1961 how, during a visit to a distant town in Morazán Department, a schoolteacher "read the entire text of the 'Kennedy Plan for Latin America' to a group of peasants, emphasizing the food program."[55] But in the context of Latin America, the Alliance's presence in El Salvador was small. Throughout the years of the Alliance for Progress, El Salvador lagged behind most of the rest of Latin America in terms of the amount of U.S. aid it received. Measured in per capita terms, El Salvador averaged twelfth in loans and grants to Latin America. Between 1962 and 1976 it never rose above seventh and fell as low as seventeenth; during that same period El Salvador ranked thirteenth in per capita military aid. During the first five years of the Alliance, the country received US$80 million in economic assistance and US$5 million in military aid. In this context the US$11 million devoted to educational television represented a large sum of money and a departure from the norm for U.S. aid to El Salvador.[56]

One reason that U.S. support for El Salvador's education reform increased at the same time that overall U.S. aid to Latin America was decreasing is that President Johnson took a keen interest in educational television. It was under his watch, in 1966 and 1967, that the Corporation for Public Broadcasting was created in the United States after a vigorous public debate over its merits. Johnson believed that just as educational television had the potential to promote learning at home, it could also promote economic development abroad. During a stopover at American Samoa in October 1966, he celebrated the island's cutting-edge use of television in classrooms. Upon his arrival at Pago Pago's airport, the president said that the island had "become a showplace for progress," and that "the pilot program of education which you have started may point the way to learning breakthroughs throughout the Pacific islands and Southeast Asia. Samoan children are learning twice as fast as they once did."[57] A month after returning from Pago Pago, Johnson created a task force to "assess the value of educational television broadcasting for primary and secondary schools in less-developed countries."[58] It came to be called the White House Task Force on Educational Television in Less-Developed Countries.

In April 1967 Johnson attended a summit with the Latin American heads of state at Punta del Este, Uruguay, to discuss how to "work toward modernization of Latin life."[59] The meeting was meant to reaffirm the U.S. commitment to the Alliance for Progress, even though congressional support for funding was waning. The White House Task Force on Educational Television in Less-Developed Countries had told the president in March that the Uruguay conference would provide an ideal opportunity to promote educational television and recommend a pilot project in El Salvador.[60] While at Punta del Este, Johnson met with the president-elect of El Salvador, Sánchez

Hernández, to discuss "the potentialities of instructional television for speeding educational development." The project was of sufficient importance that Johnson mentioned it explicitly in his formal remarks at the opening session with the other heads of state. He promised U.S. technical and monetary support to create "an inter-American training center for educational broadcasting" and to set up "a pilot educational television demonstration project in a Central American country that will teach the children by day and entertain and inform their families at night."[61]

In early December 1967 the Inter-American Committee of the Alliance for Progress met in Washington, D.C., to review El Salvador's development efforts. The committee made a list of recommendations for El Salvador that included the need for an educational system "with particular emphasis on modernization of curricula, intensification of teacher training, strengthening secondary and technical education, and the realization of projects for instructional television."[62] In June 1968 USAID produced a detailed document outlining the details of the education reform and recommending the authorization of a US$1.9 million loan.[63] In July President Johnson traveled to El Salvador for a meeting with the five Central American presidents. During the trip he visited a teacher training school, where he announced the loan and an additional donation of US$700,000. In his official remarks Johnson mentioned that he had been "greatly inspired" by the educational television experience in American Samoa and was delighted that the Samoan accomplishments were "going to be done and improved" in El Salvador.[64] Since the television initiative in El Salvador was a pilot project, USAID, the agency responsible for overseeing the initiative, planned to follow its progress with rigorous social science investigations. To design and carry out the research, USAID hired a team from the Institute for Communications Research at Stanford University, headed by Wilbur Schramm. Not coincidentally, Schramm had been the main author of the reports that persuaded President Johnson that the experiment with educational television in American Samoa had been a rousing success. Johnson was well aware of Schramm's work; in 1964 he wrote a foreword for one of his books.[65]

The selection of Schramm to head the investigation team in El Salvador demonstrated the importance that the Johnson administration placed on the Salvadoran project. By that time Schramm was a senior expert in the field of communications and development, and he had been instrumental in transforming the perception of television from a mere technological innovation with educational benefits to a tool of development and a weapon in the Cold War. Schramm had been a highly prominent advocate of educational television in the United States in the 1950s, and then in the 1960s he promoted it as a way to modernize traditional peoples in developing countries.

Wilbur Schramm and the Use of the Mass Media to Promote Development

It is no surprise that U.S. education experts came to see television as a potentially useful tool. Earlier mass media technologies had similarly captured their imaginations. In the first decades of the twentieth century, educators considered using films to teach. Forward-looking school administrators were the first enthusiasts. As early as 1904 the state of New York founded a visual instruction department. Five years later there were enough educational films on the market for an enterprising author to edit a catalog. The following year the public schools of Rochester, New York, began using instructional films in the classroom. By 1923 the U.S. commissioner of education predicted that "the educational use of motion pictures will gradually overshadow the commercial."[66]

When radio found its way into most households in the developed world, educators saw it too as a natural way to enhance education. From the mid-1920s to the mid-1930s, educational radio expanded rapidly to include "schools of the air," educational hours, and even full-time educational stations.[67] After World War II, television quickly supplanted radio as the cutting-edge mass media technology, and innovators saw it as having revolutionary potential for education.

Even before television was ready for mass production, some people were predicting that it would assume a prominent place in the classroom alongside radio. A Columbia Teachers College professor stated in 1930 that radio and television "may work profound changes in education that will enable the best teachers to reach all pupils of the country in their school rooms." He even suggested that teachers would be supplanted and would become mere "disciplinarians."[68]

At the 1939 World's Fair, David Sarnoff, the president of RCA, introduced market-ready television to the American public, saying that the new medium was "a creative force which we must learn to utilize for the benefit of all mankind."[69] A mere two years later, Francis Henry Taylor, the director of the Metropolitan Museum of Art, broadcast the first televised images of the museum's collections to American living rooms and predicted that "television will be the instrument which will create as complete a revolution in the education of the future as the discovery of movable type and the invention of the printing press 400 years ago."[70]

After the end of World War II the popularity of television increased rapidly in all industrialized nations. Many individuals and institutions were eager to turn Taylor's words into reality. The late 1940s and 1950s witnessed various innovations in the educational use of television, from experiments with closed-circuit TV in the school system of Hagerstown County, Maryland, to rural teleclubs in France, to the Telescuola in Italy, to NHK in Japan.

However, the grandiose hopes of television advocates were seldom realized. Matching the reformers' enthusiasm to integrate the latest technologies into the classroom was the resistance of administrators and teachers who questioned its cost and utility. While various policymakers and community leaders wanted to use film, radio, and television to resolve problems of productivity, equity, and cost, teachers considered using media only if it supported classroom teaching. They wanted simplicity, reliability, versatility, and durability, and most of all, they did not want media to undermine their authority in the classroom.[71]

Even though there were many naysayers in the developed world, the career of Wilbur Schramm reveals how television was transformed into a tool of development and a weapon in the Cold War despite reservations. Schramm was a founder of the academic field of communications. His interest in the use of television in education combined with his leadership skills and his broad social connections in academics, philanthropy, and politics to make him one of the most effective advocates for instructional television in the world.

Schramm's interest in communications as a social science grew out of his experience in World War II. He was part of a group of intellectuals dedicated to psychological warfare.[72] The informal beginnings of that group can be traced to a seminar in 1939 sponsored by the Rockefeller Foundation that provided the guidelines for the use of mass communications in war situations. The premise of the seminar was that government authorities and the ruling elite "should automatically manipulate mass sentiment in order to preserve democracy from threats posed by authoritarian societies." Communications scholar Christopher Simpson makes the point that during this period the goal of mass communications was to "engineer consent."[73] This description may or may not have applied to the entire field, but it certainly did to Schramm's work.

Although Schramm did not participate in the Rockefeller seminar, he became part of an emerging network of like-minded social scientists when he started working for the Office of Facts and Figures (soon to be renamed Office of War Information, OWI) in January 1942. By the time he arrived in Washington, D.C., and turned his attention to the social sciences, Schramm, at thirty-two years of age, had already founded the legendary Iowa Writers' Workshop and had won an O. Henry Prize for one of his short stories. He was an established writer with excellent connections.[74]

During his few years in Washington, Schramm established relationships that helped him advance projects later in life. Most of the postwar authorities in communications research had been active in the war propaganda effort, either at OWI or at other organizations participating in psychological warfare, like the Office of Strategic Services, the Psychological Warfare Division of the U.S. Army, and the War Communications Division at the Library of Congress.[75] The remarkable group of social scientists working in Washington, D.C., at this time became part of what has been called "one of the best old-boy (or girl) networks ever."[76] One of them would later characterize its impact on his career: "[The World War II experience] (1) Led directly to my main academic positions; (2) strongly influenced my major research interests; (3) established a continuing network of crucial personal/professional relationships with individuals."[77]

The impact of this network on Schramm's career was similar. At OWI Schramm collaborated with social and behavioral scientists on a variety of programs, such as surveying public attitudes, crafting propaganda messages, and monitoring broadcasts. One of his responsibilities was to help draft President Roosevelt's "fireside chats."[78] His World War II experiences provided excellent training for the Cold War. After the Chinese invasion of Korea, the Air Force sent him, along with John Riley and Frederick Williams, to survey the situation in Seoul. Their report was later published in a widely circulated book, *The Reds Take a City*.[79] Schramm later described the smooth transition between his participation in the "psychological warfare team" in the OWI to his new work in Korea.[80]

The Reds Take a City helped delineate Schramm's preoccupation with the role of communications as a weapon in the Cold War. One of the book's goals was to describe how a "communist blueprint," created in Moscow and previously applied in Eastern Europe, operated in Seoul. Since "ideas in any totalitarian state are an aspect of power, the control of information is considered of equal importance to other controls," and therefore democracies had to be equally forceful in the use of mass communications to counteract communist influence.[81] His interest in putting mass communications at the service of the Cold War became a recurrent theme in his writings in scholarly journals.[82]

To Schramm, psychological warfare was "nothing that a citizen of a democracy need to feel ashamed of doing, and it is conceived of as a fourth arm for attaining national objectives; the others are diplomatic, economic, and military." In 1960 he advocated that high priority be given to an "active, militant, political communication."[83] In other words, at exactly the moment when Schramm was redirecting his career from that of psychological warfare to academics in the field of international communications, his mentality as a cold warrior was being solidified.

Schramm described mass communications as a way to transmit societal values. In 1957, barely five years after publishing his work on Korea, he wrote, "Mass communication helps us transmit the culture of our society to new members of society. We have always had teaching at mother's knee, and imitation of the father—and still have. For thousands of years we have had schools of some sort or other. But mass communication enters into this assignment by supplying textbooks, teaching films and programs, and a constant picturing of the roles and accepted mores of our society."[84]

It was no great leap to move from this paternal metaphor to the idea of using communications to modernize "traditional societies," a theme that Schramm developed in *Mass Media and National Development: The Role of Information in Developing Countries*.[85] In that influential work, which was translated into many languages, Schramm put communications theory in the framework of modernization theory. He did so at a critical time, when some theorists considered modernization to be inexorable and many Latin American nations to be in the "preconditions for take-off" stage. It was at that juncture that they dreaded the "disease of transition," communism. Thus, they argued that the United States needed to devote large amounts of money to foreign aid programs to help countries along in the development process and to stop communism. Books by leading proponents of modernization theory, like *A Proposal: Key to an Effective Foreign Policy*, published in 1957, and *The Emerging Nations: Their Growth and United States Policy*, published in 1961, made the case for a dramatic increase in U.S. foreign aid.[86] Modernization-theory advocate Walt Rostow used his powers of persuasion in person when he became an adviser to Senator John F. Kennedy. He prepared speeches in which Kennedy, first as a senator and later as a presidential candidate, framed his foreign aid proposals in the language of modernization.[87]

After Castro's rise to power and the heightening of anxiety among U.S. leaders, modernization theory became highly influential. Directly and indirectly inspired by modernization theorists, the Eisenhower administration identified foreign aid as an instrument to promote development and limit the influence of communism. As discussed in chapter 1, in his last year in office Eisenhower offered financial support to fund the policies advocated by the Act of Bogota, a list of "measures for social improvement and economic development" drafted by U.S. and Latin American representatives. Kennedy followed up in 1961 with the much more ambitious Alliance for Progress. Replacing tradition with modernity in Latin America became a matter of strategic importance to the United States.

Schramm was one of the most influential authors linking modernization to mass communications and eventually to educational television. To overcome politically dangerous backwardness the citizens of poor countries had to change their traditional mores. "Unless they change," Schramm argued in *Mass Media and National Development*, "they will have to watch technological growth from the sidelines; social change will happen to them, rather than their playing an active part in bringing it about."[88] Schramm cited Max Millikan and Donald Blackmer, who had stated that "the paramount requirement of change in any society is that the people themselves must change." To this comment Schramm added that "this is the point where modern communication becomes so important to economic development."[89] By citing other scholars, like his frequent collaborator Daniel Lerner and the economist Theodore Schultz, Schramm focused on the dichotomy between traditional and modern societies and promoted the classic modernization theory belief that traditional societies could abandon their counterproductive mores and structures. At a time when development theorists defined investment in capital formation as the main requirement for economic growth, Schramm argued that "traditional social patterns and structures are not capital-creating." For Schramm mass communications was the most effective instrument to turn traditional social structures into modern ones. Mass media would increase the flow of information from industrialized countries and create a climate of change by raising people's aspirations. "In the service of national development," he wrote, "the mass media are agents of social change. The specific kind of social change they are expected to help accomplish is the transition to new customs and practices and, in some cases, to different social relationships. Behind such changes in behavior must necessarily lie substantial changes in attitudes, beliefs, skills, and social norms."[90]

Schramm believed that the way to achieve these changes was through the educational system. "Public education is both a leading channel of information to the people and a chief support of the mass media. Schools build literacy. They instill the kinds of interests and needs that require mass media." Such an argument about the link between education and mass media converged perfectly in the policy of instructional television: "Where teachers and schools are scarce they [the mass media] have proved to be of great help in adult education and literacy training. . . . These facts are important because, as we know, teachers and schools are scarce, and many of the available teachers are trained for yesterday's rather than today's teaching job. Technical skills are in short supply."[91] Schramm had profound faith in the effectiveness of educational television, and he became its paramount proselytizer, convinced that it could only help a needy society.

> There is no longer doubt of the potency of media as teachers. Textbooks, of course, have long ago proved what they could do. Radio and film in many lands have proved helpful in adult education and schoolrooms. Now the evidence comes in on the newer devices. For example, out of 393 experimental comparisons of classes taught chiefly by television with classes taught by conventional classroom methods, there was no difference (in what the pupils could do in the final examination) in the case of 65 per cent of all the comparisons; in 21 per cent of the cases, the television class wrote significantly better examinations than the conventional class, and in only 14 percent was the conventional class superior.[92]

Television technology was an effective way to disseminate quality instruction at minimal cost.

> But countless men have read law and learned mathematics by themselves from books. Men have learned engineering, electronics, radio repairing, and such skills by correspondence lessons. In Chicago, the entire curriculum of a junior college is offered by television and studied quite successfully by hundreds of students who have no other contact with the college except at examination time or when they send in written assignments or ask questions. It may well be that in the atmosphere of need in a developing country, the media can carry a much larger share of the teaching load than they have been asked to carry in economically better developed countries. . . .

... To a country where highly trained teachers are scarce they
[radio and television] offer the opportunity to share its best teachers widely. Where few teachers are trained to teach certain subjects,
these media offer the hope that those subjects can be taught even
before qualified teachers become available.[93]

Finally, Schramm promoted the merits of rapid social change because "swift
change is often less painful than slow and gradual change."[94]

Schramm's work in El Salvador was the result of his success, first, in cast-
ing his ideas in the dominant paradigm of modernization theory, and second, in skillfully placing them in the agenda of international development.
Mass Media and National Development was a decisive work in advancing
those ideas. It also accounts for the depth of his collaboration with UNESCO
in the mid-1960s. In fact, the book was commissioned by UNESCO and published on its behalf.

UNESCO and the Use of Television in Education

UNESCO had been interested in the mass media since its inception, but it did
not have special policies regarding television until the 1950s. Television was
not even included in the mass media resolution passed by the First Regional
Conference of National Commissions of the Western Hemisphere celebrated
in Havana in 1951.[95] This omission does not mean that the institution ignored
the new medium. The *UNESCO Courier* in the early fifties carried articles
about the first experiments in educational television, such as the Johns Hopkins
University project that started in 1948 to televise science classes.[96]

In 1951 the General Conference of UNESCO authorized the director
general "to bring to the attention of Member States information and suggestions to stimulate the more rapid development and application of television" for the purpose of furthering international understanding through
education, science, and culture. As a result, the following year the director general convened a committee of experts that recommended UNESCO
do such things as create a clearinghouse of information on the educational
prospects for television, undertake studies, organize pilot projects to explore
educational uses of television, and advise member states.[97] The work of the
committee marked UNESCO's initial involvement with television.[98] Later in
1952 the General Conference authorized the director general to carry out the
tasks suggested by the committee of experts.

In 1952 UNESCO published Charles Siepmann's important and extensive survey on the educational use of television in the United States.[99] This publication was followed by an entire issue of the *UNESCO Courier* in 1953 titled "Television: A Challenge and a Chance for Education." It included a number of articles, some based on Siepmann's book, that amounted to a complete overview of educational television.[100] The article titles included, "What Has TV to Say to Us?," "The British Approach to Educational TV," "France's Unique Contribution to TV for the Many," "College Courses by TV," and "The Case for and against School TV." This issue of the *Courier* undoubtedly reached far more people (particularly policymakers, the main target audience of UNESCO publications) and was more accessible than Siepmann's book. It constituted an all-out effort to highlight the potential of television in schools. The cumulative result of the *Courier*'s articles was that television was seen as the future of schools and a valuable tool for modernization.

Although the authors appearing in the *Courier* were generally enthusiastic about the value of educational television, they provided warnings too. Siepmann's work stated that "television can't replace the teacher. It is a most effective supplementary tool in the hands of the gifted teacher. The poor teacher usually botches the job, and despite its superficial attractiveness, the screen is likely to be a distractive influence rather than a teaching aid." And a new UNESCO staff member, Henry Cassirer, wrote an article for the *Courier* in 1953 that on the one hand embraced the potential of educational television for development:

> Television is taking root today in countries where illiteracy and utter poverty, ignorance of healthy living and of modern methods of production, are widespread among large sections of the people. Advertisers have long realized television's uncanny power of persuasion and demonstration. Cannot these same powers serve fundamental education and change our entire approach to the problem of informing people in less developed countries on ways to improve their conditions of life? This is a subject, rich in promise, to which UNESCO is now giving particular attention. Here is a challenge for constructive forces to bring their influence to bear upon the future shape of television.[101]

But on the other hand, Cassirer's article foresighted the potential for educational television to empower centralized, authoritarian governments. He

TV lessons in 24,000 Japanese schools

All-India Radio broadcasts courses in science, English and Hindi for secondary schools from its experimental transmitter. Japan, in contrast to most Asian countries, has a highly-developed TV network and its educational programme, which covers 42 per cent of the population is received in 24,000 schools. In Oceania, an extensive educational service is being organized for American Samoa.

In the United States, more than 60 educational stations are run non-commercially by schools, universities and foundations. TV instruction beamed from transmitters in high-flying aircraft and covering 78,000 square miles has been developed, indicating what communication satellites might do on a much larger scale for educational broadcasting.

Television for schools is receiving increasing attention in Europe and has been particularly well-developed in Italy and the United Kingdom. In the U.S.S.R., a high percentage of viewing time is devoted to educational programmes for children and adults. The "People's University" programme offers courses in science and technology, arts and English.

DOCUMENTARY and educational films have spread throughout the world and are being produced in increasing numbers by feature film producers, government agencies, industrial concerns, foundations and various non-profit organizations of a cultural, scientific or educational character. In many countries, the film has become an accepted part of the school curriculum, sometimes being used to enrich an already adequate course of instruction, sometimes to supplement instruction where

there is a deficiency of textbooks, equipment and qualified teaching staff. With the aid of mobile units, educational and documentary films reach audiences previously uninfluenced by the cinema. Throughout Africa, Asia and Latin America, these units find their way to remote villages whose inhabitants can often neither read nor write. Particular use of these mobile units is being made in Africa.

In South America the employment of films for education in rural areas is mainly in the planning stages. In Asia, the cinema is regarded mainly as an entertainment medium. However, Japan, India and Israel all have outstanding information film services.

While many European countries use the film for educational purposes to a limited extent, only a few countries, such as Finland and the Netherlands have made it an integral part of school curricula.

Canada has one of the world's most highly-developed educational film services and widespread use is also made of such films in the United States. Cuba, Australia and New Zealand, among other countries, maintain units for the production of short information films.

The U.S.S.R. produces several hundred instructional films yearly and 23,400 mobile units screen them throughout the region.

In a foreword, *World Communications* draws attention to the programme UNESCO has undertaken at the request of the United Nations to help the developing countries build up their mass media. The United Nations emphasized that the information media have an important part to play in education and in economic and social progress generally and that new communication techniques offer special opportunities for spreading education swiftly.

A TV history lesson for Italian schools makes a greater impact because of its authentic classroom atmosphere. Cameras switch from teacher and blackboard to a live class in the studio. These lessons are part of a three-year course of vocational education for boys and girls who have completed their primary schooling.

Unesco-Eric Schwab

FIGURE 13. *The UNESCO Courier* included this image with a story on the use of educational television in Japan and Italy. *UNESCO Courier*, February 1964, 14.

deplored "the obstacles to a challenging free-for-all communication with the poor, the trends towards centralization and top-down paternalism."[102]

Although Cassirer held his position at UNESCO until 1970, his writings reveal that he did not draw influence from Schramm. Cassirer's autobiography goes to great lengths to stress his humanistic (as opposed to social science) background. Moreover, the fact that Cassirer's work never mentions Schramm, who undoubtedly not only defined the field of mass media and development but also influenced UNESCO policies, suggests that there were divisions within the organization as to the merits of educational television.

The early literature on educational television coming out of UNESCO was open to a great variety of opinions, but this situation was about to change under the influence of Schramm, who would focus it in a more singular direction. The turning point was UNESCO's General Conference of 1960, "which re-shaped UNESCO's policy and organization in development terms."[103] During the 1960s the organization's ideas on development came to be heavily influenced by modernization theory, a transformation that took place, by and large, during the tenure of René Maheu as director general (1962–1972). Maheu was in full synchronicity with the ethos and can-do spirit of the emerging development community. He perceived of the 1960 General Conference as driving the institution in a new direction when it decided that "priority should be given to education for the implementation of national plans for social and economic development."[104] One of the statements that Maheu made in his first report as acting director general was to applaud "the quick recognition by many governments and international authorities in 1961 that the contribution of the social sciences is vital to sound national development." In the same report he announced the creation of a Department of Social Sciences and an Analysis Unit to "study the role of education, science and technology, and mass communication in economic development."[105]

Maheu received the backing of UNESCO's executive board, which in 1961 endorsed the Alliance for Progress and directed the director general to ensure UNESCO's "closest possible participation" in the development of the educational and social program adopted a few months earlier at Punta del Este. The board also told him that UNESCO should help countries prepare projects to be presented as part of the Alliance program.[106]

One of the first initiatives emerging from these pro-Alliance positions in UNESCO was a regional conference on education and development that took place in Santiago, Chile, in March 1962. The executive board of UNESCO asked the acting director general to take into account the objectives defined in Punta del Este when drawing up the conference agenda.[107] The meeting of the executive board had taken place in November 1961, that is, only a few months after the Punta del Este conference. The United States attached similar importance to the meeting, such that President Kennedy himself was kept informed on its developments.[108]

The regional conference was meant to propagate a new way of thinking about education as a component of development planning. The event was cosponsored by UNESCO, the UN Economic Commission for Latin America (ECLA), the OAS, the ILO, and the FAO and was coordinated with the newly created USAID. The conference was preceded by careful preparations and followed by numerous press releases and other marking initiatives to disseminate its message.

Prior to the conference, UNESCO representatives in Central America worked hard to prepare their local representatives for it. The UNESCO representative to El Salvador, José Lanza Diego, and the other UNESCO representatives in Central America met in San José, Costa Rica, to discuss strategies to promote the conference and advance its goals. In the case of El Salvador, the conference's objective to link education to economic development marked a departure from previous thinking. Thus, there was a learning curve for the Salvadorans, and Lanza Diego and UNESCO considered it especially important that the individuals attending the conference in Chile be fully prepared. UNESCO encouraged local representatives to arrive at the conference with specific plans as to how their nation would coordinate education with economic and social development. This advice was particularly relevant to El Salvador, because the meeting in Chile coincided with the United States preparing to commit aid for development projects.[109] All of these various preparatory meetings received extensive press coverage.[110]

The opening of the Santiago meeting was front-page news and a topic of editorials in Salvadoran newspapers.[111] The Salvadoran representative to the meeting in Chile outlined the objectives that El Salvador had at that point: (1) expand primary education to the entire population, (2) construct new schools, (3) train teachers, (4) improve the status of teachers, (5) reduce illiteracy, (6) train skilled labor, (7) update the curriculum, and (8) promote agricultural education and train people with skills in agriculture.[112] The press also informed the public about the results of the meeting.[113] The Santiago conference was followed by a meeting of ministers of education of Central America and further publications written by UNESCO staffers highlighting the link between education and development.[114]

Between the conference in Chile and corresponding U.S. economic support, a great deal of developmental momentum was being generated in the early 1960s. Shortly after the return of the Salvadoran delegation, the minister of education announced his desire to implement an education reform. According to the minister, "this reform will be in accordance with the economic realities that will arise in the country as a result of the loans received from the Alliance for Progress."[115] The complex organization of the conference and the publicity surrounding it offer prime examples of how international and bilateral donor agencies influenced education policy in poor countries through the creation of models of good practice.

UNESCO had little money of its own to finance major projects. A UNESCO-sponsored meeting in Asia in 1958 highlighted this reality. The participants strongly embraced the merits of educational television, saying that "this most powerful new medium was desperately needed for educational purposes," yet funds were not available to put it to use.[116] Instead, UNESCO exercised influence through technical assistance teams that incorporated their ideas into the educational planning documents of poor countries.[117] According to Maheu, UNESCO "played a pioneering role in securing the recognition of educational planning as an essential element in the general planning of development."[118] For him, educational planning was "the basis of everything else."[119] The synchronization of educational and economic planning proved an excellent vehicle for the introduction of such ideas as educational television.

UNESCO and Schramm Come Together

Schramm's relationship with UNESCO started with his work as a consultant, and the organization later sponsored his writing of *Mass Media and National Development*. In 1965 the *Courier* described him as someone who had "been closely associated with UNESCO for a number of years as a consultant, researcher, writer and editor and as an adviser to governments on UNESCO's behalf."[120] His work shaped UNESCO's communication policies in the 1960s and early 1970s in accordance with modernization theory.

In 1958 the UN General Assembly called for a "'program of concrete action' to build up press, radio broadcasting, film, and television facilities in countries in the process of economic and social development." In response, UN staff members organized meetings on mass communications for Asia (Bangkok, 1960), Latin America (Santiago, 1961), and Africa (Paris, 1962).[121] UNESCO took a keen interest in the issue and hired Schramm, already an established authority in the United States in the field of communications, to synthesise the discussions.

The result of this project was *Mass Media and National Development.* The book became highly influential, in part because it included discussions that had been carried out on three different continents.[122] But in fact the book was more a distillation of Schramm's ideas than a mere summary of what was said at the UN meetings. Schramm had actually advanced his main argument earlier, in a document submitted to UNESCO prior to the Santiago meetings. In that document he discussed how "other countries have found that the media grow with, and contribute to, the general economic growth of a nation," and he also talked about the need to spread "the new skills and behaviors" of modernity. The precise ideas presented in *Mass Media and National Development* bore little resemblance to the generalities expressed in a bureaucratic language by the international delegates in Bangkok, Santiago, and Paris.[123] The report of the Santiago meeting, for example, included such generic bureaucratese as saying that the participants "considered that while each media had a special role to play, much could be done to improve their coordinated use in the service of education." It is also worth noting that in the book Schramm did not mention the connection between economic development and the prevention of communism, as Pool and Rostow had done so explicitly in other publications. After all, the book was sponsored by an agency of the United Nations, which would have made such a statement impolitic.

Schramm then participated in one of UNESCO's most important initiatives to promote instructional television, the three-volume *New Educational Media in Action: Case Studies for Planners*, which was published by UNESCO's International Institute for Educational Planning in 1967. The three volumes were accompanied by a memo to educational planners that analyzed case studies and discussed their implications for policy making; Schramm was the main author. Once again, presenting the work as the synthesis of a major international effort gave it an aura of importance and legitimacy.[124] The volumes described experiences with educational mass media in areas as diverse as American Samoa, Hagerstown (Maryland), Japan, Australia, Niger, Colombia, Palestinian refugee camps, Italy, New Zealand, and Honduras. Many years later, in 1994, Professor Colin N. Power, UNESCO's assistant director general for education, singled out the memo to educational planners as the document that started the organization's move from research to concrete action.[125]

Schramm shaped UNESCO's approach toward instructional television so much that scholars referred to it as "the UNESCO-Schramm" strategy of communications.[126] Schramm's writings became obligatory reference materials for anyone interested in instructional television, and his outlines reappeared in narrative form in countless reports by international aid missions. Schramm's perspective pervaded UNESCO's mass media–related publications throughout the 1960s. In his various works he described three settings in which a developing country should benefit from instructional television: when the country needed to modernize (mainly in the form of industrialization); when teachers were scarce; and when the system could be implemented cost effectively. In the UNESCO series Reports and Papers on Mass Communications, a section devoted to education and development in Asia described instructional television in terms of modernization theory, as helping individuals overcome traditional mindsets: "In a general way, it may be stated that nation-wide broadcasting promotes national integration and the creation of a national market. As a nerve centre of society, broadcasting assists in the coordination of national economic activities and the promotion of a money economy. Broadcasting is both the result and the stimulator of modernization. It is part of an evolution towards a way of life which includes the much wider use of the products of industrialization."[127]

A similar sentiment was echoed in a report issued by a mission to the Ivory Coast. The mission perceived Ivorian society as suffering from traditional values and needing something to spark national integration. The report argued that good access to mass media would help solve the problems by promoting rapid economic and social evolution. The proposed solution was a large-scale instructional television project.[128] In another example, UNESCO convened an international panel of consultants on communications research in April 1971 "to formulate a 4-year programme of studies on the effects of communications on relations between changing societies and social groups, as well as its effects on the individuals comprising them."[129] The meeting concluded that communications research could "play a vital role in showing the ways in which communication can be activated in those sectors of the society which are in the greatest need of the 'developing impulse' but are precisely those which barely participate in matters of public interest. This is the case with rural people in so many countries."[130]

A constant theme in all of UNESCO's reports was the need for developing countries to modernize, and one of the main problems was a scarcity of teachers. Thus, media was seen as the way to overcome that hurdle. The meeting in Asia concluded, "an even more radical approach, which educational planning authorities might take into consideration, is to meet the pressing lack of teachers and schools in certain geographic areas through the creation of schools organized around a television receiver which provides the main burden of overall instruction, along the lines of the school system in Western Samoa, the Television High School in Japan, or Telescuola in Italy."[131]

One of the basic premises of modernization theory was that its prescriptions were universally applicable. As Rostow put it in *Stages of Economic Growth*, "there is emerging from the intensive work of social scientists on the development problem a recognition that there are common elements in the patterns of development of different countries which have implications for development policy elsewhere."[132] Cultural differences received attention insofar as they could delay industrialization, but they were seen as "mere 'obstacles' destined to the dustbin of history."[133] All countries, regardless of their history, could follow the same path to modernity and could eventually resemble industrialized countries. And so, if educational television could help one country advance along the path to modernity, then it could help them all. The Japanese experience and Italy's Telescuola became models to be followed. According to one UNESCO report, "It may well be envisaged that classes in Asian countries will gather around the television screen and that the bulk of instruction will be provided over the air."[134] UNESCO sent missions from one country to another to instruct willing government functionaries on what to do, regardless of the distinctiveness of the local context. Government officials from the Ivory Coast, for example, were sent to American Samoa, Niger, and El Salvador to learn from their experiences.[135] A mission from Ghana also visited El Salvador.[136] Using its supposed success stories as evidence, UNESCO officials promoted educational television in Thailand, Upper Volta, the United Arab Emirates, Syria, and Iraq, among others.[137]

It would be easy to frame El Salvador's educational television project as a U.S. initiative. Historian Thomas Leonard reached that conclusion after reading U.S. government documents. He argued that "the origins of Salvador's Educational Television (TVE) dated to the 1967 Punta del Este Conference where Lyndon Johnson offered U.S. support for a pilot educational demonstration project. Following extensive studies, USAID determined El Salvador to be the location, in large part because of the educational reform efforts being undertaken by Salvador's Minister of Education, Walter Béneke."[138] One constituency that had advanced the same conclusion as Leonard years earlier was leftists and progressives in El Salvador, who in the late 1960s and early 1970s portrayed educational television as an imperialist conspiracy of the United States.

It would be equally possible to portray El Salvador's educational television project as originating primarily from the minds of domestic actors. Debates over education and the need for education reform went back many years and were deeply rooted in El Salvador's distinct political history. Educational television was simply a latecomer to that long history. Furthermore, one of the most avid proponents of educational television in El Salvador, Walter Béneke, came to believe in its merits independently and of his own accord during his diplomatic posting in Japan. When he and other government officials proved so receptive to UN and U.S. encouragement to implement educational television, they might have just been taking advantage of an opportunity to receive large amounts of money from foreign sources to help them with an idea they had embraced on their own.

But in fact, neither of these explanations is sufficient by itself. The United States and President Johnson did not have a blank slate when they advanced educational television in 1967, nor did Salvadoran authorities conceive of their approach to education in isolation. Rather, educational reform and its television component came to be seen by policymakers as "the" logical choice because of a complex amalgamation of factors that converged in unpredictable and indeterminate ways. The emphasis on education flowed naturally from the modernizing ethos of the military regime in the middle of the twentieth century. Powerful members of the economic elite envisioned the country's future as being tied to industrialization, and they worried about the availability of trained labor. At the same time, influential international actors were promoting modernization theory, and an entire sector of the development apparatus was taking an intense interest in countries like El Salvador. Development experts, backed by money, Western governments, and the latest in intellectual trends, helped to define problems, shape solutions, and implement policies. And once policies were up and running, they often took on lives of their own. Educational television in El Salvador seemed to provide such a case. In the words of one of the Stanford team's reports, "A major technological change has forced its own logic upon those who had

decided to use it. . . . El Salvador's educational leaders seem to have understood and accepted the implications that this innovation has for structural
changes that go far beyond the placement of a piece of hardware in a classroom. . . . To our knowledge no other country has accepted so completely the
implications that educational technology carries with it."[139]

CHAPTER 4

"A Feverish Laboratory"
The Education Reform of 1968

In a few years, thanks to the Education Reform, the country will have a generation intellectually and professionally capable of efficiently participating in the modernization of the fatherland in this era of science and technology.

—Fidel Sánchez Hernández, 1971*

✢ IN OCTOBER 1966 A BOISTEROUS GENERAL ASSEMBLY OF THE PCN NOM-inated Col. Fidel Sánchez Hernández, Julio Rivera's interior minister, as its candidate for president. There was little doubt that he would prevail in the March elections. That night a group of friends, well-wishers, and even a mariachi band crowded into the small living room of the Sánchez Hernández residence. In the midst of the revelry a reporter from *El Diario de Hoy* managed to grab a few minutes with the candidate. "I believe that education ought to be ahead of everything," Sánchez Hernández said, claiming that education would be a priority during his administration. Then he turned to the issue of communism and made a firm promise to fight the "red danger." Indeed, education and anticommunism dominated the next seven months of his campaign. After he won the election and was sworn in as president in July 1967, he did his best to translate those two promises into policy.[1]

Contemporary evidence suggests that Sánchez Hernández's preoccupation with communism may have been misplaced. In 1968 the CIA considered El Salvador's Communist Party to be "small, illegal, intimidated, and generally ineffective."[2] Che Guevara had been killed in Bolivia, and most Latin American communist parties were sticking to the Moscow line of downplaying insurrection in favor of labor organizing and electoral coalitions. If the new president's concern with the communist threat was overblown, his attention to education was justified. A report prepared in 1968 by John Ross, a UNESCO expert in educational planning, offered a long litany of educational deficiencies in El Salvador, including a high dropout rate, a small number of schools (many housed in inadequate buildings), poorly trained secondary school teachers, outdated curricula and pedagogy, and a dearth of teaching materials.[3]

The first PCN administration under Julio Rivera (1962–1967) made significant strides in drawing attention to the problem of education and designing programs to improve the situation. It also reoriented the manner in which education was conceptualized. Instead of being a tool to form citizens, education began to be described as a key component in economic development.[4] President Sánchez Hernández built upon Rivera's foundational steps and in his education reform retained many of the programs that Rivera had initiated, especially educational television.[5]

The 1968 reform was the most ambitious reorganization of education in the nation's history, before or since. The reform's designers conceived it as the mechanism by which El Salvador would create the workforce to industrialize its economy. The reform was sprawling and multifaceted. Its different parts were not always consistent with each other, but it was an exuberant effort that sought to bring fundamental change to the system of education. The reform was presented as a technical response to problems identified by the best national and international experts. Yet systemic changes of such importance were bound to have political implications, particularly when they affected the working environment of teachers, the largest group of civil servants in the country. This chapter is dedicated to describing the reform, its planning, its various elements, the reaction of teachers, and the significant role played by the minister of education, Walter Béneke.

Introduction and Planning of the Reform

Thanks to the preliminary steps taken by the Rivera administration, Sánchez Hernández and his education policymakers hit the ground running. Three weeks after Sánchez Hernández's inauguration, the newly appointed minister of education, Walter Béneke, announced a sweeping reorganization of the Ministry of Education.[6] Talk of education reform was ever present, and educational television was always at the center of the discussion. The government made great efforts to create a positive climate for reforming education, fully aware that introducing major changes could incite opposition. The new television system, Minister Béneke explained to the press, "will not displace teachers and it will not be in foreign hands." He insisted that many good things could be expected of TV; the small screen was an "efficient, direct, scientific and didactic [tool] that has been used in the most advanced countries to solve the problem of educating the masses at a minimal cost."[7] In the meantime a team from the National Association of Educational Broadcasters had been hired by USAID to consult on how educational television could be implemented in El Salvador.[8] The minister created the Comisión Nacional de Educación por T.V. (National Commission of Education through Television), a group of high-level stakeholders that included members of the business community. They lent credibility to the government's endeavors while providing suggestions on how to make the television initiative work.[9] Changes to the education system began barely two months after Sánchez Hernández's inauguration, with the publication in early September of a series of op-ed articles authored by the commission.[10]

The government's grandiose pronouncements about the reform and its frequent references to detailed plans masked the highly improvisational nature of the implementation process. Béneke, Sánchez Hernández, and the education commission were all anxious to get the process underway, and they imbued implementation with a sense of urgency. They saw themselves as working against time. The nation's economy needed to be modernized, and they believed education was a key mechanism in the process. They saw the existing education system as counterproductive to that goal. Therefore, it was more important to get the process of change underway rather than to insure that every *i* was dotted and *t* crossed. "Our educational system is deficient and our problems are so grave," Sánchez Hernández said, "that it would be impossible to solve them with the traditional systems and methods. We have to move forward in big steps."[11]

Critics of the reform noted that implementation of some programs began in advance of the creation of relevant planning documents. UNESCO adviser Bruno Stiglitz confirmed this to be "absolutely true," but he said it was acceptable given the dismal state of education. Stiglitz supported the attitude of the education designers under Sánchez Hernández, saying that the reform was indeed the product of planning, "as long as we understand [planning] as a general picture, very superficial [*somera*] and flexible." In his view, the lack of specificity "made it possible to gradually adapt to the solutions to each of the problems that they wanted to solve."[12] The reformers' approach to curricular redesign seemed to confirm the critics' accusations of reliance on unplanned and unorthodox methods. The reformers planned to initiate their program at the middle school level (seventh, eighth, and ninth grades) and then proceed on to primary and high school.[13] This ran against standard practices of education reform, which start at the primary level and work up. The introduction of new math also fueled critics' concerns. As Stiglitz described it, "A 1968 trial in a 6th grade class that had never in prior years received training in the new math indicated that, even though the subject was completely unknown to the children, and that under normal conditions they would have had five years of preparation, sixty percent of the material was understood by them. . . . This experiment gave us a road map and the curriculum was introduced at once in grades first to sixth."[14] According to a later interview with a USAID official who had participated in the early stages of the reform, Béneke expressed exasperation with the amount of proposed planning: "I have planning teams coming out of my ears—from the World Bank, the United States, Sweden and so on. They all give me books of plans. But by the time I would do everything they say I should do I would be out of office. I have to get this baby born and on its feet before I worry about planning."[15]

If this USAID official's memory was correct, then Béneke expressed a view that stood in stark contrast to the public image being cultivated by the Sánchez Hernández government. After the 1962 education and development meeting in Chile, and with the encouragement of Alliance for Progress advisors, education policy was conceptualized as part of a grand development strategy to be carried out according to planning instruments prepared by technically trained staff. The five-year plan of 1962–1967 prepared by the Rivera administration included a detailed section on education. Following that example, the Sánchez Hernández administration produced a five-year plan solely for education, the Plan Quinquenal de Educación (Five-Year Plan for Education). Interestingly, Rivera's plan did not mention educational television, the most expensive, innovative, and controversial aspect of the reform. Similarly, Sánchez Hernández's five-year plan was published in September 1970, after many of the most important decisions regarding education reform had already been made. Not surprisingly, the government ultimately introduced programs that had not been mentioned in the plan, like the prolongation of primary school to nine years and the introduction of specialized high schools in specific trades like tourism and fishery.[16] Gilberto Aguilar Avilés, an important member of Béneke's team, said that planning was an afterthought. Instead, programs were implemented as they grew out of basic ideas put forth by the minister, who was the main force behind all the important decision making in education policy.[17]

Minister Béneke

Sánchez Hernández intended the education reform to be his main legacy, so his choice for minister of education was no small matter. Walter Béneke's energetic approach to policy making was apparent from the moment he took office. Journalists never lacked for stories about the flurry of activities taking place in the ministry; every week brought something new. In his first few months in office Béneke promised to stamp out corruption; he visited schools; his staff drafted a new law of "teacher stability"; he announced that the ministry would close most of the teacher-training normal schools; he declared that *plan básico* (middle school) would be the main target of the reform; he said the budget of his ministry would increase by an unprecedented 6 percent and that the ministry would have a new Department of Student Welfare; and he announced that in the first year the Sánchez Hernández government was going to create seven hundred new teaching positions, build twenty-seven new high schools, standardize middle school fees, and replace hourly jobs with full-time teaching positions. There is no question that Béneke's tenure proved to be transformative. Under his tutelage the Ministry of Education was "a feverish laboratory," to use a metaphor that Béneke included in a report to UNESCO in 1968.[18]

Béneke epitomized the modernizing leader that the architects of modernization theory believed to be essential in the transition to modernity.[19] There was no problem "more critical in a modernizing society," wrote Daniel Lerner, than recruiting a new elite.[20] For some contemporary analysts, like the U.S. historian John Johnson, the military could fulfill this crucial role in Latin American nations.[21] This line of thinking prompted New York governor Nelson A. Rockefeller to say in his 1969 report on Latin America that "a new type of military man is coming to the fore and often becoming a major force for constructive social change in the American republics."[22] The PCN regime in El Salvador provided a veritable template for this understanding of the role of the military in modernizing Latin America. The military officers in government were convinced of their ability to implement modernizing change and avoid potential destabilization, and Minister Béneke was their ideal civilian counterpart. He was instrumental in designing and implementing the education reform but could not have pursued his ambitious agenda without the full support of President Sánchez Hernández and a significant portion of the armed forces. Schramm considered Béneke to be a model of modernization and compared his importance to that of Governor Rex Lee, who had introduced educational television in Samoa.[23]

Béneke was born in 1930 to an upper-middle-class, landowning family. His father was of German ancestry, and his mother came from a well-connected Salvadoran family. After attending private school in San Salvador he studied economics and political science in Spanish universities in the early 1950s. During that period he befriended the future president of El Salvador, Fidel Sánchez Hernández, who was taking advanced military courses in Madrid. Béneke furthered his education with courses and seminars in Brazil, Denmark, and England. In London he attended a seminar on educational television organized by the Centre for Educational Television Overseas (CETO). After returning to El Salvador he worked for the Ministry of Economics and then returned to Europe as a diplomat in Germany before being appointed as consul general in Tokyo and then as ambassador to Japan. Parallel to his official duties, he pursued a literary career writing award-winning plays.[24]

Contemporary accounts and later interviews shed light on Béneke's distinct personality.[25] He was a small, youthful-looking man with a receding hair line, barely thirty-seven years of age when he became minister. He "spit words" in rapid succession. "He was at discothèques, lunching here, traveling there. He was completely tireless," said Madeleine Imberton, a personal friend who also worked at the ministry.[26] His charismatic personality helped him draw young, talented people around him. He gave his assistants considerable latitude, but they knew that he had strong views about everything. Gilberto Aguilar Avilés, who was put in charge of the new Ciudad Normal, described him as "a man passionate about everything he did. Walter was one of those people who detest mediocrity and disloyalty. . . . [He] gave his trust to high performers; perhaps he stated his ideas bluntly, but we helped him to systematize everything. When he gave me [the leadership of] Ciudad Normal he didn't provide guidance . . . we simply did it."[27] Imberton offered a similar description: "He let you do, he was always sure that you were able to do it." He may not have provided specific directions, but no one had any questions about his overall vision or even questioned it. "You could not doubt that his project was correct, he was so convinced of it; it was so feasible."[28]

Béneke's brilliance and charisma were mitigated by his ability to alienate opponents, sometimes with sharp and unforgettable insults. This trait emerged in part from his approach to people: "He was a man who either liked you or didn't like you at all," said Salvador Choussy, an architect who worked in the culture section of the ministry. His penchant for swift action and sweeping solutions to institutional problems created adversaries. His decision to close dozens of teacher training schools created a lot of animosity among the people who ran them. He did something similar with other established cultural institutions. For example, he shut down the Directorate of Bellas Artes (Fine Arts), the old section of the ministry that was in charge of cultural affairs, and replaced its tradition-minded officials with his young, new recruits. The traditionalists reciprocated with lasting enmity.[29]

One of the most remembered anecdotes about Béneke's style was his use of a helicopter to bypass striking teachers in early 1968 while negotiating a loan with the World Bank (the strike is discussed below). The bank's team had arrived in San Salvador when striking teachers blocked access to the National Library, home to the Ministry of Education. "No one has been able to penetrate the Ministry of Education building by normal means, for over three weeks" reported a UNESCO representative who attended the talks, "because barricades have been set up by striking teachers around the building." Béneke was not deterred. The director of national police provided a helicopter, and Béneke flew the one kilometer distance from the roof of the police building to the roof of the National Library, right over the striking teachers.[30] In the words of the UNESCO representative, "The Minister, however, has reached his office on several occasions by landing atop of the building, in a helicopter."[31] Photos of Béneke and his vice minister entering and leaving the building via helicopter made the front pages of the newspapers.[32] As for the teachers, they never forgot it or forgave him. They interpreted it as a metaphor for Béneke's willingness to go over their heads with every major decision. It is difficult to see how negotiations with the World Bank would have been affected by a lack of access to the ministry. But true to form, Béneke delivered a message to his adversaries that he was unaffected by their demands.

Teachers resented Béneke for other reasons as well. Gilberto Aguilar Avilés, who was appointed by Béneke to lead the new teachers' school, explained in an interview that Béneke burned bridges with the teachers through "the harshness of his statements, his drastic approach to the strikes, his incapacity for

FIGURE 14. One of the many newspaper images of Béneke and the helicopter
he used to gain access to the building housing the offices of the
Ministry of Education. *El Diario de Hoy*, February 21, 1968, 2.

dialogue and consensus. He uttered very callous and ironic judgments. The
teaching profession is ultra sensitive and his way of handling the strikes was
perhaps what caused such dislike."[33] As one of Béneke's critics later described
him, "he had an authoritarian side and an ego that surpassed all limit of com-
prehension, ruling with 'yo mando' [I command] and 'yo ordeno' [I give the
orders]." He followed up that criticism by saying that "the thing with Béneke
is that he never wanted to listen to the people, and especially to the teachers,
who would be responsible for the success or failure of the education reform."[34]
A class dynamic contributed to the gulf. Béneke was a cultured member of the
upper crust, as were many of the brilliant young team members that he had
hired. The average teacher came from the lower middle or working class and
had little or nothing in common with the private education and country-club
life of the officials in the ministry. Furthermore, the president's selection of
Béneke symbolized a shift in education policy making, away from teachers
and career educators and toward technocratic bureaucrats pursuing economic
development. In the words of Victor Valle, a student and political activist in
the 1960s, "he [Béneke] did not come from the ranks of educators, but to the

contrary, by his class, his upbringing, his reputation as an intellectual, he had disdain for teachers."[35]

Béneke's self-assurance was apparent to everyone who dealt with him, including foreign advisors. A UNESCO expert who helped prepare the documents for the World Bank loan in 1967 explained that he and his colleagues had limited influence on decision making; the determining factor was the opinion of "the Minister of Education, whose views on secondary education seemed to reflect his relations with other Latin American Ministers of Education as well as his own ideas." Béneke was such a strong presence in the discussions that "the job of the UNESCO mission and most of those who collaborated in the project was limited to include in it, and to logically organize, the programs drawn up by the Minister."[36] When foreign advisors tried to push too hard to change the education agenda, Béneke did not hesitate to show them the door, as happened on one occasion when UNESCO officials tried to sell him a literacy and adult education program.[37] On another occasion when a U.S. official said that the United States and El Salvador were equal partners in the reform, Béneke replied, "Whoever told you that? We invited you here to help us, but we're not partners, I have to live with what happens—you don't."[38]

Teacher Discontent

As much as they may have wanted to, Minister Béneke and President Sánchez Hernández could not implement their reform in a vacuum. Powerful interest groups throughout society had strong opinions about their plans for education. Among those groups, teachers emerged as one of the most organized and stalwart. Béneke and Sánchez Hernández knew all too well that teachers had organized themselves into a union and were determined to continue pressing the requests that had been rebuffed by the Rivera government. In hopes of dealing with this problem, Béneke and Sánchez Hernández included in their education reform programs to address teachers' concerns, but ultimately they failed to win teachers' support. The growing tensions between teachers and the state had repercussions for the urban labor movement more generally, making it all the more difficult to carry out their massive overhaul of education.

On September 20, 1967, President Sánchez Hernández made a televised speech in which he officially unveiled the education reform. The goal of the reform, he claimed, was "to extend the democratization of teaching and modernize it with new pedagogical methods." He addressed his presentation directly to teachers, assuring them that they would be "the irreplaceable axis" of the reform. The main point of the speech was not to explain the reform or its television component; the education commission had already done that. Rather, it was to announce a benefits package for teachers. There were economic and political reasons not to go along with the requests of the teachers' union. The teachers' plan was a costly proposition, and "giving in" to the new union's demands could strengthen and embolden it. The prior administration of Julio Rivera had run into opposition when it tried to amend the retirement plan for teachers and eventually the teachers presented their alternative plan, IMPRESS. Sánchez Hernández opposed that plan and proposed his own alternative, believing it to be sufficiently generous although less expensive.[39] He told teachers that their benefits would be covered in the new pension plan for government workers and would include full health benefits for an additional 2 percent deduction from their annual pay, along with a few perks, like a vacation spot on the beach for teachers and their families. In regard to pensions, Sánchez Hernández ignored IMPRESS and said the teachers would have to accept the new plan. He closed his address by appealing to the teachers' patriotism: "Finally, I ask you teachers, Salvadorans one and all, to reflect seriously and conscientiously on these issues, and to not demand more of the fatherland than the fatherland is able to give."[40]

ANDES considered Sánchez Hernández's offer offensive. Its secretary general, Flavio Jiménez hijo, described it as like a "father giving a toy to a crying child." He said that "teachers have endured years of struggle, suffering and sacrifice to achieve just demands, and they are being offered a toy."[41] As a former teacher later put it, "teachers were expected to give everything and ask for nothing."[42] As a response to Sánchez Hernández and in hopes of pressuring the Legislative Assembly to accept IMPRESS, ANDES declared a three-day work stoppage in early October. The union's well-honed organizational capabilities were in full evidence during the work stoppage. Union leaders sent out specific instructions to local affiliates telling them how to conduct themselves and what exactly to do during the strike. "On Monday and Tuesday, teachers should arrive for work and then at the designated hour leave the school and remain outside the building for those two days. On Wednesday they may remain inside the building to finalize the strike." As part of their organizational duties, teachers were told to go to their students' families and explain the reasons for the strike, so that "they do not send their children to school on those days."[43] The union's organizational work paid dividends in the form of widespread participation throughout the entire country.

Recognizing what he was up against on the first day of the strike, Minister Béneke denounced the stoppage as "illegal," called the striking teachers "terrorists," and ordered all schools throughout the country closed indefinitely "in order to protect the personal security of teachers and students."[44] He also called on teachers not to fall victim to "outside pressures," which in the parlance of the day meant Soviet- or Cuban-inspired communism. Béneke's accusation of communism marked the beginning of a rhetorical attack that the Sánchez Hernández government would employ constantly in its battles with teachers. They would accuse rank-and-file teachers of being duped by leaders who were communists operating on orders from Moscow.

When the IMPRESS bill went before the Legislative Assembly on October 9, 1967, thousands of teachers surrounded the National Palace, where the assembly was meeting. The debate among the deputies in the assembly went on for nine hours, and local newspapers reported that teachers hooted and hollered when reports of PCN deputies speaking against the bill made their rounds. The Christian Democratic deputies argued in favor of the bill, but the PCN had a majority and voted to table the bill until the following year.[45] In a preemptive move to forestall teacher mobilization in response to the vote, the government canceled classes for the rest of the year. With the year-end vacation scheduled to begin in November, the impact of the lost classes was minimal, but October was when annual exams were administered to determine whether students advanced to the next grade. The Ministry of Education announced its intention to hold the exams anyway, but there are conflicting reports as to whether any exams were given.[46] Regardless, ANDES continued to mobilize during the three months of vacation. In January 1968 the union launched recurrent demonstrations and marches throughout the streets of several cities, especially San Salvador.

The conflict between ANDES and the state in late 1967 represented a significant development in the history of mass mobilization in El Salvador. Teachers were public employees and had been loyal supporters of the military regime for many years. But now they were mobilizing against the state and making demands as employees before an employer. Furthermore, their movement did not occur in isolation but rather amid a rising tide of labor activism, beginning with the strike by workers at the ACERO metal factory in Zacotecoluca in April 1967.[47]

The ACERO strike was the first major work stoppage during the reign of the PCN, and although no one knew it at the time, it would initiate a new era of labor mobilization in El Salvador. The roughly two hundred ACERO workers began the strike in early April, demanding higher wages, safer working conditions, and job security. They received support from the Unitary Federation of Salvadoran Unions (FUSS), one of the two main labor federations at the time. Some of FUSS's leadership was linked surreptitiously to the Communist Party. The other main labor federation, the General Confederation of Salvadoran Unions (CGS), was more conservative but nonetheless supported the striking ACERO workers. The strike dragged on throughout April with intense and sometimes violent standoffs between striking workers and police at the gates of the factory. Toward the end of the month, FUSS organized a solidarity strike of all its affiliated unions to pressure ACERO. The federation also called on all other labor sectors to join a *huelga general* (general strike). By all indications, at least ten thousand and perhaps as many as thirty thousand workers in various economic sectors joined the strike. In response, ACERO negotiated an end to the strike that favored striking workers.[48] Perhaps not coincidentally, at the end of the year the government passed a new law raising the minimum wage for industrial workers, despite the strong objections of business owners.[49]

Unionized bus drivers went on strike six months later, in early October. The bus drivers' strike was resolved in two weeks with some concessions to the strikers, marking yet another groundbreaking moment in labor mobilizing.[50] In interviews, former teachers and students cited recurrently the motivational impact of the strikes by the ACERO workers and bus drivers.[51] Thus, the evolving conflict between teachers and the state did not occur in a vacuum but rather in an environment of intensifying labor mobilization. Both the teachers and the state drew lessons from these other movements. Realizing that each conflict set a precedent for the next, the state chose to take a hard line with the teachers in hopes of forestalling future demands, as teachers in turn drew inspiration from the successes of other striking groups. As one former teacher summarized the situation: "The government was nervous as a consequence of the triumph of the Cuban Revolution and the strike by the ACERO workers, and it became especially worried about the teachers marching."[52]

During the effervescence of labor activism in 1967, signs of the ideological factionalism that would eventually lead to the formation of various guerrilla fronts were already in evidence. During the ACERO strike, FUSS asked

ANDES for support, and many teachers wanted to join, but Mélida Anaya Montes opposed the idea, saying that teachers should stay out of the ACERO conflict and not participate in the general strike at the end of April. She knew of the ties between FUSS and the Communist Party, and she strongly opposed the communists, believing them to be opportunistic and overly centralized. Moreover, she believed it essential for teachers to limit their affiliations with other organizations and instead remain focused on issues pertaining to education. The secretary general of the Communist Party at the time of the ACERO strike was Cayetano Carpio. Ironically, he would be the first leader to break with the Communist Party and form a pro-insurrectionary guerrilla front, the Farabundo Martí Popular Liberation Forces (FPL) in 1969. Even more ironically, in the mid-1970s Anaya would oversee the integration of ANDES into the FPL's mass front organization, the Revolutionary Popular Block (BPR), and she would eventually become the FPL's second in command, behind Carpio. These events were still years away, but in 1967 lines of division that individual teachers would eventually have to negotiate were emerging within the left.[53]

The Teachers' Strike of 1968

As the year 1967 drew to a close, tensions ran high. The government was trying to overhaul education, and teachers were not pleased with what was happening. They had launched a successful, albeit short, strike and had been organizing various marches and demonstrations throughout the country. The education reform and teacher discontent became daily topics in the press. Photographs of well-organized and determined groups of teachers appeared regularly in newspapers, alongside articles describing events and editorial debates. Teachers were already in uncharted territory for themselves and for collective organizing more generally. A sense of the historic importance of the moment was looming, and no one knew where the conflict was going to lead. ANDES leader José Mario López opened the union's general assembly in December 1967 with words that captured the gravity of what was transpiring, emphasizing the union's determination to press forward with its demands: "We were born in struggle and have made it this far and our existence will continue to be one of eternal struggle; this is our normal state. Three years have now passed [since the union's formation] with fruitful results, our collective conscience is formed and no one who tries to broker in human dignity will break this consciousness. We have

made history and no one will force us back to the past."[54] As school vaca-
tions began winding down in February 1968 and the start of school loomed
on the horizon, ANDES claimed that the government had taken advantage
of the three-month hiatus to exact retribution on its members.[55] The union
accused the government of firing or transferring activist teachers, thereby
disrupting their lives and increasing their transportation costs to get to
and from work. The ministry responded by claiming that only 150 teachers
had been affected and that such terminations or transfers were normal.[56]
ANDES claimed that many hundreds more teachers had been affected, and
it demanded that all those who had been fired or transferred be returned to
their previous posts.

ANDES leaders scheduled a massive march on February 2, the first
day of the new school year. They had repeatedly asked President Sánchez
Hernández to meet, but all their overtures had been rebuffed. Throughout
the night of February 1, thousands of teachers from across the country
arrived in San Salvador. With the number of teachers gathering in Cuscatlán
Park growing quickly, Sánchez Hernández relented on February 2 at 7:30 a.m.
and agreed to meet with ANDES leaders. Arnoldo Vaquerano, one of the
ANDES representatives who attended the meeting with the president,
recalled that Sánchez Hernández reiterated his and Béneke's past statements
about the teachers' demands and the educational reform. ANDES leaders left
the meeting frustrated and decided to march at 2:00 p.m. The marchers followed the customary route from Cuscatlán Park through the center of town,
past the National Palace, to the front of the Presidential House, where they
shouted demands. The teachers were joined by market women, workers, and
university and secondary students. Vaquerano insists the total number of
marchers was close to thirty thousand.[57]

After leaving the Presidential House, the marchers gathered in Plaza
Libertad in the center of town for a rally at 5:00 p.m. Vaquerano remembers
it as a very powerful and emotional setting, with thousands of people shout-
ing and chanting. When López took the stage, he announced that ANDES
was declaring an indefinite work stoppage until the government acceded
to its demands. Vaquerano says that the rest of the ANDES leadership was
surprised because they had not planned for a strike when López made the
announcement. He claims that López got caught up in the heat of the moment
and made the declaration independently. Regardless of whether that is true
or not, the 1968 teachers' strike was underway. In Vaquerano's words, "it was
historic; never had anything like this occurred, notwithstanding the strikes

by ACERO workers or taxi drivers." As Julio César Portillo put it, "teachers marching in the streets indicated their rupture with the state."[58]

Around midnight, police and military personnel arrived in the plaza and a violent confrontation occurred. Seasoned members of the FUSS and the Salvadoran Communist Party (PCS) who were present advised the teachers to abandon the plaza in favor of a more secure location. Accepting their advice, ANDES gathered in the plaza in front of the National Library, which housed the offices of the Ministry of Education. According to Vaquerano, ANDES had no plan to occupy the plaza, but the marchers had been forced out of Plaza Libertad by the police. Once teachers began to gather in the plaza outside the library, the movement took on a self-reinforcing quality. Over the coming days, the plaza was converted into an occupied site with hundreds, even thousands, of people constantly present. ANDES scheduled daily rallies at 5:00 p.m. to coincide with the end of the workday so that by 7:00 in the evening the plaza was filled with people. The plaza became a gathering point for striking teachers and other opponents of the government. Police maintained a cordon around the plaza to check people for weapons, but they permitted the occupation to proceed. Julio César Portillo, a young teaching student with little political experience, met his revered fifth-grade teacher in the plaza and was encouraged to stick around. "Frankly, I didn't want to stay," he writes in his memoir, "but I stayed the whole afternoon. And what a remarkable afternoon it was! Especially, the speeches! People expressed clearly the problems and offered solutions! The speech of Mélida Anaya Montes, in particular, directed me towards the struggle."[59]

Elections for mayors and deputies to the Legislative Assembly were scheduled to occur just a few weeks later, and the Christian Democrats had high hopes. During the occupation of the plaza, PDC supporters also took up residence to support ANDES and rally support for their party. According to Vaquerano, Anaya was concerned about the PDC presence and the potential misperception that ANDES was affiliated with an opposition political party, but she recognized the unique and spontaneous energy of the plaza and decided to tolerate the proximity of the Christian Democrats. As it turned out, the PDC delivered a strong blow to the PCN in that election by winning a near majority in the assembly and a large portion of the mayoralties.[60]

Vaquerano claimed that ANDES had not planned to declare an indefinite strike, but the emotional environment of the February 2 march, preceded by years of steady mobilization, acted as a catalyst. It compelled López to declare a strike without a prearranged plan. The following day, the strong

FIGURE 15. A newspaper image of one of the teachers' marches during the 1968 ANDES strike. The orderly lines were a purposeful and highly valued aspect of the teachers' organizational plans. They were meant to indicate the reasonable and professional nature of the teachers' demands. *La Prensa Gráfica*, February 16, 1968, 1.

emotions of common desires resulted in a spontaneous and indefinite occupation of the plaza outside the library that contrasted with ANDES's normal, organized and orderly marches. Once the occupation began, it took on a self-reinforcing quality. Anaya chose not to oppose it, even though under normal circumstances she would have objected to such a close association with the PDC. Young teachers like Portillo found themselves caught up in the moment and drawn to the collective environment. "My heart was pounding in my chest," he recalled, "and I had a lump in my throat and I shed tears listening to those speeches."[61]

The demands put forth by ANDES during the strike included improvements in pensions and health care as well as the reversal of recent firings, the return of transferred ANDES teachers, the resignation of Minister Béneke and his vice minister, and a reevaluation of the 1968 reform, even though at this point the reform was still mostly on the drawing board. In regard to the reform, ANDES stated its support in principle, but the union wanted both the content and the process of the reform to change. In the words of one of its statements, "an educational reform can never be produced by a closed circle; the backing of public opinion is essential to efficiency."[62]

The government responded to the strike in much the same manner as it did to the teachers' work stoppage in October 1967. It rejected ANDES's demands, declared the strike illegal, and unleashed a propaganda campaign that denounced the strikers as immoral and unpatriotic. The government repeatedly claimed that ANDES's leadership had been taken over by communists and employed the trustworthy trope of portraying rank-and-file members as victims of their crafty communist leaders, who were in league with the Soviet Union. President Sánchez Hernández warned teachers about the union's leaders: "During these days, the Salvadoran teachers are being subjected to a trial by fire from foreign elements whose interests lay outside their noble mission." He defined it as his "obligation to warn the teachers who in good faith innocently follow leaders who have been led astray by outside forces." He presented himself as a defender of democracy against "subversives" who "do not believe in the popular vote and whose only method of taking power is through force."[63] In the words of conservative columnist Sidney Manzinni, "communist criollos" (domestic communists) served the interests of "Soviet imperialism," which represented the greatest threat to El Salvador's future.[64]

The intense electoral competition between the PCN and the PDC fueled the government's rhetorical attacks, leading it to say that the future of Salvadoran democracy was at stake in the elections and in the teachers' strike. The PCN took out full-page ads in the daily newspapers declaring that communists had taken over both the PDC and ANDES and were planning to violently overthrow the government and install a totalitarian dictatorship.[65] Béneke added in an editorial of his own that "I am an enemy of violence, but am not opposed to using it to prevent democracy from being turned into a [communist] dictatorship."[66]

Béneke's personality exacerbated the conflict with the teachers. His tone with the teachers ranged between indifferent, insulting, and threatening.[67] He opened one of his defenses of the government's position by writing, "It is said there is no worse kind of deafness than that of the person who chooses not to listen, but I will never grow weary of demanding that ANDES leaders explain their stance."[68] The government published poems in newspapers that supposedly had been written by schoolchildren bemoaning the teachers' affront to students, who after all "had brought them flowers on Day of the Teacher."[69]

TRISTEZA DEL NIÑO	THE SADNESS OF A CHILD
Maestro, yo que tengo sed	Teacher, I am thirsty
De la ciencia,	for science,
¿por qué me ofendes	Why do you offend me
Con tu ausencia?	with your absence?
Yo que he puesto en tus manos	I have placed in your hands
De la inocencia	the purity
Su blancura,	of my innocence,
¿por qué me la manchas de	Why do you stain it with
amargura?	bitterness?
Yo que el 22 de Junio	On the 22nd of June
Te llevo muchas rosas	I bring you roses
¿por qué me las deshojas?	Why do you pull off the petals?
Tú que me diste en la Escuela	In school you gave me
Abrigo luminoso	enlightened guidance
¿por qué hoy te has vuelto	Why have you become spiteful?
rencoroso?	
Maestro, me hablaste de la Patria	Teacher, you spoke of patriotism
Con palabras de amor,	with loving words,
¿por qué quieres sumirla en	Why do you bring pain to our
el dolor?	Fatherland?

President Sánchez Hernández agreed to meet the leaders of ANDES on February 18, 1968. Of ANDES's ten demands, the government agreed to only six minor ones. Both sides accused the other of intransigence, and after the meeting Sánchez Hernández once again declared the leadership of ANDES to be controlled by radical leftists.[70] With the failure of negotiations, the strike continued. ANDES tried to pressure the government with continual demonstrations. One of the larger ones occurred on February 23, with participants numbering in the tens of thousands. Even the deeply conservative newspaper *El Diario de Hoy*, which opposed the strike, admitted that the march was massive, orderly, and consisted of a diverse array of workers, public employees, and students.[71]

FIGURE 16. ANDES leaders entering their meeting with President Sánchez Hernández on February 18, 1968. Mélida Anaya Montes is in the center. President Sánchez Hernández is to the right of Anaya. José Marío López is to the far left. Arnoldo Vaquerano is on the far right. *La Prensa Gráfica*, February 18, 1968, 1.

Three days later, FUSS called for a general strike to show solidarity with the striking teachers.[72] Apparently, FUSS hoped to pressure the government to relent through mass collective action, just as it had done with the general strike against ACERO in April 1967. In the newspaper announcements calling for the strike, ANDES and FUSS listed themselves as cosponsors.

The involvement of FUSS and the call for a general strike in solidarity triggered the government's turn to violence and repression. Five days
earlier, army leaders had met with President Sánchez Hernández to discuss
the potential threat to national security represented by the striking teachers.[73] When FUSS put forth its call for a general strike, the army blockaded
roads leading into the capital in an effort to prevent an influx of sympathizers. It then resorted to murder. Two known FUSS members, Saúl Santiago
Contreras and Oscar Hilberto Martínez, were killed in a manner common
among paramilitary death squads. Contreras was arrested on the highway
entering the capital and Martínez was picked up at a construction site where
he worked. They disappeared for four days, and then their mutilated bodies
showed up on roadsides.[74] In the rural areas, ORDEN and other paramilitaries intensified their opposition to striking teachers and the PDC. Interviews
with people who were students and teachers at the time reveal memories of
rising paramilitary repression in early 1968. Julio Flores recalls that at this
time his house was stoned and threatening slogans were painted on walls.[75] A
former student from Suchitoto, whose parents were teachers, recalls returning home during the strike and coming across a crowd of people on a road-
side looking at a burned body stuffed into in coffee sack.[76] Portillo refers to
"the organization of rural patrols and armed civilians to control teachers."[77]

With FUSS's call to strike, conservative sectors began to close ranks.
The day after FUSS issued its declaration, the conservative organization
of private business owners, ANEP, called on the government to employ a
strong hand in defense of private enterprise and private property.[78] The next
day the National Guard arrested hundreds of people in a sweeping crack-
down. Gen. José Alberto "Chele" Medrano, head of the National Guard and
founder of ORDEN, assured Salvadorans that most of those detained were
communists: "From their clandestine positions, communists are unleash-
ing threatening plans: leading students and workers against public forces
in order to incite a violent confrontation. . . . Confidential sources tell us
that indoctrinated and fanatical communists trained in terrorism in Cuba
plan to unleash a wave of violence and terror. . . . Heads of families are
obligated to not allow their children to be victims of the communists who
want to subordinate the country to the designs of the Soviet Union. . . . [To]
achieve this they use innocent people."[79] The main student organization
at the university, AGEUS, denounced the arrests, saying that at least five
hundred people had been detained, including two hundred in Santa Ana
and fifty students in the capital.[80] ANDES renamed the plaza in front of the

library in honor of Saúl Santiago Contreras, one of the two FUSS activists kidnapped and killed, and labeled both Contreras and Martínez as martyrs. Today, portraits of the two men still hang on the walls of the ANDES meeting hall in downtown San Salvador.

Another tactic that the government employed to force ANDES to the bargaining table was to threaten the loss of an entire month's salary unless teachers returned to work. Already suffering from what they perceived as inadequate compensation, individual teachers had little room to absorb a month's lost wages. Portillo said that the government's control of teachers' salaries was its most effective weapon in breaking the strike. "They [government officials] took it to the level of the stomach and this weakened the movement."[81] ANDES responded by saying that they would not negotiate unless the government rescinded the threat of salary reduction.

The government's tactics proved effective. FUSS withdrew from the strike and ANDES went to the negotiating table. ANDES now had little bargaining power and the government was not going to relent. At the beginning of the strike the government had proposed Archbishop Luis Chávez y González as arbiter, but ANDES had rejected him as being too conservative. But now ANDES agreed to accept the archbishop's arbitration. In the new negotiations ANDES gained none of its main demands. It accepted the government's pension plan, failed to win back the lost month's pay, and received no guarantee that the fired and transferred teachers would be reinstated but only that a commission would be established to investigate the matter. For its part, the government only had to promise that it would not enact reprisals against ANDES members after the strike was over.

The strike officially ended forty-two days after it began. If measured against ANDES's demands, the strike was a dismal failure. At its general assembly meeting later that year, when ANDES's leaders summarized their year's activities, they made clear that the strike had caused problems for the union's organization and finances: "Various departmental committees remain incomplete and disorganized, caused partly by the flight or resignation of 7 departmental general secretaries. . . . Among the organizational problems caused by the strike are irregularities in the collection of members' dues in various parts of the country." They went on to say that the strike "produced lasting conflicts, especially denunciations [by the government] against individual teachers."[82]

The union's leaders refused to portray the strike as a failure, however, and in fact they defined it as a great moment in their ongoing fight for

teachers' rights. In that same year-end summary, they listed numerous posi-
tives coming out of the strike and offered a resoundingly positive conclusion. "The strike has a great historic value. . . . A primary achievement was
preserving the union and considerably increasing the Salvadoran teachers'
consciousness of struggle."[83] Forty years later, one of those leaders, Arnoldo
Vaquerano, still looked back on the strike as a crowning achievement. He said
that the teachers made tremendous organizational gains after years of hard
work and won a moral victory by exposing the state's repressive obstinacy.[84]

The strike had wider implications. In his study of popular mobilization in 1960s El Salvador, sociologist Paul Almeida described the strike as
the largest demonstration of civic collective action up to that moment and
as a "major force in creating political awareness not only for teachers, but
for a whole generation of sympathetic social sectors."[85] An interview with a
former teacher suggested the dramatic impact of the strike on teachers' consciousness. "Before 1968, I hadn't heard much of ANDES," he said, "but after
the strike, a teacher's world revolved around ANDES."[86]

The Main Elements of the Reform

President Sánchez Hernández and his political team did not grasp the long-
term implications of the mobilization of teachers. From their point of view,
they had just won a test of wills. The striking teachers returned to work and
the government didn't have to give them IMPRESS. After the 1968 strike
educational authorities acted as if they could safely ignore teachers' concerns. The plans for the educational reform continued undeterred.

A five-year presidential term was a short time to accomplish all that
Sánchez Hernández and his team wanted to do. The main elements of the
reform—educational television, teacher training, administrative changes,
school supervision, expansion of enrollments, diversified high schools, new
cultural policies, and curriculum changes—were introduced implacably in
overlapping steps. For the sake of clarity we will describe them separately.
Table 4.1 lists the main elements and the year each was introduced.

We begin the discussion with educational television because it determined almost every other aspect of the reform; the Stanford reports called
educational television the "catalyst" for the entire reform. For example, the
revision of teacher training in 1968 emerged directly from the need to retrain
teachers to become "partners" with the teleteachers. The reorganization of
the ministry's administration eased its ability to implement an ambitious

project like TVE. The new teaching style that accompanied the use of television required more support for teachers, which in turn prompted the creation of a new system of school supervision in 1969. Television also addressed one of the main problems faced by the reform's designers—increasing the percentage of children in school without adding to the cost of educating each student. Television had high start-up costs, but once the system was operational, it was a cheap way to reach large numbers of students. In late 1971 and early 1972 the curricula, textbooks, and teacher manuals were thoroughly revised for all levels, particularly at the middle school level, with the goal of facilitating teleclasses.

Educational Television

The National Commission for Education through Television appointed by President Sánchez Hernández in his first weeks in office got right to work. It built upon the foundation set by the Rivera administration. Less than two months after Sánchez Hernández's inauguration, the commission produced a detailed report explaining how television would transform education. One of the document's defining features was its description of education as a key to national economic development. It said that overcoming educational deficiencies and promoting development were costly and time consuming; after all, tasks such as training teachers took time. The document explained that El Salvador was caught in a vicious circle, "we cannot achieve economic growth to improve the living conditions of the Salvadoran people without improving the training of our human resources, and we cannot improve training without the economic growth necessary to finance the extremely high costs involved." The commission's solution was to rely upon television, following the example of nations that had done so with success, in particular Italy's Telescuola. The premise behind the commission's recommendations was that television could provide a "surprisingly economical and comparatively rapid" means of solving the problem of a scarcity of qualified teachers.[87] Those who had limited training could perform as "monitors," while the teleteachers could handle the highly specialized topics. An added advantage is that teleclasses could be offered in non-school buildings.

One controversial recommendation was that educational television be implemented first in grades seven through nine—middle school, or what was known in El Salvador as plan básico.[88] The National Association of Educational Broadcasters disagreed with this view and had recommended that

Table 4.1

Main Elements of the 1968 Education Reform

1968

Educational television. Staff training. Opening of the TVE studio at San Andrés. Tests in twenty classrooms.

Teacher training. Closing of old teacher training institutions and creation of Ciudad Normal Alberto Masferrer. Forty middle school teachers trained to participate in TVE test.

Administrative reform. Changes in organizational chart. Move of dispersed ministry units to a central location. Beginnings of study of comprehensive administrative reform.

School supervision. Planning activities. Staff training.

Expansion of the system. Creation of eight hundred positions for primary school teachers.

High school reform. Planning activity. Negotiation of foreign loans to finance the program.

Curriculum. Planning activities. Elaboration of "transitory curriculum" to use in seventh-grade classrooms selected for TVE tests.

1969

Educational television. TVE test in seventh-grade classrooms in thirty-two schools.

Teacher training. Selection of 260 middle school teachers for training at Ciudad Normal Alberto Masferrer. Three-month training for teachers who would participate in TVE tests in 1970.

School supervision. Middle school supervisors organized in a separate unit, the "TVE utilization supervisors." Staff training.

Expansion of the system. School construction planning.

High school reform. Approval of loans to finance diversified high schools.

Curriculum. Preparation of curricula drafts for primary and middle school.

1970

Educational television. TVE test extended to the eighth grade. TVE introduced in 219 seventh grades. Taping of teleclasses.

Teacher training. Training of 260 middle school teachers. Selection of 264 middle school teachers to be trained at Ciudad Normal in 1971.

School supervision. Increase in the number of middle school supervisors.

Expansion of the system. Beginning of first stage of construction of 720 rural and 80 urban classrooms for primary school, 180 classrooms for middle school, 303 classrooms for diversified high schools.

High school reform. Training for teachers in industrial and agricultural high schools.

Curriculum. Seventh grades receive new textbooks. Revision of curricula for diversified high schools.

1971

Educational television. TVE extended to the three years of middle school. TVE used to give refresher courses to primary school teachers.

Expansion of the system. Plan básico becomes part of primary school, enrollments increase. Beginning of construction of 100 classrooms for diversified high schools. Beginning of second stage of construction of 720 rural and 80 urban classrooms for primary school, 300 classrooms for middle school.

High school reform Test of new curricula in the first year of high school. Elaboration of definitive curricula for diversified high schools.

Curriculum. Introduction of new curricula for eighth grade.

1972

Educational television. Continuation of use of TVE in middle school. Comprehensive evaluation of the project.

School supervision. Middle school and primary school supervisor units merge.

Expansion of the system. Completion of second stage of construction of 720 rural and 80 urban classrooms for primary school, 300 classrooms for middle school, and 100 for high school. Construction of an additional 120 classrooms for middle school, 540 for rural primary schools, 60 for urban primary schools, and 74 for diversified high schools.

High school reform. Introduction of diversified high schools in existing high schools.

Curriculum. New curricula extended to all three grades of middle school.

Source: Compiled from Stanford University, Institute for Communications Research, "Television and Educational Reform in El Salvador," yearly reports. The classroom construction data are based on planned figures that appeared in *El Diario de Hoy,* February 21, 1970.

television be used first in primary school, where curricular deficiencies were most glaring. Almost 40 percent of primary school–age students (most of them in rural areas) could not attend school due to the lack of classrooms. In 1967, 453,000 students attended primary school, more than half of them concentrated in the first two grades. Only 31,300 attended sixth grade. (See table 4.2). Only 53.8 percent of the nation's schools, mainly those in urban areas, even offered classes beyond the third grade. Of the primary school–age children in rural areas (64 percent of the total), only half attended school.[89] By comparison, the total number of Salvadoran students attending middle

Table 4.2

School Enrollment in 1967, Public and Private (thousands)

Primary School		Middle School		High School	
Grade	Enrollment	Grade	Enrollment	Grade	Enrollment
1	158.5	7	13.6	10	7.1
2	99.8	8	10.4	11	4.23
3	69.9	9	8.6	12	0.51
4	54.0				
5	39.6				
6	31.3				
Total	453.1		32.6		11.84

Source: El Salvador, Ministerio de Educación, Documentos de la reforma
educativa #2, 20, 24, 28.

school was only 32,600 (see table 4.2), and more than half of them attended private schools.[90] Middle school students accounted for less than 2 percent of all school-age children and 6.5 percent of all students attending school.

In the face of opposition, the commission defended its position by saying that primary school attendance had been prioritized in the past without corresponding attention to middle school. Hence, middle school had become a bottleneck in the system. The commission also reasoned that the cost-saving aspects of television would be greatest at the middle school level because the cost of teaching each middle school student was relatively high. Television would also be easier to implement in middle school because most of the classrooms were located in urban areas with easy access to electricity. In contrast, the commission recommended against using television to aid literacy programs because it would be costlier to set up and the people who needed it were spread throughout the countryside. The best strategy, according to the commission, was to start the television experiment with middle school and then extend the program into earlier grades.

Another defender of implementing television in middle schools was Bruno Stiglitz, Minister Béneke's main UNESCO advisor. Stiglitz claimed that the existing middle school curriculum was the most deficient, neither complementing primary school nor providing adequate preparation for high school. Teaching at the middle school level was also the worst. Many teachers were not full time but rather worked as hourly employees; some of them were trained as primary school teachers or were moonlighting professionals, like lawyers and dentists, with time to spare. Stiglitz claimed the equipment and teaching materials in middle school were inadequate, and finally he observed that enrollments were low. He also added an economic justification, albeit one different than that put forth by the commission, noting that few students who finished sixth grade went on to middle school. This meant the government was wasting money. By the time students reached the sixth grade, the state had spent a lot of money on them, without transmitting skills needed for economic development. If students left after the sixth grade, the state was not getting much return on its investment. Strongly echoing Wilbur Schramm, Stiglitz said it was inefficient to lose students just as they were ready to "absorb knowledge and attitudes useful for economic development."[91] A former ministry official who worked closely with educational television described middle school as a barrier, or "levee," between primary school and high school.[92]

The architects of educational television debated how to use it in the classroom. One possibility was to follow the lead of countries like France that used TV to show cultural programs that enriched the curriculum and complemented the classroom experience. Béneke strongly opposed this approach; he was "not interested in that open ended use of television, he preferred educational television for a captive audience."[93] He wanted a structured system where students sat in front of a TV monitor at scheduled times to receive the message that the education authorities considered appropriate. Béneke wanted to find the best teachers he could and "can" their taped lessons so he could make the highest-quality product available to the largest number of consumers.[94] His views prevailed over the recommendations of foreign advisors. Ministry officials spent the first half of 1968 training technicians and staff with U.S. advisors and securing financing to install a TV studio at the San Andrés campus in La Libertad Department. In June, less than one year after Sánchez Hernández had come to power, the U.S. Congress approved a loan package for the education reform, and Salvadoran authorities began building production studios, installing equipment, and getting ready to launch experimental classes in September 1968. The ministry claimed that students would learn "by means of the ultra-modern TV system."[95] In the meantime, Béneke flew to Washington, D.C., to finalize the negotiations of a $6 million loan with the World Bank to build new high schools.

Three and a half weeks later President Lyndon B. Johnson arrived in San Salvador to meet all of the Central American heads of state. Along with his wife, Lady Bird, and daughter Luci, he traveled to La Libertad to cut the

FIGURE 17. President Sánchez Hernández, President Johnson, and
Minister Béneke during the inauguration of the educational television studios.
El Diario de Hoy, July 8, 1968, 1.

inaugural ribbon at the new educational television studios.[96] He expressed
repeatedly his vision of television as the future of education. He wanted the
"fruits of technology in this great, new technique of television . . . brought
to the homes of all the people of all the world." In his speech Johnson envisioned educational television becoming as common as "the little red school-
house was in my own country when I was a boy."[97]

In August 1968 the government announced its plan to experiment with
televised teaching in fifteen classrooms of seventh graders taking modern
math and fifteen classrooms of eighth graders taking organic chemistry.[98]
The formal launch of educational television would occur on February 17,
1969. President Sánchez Hernández traveled to the studios at San Andrés to
give the inaugural speech. In his remarks he addressed some of the issues
that were worrying students and the general public. He reiterated that the
new system would not displace teachers: "television is just an instrument
put at the service of the teacher." He also addressed the matter of cost, indicating that so far the project represented only 1 percent of the government's
education budget and that when the plan reached full capacity, its share of
the budget would only be about 2 percent.[99]

By 1969 the trial for educational television had been expanded to roughly one thousand seventh graders in twenty-eight public schools and four private schools, covering their full curriculum (social sciences, Spanish, math, science, and English).[100] The format of the televised class was relatively simple. Students watched a twenty-minute lesson on TV, and then the classroom teacher elaborated and answered questions. Education authorities defined the classroom teacher and the teleteacher as "partners." By 1970 the system covered 219 public seventh-grade classrooms, which meant that more than half of all students at that level received some of their education through television. That same year's trial run in the eighth grade covered thirty-two classes.[101] Initially some private schools experimented with the system, but most of them quickly rejected it.[102] By 1972 most students in all three grades of public middle schools received their classes from teleteachers. Plans existed to experiment with teleclasses in primary schools by 1972, but they never had the chance to come to fruition.

The international supporters of educational television—UNESCO, USAID, and the Stanford team under Wilbur Schramm—celebrated the uniformity and centralization that television introduced into the system. UNESCO's consulting team saw virtue in each classroom having the same specialized teacher, "with the same curriculum and the same quality control, and experiences that require high cost laboratories and aspects of modern scientific development." They also saw television as a way to solve the problem of poor-quality teaching, because even teachers with "short and general training" could teach effectively with TV with a modest amount of additional training.[103] The Stanford team concurred, saying, "Television can present exactly the same instruction to all students at the same time. This makes possible a common evaluation of learning since a common curriculum was used and core instruction was identical." Following suit, USAID advisors envisioned "periodic common examinations created by a testing section of the Ministry." Since the TV schedule imposed the same regimen on every school, "principals do not have to solve scheduling problems." [104] Or to put it another way, the ministry decided for the principals how to organize their school day.

Teacher Training

Educational television forced the reform of the existing system of teacher training. Teachers had to learn new skills to work in tandem with the televised classes, whereas the existing system prepared teachers to work independently in the classroom. In 1963 teachers were trained in fifty-four *escuelas nor-males* (teacher training schools) distributed throughout the country. Eleven were public, twelve semipublic (heavily subsidized), and thirty-one private. Together they had 7,231 teacher training students. By 1966 the number of escuelas normales had increased to sixty-three.[105] The various schools pursued diverse goals. Some specialized in training only primary or secondary teachers. Some trained teachers during the day, others in the evening. There were both single-sex schools and mixed schools. A few institutions trained teachers exclusively for rural areas.

The new education authorities under Béneke believed that the existing system trained too many teachers for the number of available jobs and that it was disorganized and decentralized. Many of the private schools, for example, were merely for-profit operations more interested in filling their classrooms with paying customers than in providing quality training.[106] Believing the system to be poorly regulated, of questionable quality, dispersed, and nonresponsive to the needs of the country, Béneke dismantled it with the stroke of a pen. He closed all the existing schools and created a new one on a campus surrounded by woods in the idyllic environs of San Andrés, coincidentally on the same grounds as the TVE studios. The new facility was called Ciudad Normal Alberto Masferrer, after the renowned philosopher of the 1920s and 1930s, and it became the sole institution for teacher training in the country. The person in charge of the new school was Gilberto Aguilar Avilés, a well-respected professional in the ministry. In the Rivera administration he had been charged with preparing the terrain for educational television.[107] Some of the professors in the old escuelas normales were recruited to teach in the new institution, but most of them were not. The government particularly ignored professors from one of the leading normales, the Escuela Normal Superior, because it considered them to be too opinionated and too opposed to the new system. One of those professors was Mélida Anaya Montes, co-founder of the teachers' union.[108] Opponents of the Ciudad Normal saw it as a ploy to demobilize teacher activism.[109] No evidence exists to corroborate that view, but as we will see in the next chapter, if the authorities thought that closing the normales would end teachers' opposition, they were sadly mistaken.

The first task of the new officials of the Ciudad Normal was to train forty teachers to participate in the pilot program for educational television. Those teachers received three months of special training in late 1968 and early 1969. At the same time, 260 middle school teachers were uprooted from wherever they were living to be brought to San Andrés for a yearlong training in teaching with television. During their year at San Andrés, they received full salary and room and board.[110] As the authorities explained, few of the recruits had been teaching with the benefit of full-time positions or appropriate training to teach their current level. By retraining them, the government hoped to achieve its goal of staffing all middle school and high school classes with full-time teachers.[111] In its heyday the Ciudad Normal had one thousand boarding students.[112]

Regardless of the fact that the creation of Ciudad Normal was a direct byproduct of the education reform, which teachers generally opposed, most of its alumni have fond memories of the school. They still have an esprit de corps and miss the sense of mission (*mística*) that the institution instilled in them. Young teachers learned constructivist pedagogic techniques and gained pride in their ability to teach. But when the graduates went on to teach in classrooms with television, they were second to the teleteacher.[113]

Administrative Reform

The old administrative structure of the ministry could not accommodate the fast pace of reform and the volume of innovation. Béneke wanted the ministry to be "modernized according to methods used by the U.S. firm IBM."[114] USAID hired Clapp and Mayne, Inc., a Puerto Rican–based consulting firm, to prepare a blueprint for the reorganization.[115] By the end of 1968 the consultants had submitted the plan, and ministry authorities proceeded with the reorganization. The ministry's twenty scattered offices were relocated in a single building, and a simplified organizational structure was put in place. Since the legislation to create an autonomous institution for educational television had failed under Rivera, the new organizational chart of the ministry included a new unit for educational television directly under the minister and separate from the National Directorate for Education, the main unit in charge of educational issues. That placement on the ministry's organizational chart highlighted television's privileged status.[116]

School Supervision

The use of television required an overhaul of the system of school supervision. School supervisors worked under difficult conditions. They were poorly paid, did not have access to adequate transportation to move from school to school, and were organized in a highly centralized manner. Teachers and school officials did not trust them, seeing them as police enforcers. During their visits to schools the supervisors looked for infractions and reported everything to higher authorities. Needless to say, supervising was contentious, and the job involved little in the way of providing support or pedagogic advice.

The first change to that system was directed, not surprisingly, at the middle school level and was directly linked to the TV experiment. A new class of supervisor, called the "TVE utilization supervisor," was introduced in 1969.[117] A supervisor's primary function was to help middle school teachers adjust to the changes introduced by television. After a year of operation, the new system still failed to satisfy researchers from the United States, who felt that it "neglected to face squarely the problem of what 'improvement in the quality of teaching' really meant." Further amendments were introduced that drew upon the latest pedagogical techniques. Supervisors now conducted class observations and focused on student interaction, group exercises, and homework assignments that taught the difference between "memory" and "thought."[118] The new supervision unit was attached directly to the division that oversaw TV production. Some of Béneke's critics saw that organization as evidence that the minister promoted his pet project of educational television at the expense of other ministry activities.[119]

Despite Béneke's strong support for the changes to supervision, the innovations faced implacable resistance and bureaucratic problems from an old guard in the ministry. In 1970 the ministry had created seventeen new positions, but most of the school year passed before a majority of the new supervisors were in the field. The Stanford team reported that the supervisors "were hampered by a lack of cooperation, leadership, and support on the part of the leaders of the Division of Secondary Education in the Ministry."[120] Soon thereafter the training course for supervisors was scuttled for political and legal reasons, and the newly trained supervisors went back to their old positions. The supervision unit was even moved to the Division of Secondary Education. The supervision system was reorganized once again when middle school became part of primary education in 1971. As the Stanford researchers reported with dismay, "supervisors who had been trained to work in middle school were placed in a unit with former primary school supervisors to work in all nine grades of basic education. This change also meant that supervision, in most cases, retained its administrative function and lost its pedagogic role."[121] Supervision represented one of the few areas where Béneke's vision did not prevail.

Table 4.3
Middle School Enrollment, 1967–1971

Enrollment date	# of students
February 1967	40,123
February 1968	43,222
February 1969	46,913
February 1970	49,588
February 1971	60,334

Source: R. V. Piriz, El Salvador, Supervisión Escolar, 1965–1971, Misión marzo de 1965–diciembre 1971, p. 32, UNESCO Archive Reg. X07.21(728.4), AMS Aid to Member States Programme—Salvador.

Expansion of the System

Low enrollment at the middle school level was a constant concern to ministry officials, and they took dramatic steps to resolve the problem. One strategy was to eliminate the term *middle school* (plan básico) in 1971 and place seventh, eighth, and ninth grades in the category of primary education.[122] That seemingly small step had profound implications, as revealed by Article 198 of the 1962 Constitution. It said, "All the inhabitants of the Republic have the right and the duty to receive basic [primary] education" at no cost in public schools. Thus, by simply reclassifying grades seven through nine as primary school, ministry officials made middle school compulsory and free.

Following the reclassification, the government eliminated tuition payments in grades seven through nine, and enrollment increased rapidly. As shown in table 4.3, the number of students in middle school had been increasing by about three thousand per year since the beginning of the reform, but in February 1971 the increase from the previous year more than tripled (it increased by 10,746 students to be precise).

By increasing the number of students in those grades where television was being implemented, the government lowered its per-student cost of providing education. But the expansion also created some problems that forced the ministry to take extraordinary measures. Because the number of classrooms and teachers could not increase as quickly as students enrolled, the school day had to be divided into two shifts, morning and afternoon, and teachers would have to work more hours. Mandatory teaching time for teachers increased from twenty-one to twenty-five hours. As one of the Stanford reports explained:

> Even this was not enough. Most schools were short one or more teachers for the first several months of the [1971] school year. Each school solved this problem its own way. In some places, students watched the television classes without teachers, and thus without motivation or reinforcement sessions. In others, two classes of up to 45 students each crowded into a single classroom with one teacher. In other schools teachers took extra classes with or without overtime pay.
>
> Finally in May and June a supplemental budget was passed by the National [Legislative] Assembly and more teachers were hired. Even so, throughout the school year, specialists in Science found themselves teaching Humanities and vice versa. Teachers trained to teach primary school found themselves instructing in ITV [TVE] classes without any retraining at San Andrés. [123]

Another strategy to resolve the problem of increased enrollments was to initiate an aggressive plan for building new schools. The pace of construction was unprecedented in the nation's history. With Alliance for Progress funds, the government launched a program called "one school per day." Plans for the first stage in 1970 included constructing 180 middle school classrooms and 720 rural and 80 urban primary school classrooms in addition to 303 for the specialized high schools. The second stage included adding 300 more middle school classrooms, 720 primary school classrooms in rural areas and 80 in urban areas, and 100 high school classrooms. The third stage called for 120 additional classrooms for middle school, 540 for rural primary schools, 60 for urban primary schools, and 74 for high schools.[124]

"Social promotions" was yet another policy put forth as a means of increasing enrollment. It entailed automatically passing students from one grade to the next regardless of performance. This policy replaced the old practice of making students repeat grades if they failed. Ministry officials saw it as a way to ease the problems of high dropout rates and of older students remaining in early grades. The plan was highly controversial. Many teachers and parents disliked it immensely, believing that it worked against academic standards. The controversies surrounding social promotion and educational television overshadowed the magnitude of school construction, one of the indisputably positive legacies of the reform.

High School Reform

Although reformers in the ministry were focused on middle school, they believed that reforms at the high school level were essential for producing a trained labor force to promote economic development. The traditional high school curriculum was not designed to train people to be middle managers, so education planners decided to complement traditional high schools with a system of specialized schools that focused on different trades. The idea first arose in early 1968 during negotiations with the World Bank for a loan to build new high schools. The negotiations had started merely as a discussion about financing high school buildings and then evolved into a thorough revision of the role of secondary education in economic development. One of the UNESCO officials who participated in the negotiations surmised that "the labor pyramid of the country lacked training for the lower-medium managers, particularly in the most important sectors for the socioeconomic development of the country." Moving from that general proposition to an effective plan of action required knowing which economic sectors were lacking middle managers, but the country "didn't have any human resource studies at any level."[125] Based on modest research done at the last minute, authorities decided to use the loan to make significant changes to secondary education. The main byproduct of that decision was the creation of specialized high schools (*bachilleratos diversificados*).

Traditionally almost every high school student studied a common college-preparatory curriculum. Under the new system students had to choose among a variety of specialized options, including fishery and navigation, health, agriculture, tourism, and the arts. "Even though [the new options] did not have a well established market," reported the UN official Bruno Stiglitz, they "represented sectors of certain potential for the economic development of the country." The number of students to be affected was not great (in 1966 only 23,892 students attended high school), but it was expected to grow.[126] By 1972 the new bachilleratos diversificados were fully operational, but most students continued to enroll in the traditional schools.

Cultural Policy

One aspect of the reform, cultural policy, was not directly tied to television but had great visibility and a long-lasting impact. By law, cultural policies and all related institutions operated under the jurisdiction of the Ministry of

Education. As would be expected, this fact did not escape Béneke's reformist enthusiasm. Béneke took great interest in the arts, particularly theater (he was a published playwright). The arts high school (Bachillerato en Artes), one of the new bachilleratos diversificados, stood at the intersection of education and cultural policy. It was a bold experiment that transformed many lives. The student body was made up of young men and women who were recruited from all over the country. Their regional diversity represented a major innovation in a country where "high culture" was traditionally concentrated in the capital. In another extraordinary innovation, the government offered all students full scholarships, including room and board. For small-town, artsy high school students, living away from home in a community of people who shared their interests was an unprecedented experience. One of the teachers reminisced that he was surprised when all the students wanted to join the water polo team. "They had never seen anyone play with a ball in a swimming pool."[127] Their small towns probably did not have swimming pools.

The arts school also promoted an environment of freedom and exploration. The principal was Magda Aguilar, a woman who, with Béneke's full support, hired a very young and talented staff ready to take on the world. Béneke was so interested in the high school that he hired some of the teachers personally. Roberto Salomón, the person placed in charge of the theater program, explained the circumstances of his appointment in a later interview: "Walter Béneke had started this entire dynamic of young people, young idealists, people working in a totally idealist way towards bettering education and bettering social conditions in Salvador. He offered me a job as—he said, 'You're going to—' Didn't ask. He said, 'You're going to create a theater department at a new National Arts Center which I'm founding as of last—it's been working for six months but doesn't work. I need somebody to run it.' I had never done any teaching. (How old were you at this point?) Twenty-four. Twenty-three."[128]

Students and teachers at the school believed themselves to be producing cutting-edge alternatives to traditional work in all media. The school had regular theater seasons and a symphony orchestra. The young staff were well trained and cosmopolitan, and they introduced students to new perspectives. The theater department included Argentines who had fled the military dictatorship in their country and Spaniards escaping the Franco regime. Their political ideas permeated group discussions of the plays under study. For example, the young actors presented a production of Peter Weiss's play

Marat/Sade, shocking elite theatergoers. Yet when they were invited to perform the play in Costa Rica, Béneke showed his support by being the guest of honor.[129] To staff the music department, Béneke persuaded the Peace Corps to add music teachers to the standard group of community development workers and public health specialists sent to El Salvador. In September 1970 four Peace Corps volunteers—a bassoonist, a soprano singer, an organist, and a cellist—arrived in San Salvador. The second day of their stay in the country they were ushered to Béneke's office for a press conference, just the beginning of their hectic and fruitful stay in El Salvador. The Peace Corps contributed three more musicians and then two dancers and a sculptor. The Japanese equivalent of the Peace Corps sent a sculptor and a painter.[130]

Life in the student dorm represented another kind of challenge to tradition: "total sexual freedom," said one of the former teachers. Their attitude distinguished the students from the rest of society. To conservative Salvadorans "the girls were prostitutes and the boys gay." They experimented with sex, drugs, and politics. One of the teachers remembers that he and the principal had to make frequent trips to the police to get students out of jail, "some for marijuana smoking, others for subversive activities."[131] But Béneke had no regrets. He saw himself as an artist and valued the potential of young people even if he disagreed with them. Salvador Choussy, a young architect hired personally by Béneke to work in cultural affairs, illustrated that side of the minister's personality. After the 1968 teacher strike Choussy organized an art exhibit that was critical of the government. Since the exhibit had good art, Béneke offered him a job on the spot. The open environment of the school led many students to question not only traditional art forms but also the social conditions around them. Many alums joined opposition political movements, and a few even became guerrillas.

The vice minister for culture, youth, and sports was considered to be Béneke's right-hand man. He was Roberto Murray Meza, the young (early twenties) heir to a beer fortune. The ministry organized music festivals, art exhibits, and lectures at a pace and with a level of ambition unprecedented in the country's history. Carlos de Sola, the young man selected to be director of culture, was one of the most promising members of his generation until his early death in 1979. "It was a fantastic time," said Madeleine Imberton, one of his assistants in charge of a publication dedicated to popular art.[132]

The ministry of education became a virtual nursery for top talent. Murray Meza became a prominent business and political leader. He has often been mentioned as a possible presidential candidate for the right-wing

ARENA party, and he sponsors nongovernmental organizations active in education-related issues. Salomón, the theater teacher, has had a successful career producing plays, mainly in Switzerland (where he lives most of the year), as well as in El Salvador and the United States. Other teachers at the arts high school included the painters Roberto Huezo and Roberto Galicia and the writer Eduardo Sancho, all of them members of Salomón's generation. In 2008 Galicia was serving as director of El Salvador's art museum. Huezo, a successful artist, has held important positions in the Salvadoran cultural world. Sancho had a different kind of prominence; he was a commander of a guerrilla front during the civil war. David Escobar Galindo, head of the National Library (seen by other Béneke appointees as a relative veteran because he was in his late twenties), became an internationally respected author and was one of the government's representatives in the negotiation of the Peace Accords in 1992. In 2010 he was a university president. The ability of Béneke and his top aides to identify the country's best talent at an early age was impeccable.

Curriculum

The linking of education to economic development mandated a revamping of the curriculum. The content of the new curriculum, with its complementary teacher guides and textbooks, reflected the PCN regime's modernizing vision for El Salvador. A scholar of education and nationalism in twentieth-century Latin America, Matthias vom Hau, has demonstrated the important role that textbooks and educational curricula play in promoting development projects. "Textbooks do not reveal the 'facts,'" he says, "they convey particular visions of reality by emphasizing and downplaying certain aspects of the world. As cultural artifacts, textbooks are planned, designed and distributed by actors with real interests. In particular, states are the key actors in shaping textbooks."[133] Not unlike the socialist idea of using education to create a "new man," the revised curriculum that emerged out of El Salvador's 1968 education reform set out to develop a "modern person" with all the attitudes, beliefs, skills, and social norms necessary to overcome traditionalism. The plan was for students to gain an appreciation of the importance of development and the crucial role of the state in promoting it and acquire favorable opinions of elite business organizations and projects sponsored by the Alliance for Progress. As per modernization theory, the new student would understand history as an evolutionary progress, with industrialized countries like the United States providing an image of El Salvador's future. The new, modernized student would appreciate the importance of science and technology for bettering their surroundings.

The new social science curriculum for seventh, eighth, and ninth graders set out to instill students with a sense of responsibility for developing their country. Among its stated objectives was "encouraging attitudes to interpret the continuity of history and to promote changes in the country."[134] Students were expected to nurture in themselves the attitudes, beliefs, and skills that it took to be a modern person, such as appreciation for wealth maximization and a desire to better oneself, engage in teamwork, and participate in society.

The curriculum related as many topics as possible to economic development. When it came to geography, one goal was "to analyze how the geographic position of El Salvador in Central America contributes to its development." When it came to citizenship, students were supposed to organize a roundtable to discuss "the duty of citizens to contribute to the development of the country." The authors of the curriculum wanted to make sure that students understood the need to employ the latest techniques, and they presented government as a positive force for change. The curriculum included suggestions for teachers to "comment with learners on the need for the State to carry out public service works" and for students to "investigate how branches of the State contribute to the commercial development of the country."[135]

In addition to presenting the state as a positive agent for development, the new curriculum also hailed private enterprise. The role of business leaders in designing some sections of the texts is all too apparent, as seen in a two-page section devoted to the Salvadoran Industrial Association (ASI). It portrays the association as a national leader and as one of the foremost representatives of private enterprise. The section's glowing description sounds more like a glossy brochure than a dispassionate educational tool. It describes the association as improving "the quality of domestically produced goods" and "making sure that its associates promote the well-being of their workers and employees."[136]

The textbooks presented foreign donors as yet another beneficial team member in the process of national development. Salvadoran students learned that one of the government's many positive activities was taking out loans from foreign banks and soliciting technical assistance from international agencies like "the Inter-American Development Bank, the World Bank, the Alliance for Progress and the Ford, Kellogg and Rockefeller Foundations."[137] One textbook also went to great lengths to show the benefits of government

FIGURE 18. "A Comparative Look at the Central American Common Market," as it appeared in the new seventh-grade social studies textbook. El Salvador, Ministerio de Educación, Dirección de Televisión Educativa, *Estudios sociales, 7º grado*, 166.

programs that had been backed by the Alliance for Progress. The subject of family planning received an entire section in the seventh-grade social studies book, as did the Central American Common Market.[138] In the ninth-grade students learned that the Common Market permitted freer regional trade, such as was done in the European countries.[139] Once again, industrialized countries were presented as the model to emulate. One illustration showed how greater integration of the regional economies of Central America would allow the region to compete with the larger Latin American countries. It presented the Central American countries as small men in dark suits matching Latin America's giants—Argentina, Mexico, and Bolivia—by standing on each other's shoulders.

The textbooks openly promoted topics that conservative business leaders opposed, like the Alliance for Progress and land reform. An entire section of the eighth-grade social sciences text discussed the need for land reform and the importance of a more balanced distribution of income. The country's current income distribution was presented as hindering development because "in our countries the very unequal distribution of income has permitted the privileged few to enjoy great personal and familial satisfactions, but that does not benefit the progress and welfare of the community." The book was published shortly after the government had organized the First Conference on Agrarian Reform and was beginning to pursue land reform on a small scale. The goal of land reform, according to the text, was to "both eliminate the large estates [*latifundios*] . . . and create agricultural units that modify the socio-economic organization of the country to improve it." The text even promoted rural unions to benefit peasants and laborers in the countryside. It reproduced recommendations from the Agrarian Reform Conference of 1970, including one that said, "campesinos and agricultural workers should have their own organizations such as unions and communal cooperatives, and laws that deprive them of the right to organize should be abrogated."[140] Landed elites and conservative business leaders eventually stopped the government's plans for land reform, but the textbooks remained unedited, providing food for thought for many a teenager who could relate to the problems of low income and lack of access to land.

The seventh-grade textbook *Estudios de la naturaleza* (Natural studies) celebrated the ability to engage in teamwork as a sign of being modern and as evidence of good mental health.[141] The books infused students with respect for science and technology. The teacher's handbook suggested that students engage in activities to "investigate how science and technology have influenced the factors of production" and to analyze "the experiments undertaken in the country thanks to the introduction of the hydroelectric and geothermic industries." Other activities should show students how to analyze economic changes brought about by "the application of new methods and techniques."[142] The text told students that when science and technology advance, "they offer humanity conditions to live a better life." The United States was promoted as the model of scientific and technological development. The text celebrated El Salvador's strides in science and technology thanks to government initiatives, especially in education, where the country "was testing modern technologies. The most recent and novel being the application of television to the educational system."[143]

The new textbooks and teaching aids contrasted the pursuit of modernity with traditional stasis. The teaching manuals informed social science teachers to "direct the analysis to the indigenous problem [*el problema indígena*] and suggest solutions."[144] In other words, El Salvador's indigenous population was assumed to be traditional and thus a problem for the country rather than an asset. One exercise invited students to contrast traditional

FIGURE 19. This exercise from a seventh-grade social studies text asked students
to compare traditional and modern life. Ministerio de Educación,
Dirección de Televisión Educativa, *Estudios sociales, 7° grado*, 171.

and modern ways by selecting examples of how science and technology
improved people's lives. Figure 19 shows how students were asked to contrast the experience of riding a horse or an oxcart with riding in an airplane
or a car, doing laundry by hand with using a washing machine, and doing
calculations by hand with using a calculator.

There was also another textbook initiative, outside of the education
reform, that reinforced the values of the TVE books at the primary school
level. The initiative was promoted by the Organization of Central American
States (Organización de Estados Centroamericanos, ODECA) and by the
USAID Regional Office for Central America and Panama (ROCAP). Hundreds of thousands of ODECA-ROCAP textbooks, as they were known, were
distributed throughout Central America. One of the main incentives behind
the program was to promote Central American integration by having primary students throughout the region study the same Spanish, mathemat-
ics, natural sciences, and social sciences curriculum. Their distribution in
El Salvador began in 1968 and soon generated hostility among teachers, who

criticized them for being ideological, glossing over social problems, and promoting the agenda of the United States.[145]

W. Phillips Davison, a prominent professor of communications at Columbia University, had stated that the role of communications in development programs was "not only to teach new techniques but to activate and reinforce *desires* for change—to prepare the ground for the adoption of improved techniques and to focus attention on the desirability of new ways of behaving."[146] After reading the curriculum and textbooks of the 1968 reform, there is plenty of evidence to conclude that they were entirely consistent with Davison's goals. All of the new curricular materials—teacher's guides, textbooks, and teleclasses—along with printed and verbal media, were part of a collective package designed to deliver a coordinated message and a shared vision. It was McLuhanian redundancy at the service of development.

Not all of the curricular innovations were defined by modernization theory. Some followed a nationalistic agenda, such as the new Spanish curriculum that included significant amounts of Salvadoran literature. Others were motivated by good pedagogy, such as the emphasis in the natural science curriculum on students doing experiments. One of the most debated curricular innovations, "new math," had nothing to do with modernization theory. It was supposed to help students think in abstract terms by introducing concepts like set theory, which proved as puzzling and unpopular in El Salvador as it did in the United States in the 1960s. Generally, the new curriculum was inspired by constructivism, the idea that learners construct knowledge by themselves and teachers are facilitators. Thus students were encouraged to participate in class, have group discussions, investigate their surroundings, and carry out experiments. Independent of both educational television and modernization theory, the reform introduced extraordinary innovations in teaching and learning.

The architects of the 1968 education reform believed that El Salvador's prosperity depended upon economic modernization and industrialization and that education was the key to achieving those goals. A newly educated workforce with a modern mindset would provide the requisite human capital to promote industrialization. The Salvadorans were joined in these views by a host of international development agencies that backed them with money and technical advice.

The planning of the reform was haphazard. In the end it seemed like an afterthought, an after-the-fact repackaging that helped manage programs already underway. But planning was an essential component because the international development constituency required it. They found it much easier to adopt a planning document than the exuberant ideas of a brilliant and powerful minister of education who was prone to improvisation.

One could construct a credible narrative about the education reform that casts international actors as secondary, supporting actors. Béneke's notorious assertiveness and his overarching role in designing and implementing the reform would be exhibit number one. The Salvadoran business community (empresa privada) could also be included in that narrative. Its members played important roles at key stages of the reform, including participation in the National Commission of Education through Television and on the curriculum design teams. The cooperation between the modernizing military regime and reformist members of the business community helped ensure that the new educational system would promote industrialization under the leadership of business elites.

Pedagogues within the ministry, particularly those who couched their arguments in terms favorable to the minister, also imprinted the reform, particularly in teacher training, curricula, and textbooks. Béneke's penchant for selecting bright assistants who shared his overall vision and then giving them plenty of leeway allowed them to advance their own agendas. But all of the reformers had to contend with powerful domestic actors who were resistant to change, such as the old education bureaucrats. The prime example of resistance was their ability to prevent Béneke from changing the culture of the supervising unit.

The main domestic actor to emerge in opposition to Béneke and his reform was teachers, the largest sector of public servants and a cornerstone of a growing wave of civil society opposition to the PCN. Teacher organizers worked diligently to create a sense of cohesiveness and shared purpose among the nations' rank-and-file teachers. Their success in doing so was made evident in the size and strength of their new union, ANDES 21 de Junio, and in the union's ability to launch a highly organized, long-lasting, albeit unsuccessful, strike in 1968. Just as Béneke was an independent variable who guided the story of the reform, so too were teachers, their organizational leaders, and their ability to articulate their understanding of the reform and provide an alternative vision to that of the PCN regime.

Thus, are we to conclude that the reform was by and large a local product with everything else being a side story? Does the Salvadoran reform offer an argument against the alleged power of the development community?

The answer to those questions is a resounding "no." In every element of the reform one can see a constant negotiation and struggle, implicit and explicit, between the ideas hatched in international organizations and bilateral aid agencies and the goals of their local, state-based counterparts and various non-state stakeholders. A good example is the decision to carry out the reform at the middle school level. While the consultants hired by USAID recommended that the reform concentrate on primary education, Salvadoran policymakers insisted that it was necessary to break the "bottleneck" that they thought existed at the middle school level. They even persuaded the UNESCO expert to side with them.

The agendas of the international advisors, Salvadoran government officials, and Salvadoran business sector all had distinct origins, and they stressed different aspects of the educational situation in the country. But generally they pointed in the same direction. In the end, their visions reinforced each other, sometimes in ways that proved to be problematic. A case in point is centralization. The military regime, following its own traditions, promoted a strong role for the state in education that accorded with a vision of development being promoted by the Alliance for Progress and modernization theorists: the modernizing elite leading the traditional sectors into modernity. One of the overriding impacts of the new system was to increase greatly the centralization of education administration, which had already been quite centralized. The modernizing ethos of the Salvadoran military regime, including the vision of civilian officials such as Béneke, shaped the reform, but international development experts helped define how they understood and approached the problems of their country. Modernization theory, the Alliance for Progress, UNESCO, USAID, and various individual foreign advisors were influential at every step, contributing ideas, technical expertise, and a substantial amount of cheerleading. Most importantly, the scale of the reform and its ambitious goals were entirely determined by the availability of international funding.

The reform was an expansive exercise ranging from managerial aspects to pedagogy, from technology to the arts. As such it was often inconsistent and all over the place. Despite this, or perhaps because of this, the intellectual energy around the reform and the charisma of Minister Béneke attracted an impressive and varied team of young people eager to change everything. Even today many of them, now in prominent positions, have fond memories of working at the Ministry of Education during the Béneke era, even though a good portion of them held political opinions that diverged from the official view. The lives of the individuals on Béneke's team took markedly different directions. Some became captains of industry, others leaders of the guerrilla movement. Some became intellectuals tirelessly promoting negotiations, others left the country in the 1980s to pursue intellectual or artistic careers. These disparate directions are testimony to the internal debates about the nature of modernization that were brewing in the 1960s. The sharp ideological differences that divided the country in the 1970s and 1980s were still taking shape. In fact, the experiences that people had during the reform and the conflicts it produced contributed to the country's polarization.

CHAPTER 5

Modernization Projects and
Authoritarian Practices in the 1970s

We have initiated an education reform based on the conviction that education fulfills the dual task of giving a person consciousness of the human condition and preparing him for efficient work in a modern world.

—Walter Béneke, 1968

I understand that not having implemented the Agrarian Reform project meant a return to past economic and social inequalities, a past full of injustices and disappointments that shortly after led the country to an armed conflict.

—Arturo Armando Molina, 2006

✛ WHEN THE COFFEE-PICKING SEASON ENDS IN FEBRUARY, CHILDREN IN El Salvador go back to their books and begin another year of school. The 1969 school year opened with a bang. On February 13 Minister Béneke announced a "massive" school construction project.[1] Later that week President Sánchez Hernández went to Ciudad Normal Alberto Masferrer to inaugurate, once again, a TVE initiative. This time he was announcing the regular transmission of classes to more than one thousand middle school students.[2] "No one can overcome our determination, and no one will bend our resolve, to give El Salvador the educational system it needs," he said at the inauguration.[3] He was talking about the ambitious, sprawling, and not-always-consistent package of education reforms led by Béneke. It is no coincidence that he did so at an event dedicated to educational television. As we will see in this chapter, TVE brought about the greatest changes in the classroom.

As with other modernization projects introduced by the PCN, and as with other Alliance for Progress initiatives throughout Latin America, TVE was presented as an apolitical, technical solution to a development problem. But in both its execution and its consequences, TVE was profoundly political. President Sánchez Hernández hinted as much in his oblique reference to forces that wanted to bend his resolve.

This chapter focuses on the political implications of the educational reform and other PCN modernizing projects. It starts with an analysis of the education reform as it was experienced by students and teachers. The students' initially positive reactions, especially to TVE, seemed to justify the reformers' plans, but the burdens of the new system rested more squarely on the shoulders of teachers. They, however, could not express reservations without paying a price. President Sánchez Hernández was serious when he said that no one was going to bend his resolve.

The government introduced the various elements of the reform systematically, one after the other, in an increasingly complex political environment. During the years of the education reform, El Salvador went to war with Honduras, the government attempted to enact a highly polarizing land reform, extremists carried out the first high-profile political kidnapping and murder, teachers organized a massive strike, and the country witnessed a bitterly contested presidential election. Yet the reform continued without concessions. Under these circumstances only an authoritarian style of rule could get the job done on schedule. While the reform proceeded briskly, it produced significant collateral damage, including alienating teachers and causing deep polarization throughout the political system.

The education reform was emblematic of a particular style of governance, one impervious to the concerns of civil society. Such a style incited alienation, resistance, and government repression, which were then followed by polarization, popular mobilization, and more government repression. The second great teachers' strike of 1971 illustrates that degrading cycle, as do two big projects undertaken by the PCN in the 1970s, the building of the Cerrón Grande Dam and a second attempt at land reform.

The Reform in the Classroom

The array of changes introduced by the education reform was supposed to transform the classroom, first in middle school and then at all levels. Middle school students received their English, social studies, and Spanish lessons in new ways, with a new curriculum and a retrained teacher fresh out of the Ciudad Normal who worked in partnership with a teacher who appeared at regularly scheduled times on the TV monitor. School supervisors were supposed to drop by at regular intervals to provide helpful advice. More and more students were being taught in airy new school buildings with wide corridors. It was not unusual for the reformed classrooms to receive visits from researchers and international visitors interested in the pilot project.

Each aspect of the education reform—the administrative restructuring, teacher training, school supervision, enrollment expansion, curriculum upgrades, and televised classes—converged in a concrete way in the middle school classroom, where the first of many students' minds were supposed to be modernized. At least that was the plan, but daily reality in the school did not necessarily conform to the expectations of international development specialists and government policymakers in San Salvador, Washington, and Paris. What did the reformed classroom mean for students? How did teachers' perceive the radical transformation of their daily experience?

Students

For students the indisputable star of the reform was the television monitor. Television was a novelty for most students in 1970s El Salvador, and most of them responded to its presence in their classroom positively and with curiosity. The Stanford research team captured that sentiment in one of its observations:

> On May 12 [1972], the TV set from the Ministry arrived, two months late. The set had been placed in the classroom the night before; the students caught their first glimpse of it as soon as they entered the room. The reactions were varied and enthusiastic. How handsome! . . . How beautiful! . . . How big! . . . How cute! . . . Some students simply stood in front of the set and stared. Others touched it, and one went so far as to put his arms around it lovingly. Another wrote on the board in bold letters, "Do not touch the television set." The rest of the students walked around the room selecting the best seating position to view their first lesson.[4]

Historian Carlos Gregorio López was a student of TVE in the early 1970s. In a 2007 interview his memory of the new system paralleled the Stanford team's observation. López had grown up in a rural area, and his family could not afford a television set. He described the appearance of a television in his classroom as a "novel touch that took us by surprise." He recalled liking the experience since it was the first time in his life that he had had the opportunity to watch television for two hours in a row. He said the televised classes expanded his horizons.[5] Most other families were like López's and did not own televisions. One TVE alum recalled in an interview that he was the only one in his grade with a TV at home, and another one said that only five families in his entire town had televisions.[6] Their descriptions of students' reactions to TVE echoed López's. They said that, as teenagers, especially for those students who did not have a TV or had hardly ever seen one before, having daily access to television appealed to them in a way that is hard to imagine today.

Students also generally admired the teleteachers, although for different reasons. One former student reported having a crush on the natural science teacher, a young, attractive woman; another one reported that the English teacher was from Suchitoto, his hometown, which made him popular with him and his classmates. "One felt proud . . . we saw him in the streets," the former student said.[7] The teleteachers became something like heroes to some students. One student recalls how disappointed he was to discover that his teleteacher in English was just a normal person. On TV the teacher was wonderful; he wore a distinguished coat and tie and spoke with an appealing American accent. But when the student visited the facilities of educational television on a school outing, he and his classmates saw him sitting in shorts and flip flops. He did not greet the adoring students, who were certain that "he was going to recognize us." "I felt deceived," the student recalled; his idol was a perfectly normal, scruffy man.[8]

Students liked the new curricular materials and textbooks that accompanied the teleclasses. In fact, those materials have been one the most enduring products of the reform. The public school system had never had a collection of professionally produced textbooks made specifically for its curriculum. The textbooks were photocopied and even reprinted illegally. Some teachers still use them today. A well-known author who used them as a student reminisced that he "loved the language books . . . they included poems, excerpts of plays . . . I loved them."[9]

TVE generated plenty of negative feedback as well. Some students found it difficult to incorporate new material that came at them in such a relentless succession. Some of the teleclasses left doubts or gaps, but since the pace of learning was set by education officials in San Salvador, the classroom teacher could not slow the process down. Thus, it was hard to keep all students at the same level of understanding. "Not all of us learned at the same rhythm," recalled a former student.[10] If the class happened to fall behind the pace imposed by the teleteacher, there was no hope of recovering. One interviewee recalled how his eighth-grade class had a difficult time: "we were seriously out of sync with the teleclass; the teacher did not insist . . . because neither he nor we followed [the rhythm of the teleclass]."[11]

López contrasted his generally positive memories of TVE with a bad experience in his Spanish class. He had a "fantastic" classroom teacher for Spanish, and thus the teleclass bored him.[12] Another former student remembered resenting the discipline of sitting in front of a monitor: "to me it was dictatorial."[13] The teleteacher "was never wrong" and "never had to answer any questions," while the classroom teacher could be confused, particularly when it came to math.[14]

Teachers

Teachers' memories of educational television complement the students', although their tone is generally more critical. At first many teachers seemed open to the innovation of televised teaching. The Stanford team surveyed a sample of teachers in 1969 (including users and nonusers of TVE) and reported that 73 percent believed that "students learn more by television than by teaching without TV" and 76 percent felt that "classroom teachers improve their teaching method by observing the television teacher."[15] Former activists in the teachers' union phrased the issue differently in a 2005 interview. According to them, "there were teachers who believed in government propaganda."[16]

Teaching with television altered radically the traditional class routine and the teachers' professional responsibilities. "It was no longer a matter of simple class planning. . . . [There were] too many books," said one former teacher, commenting on the extra work required.[17] Various teachers stressed that television would have been good if it had been used in support of the classroom teacher, because "children preferred a [live] lecture class" and "the best thing is the teacher-student interaction."[18] With television, the children became "mere spectators; without participation, they did not learn."[19] Coincidentally, a former student said that in the presence of the teleteacher the classroom teacher became "a passive person."[20]

Many teachers found the rigidity of the schedule imposed by the centrally broadcast teleclasses to be jarring. Some teachers remembered the system as "impersonal and unidirectional."[21] A former teacher described how "teachers could not incorporate a new activity into the class; if you missed a class you lost it . . . educational television enslaved you."[22] For another teacher the problem was that the classroom teacher had only ten minutes to answer the questions raised by the teleclass and reinforce the key points; "the annoying thing is that teachers had no time. . . . after one teleclass came another one, and another one."[23] It was as if education was happening on an assembly line. The rigid schedule of the broadcasts put time constraints around every aspect of school. For the most responsible teachers (and for those who had time to spare), this situation forced them to spend time with students after school, helping them catch up on the material covered by the teleclasses.[24]

Only 20 percent of teachers had training appropriate for the class level they were teaching. Not surprisingly, many teachers found the experience of teaching a new curriculum in tandem with the teleteacher to be demoralizing because it exposed their limitations before the students. The Stanford team's class observations provide ample accounts of this happening. In a social studies class, the teacher had an authoritarian style that the students contrasted unfavorably to the charming teleteacher.[25] English teachers had an almost impossible task of matching up to the teleteacher, whose accent was almost flawless. The report from one class observation said, "Attitudes toward English benefited most from the introduction of ETV, since English was little liked by non ETV students but well regarded by ETV students." A footnote to the report used that evidence to justify the use of educational television, saying that English teachers in the country were ill-prepared, and therefore TV was particularly effective for that subject.[26]

Seemingly unaware of the implications of the statement, a Stanford report said, "The classroom teacher's word is no longer the only word." Advocates of the system promoted the teleteacher as someone to imitate, "a model of good teaching techniques that can be emulated by the classroom teacher." The Stanford report did not see the interaction as a threat to the self-esteem of the classroom teacher but rather as an incentive to improve: "In some instances, the classroom teacher develops a feeling of competition with the teleteacher, and he works very hard to show his students that he is as competent and creative as the teleteacher."[27] Interviews with TVE alums revealed more about how the competition played out in real life. One former student from a rural area reported that in his school a teacher went to great lengths to imitate the teleteacher, such that he and his classmates gossiped about it during recess. The classroom teacher began dressing like his urban, televised counterpart, including wearing cufflinks, an unusual affectation for a small, rural town.[28] A female teacher remembers that children were "more motivated" looking at a well-dressed teleteacher "with resources." In contrast, "the village instructor, with her presentation, would not be equally motivating . . . it affected the self-esteem of the rural teacher, the teleteacher left her lacking in every aspect."[29]

Some teachers believed that TVE was part of a grand plan to replace the classroom teacher by "trying to tell the teacher that she or he didn't know anything."[30] Some reasoned that the teachers were chosen to appear on TV based less on the quality of their instruction and more on their being political hacks: "the government was always interested in the sycophantic ones" at the expense of independent teachers.[31] In the power conflict between flesh-and-blood teachers and the image on television, the latter invariably won. During the height of the reform, teachers came to feel their sense of professionalism threatened by television. One of them, a union activist, felt that he had been "trained with great humanism" in the normal school and that no television could replace him.[32] Older teachers lamented the end of the old system of normal schools, feeling that their time in school had built an esprit de corps and a sense of collective mission. Yet those trained at the new Ciudad Normal Alberto Masferrer looked back just as fondly on their years in school, where they received an "integral education."[33]

Two aspects of the reform received unanimous criticism from former teachers, "social promotions" and new math. Social promotions—automatically promoting students to the next grade—were inconsistent with the traditional culture of education. Like everything else in the reform, implementation was not preceded by significant discussions with teachers, which could have helped them understand the rationale behind the policy. To some teachers, the only possible result was to "weaken academic standards."[34] Similarly, the new math "was not well received" and was considered "unnecessary."[35] Parents could not help students with their homework, and from what they saw, the new math was a waste of time. Some students "didn't understand it and did not see its usefulness."[36]

Some teachers described both TVE and the entire 1968 reform with blanket condemnation. One union activist remembered it as an example of the "vertical attitude of the government that demonstrated contempt for teachers."[37] A veteran teacher said that "Walter Béneke's reform destroyed

education in order to deliver classes by television."[38] Another teacher suggested that Béneke's motive for pushing TVE was personal greed: "the rumor
was that he has done great business with Japan in the television deal."[39] That
charge is inaccurate since the monitors were purchased in the United States,
but it reveals a level of anger and suspicion that has survived decades.

Some teachers expressed their resistance to TVE by simply "declining
to turn the TV on."[40] This attitude of resistance can be inferred from a class
observation carried out in 1976 in a rural school by a U.S. doctoral student:

> Since there was only one set, the fifth grade students who had been
> to the previous class were moving their supplies and chairs into the
> other classroom, while those who were going to have the teleclass
> entered the room with the set. The teacher came and turned on the
> set five minutes after the class had begun; meanwhile, the change
> of groups and furniture was not yet finished, so students continued
> to come and go with books and benches; two students swept the
> floor of the classroom while the teacher, seated at her desk totally
> removed from what was going on, wrote something in a notebook;
> and in the front of the room the television, uncovered and plugged
> in on its pedestal, transmitted the day's teleclass.[41]

By the early 1980s the rigid application of the televised system was a
thing of the past. Instructors used the teleclasses as a supplement or to cover
for them when they felt unwell or unwilling to teach. New classes were no
longer being produced, and the only classes being broadcast were in black
and white and thus old-fashioned looking. Students had become accustomed
to higher production values and found the classes boring. Occasionally the
TV monitors were used alternatively. One student remembers the 1982 World
Cup match between El Salvador and Hungary because school authorities
brought a monitor out to a central place in the school for everyone to watch
the match. When it became clear that El Salvador was going to lose, the principal ordered the monitors turned off and returned to the classroom. Inside,
the students turned the TVs back on and watched in despair as their team
lost ten to one.[42]

Students and teachers viewed the reform through the lens of their daily
lived experience. Students enjoyed the novelty of the new technology. Even
in the late 1960s television was not the main feature in households of families
with modest resources. Many students enjoyed the textbooks and were fas-
cinated with the teleteachers and the world they brought into the classroom.

But even they realized the limits of the system when they discovered that they would be left behind if they could not maintain the pace set by the implacable succession of teleclasses.

The quotidian experiences of teachers were far more complex. Even though they were open to innovation, their disenchantment grew steadily. The system put new demands on them. They had to go through retraining. Students inevitably compared them to the teleteachers, rarely to their advantage. As the system progressed, many had to teach two shifts and work longer hours without commensurate compensation. Moreover, the reform, with all its alienating features, came at a time when they were already unhappy with their working conditions and the benefits they were receiving.

The blinders imposed by a narrow, technology-oriented vision, an aspect of the reform where the local and international visions reinforced one other, caused some leaders to misunderstand teachers' disenchantment and their support for opposition political movements. Government authorities were so enamored of their project and so eager to put it in place that they were oblivious to how teachers perceived it. The Sánchez Hernández administration, true to the authoritarian nature of the military regime, steamrolled every obstacle in order to impose its vision of modernity. It is not surprising that teachers felt increasingly estranged, powerless, and ignored by the authorities.

From the political point of view the gradual alienation of teachers was part of a wider picture. As we will see in the following sections, the education reform took place in a political environment that was becoming increasingly unsettled and polarized. To understand the activism of teachers and the importance that the teachers' union achieved, it is necessary to situate teacher grievances in the larger context of the political polarization occurring in early 1970s El Salvador.

The 1969 War and the Limits of Political Liberalization

When Lyndon Johnson arrived at San Salvador in 1968, he may have distributed money for some television monitors, but he had more pressing items on his agenda, namely reducing tensions between Central American countries and thereby saving one of the key elements of the Alliance for Progress in the region, the Central American Common Market. The main point of conflict was between El Salvador and Honduras. Salvadoran industrialization policies had been relatively successful, giving the country a clear trade advantage over Honduras. In addition to a serious trade deficit with El Salvador,

Honduras also had Salvadorans placing industrial plants in Honduran territory. Honduran entrepreneurs felt marginalized in their own country. Also, the modernization of Salvadoran agriculture had displaced thousands of peasants from their subsistence plots, creating a large contingent of landless peasants. Many of them migrated to land-rich Honduras, where they cultivated government-owned land as squatters. By 1969 Salvadoran authorities estimated that between two hundred thousand and three hundred thousand migrants were in Honduras, a country of only 2.5 million people.[43] The immediate irritant that prompted Johnson's visit had to do with tensions created by President Rivera's alleged interference in Honduran internal politics more than a year earlier. The tensions between Honduras and El Salvador threatened to destroy the spirit of collaboration necessary for a common market to function.

President Johnson's 1968 visit to Central America delayed a confrontation but did not avoid it all together. The trigger for the military conflict between Honduras and El Salvador was a land reform promoted by Honduran president Oswaldo López Arellano to bolster his faltering political standing at home. Citing a land reform law from 1962, the president of Honduras's National Agrarian Institute (Instituto Nacional Agrario, INA) sent letters to Salvadoran settlers in April 1969 telling them that they were illegally occupying national land targeted for redistribution. He told them that "the law establishes, as the prime requisite [to benefit from the land reform] being Honduran by birth" and asked them to return the land to the Honduran state.[44] The letters were followed by acts of harassment, intimidation, and expulsion. Salvadoran authorities denounced Honduras before the Organization of American States and claimed that it was violating the migrants' human rights.

The sight of thousands upon thousands of dispossessed peasants crossing the border back into their country fueled nationalistic sentiment in El Salvador. The recently organized opposition parties, particularly the Christian Democrats, chose to ride the wave of nationalism and demanded strong action. Conservatives naturally took a similar position. The main daily newspapers, always a reliable gauge of conservative sentiment, printed countless dramatic stories on the suffering of Salvadorans expelled from Honduras after being abused by "barbaric" mobs. Nationalism was fueled by another powerful force: soccer. The expulsion of Salvadorans took place at the same time that Honduras and El Salvador were competing to represent the region in the 1969 World Cup. Every match between the Salvadoran and Honduran teams was an excuse for both sides to display their capacity for blind chauvinism. People were ablaze with nationalist fervor regardless of their political persuasion. The conservative press fanned the flames with articles demanding that Honduran authorities respect the human rights of Salvadoran peasants (a demand Salvadoran conservatives never made to Salvadoran landowners or the armed forces before, during, or after 1969). Even *Opinion Estudiantil*, the radical student periodical, supported the idea of going to war with the neighboring country. President Sánchez Hernández called for a meeting of all political groups to unite against the country's enemy. He formed a National Unity Front (Frente de Unidad Nacional), including all political parties and many civil society organizations. Even the teachers' union and the Communist Party supported the National Unity Front.[45] The demands for action grew louder as more and more Salvadorans who had been expelled from Honduras crossed the border. El Salvador invaded Honduras on July 14, 1969; the war lasted one hundred hours.[46]

After the war, both the government and the opposition parties tried to maintain the momentum of national unity. José Napoleón Duarte, the popular leader of the Christian Democrats, helped the government organize a massive rally to welcome the troops returning from the front.[47] He organized the rally in direct collaboration with Walter Béneke, who worked closely with the president to manage the political aspects of the war effort.[48] The war was followed by a discussion in political and intellectual circles about its causes. There was a general feeling that the events had highlighted the profound problems of the country and the need for fundamental solutions. Many important voices mentioned the need to carry out land reform. In August the Conference of Bishops proposed a modest land redistribution plan.[49] Simultaneously, Sánchez Hernández's cabinet met and agreed to study a "democratic" land reform plan.[50] Five days later ANDES, even though it had been in a constant state of conflict with the government, particularly after the contentious strike in 1968, took out full-page newspaper advertisements to encourage its members to support the president by buying bonds that had been issued to finance the war: "The funds created by the sale of Bonds of National Dignity should be used to carry out the announced social reforms. With the desire to see that this is the case, ANDES supports decidedly this campaign and calls on its members to voluntarily purchase said Bonds."[51] In his Independence Day (September 15) speech President Sánchez Hernández told the Salvadoran people that the country was experiencing a decisive moment and that it was necessary to carry out long-delayed changes. He singled out "three transcendental reforms: Education Reform, Agrarian Reform, and Administrative Reform."[52]

The administrative reform did not generate a great deal of popular excitement, but agrarian reform was an entirely different matter. The subject of land reform was traditionally taboo, but after World War II it entered into public discourse occasionally. The opinions expressed about it varied widely across the political spectrum, but everyone tended to define land reform in the context of social revolution. Centrists advocated it as an alternative to revolution; conservatives opposed it as equivalent to revolution; and the left embraced it as part of a coming revolution. Among those who supported land reform, opinions differed about which model should be used and how fast it should proceed. But all of them shared the belief that national progress depended upon the government adopting a redistributive land policy. Opponents of land reform believed that any such policy was tantamount to socialism.

When Sánchez Hernández entered office in July 1967, the precedents for land reform were few. Very limited and unthreatening land distribution projects had been carried out by Mejoramiento Social under President Martínez and by the Instituto de Colonización Rural under President Osorio. There were plenty of foreign case studies to fuel debate among Salvadorans, including the notorious example of Jacobo Arbenz in neighboring Guatemala between 1952 and 1954 (which led to a coup d'etat orchestrated by the U.S. Central Intelligence Agency). By the early 1960s international development agencies operating within a modernization theory framework began to pressure countries like El Salvador to initiate land reform as a necessary component of economic growth.[53] An explicit expression of this view emerged at the meeting of American heads of state at Punta del Este, Uruguay, in August 1961. Their "Declaration to the Peoples of America," signed by all the participating nations except Cuba, stated: "The representatives of the American Republics hereby agree to establish an Alliance for Progress. . . . To encourage, in accordance with the characteristics of each country, programs of comprehensive agrarian reform, leading to the effective transformation, where required, of unjust structures and systems of land tenure and use; with a view to replacing latifundia and dwarf holdings by an equitable system of property."[54]

As part of this reformist impulse, some Latin American governments initiated land reform programs in the 1960s, including Chile under President Eduardo Frei Montalva (1964–1970) and Peru under a reformist military regime in 1969. Of course, every Latin American nation had the example of Mexico in the 1930s as the original case study and Cuba after 1959 as the radical alternative.[55]

In El Salvador it remained dangerous to talk about land reform throughout the 1960s. Any mention of it in the rural areas, and especially any sign of organized action against private property, resulted in brutal repression by the security forces or by paramilitary organizations. Sánchez Hernández began to change the climate around the discussion of land tenure starting in 1967, when he made land reform one of the three pillars of his presidency. In early 1969 he selected the wealthy, reformist landowner Enrique Alvarez to serve as minister of agriculture. Alvarez had served as undersecretary of agriculture the year before but resigned in the face of resistance to reform by other members of government. When Sánchez Hernández offered him the head post, Alvarez reportedly told him that he would accept it only on condition of having the freedom to enact change, and Sánchez supposedly agreed.[56]

The negative impact of the war with Honduras in July 1969 heightened the reformers' call for action. Even though the nation was riding a wave of nationalistic patriotism, the economic consequences of the war were immediately apparent. As Lyndon Johnson had feared, the Central American Common Market collapsed and more than one hundred thousand landless peasants returned from Honduras. According to reformers, the time had come for land reform. The government's efforts to sell the idea of a land reform did not stop with Sánchez Hernández's Independence Day speech. In a meeting with the Junior Chamber of Commerce in October, Alvarez told his fellow wealthy listeners that the rich had to make some sacrifices to preserve the peace, that reform would be their "insurance policy" against revolution.[57]

It is apparent that Sánchez Hernández was interested in pursuing land reform, but it is not clear what political strategy he had in mind. What is certain is that events unfolded in an unexpected way. The moment of national unity created opportunities for politicians of different persuasions to cooperate with one another, such as in the Legislative Assembly, where many PCN deputies had demonstrated an independent streak and were on friendly terms with their Christian Democratic counterparts. Some members of the PCN delegation deemed their party's leadership to be too conservative and opened conversations with opposition deputies. Ultimately, six PCN deputies joined forces with the Christian Democrats, the Social Democrats (Movimiento National Revolucionario, MNR), and a small party on the right

(Partido Popular Salvadoreño, PPS) to replace the assembly's leadership. For the first time in memory, the sitting president's political party did not control the Legislative Assembly.

The change in the assembly was a logical consequence of the political reforms that President Rivera had launched in 1963, which had brought opposition deputies to the legislative body. President Sánchez Hernández was unhappy with the turn of events. After November he vetoed every single law passed by the assembly. According to the account of Julio Adolfo Rey Prendes, one of the leaders of the Christian Democrat legislative delegation, the inability to pass legislation motivated him and his colleagues to concentrate on a discussion of the possibility of land reform.[58]

Land Reform and the Debate over Modernization—1970

The eventual forum for the debate was a week-long Congress on Agrarian Reform organized by the Legislative Assembly that occurred in January 1970.[59] It gathered representatives from diverse sectors of Salvadoran society. While findings would be nonbinding, the delegates were charged by the assembly with producing recommendations that the next legislature could use as guidelines for drafting legislation. Elections for the next assembly were scheduled for March.

In hindsight, there have been few moments in Salvadoran history when so many diverse representatives came together to discuss openly such a politicized subject. The assembly sent out invitations in early December to more than fifty prospective stakeholder organizations divided into four sectors—business, labor, government, and nongovernmental. The list of invitees included business leaders, landowners, nonradical labor unions, the nation's two universities (UCA and UES), all the legalized political parties, and various governmental and nongovernmental entities, such as CONAPLAN, that had a vested interest in land reform and national development. Notably absent were political parties or organizations that the government had branded as communist or "terrorist," such as the Communist Party, the Party of Renovating Action (PAR), and the autonomous peasant organization, the Christian Federation of Salvadoran Peasants (FECCAS). Nevertheless, Shafik Handal, who at the time was serving clandestinely as the secretary general of the Communist Party, attended the conference as a delegate of a legal political party.[60] The list of invitees also showed an urban bias, as pointed out by one of the left-leaning delegates: "We have to lament the absence of the

Salvadoran peasant ... [who] must be an active player in constructing his own destiny. . . . Without the peasant, a true agrarian reform will be impossible to achieve."[61] Actually, peasant representatives were present, but they were from the progovernment cooperative organization, the Communal Union of El Salvador (UCS), and they served as audience members rather than delegates.[62] Also notably absent was Enrique Alvarez, the new minister of agriculture. According to one biography, he did not feel ready to tackle the issue of land reform and therefore did not attend.

Regardless of the noteworthy absences, more than one hundred delegates attended the congress and many dozens of other people observed as audience members. Delegates included prominent figures in Salvadoran political and intellectual life, including Father Ignacio Ellacuría for the UCA; the liberationist priest from Suchitoto, Father José Inocencio "Chencho" Alas, for the Catholic Church; one of the most prominent captains of industry, Francisco de Sola, for the state bank; the conservative writer Ricardo Fuentes Castellanos for a nongovernmental think tank; the rising political leader Rubén Zamora for the Christian Democrats; Guillermo Manuel Ungo for the center-left political party the MNR; and the conservative lawyer José Antonio Rodríguez Porth for the business sector. The congress generated a steady buzz of editorial commentary in the newspapers, and the entire proceedings were published by the government and the UES.[63]

Any sense of collective mission that might have existed among delegates as they arrived for the congress quickly dissipated when the proceedings opened with discord.[64] Representatives of the business sector threatened to withdraw unless the rules were changed. They insisted that the congress only allow discussion and produce no resolutions. In outlining their reasoning, the business sector's representatives provided a rarely heard expression of its members' view on modernization and development. "No one disputes the fact that the condition of the peasant needs to be improved," said one representative.[65] What he and the other members of the business sector opposed was the idea that land reform would solve the problem. Instead, a version of agrarian modernization should be considered that would not affect land tenure. "Improving the living standard of the rural worker," said the business sector's main spokesperson, Rodríguez Porth, "can only be achieved by improving the techniques of production, which naturally increases productivity and the savings of individual workers." Rodríguez Porth realized that modernizing agriculture would reduce the need for manual labor and thereby increase unemployment in the countryside. He said the solution lay in absorbing "the jobless into other economic activities such as industry or services."[66]

In defending his position, Rodríguez Porth articulated the fundamental beliefs of conservatives, that "the business sector takes all the risks of entrepreneurship and improves the country's capacity to increase wealth." Thus, whatever progress El Salvador had made was due to "men living under the banner of liberty." Expropriating land or wealth from the private sector would be theft and would destroy the country's future. What Rodríguez Porth called "compulsory and arbitrary actions by the State" would turn El Salvador into a country where individuals lacked incentive to work for fear of having their wealth taken from them. Land reform would "impede the appearance of new enterprises and provoke situations of hardship and misery and . . . cause grave damage to the national economy and to all Salvadorans."[67]

The business sector's threat unleashed a torrent of debate that lasted the rest of the first day. Ultimately, the congress did not change the rules, and the business sector chose to withdraw. Its two dozen members marched out of the meeting hall amid cheers from supporters in the audience. Outside the congress, conservative opponents launched a media blitz to criticize land reform.[68] The remaining delegates overwhelmingly supported land reform, just as the business sector feared. They concluded that the Salvadoran state had the legal right, the moral responsibility, and an economic justification to carry out land reform. Individual delegates disagreed about the scale of reform. One member of the labor sector argued for a "rapid and massive" reform, while most others promoted a more moderate version.[69] Nonetheless, the four remaining days allowed delegates to coalesce around the idea that El Salvador's problems of inequality and economic backwardness could be alleviated only by "a profound reform based upon a massive expropriation of land."[70]

This vision of modernization had been articulated earlier by ANDES, back in August 1969. If a greater proportion of the population had a larger share of national wealth, its argument went, then an internal market would emerge that could promote industrialization and economic modernization. In the absence of such a transformation El Salvador's economy would remain backward, dependent, and agriculture based. The delegates to the congress who adhered to this type of view challenged the business sector's contention that it represented modern capitalism. Instead, they argued that the status quo resembled "feudal relations of production" in which the peasant lived in a veritable state of "slavery."[71] Only through a massive land reform, the labor delegates argued, would El Salvador move forward into the twentieth century.

Another critique of the status quo came from an ethical position and was provided by Father Ellacuría of the UCA. He said that it was "unjust for so few people to control most of the social and political power when the great majority of the population . . . cannot defend itself for lack of resources."[72] The delegation from the Catholic Church promoted a similar argument by citing the Bible, Vatican II, and the Papal encyclical "Populorum Progressio." Its members argued that a proper society is one in which "man is the subject of his own destiny, not an object," and that "only when man takes land into his hands and transforms it, can progress materialize."[73]

Jorge Sol Castellanos, a member of an elite family who as minister of the economy in the 1950s had been the architect of the industrialization policies and the organization of the Central American Common Market, attended the congress as a delegate of a left-leaning political party. In his contributions to the congress he used a historical argument to say that the current state of inequality was neither the norm in El Salvador nor something that occurred naturally. He said that private ownership of land was talked about "as if it were sacrosanct and has existed since our beginning." Instead, he traced the origins of the current state of land tenure to the liberal reforms of the 1880s, when liberal elites altered the laws and politics of land-ownership in their favor. The result was a massive transference of land from communal holders to wealthy individuals. For more than 350 years prior to that transformation, he said, the majority of land in El Salvador was communal property. Using irony to make his point, he said, "it is claimed that we have never had an agrarian reform in this country, but in fact we had a profound one [in the 1880s], but in reverse."[74] His references to the role of the state in creating the base for big landlords was a powerful rebuttal to Rodríguez Porth's contention that El Salvador's progress had been the product of individualist entrepreneurs operating on their own.

The contentious and potentially violent nature of these debates was revealed on the street outside the National Palace on the fourth day of the conference. Father Alas was kidnapped in the parking lot as he returned to the meeting. Alas had been inspired by liberation theology and had been working among the peasants in the rural environs of Suchitoto to train them in collective organizing and self-help. In his account of the abduction, Alas claimed that he was kidnapped by paramilitaries or undercover soldiers controlled by "Chele" Medrano, head of the National Guard and founder of ORDEN. He was beaten, drugged, and left naked by the side of the road in a remote area. This attack on Father Alas was the first "death squad"–style attack on a Catholic priest in El Salvador. Many more were to come, but this event makes clear what was at stake in promoting land reform.[75]

Conservatives saw the congress as a direct threat. For reformists it was a way of forcing the hand of the president to live up to his rhetoric. For the president it was an example of the dangers of losing control of the management of a complex political issue. One of the main legacies of the congress was that it put in sharp relief the unyielding resistance of the big landowners and their allies to any mention of changes in land tenure. The intra-right debate between PCN reformers and the traditional elite became sharper.

The president recovered his footing with the legislative and municipal elections in March 1970. During the electoral campaign the PCN emphasized nationalism and the popularity of the war. Its main slogan was "be a good Salvadoran, vote PCN!"[76] The strategy worked, and PCN deputies loyal to the president gained complete control of the Legislative Assembly. Opposition parties argued that the government party had used fraud, which is very likely, but opposition leaders also acknowledged that the nationalist card had played in favor of the PCN.[77]

Back in control of the legislature, the Sánchez Hernández administration continued its reform program but calibrated its implementation by remaining wary of conservatives' power. The new Legislative Assembly passed moderate land reform legislation in November 1970. It was limited to a single, forty-five-hundred-hectare region known as the Zapotitán Valley in western El Salvador. The government had purchased this land in the 1930s under one of Mejoramiento Social's halfhearted attempts to provide land to peasants. It then sold off three- to five-hectare blocks to peasant families in the 1940s without providing the necessary assistance to make them economically viable. Wealthy outsiders then bought these properties from the struggling peasants. By 1971, 2 percent of the region's landowners owned more than half the valley, and a single landowner, Miguel Dueñas, owned more than one-third of it.[78] Despite the modest scale of the government's reform legislation, landowners considered Zapotitán a trial run for nationwide land reform, and so they resisted the project. The large landowners outmaneuvered the new legislation by carving up their properties into fifty-hectare chunks and distributing them to friends and family.

By the end of 1970 the war, the land reform discussions, and the legislative and municipal elections had substantially changed the political landscape. The fluid environment that followed the war encouraged reformists within and outside the structures of the state to push the envelope. Their assertive promotion of land reform terrified conservatives, who began to distance themselves from the government and to vilify reformist opposition parties like the Christian Democrats.

Events like the war with Honduras and the congress meant that the teachers' union had to figure out how to promote its agenda in a rapidly changing political situation. The union's support for the National Unity Front and its effort to encourage teachers to buy government bonds are examples of its attempts to participate in the most important national debates. But ANDES's constituents were restless. During the preceding couple of years teachers had to adjust to a new, harder, and constantly changing work environment. By the early 1970s the education reform was becoming a tangible reality. Hundreds of middle school teachers were receiving training at the San Andrés teachers' school, learning how to be "partners" with a teleteacher. When seventh-grade teachers entered their classrooms in 1970 their first sight was a television monitor that would dictate their daily schedule. Other teachers saw a portent of things to come in the experience of their seventh-grade colleagues. In the meantime, the union's leadership devoted countless hours to organizing teachers throughout the country.

The Teachers' Strike of 1971

In December 1970 ANDES convened a national congress to discuss the education reform, and it later organized regional seminars for students and teachers. According to Mélida Anaya Montes, the first months of 1971 saw "an intense evaluation of the curricula by the teachers."[79] Salvador Sánchez Céren, who by then had risen in ANDES to the level of secretary general of La Libertad Department, describes in his memoir the process of "visiting all the municipalities in La Libertad [Department] to organize and inform."[80]

The relationship between the educational reform and the teachers' struggles was complex. Many of the teachers' demands preceded the reform and had deep roots in decades of government policies. When the reform was enacted, it fueled a fight that was already underway. Arnoldo Vaquerano mentioned in an interview that teachers resented that they had not been consulted in the design of innovations that were going to have a profound impact on their profession. Educational television was a classic example. Even if it affected only a small number of teachers at the middle school level at first, teachers saw it as an indication of their endangered future. Vaquerano explained that he believed the government intended to replace teachers with televisions: "One of their [government officials'] objectives was to stop producing new instructors, that is, with a TV monitor in the classroom and a team of educators teaching classes from the headquarters of educational TV . . . they needed no more than two or three teachers for several grades." The reform also implied a sense of direction for the economic development of the country that union leaders did not agree with. "The development of the country had to be based on an education reform; the mistake was the way they tried to develop [the country]."[81] Victor Valle also referred to the fear "that television was going to displace teachers" and said that the union came "to see it as a threat."[82]

Numerous and diverse factors increased the state of conflict between teachers and the PCN. But as is often the case with social mobilization, a particular issue became the rallying point. In 1968 it was retirement benefits, and in 1971 it would be salaries. By 1971 teachers had come to believe that they were woefully underpaid. They had not received a raise since 1962, and the government was using a 1941 formula to set base pay and determine raises.[83] Furthermore, as a consequence of the education reform, teachers were required to work longer hours each day and teach many more students with only a modest raise in the offing as compensation.

Typical of its approach to negotiating with the government, the union addressed the issue of salaries with a well-researched, social science–based study. ANDES leaders assembled an investigative team in 1969 to study the issue of salaries and determine what would constitute a "dignified" lifestyle in light of El Salvador's cost of living. The team was co-led by none other than Mélida Anaya Montes. After a detailed examination of the cost of living, the team determined that an appropriate salary for an unmarried teacher would be 314 colones per month; for a married teacher with three children it would be 645 colones per month. The two figures averaged out to 484 colones per month. At that time, almost no teacher earned anywhere near that amount. The most highly paid category of teachers received on average only 270 colones per month. The investigative team added together every teacher's current salary to arrive at a national average of 213 colones per month, which left the government more than 270 colones per month short.[84]

Naturally, the definition of a "dignified" salary was open to debate. Critics of the teachers' study, for example, could point out that the investigators did not differentiate between urban and rural areas, where the cost of living differed—although most teachers lived and worked in cities. Critics could also accuse teachers of seeking a luxurious lifestyle at the nation's expense. ANDES would respond to such accusations by saying that its definition of "dignified" would place teachers in the middle to lower-middle class of society, in contrast to the current pay scale that was forcing them to live like paupers, constantly on the edge of survival. By comparison, the average wage for skilled workers in urban manufacturing in 1966 was between 113 and 222 colones per month. That same year white-collar workers earned between 204 and 496 colones per month.[85] Comparing these data with the salaries proposed by ANDES indicates that union officials were placing the desired socioeconomic status of teachers closer to that of white-collar workers than to that of skilled laborers. An editorialist in *La Prensa Gráfica* voiced the teachers' complaint about the government's plan to overhaul education without improving teacher pay significantly: "You can't operate a new Cadillac without gasoline."[86] Teachers had many points of contention with the government coming out of the 1968 strike, but salaries and the formula used to determine raises became focal points for a new wave of civic action.

Throughout 1970 the leaders of ANDES consulted their rank-and-file members to determine their views on salaries. The union decided to demand a 35 percent pay raise and the creation of a new formula for raises. The leaders of ANDES compiled these demands in a legislative draft titled Ley de Escalafón del Magisterio Nacional (Teachers' Salary Scale Law), which they presented to the Legislative Assembly in January 1971.[87] Once again, the document was a highly technical, well-researched proposal. Just as in 1967 when ANDES presented the assembly with its IMPRESS proposal, the PCN-dominated assembly promised to consider the legislation but then did nothing for months. ANDES eventually resorted to threatening a strike if the assembly did not move forward. Meanwhile, in an April 1971 broadside, Béneke chastised the teachers and accused them of betraying their students and failing the profession of teaching. As usual, his sarcastic tone aggravated the teachers: "Gentlemen: Is there not among your sympathizers even a first-year law student that could explain to you that a Minister cannot carry out an act that has been suspended by order of the Supreme Court?"[88]

The breaking point for ANDES came when the assembly approved the PCN's counterlegislation, the Ley General de Educación, on July 8, 1971, after a three-week debate. The Ley General de Educación was the comprehensive legislation for the education reform. Its contents addressed almost every aspect of the reform, including a 10 percent raise for teachers and an amended formula for raises, one less generous than ANDES's proposal. The president of the assembly claimed that the Ley General de Educación should be voted on before considering ANDES's proposal because it was more comprehensive and included salaries, so if it were approved, then the issue would be decided.[89] During a contentious session the opposition deputies announced that they would leave the room before the vote, and most of them did. The law did not even get all the votes of the thirty-four PCN deputies; it was approved with twenty-eight votes in favor and ten against.[90] "The law was passed," as an ANDES statement later put it, "with an amazing swiftness and without serious consideration, despite serious objections and criticisms."[91]

At about this moment the UCA published the findings of its massive study of the education reform. It provided a grim assessment of teacher-state relations, laying much of the responsibility at the feet of government and the Ministry of Education. It accused the ministry of being authoritarian and elitist in designing and implementing the 1968 reform. It said the ministry treated teachers as "mediocre employees" rather than as partners, and it defended the teachers by saying that "it is easy to understand" their response before the "Ministry's promotion of itself as omnipotent and its pronounced tendency to marginalize teachers." But true to its nonpartisan standards, the UCA team found fault with the teachers and especially with their union. It said that ANDES had become "close minded" and "blind in its opposition to any initiative put forth by the government." It also said that for all the criticism that ANDES had directed against the government in regard to education, the union offered few concrete alternatives. "Where are the activities by ANDES," the authors asked, "to promote professional excellence through studies, publications, the raising of awareness and models of community service?"[92]

After the vote ANDES spokespersons declared the union to be on indefinite strike. In explaining their reasons for doing so they mentioned teacher pay but situated their decision in broader terms. They set out a point-by-point critique of the Ley General de Educación and in so doing clarified their opposition to the government's overall interpretations of development and the role of education in society. It is here that ANDES accused the government of "continually and profoundly marginalizing education" by "favoring and accentuating the education of elites" at the expense of the rural poor. The union also expressed opposition to the bachilleratos diversificados, to TVE, and to the loans being taken out to finance the various components of the education reform.[93]

The response of rank-and-file teachers to the strike was quick and massive. Apart from the philosophical qualms that they may have had about the reform, teachers felt that it had negatively affected their daily life. Early in 1971 the ministry had begun the policy of expanding enrollments by eliminating middle school tuition. The solution to the rapid increase in the number of students was the policy of double shifts. According to one of the Stanford reports, "The double shifts and increased duties must have had something to do with that event [the strike]."[94] This was clearly an understatement. No labor force takes lightly the sudden imposition of new work rules and an increase in its workload.

The reform's impact on teachers' routines and daily schedules produced particular animosity. "Part of the reform that was highly criticized was the schedule change," said one teacher. "Before, we went [to the school] from eight to twelve and from two to four."[95] Many teachers were required to take additional training classes on Saturdays, ironically via television as an early form of distance learning. One teacher recalled that the additional classes "were not well received; many left the classroom; we were already working Monday thru Friday."[96]

The Stanford team's reports provide a snapshot of the scale of the 1971 strike. They reveal that only five of the forty-five schools they monitored operated as usual. Outside of those schools, "maybe 15 to 25 percent of the classes were carried out, but sometimes with interim teachers and few students."[97]

The government responded to the strike with rhetoric similar to that of 1968. Béneke and the various other government spokespersons defined the strike as illegal. They chastised the teachers for failing to perform their duty and abandoning their students, especially the poorest ones: "The Ministry of Education calls upon the teachers who have not returned to work with respect and tolerance to reflect upon the enormous damage they are causing, not to the government, but to the hundreds of thousands of children of humble means who attend public schools. It is for them, above all else, that they should return to work."[98]

Béneke insisted that the teachers' demands for pay raises had been met by the government, which had generously devoted an additional 20 million colones to the budget for teacher pay and whose new table of raises "favors almost every teacher, but especially those who have many years of service."[99] Throughout the strike, Béneke and other government spokespersons relied on the anticommunist trope of identifying ANDES leaders as

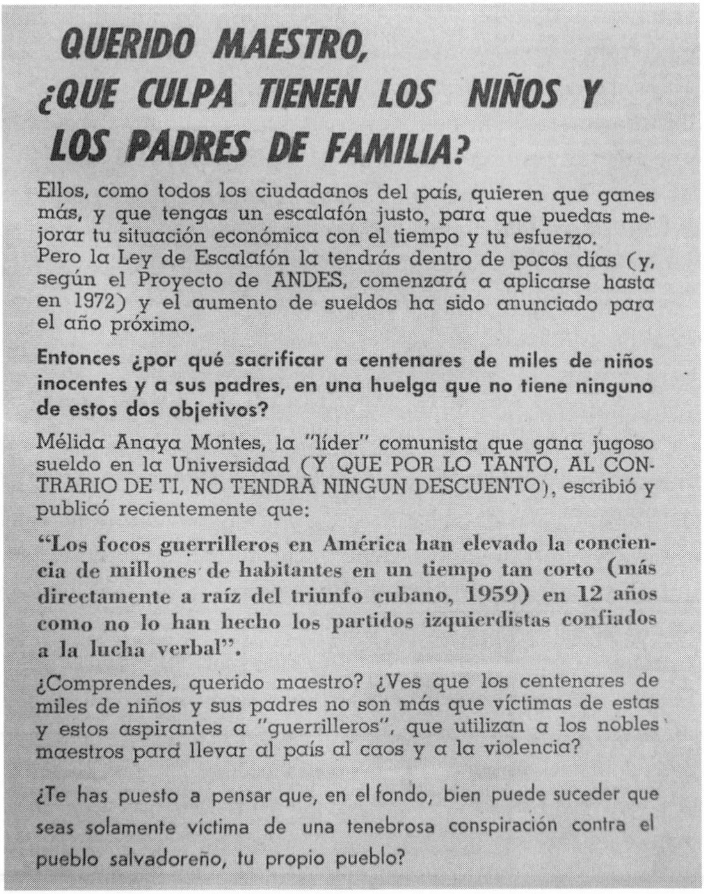

QUERIDO MAESTRO, ¿QUE CULPA TIENEN LOS NIÑOS Y LOS PADRES DE FAMILIA?

Ellos, como todos los ciudadanos del país, quieren que ganes más, y que tengas un escalafón justo, para que puedas mejorar tu situación económica con el tiempo y tu esfuerzo.

Pero la Ley de Escalafón la tendrás dentro de pocos días (y, según el Proyecto de ANDES, comenzará a aplicarse hasta en 1972) y el aumento de sueldos ha sido anunciado para el año próximo.

Entonces ¿por qué sacrificar a centenares de miles de niños inocentes y a sus padres, en una huelga que no tiene ninguno de estos dos objetivos?

Mélida Anaya Montes, la "líder" comunista que gana jugoso sueldo en la Universidad (Y QUE POR LO TANTO, AL CONTRARIO DE TI, NO TENDRA NINGUN DESCUENTO), escribió y publicó recientemente que:

"Los focos guerrilleros en América han elevado la conciencia de millones de habitantes en un tiempo tan corto (más directamente a raíz del triunfo cubano, 1959) en 12 años como no lo han hecho los partidos izquierdistas confiados a la lucha verbal".

¿Comprendes, querido maestro? ¿Ves que los centenares de miles de niños y sus padres no son más que víctimas de estas y estos aspirantes a "guerrilleros", que utilizan a los nobles maestros para llevar al país al caos y a la violencia?

¿Te has puesto a pensar que, en el fondo, bien puede suceder que seas solamente víctima de una tenebrosa conspiración contra el pueblo salvadoreño, tu propio pueblo?

FIGURE 20. The government published advertisements in local newspapers portraying the ANDES leadership as part of a dangerous communist conspiracy. The advertisement above claims that leaders like Mélida Anaya Montes were "aspiring guerrillas that use noble teachers to take the country to violence and chaos." *El Diario de Hoy*, July 9, 1971, 27.

communists who were duping the union's rank and file to serve the interests of Soviet imperialism.

In practical terms, the state turned to coercion quickly and in a heavier form than in 1968. Having learned from 1968 that the teachers' Achilles' heel was salaries, the government immediately declared that all striking teachers would have their salaries deducted for every day of missed work, and it occasionally dangled the carrot of receiving back pay if they returned to work the following day.[100] When those tactics failed to end the strike, the state turned to threats, intimidation, violence, and outright murder. When asked about the government's response to the strike, Julio César Portillo said, "the repression in 1968 was bad, but it really escalated in 1971."[101]

ANDES leaders said they received death threats and saw unmarked cars driving by their homes. They began sleeping at a different house every few nights for security reasons.[102] Meanwhile, out in the streets the army cracked down on demonstrators with tear gas, violence, and mass arrests. At least two teachers and three or more university students were killed. Not surprisingly, the murdered teachers were ANDES leaders, and they disappeared under mysterious, death squad–like circumstances.[103] So fierce was the violence that ANDES spokespersons said, "it seems the government wants the strike to continue so that it can break the teachers' resistance physically."[104] Throughout the strike TVE classes were transmitted regularly as if to show that the system could function without teachers.

Just as the government's response to the strike was more violent than in 1968, the teachers' resolve was stronger. Instead of semi-middle-class bureaucrats marching in quiet, orderly lines as they did in 1968, the striking teachers in 1971 were politicized activists. In one of the more notable events, they occupied the National Palace to pressure the Legislative Assembly to act on the union's proposed Ley de Escalafón.[105] Their street demonstrations often went from orderly marches to rowdy, violent melees. During some of the later demonstrations, teachers supposedly damaged the buildings of various newspapers, the National Palace, and the U.S. Embassy.[106] Throughout the country, striking teachers and supportive community members occupied their local school buildings and turned them into centers of "denunciation, organization, agitation, where all of the teachers in the municipality concentrated to plan activities directed towards students' families, towards the students themselves and to the community in general."[107]

Accompanying the heightened activity in the streets was a more radicalized rhetoric in which teachers identified themselves with workers and peasants. ANDES's secretary general, José Mario López, said that teachers would fight for a labor code that "represents the true interests of the working class in which not only is labor valued, but the laborer is valued as a human being, and peasants have the right to unionize."[108] ANDES received strong support from an already growing opposition movement. Paul Almeida describes how the strike "tapped into the organisational infrastructure support of Catholic labor unions, FUSS, FESTIAVTCES [Federación Sindical de Trabajadores de la Industria de Alimentos, Vestidos, y Similares de El Salvador], public sector unions, high school and public university student associations, the newly formed Jesuit university, oppositional political parties, and even the incipient peasant movement."[109] The strikes mobilized up to fifty thousand people, including teachers and their supporters. To put this figure in context, in 1970 the total labor force involved in manufacturing was around 108,000 workers.[110]

The strike ended after fifty-three days. The results of the strike were similar to those in 1968. The striking teachers had none of their main demands met, and the government's only concession was to foreswear reprisals against striking teachers. But the impact of the strikes cannot be measured in terms of the concessions obtained by the union. In the key decade of 1962–1972, the period when most of the civil society infrastructure that would play a major role in mass mobilization during the late 1970s and early 1980s was created, the teachers' strikes were pivotal moments. ANDES positioned itself "in the vanguard of the class struggle," according to an observer.[111] And if nothing else, Béneke was strategically removed from the Ministry of Education and placed in the Ministry of Foreign Affairs in October 1971.

Just as they had done after the 1968 strike, ANDES leaders took a step back and sized up the consequences of the 1971 strike at their year-end general assembly meeting. They assessed the 1971 strike in much the same way that they had the 1968 strike, as having "limited success in regard to achieving the union's demands" but as an "unqualified success in advancing the socio-political struggle."[112] Despite ANDES's similar assessments of their two great work stoppages, circumstances had changed by 1971, and the outcome of the union's failures would be very different than it had been in 1968. The intransigence of the government in 1968 deepened the union's resolve to stay the course, organize, and continue to press its demands. After the failure of 1971, a sense of frustration within the union began to push a growing radicalism, evident in the rhetoric emerging from the 1971 general assembly meeting. In describing educational television, union leaders referred to it as "an instrument of cultural penetration in the hands of Yankee imperialism," and in describing the new curriculum introduced by the education reform, union leaders used a distinctly class-based language: "The content of the various subject areas is nothing more than the consolidation, through education, of the ideology of the country's dominant classes."[113]

A conservative editorialist, Juan Ulloa, offered his assessment of the 1971 strike and ANDES's emergent radicalism. He described the strike as a "failed communist plan" and said the striking teachers proved that the "communist plague is amongst us." He went on to say that the way to handle communists had been demonstrated by General Martínez in 1932: "[He] shot them."[114] The political polarization of the 1970s had begun in earnest.

The 1972 election

The 1969 war was a moment of relative national unity that ironically set the stage for the hardening of the military regime. As the war highlighted the social problems of the country, the debate around the extent and type of reform necessary to modernize the country became more urgent and controversial. The most conservative elements in the Salvadoran elite felt that the Congress on Agrarian Reform represented a threat to their interests. They reacted by showing the government that they could not be taken for granted. The teachers' strike also prompted an authoritarian response. By the end of President Sánchez Hernández's term it was obvious that the regime was moving away from the political liberalization started by Rivera.

The presidential election of February 22, 1972, exposed the depth of the divisions within the PCN, within the army, and between the PCN and conservative business groups. The governing party almost lost control of the situation and reacted by abandoning any resemblance of commitment to democratic practices. The candidate of the PCN was Sánchez Hernández's handpicked successor, his personal secretary Col. Arturo Armando Molina. There were two other conservative candidates whose participation in the electoral process can be directly linked to the consequences of the Congress on Agrarian Reform. José Antonio Rodríguez Porth, the vocal spokesman for business interests during the congress, was the presidential candidate for the PPS. But Rodríguez Porth was not conservative enough for coffee planters from the western region. They decided to support the candidacy of the founder of ORDEN, José Alberto Medrano, who had started a new political party called Frente Unido Democrático Independiente (FUDI). His running mate was Antonio Salaverría, a prominent planter who had previously supported the PCN.

The parties to the left of the PCN had learned from their mistakes in the presidential election of 1967, when a scattered opposition was no match for the PCN electoral machine. To prepare for the 1972 election they formed a coalition, the National Opposition Union (UNO), that unified a variety of centrist and leftist parties, including a front for the still-clandestine Communist Party. UNO's candidate was the popular Christian Democrat and former mayor of San Salvador José Napoleón Duarte. He was vilified by his opponents as a communist, and a vigorous propaganda campaign was launched to portray him as such before voters. One of the right's tactics was to rely upon a tried-and-true method that it had used back in the 1967 election—drum up images of the 1932 uprising and then try to connect them to contemporary candidates. The version of 1932 that the right utilized for this campaign in 1972 was even more fantastical and gruesome that the one from 1967. It described horrific crimes and abuses being perpetrated by the rebels against innocent citizens throughout western El Salvador. It then drew a direct link between those crimes and the candidacy of Duarte, accusing him of having said that if he did not win the election, "the hour of the machetes has arrived." [115]

All objective accounts indicate that Duarte won the election despite the unrelenting propaganda campaign. Only blatant fraud at the final hour gave the victory to the PCN.[116] In response to the fraud, the opposition organized a massive demonstration on February 24. Calls for a general strike, however, did not meet with success. On March 25 a reformist faction in the military launched a coup. For a few hours they seemed to have the upper hand. The leader of the rebellion, Col. Benjamín Mejía, asked Duarte to support the movement, and he did so with a radio address that called on the citizenship to build barricades to stop the advances of progovernment forces.[117] After his radio address Duarte became the most visible leader of the coup even though he had nothing to do with its organization. The coup plotters even managed to arrest President Sánchez Hernández briefly before loyalist forces regained control. The confrontation claimed at least one hundred lives. After the coup failed, the government arrested Duarte and sent him into exile after three days of captivity. His captors treated him roughly. When his wife met him in Guatemala, she found him "with face lesions, a very damaged eye, and a back covered with bruises." [118]

Thereafter, the democratic opening closéd. President Molina was inaugurated on July 1, and on July 19 he ordered the military occupation of the UES and replaced its authorities with people he trusted. His action was a demonstration to the right that he was serious about the "communist menace" (conservatives considered the university to be a nest of subversives) and to everyone else that he was in charge.[119] He defined the university occupation as a precondition to "creating a climate of peace" for his projects.[120]

The liberalization of the political system that had been introduced by President Rivera was over, but the modernizing zeal of the PCN was alive and well and manifesting itself in new development projects. The strategy of modernizing from above found its fullest expression in the projects promoted by Molina. Before taking office he gathered a group of trusted friends, including Béneke, to devise a package of signature projects for his administration.[121] The new president was persuaded that a violent uprising was almost inevitable without rapid modernization. "I assure you that we still have time, but not much time," he said in his inaugural address, referring to the dangers of political upheaval.[122] The effect of Molina's modernization projects deepened the political polarization that had begun with the teachers' strikes and the Congress on Agrarian Reform.

Cerrón Grande—1972–1976

President Molina (1972–1977) adopted infrastructural development and electrification as critical components of El Salvador's path to modernity.[123] His government decided to promote cheap, renewable domestic electricity as a cornerstone of economic development. Domestic power would reduce El Salvador's reliance on foreign petroleum, and most importantly it would promote industrialization. In the early 1970s El Salvador was running up against the limits of production from older dams and a pair of thermal generators. Population growth alone would soon consume the remaining surplus, to say nothing of what would happen if industrialization increased. Without an infusion of cheap, reliable power, the government's plan for modernization was doomed.

Molina announced his solution to the electrification problem in August 1972, shortly after coming to office. His plan was to build the nation's largest dam to date, Cerrón Grande, in a valley along the Lempa River roughly in the center of the country, at the eastern end of Cuscatlán Department, approximately twenty miles upstream from the existing Fifth of November Dam.[124] Molina later claimed that the idea of Cerrón Grande had originated back in the 1950s under the prompting of Victor de Sola, one of the richest industrialists in the country, who was known to support modernizing reform. In Molina's own words, "Don Victor [de Sola], for his part, solicited an urgent meeting with him [President Osorio] on his third day in office because CEL [the government's electricity commission] believed it necessary to construct a dam to generate electricity. It was from this meeting that the decision was made to move forward with the Cerrón Grande dam project."[125] Although the actual decision to move forward with that plan was delayed until Molina's administration, the idea to build Cerrón Grande represented a convergence of interests between the PCN and a modernizing, industrial elite represented by de Sola, who coincidentally headed the government's electricity commission—Hydroelectric Executive Committee of the Lempa River (CEL).

Cerrón Grande would take nearly five years to build at a cost of more than 200 million colones. Because the watershed behind the proposed dam was shallow, the new reservoir would stretch back nearly twenty miles and cover more than one hundred square miles of land, including more than five thousand hectares of prime agricultural land. The majority of the cost of the project would be covered by loans from the Inter-American Development Bank. Design and construction would be carried out by a North American firm, Harza Engineering, in conjunction with CEL. The plan submitted jointly by Harza and CEL claimed that Cerrón Grande would generate power for one hundred years before silting up and would pay for itself in just over twenty years.[126]

While the government touted the benefits of Cerrón Grande, it acknowledged the risks, including the reliance on foreign loans and foreign advisors and the loss of land to the new reservoir. A major concern was the loss of agricultural land and its impact upon the undetermined thousands of people who lived on it. On flatland plains at the western end of the future lake, a few members of the Salvadoran elite grew nearly 25 percent of the nation's sugar crop and employed thousands of seasonal workers. Farther east, toward the proposed dam, thousands of peasants eked out a precarious but sustained existence through farming and fishing. The government declared its intention to remunerate landowners for the loss of their land and peasants for the loss of their homes and belongings and to pay for their relocation costs. Such expenses, Molina argued, were small in comparison to the long-term benefits of the dam.[127]

Molina's enthusiasm for Cerrón Grande was not universally shared. Some wealthy landowners who stood to lose their land adamantly opposed the project, regardless of the government's promise of indemnification. The Orellana family, which owned a large sugar plantation called Hacienda Colima, led the charge. Along with a few other wealthy landowners they created an organization called the Commission of Landowners and Affected Populations, which they used as a platform to lobby against the dam. The Orellanas were a

El Presidente Molina en una de sus giras de Gobierno Móvil

FIGURE 21. President Molina adopted a populist style and traveled around the
country in "gobierno móvil" (mobile government) tours promoting his
grand land reform and dam projects. Departamento de Relaciones
Públicas de Casa Presidencial, *El Salvador*, 1973, 101.

well-educated family whose younger members included highly trained engineers. They commissioned a technical report that refuted the government's
and Harza Engineering's claims about the dam's benefits. The commission
and its members also relied upon old-fashioned patron-client tactics to mobilize workers and peasants against the dam, giving their movement a populist
image.[128] Waldo Chávez Velasco, the PCN's propaganda chief, has claimed
that landowners and the commission spent more than 400,000 colones on
their advertising campaign against the dam; he claimed he was given half that
amount by the government to launch a countercampaign.[129]

The lobbying efforts of the Orellanas and the commission failed to generate a groundswell of right-wing opposition to Cerrón Grande. They were
unable to convince enough members of the conservative business sector that
Cerrón Grande was a bad idea. Many landowners and business leaders, like
Victor de Sola, shared Molina's view that the long-term benefits of domestic
power generation outweighed the short-term loss of land, even prime sugar
land owned by fellow elites.

Progressives and leftists offered a more sweeping critique of both
Cerrón Grande and the government's version of modernization. The main
voice of opposition came from the Jesuits at UCA. One of their main complaints about the project was the government's lack of information about

the region to be affected. The rich landowners and their lawyers had ample ability to voice their complaints and detail their losses, but the peasant majority did not. According to UCA spokespersons, the government and Harza Engineering were advancing blindly without sociological or environmental data. The government was so anxious to get construction underway that it did not even wait for the results of an environmental impact report, which the World Bank managed to produce one year later. Even at that late date, the author of the report noted the government's total ignorance of the region. "It is frightening," he wrote, "that construction can be permitted to start even before the number of people affected [by the dam] is known."[130]

Recognizing that it was impossible to conduct an effective cost-benefit analysis of the project in the absence of sound data, the Jesuits launched a massive sociological and environmental survey of the region to be inundated by the reservoir. In a remarkably short period of time, UCA assembled a team of engineers, sociologists, and economists and sent nearly one hundred student volunteers into the highly politicized region to gather survey data. The effort may have been improvised, but the team asked the right questions, and it had acted quickly. It produced a report of more than one hundred pages just weeks after Molina had announced the plan to build the dam.[131]

The authors of the UCA report acknowledged El Salvador's desperate need for power and recognized the government's desire to solve the problem as part of a broader developmental plan. But their initial evidence showed that the human and financial costs of the project far outweighed its benefits. They said moving forward without more extensive analysis would be dangerously reckless.

One of the most debated aspects of the dam project was the number of people to be affected. The government's initial report claimed that only nine hundred families, or roughly forty-five hundred people, would be affected. Even that figure represented a serious problem for the government. But soon thereafter the government revised the number of people affected to ten thousand. The UCA team said that both figures were way too low and estimated conservatively that forty-five thousand people would be directly affected by the dam.

The UCA's investigation team produced some of the most in-depth data on the region to date.[132] The survey revealed that the peasant communities there were poor but economically viable. Most residents lived in soundly built adobe homes that they had paid for themselves. The average family valued their home and belongings at more than 5,000 colones (US$2,000 in 1970 dollars), which was nearly ten times more than the government had promised to pay each family for loss and relocation. Most families had lived in the region for many years and had developed a sense of belonging. In the words of the report, "They [the residents] are poor, in the sense that they live hand-to-mouth and are unable to generate savings or incur great costs. . . . But neither are they without work . . . and it would be lamentable to destroy this model without creating an equivalent solution."[133]

The UCA team indicated that the government's lack of information guaranteed that its indemnification program would be insufficient and would result in economic destitution, social malaise, and political opposition. It pointed out the government's promise to pay large, capitalized landowners market value for their land. Perhaps the most foreboding revelation in the UCA report was the expressed willingness of survey respondents to actively oppose the dam project. More than 80 percent of respondents expressed an intention to resist the project and demand fair payment. A portion of respondents were even willing to say to the student surveyors that violence might be necessary. Only the most obtuse reader of the UCA report would have failed to see that the government had a dangerous situation on its hands.

The World Bank's environmental impact report the following year echoed UCA's findings and lobbed another bombshell at the government's claims. The author of the report was Robert Goodland, an ecologist from the Carey Arboretum of the New York Botanical Garden. Although he supported the idea of Cerrón Grande, he strongly opposed the government's specific plan. According to his summary, "if it proceeds in its present state, the overall result to the country will be strongly negative."[134]

Goodland noted that the dense population of the region had already stressed the carrying capacity of the lands above the river to the point that severe soil erosion was occurring and silt was building up in the existing downstream dam, the Fifth of November Dam. He said the proposed Cerrón Grande Dam would catch most of the existing runoff and would silt up well in advance of the government's claim of one hundred years. The silting problem would be exacerbated if the government failed to implement an effective relocation program in conjunction with an aggressive reforestation project. He predicted that silting would curtail power production in the new dam in less than fifty years, perhaps in as few as twenty-five years, almost before the dam could pay for itself. He called the plan to pay 500 colones to each peasant family "grossly inadequate" and noted that the government needed to create "economically viable and socially sustainable communities."[135]

Goodland considered the loss of five thousand hectares of good farmland to the dam to be "an expensively large area for a small country." He concluded that the only viable solution was a land reform that would transfer underutilized lands held by large, wealthy landowners to land-starved peasants. Land reform would reduce pressures on the watershed and avoid alienating thousands of poor citizens. Unfamiliar with the power of the Salvadoran landed elite, he described his proposed solution as "relatively simple and inexpensive."[136]

Goodland based his opposition to the government's plan on a simple foundation: "the World Bank's obligation [is] to promote development. The benefits of development are usually addressed at the national level but should extend to each individual. The net result of development must therefore benefit all; people are the country's most precious resource."[137] Goodland said Cerrón Grande failed to meet his and the World Bank's standard for development and if the government proceeded without implementing his recommended changes, the project would fail to achieve its developmental goals.

UCA's criticism struck deeper. The UCA team argued that the government was employing a narrow and self-defeating definition of development and therein setting itself and the country up for failure. The UCA team accused the government of embracing a "current in economic thought that understands 'development' as increasing gross domestic product per capita."[138] Of particular concern was that the government's cost-benefit analysis used market prices and ignored social costs not reflected in such prices. On the financial side, the UCA team identified expenses that were likely to occur but which the government did not list. It also noted the opportunity costs lost in not seeking out alternatives, such as collaborating with neighboring countries rather than pursuing hydroelectrification from a narrow, nationalistic stance.

On the social side, UCA basically accused the government of sacrificing the goodwill of tens of thousands of its citizens in pursuit of a modernization scheme that defined success solely by economic indicators. The UCA report insisted that while the peasants' material possessions were small in gross economic terms, they represented a lifetime of work and accumulation. Also, the peasants' loss of community would create emotional turmoil, and the process of relocation and rebuilding would be laden with stress and fear. Almost all of the peasants surveyed by UCA believed they were going to be worse off than before. In the words of the report, failure to provide

FIGURE 22. Toward the end of the dry season, in February or March, the level of Lake Suchitlán falls low enough to expose the cement foundations of household sinks (*pilas*) of former communities along the Lempa River that were inundated by the building of the Cerrón Grande Dam. Photo taken by Erik Ching, March 2008.

resolution of these problems "is absolutely inexcusable and will merit the most severe protests."[139] In short, the government was creating a powder keg.

The UCA report offered an alternative definition of development that, in concise terms, emphasized human dignity and community solidarity: "The object of development in our conceptualization is to bring about human dignity in the lived conditions of all people, to eliminate and replace with alternatives the structures that oppress human beings and prevent them from personally achieving a self-realization."[140]

Surprisingly, President Molina agreed with some of UCA's criticisms and promised to resolve the problems. In a speech about Cerrón Grande, he referenced the UCA report and outlined a series of solutions, including "organizing peasants in agricultural cooperatives, facilitating credit, technical assistance, health, education and housing, as well as the other aspects of an improved life, with an ultimate goal of assuring them permanent work in the new locations and a genuine improvement in their living conditions." [141] To achieve this end, Molina created the Commission on Relocation and Integral Development of Cerrón Grande and placed at its head Felix "Tato" Osegueda, an architect and the brother of Lino Osegueda, a close collaborator of Enrique Alvarez in the ministry of agriculture. [142] President Molina visited the region himself in response to requests from Father Alas, the priest who had been kidnapped during the 1970 land reform congress, and peasant organizations demonstrating in front of the presidential residence in San Salvador. Molina toured the region in the company of Father Alas. Together they went to some of the more remote and affected areas to meet with community representatives. Alas claims in his memoir that the tour affected Molina and strengthened his resolve to address the problems. [143]

In his memoir Alas also describes the earnestness of some members of the PCN government. He says people like Felix Osegueda and Enrique Alvarez represented a reformist tendency within the PCN that wanted to do right by the peasants. He describes a meeting with Osegueda shortly after he was charged with heading up the Commission on Relocation. He says Osegueda took his job seriously and had drawn up a comprehensive plan for indemnification and relocation, which included a land reform component, based on his prior experience with agrarian reform in Allende's Chile. The commission organized meetings with peasant communities throughout the region to explain the process. One of these meetings was held at Alas's agricultural school in mid-1973. The clarity and determination with which the peasants expressed their concerns left an indelible impression on Alas, who described the events vividly in his memoir thirty years later. [144]

An equally profound impression of the Cerrón Grande experiment was left on Francisco Altschul. He served on Osegueda's Commission on Relocation between 1974 and 1975 as a young architect and described his experience in a 2009 interview. He said he joined the six-member commission at the request of Osegueda, who had been his professor at the UES. Osegueda convinced Altschul that the commission represented a "unique opportunity" to improve El Salvador. Osegueda envisioned relocating peasants in concentrated villages where the government could more easily provide services such as water, electricity, sewers, and schools. In this effort to re-create the rural society of the nineteenth century, the peasants' farmlands would be located outside the villages and would be owned communally. [145]

Unfortunately for Osegueda, the peasants did not share his vision. According to Altschul, "the people, the peasants themselves did not accept this idea. . . . they resisted the whole notion of relocation." They may have lived in communities, but they did not live and work communally, so it was alien for them to consider living in concentrated villages far from their place of origin in strangely designed, government-built homes according to communally dictated guidelines. On the south side of the Lempa River, where community organization and Christian Base communities had a strong foothold, the resistance to the relocation plan was particularly stout.[146]

In addition to opposition from the peasantry, Osegueda and his relocation team ran up against opposition from hardliners within the PCN government. The government body charged with overseeing the building of Cerrón Grande, CEL, was a powerful institution that took pride in its technocratic ethos. It was efficient, well-funded, highly technical, and well-staffed. But its administrators defined their mission as building infrastructure, not providing social services. "Their interest was in building the dam, not in taking care of people," said Altschul. "They [CEL's managers] really didn't get it, they didn't get what it meant to people living in these areas. They deal with numbers and pipes and cement and steel and generators, not with people."[147]

The mere creation of the Commission on Relocation fueled conflict between conservatives and reformers within the PCN. The idea of relocation had been sanctioned by the highest levels of government and was under the direct supervision of the executive secretary of CONAPLAN, Atilio Viéytez. That Viéytez was in charge of CONAPLAN in 1972 was enough to rile up the conservatives within CEL. He had been a delegate for the UCA at the Congress on Agrarian Reform in 1970.[148] In addition to feeling like the relocation program had been imposed on them, the executive director of CEL, Benjamín Valiente, and his fellow conservative managers also opposed Osegueda on ideological grounds. They considered him too liberal and believed his relocation plan was a trial run at land reform.

It quickly became apparent that the reformist wing within the PCN was outflanked by more conservative sectors that dismissed the concerns of the peasantry. For his part, President Molina was either unable or unwilling to stand in their way, and so the necessary funding and political support for relocation did not materialize. Altschul resigned from the Commission on Relocation in 1975, and Osegueda followed him shortly thereafter. Reform-minded functionaries in other branches of government had been resigning as well, such as Enrique Alvarez as minister of agriculture in 1973. Ignoring the warning signs, Molina pressed forward with dam construction. As UCA and the World Bank predicted, and as the peasants feared, the government's

FIGURE 23. The National Guard was a permanent, intimidating presence in the countryside, as seen here with sugarcane workers in a newspaper image from 1973. *El Diario de Hoy*, February 28, 1973, 1.

indemnification program proved totally inadequate. Peasant residents who lived through the process claimed in interviews that the government offered indemnification for a very short period of time and if peasants failed to collect payment within that time, they lost their opportunity forever. As an interviewee from one of the affected communities, Copapayo Viejo, claimed, "they didn't try very hard to tell us when the time for payment would happen."

"Neither," she said, "did they provide any compensation for community structures, like churches and schools, and what they did offer to pay us didn't come close to replacing our losses."[149] The government made modest attempts at relocating some communities, but those failed miserably, as the process involved little more than dumping people on infertile land with minimal infrastructural support. And so, in advance of rising waters, peasants did exactly what Goodland had predicted: they climbed farther up the hillsides and tried to scrape out a living on land that was inappropriate for agriculture.

In some areas popular organizations were already well established. Many in the region had their first taste of political activism with the teachers' strikes. In 1971 the town of Suchitoto and its surrounding area, bordering the reservoir created by the dam, emerged as a strong source of peasant support for the 1971 teachers' strike. In response to the arrest of a visiting teachers' delegation to that city by local police, hundreds (and by some estimates thousands) of peasants surrounded the jail until the jailed teachers were released.[150] Another delegation of peasants from the surrounding region came to San Salvador to support the striking teachers in mid-July. Out of fear of police reprisals they took up residence for the night in the private Jesuit high school, the Externado de San José, before joining demonstrating teachers the following morning.[151] In a 2009 interview, a peasant organizer who lived in the region at the time, Fidel Recinos (nom de guerre Raúl Hércules), stated that the activism of ANDES in 1968 and 1971 had been a great inspiration to him and his fellow peasants during their incipient organizational phase.[152] In places like Suchitoto, with a history of activism, the dam radicalized people's views. Where mass organization had been minimal or nonexistent, the dam inspired people to mobilize for the first time. Recinos described the impact of the dam succinctly: "The dam came like an igniter that heated up or exploded the social situation . . . [and resulted in] a more radicalized form of struggle." He went on to say that "the phenomenon of armed, guerrilla struggle" found fertile ground for recruitment as a result of "this sentiment of frustration that had been brought on by the dam." He joined a clandestine peasants' organization and began preparing for armed resistance.[153]

Both Recinos and Father Alas described community meetings and seminars beginning in 1974 in which peasants considered their response to the dam project. Alas said that in the meetings he discouraged peasants from opposing the construction of the dam, which seemed a foregone conclusion, and instead focusing their efforts on demanding fair treatment from the government.[154] He claimed that peasant mobilization around the dam project

provided the impetus for the creation of the Unified Popular Action Front
(FAPU), one of the main mass organizations to emerge in El Salvador in
the 1970s and the one that eventually became a front organization for the
National Resistance (RN) guerrilla movement.

Alas said that he and the peasants decided to bolster their demands by
linking their grievances to those of other organized movements throughout
the country, particularly the teachers' union, as well as other labor unions
and students at the two universities in San Salvador. Alas and some peasant representatives organized an initial meeting with ANDES leaders José
Mario López and Mélida Anaya Montes. That meeting led to future organizational reunions involving teachers, students, and peasants. Soon a strong
organizational impulse emerged that linked peasants around Suchitoto to
the urban movements of teachers, students, and laborers. Alas described
his surprise at the organizational fervor of one meeting that resulted in the
founding of FAPU, held at the Basílica el Sagrado Corazón in San Salvador
in mid-1974:

> There were at least 200 people at the meeting, among them peasants,
> teachers, students and workers. I offered my perspective, which
> Mario [López] amplified and which led to a broader discussion
> about the objectives and activities we should seek to develop, and
> the organization that would be necessary to advance our cause. For
> me all of this was a surprise. It was evident that I found myself in an
> unfamiliar environment, a much more politicized environment,
> filled with ideological discussion. . . . A student from the National
> University proposed that we found the Frente de Acción Popular
> Unificada (FAPU). The proposal was put to a vote and approved.[155]

Eventually, FAPU fell victim to the ideological factionalism that plagued
El Salvador's left during the latter half of the 1970s.[156] But the discontent
and organizational zeal that led to its founding did not dissipate. The most
lasting impact of FAPU was the bond between rural peasants and urban
students and workers. In time, that bond would assume revolutionary
implications as the entire region around Lake Suchitlán (the reservoir created by the new dam) emerged as a recruiting base for militant opposition.
The two main guerrilla organizations that would eventually establish themselves there, the RN and the FPL, both had a strong involvement by teachers
and peasants.[157]

Land Reform and the Debate over Modernization—1976

The PCN's last attempt at land reform before it was thrown out of office in 1979 occurred in 1976. The targeted area was fifty-nine thousand hectares of cotton land in the eastern coastal plain. Part of the money to pay land-owners for their expropriated land was provided by USAID. Landowners launched a vociferous and multipronged campaign against the government through their organizations ANEP and the Agrarian Front of the Eastern Region (FARO). One of President Molina's public relations advisors said that 15 percent of the budget of all advertising agencies was devoted to fight the project.[158] Conservative opposition even included death squad attacks against PCN functionaries working on agrarian issues.[159] Ultimately, the landowners forced President Molina to cancel the project and renege on his oft-repeated promise that "Agrarian Transformation will advance without question and without vacillation."[160]

Some of the supporters of the PCN's 1976 land reform experiment had attended the 1970 Congress on Agrarian Reform and advocated in favor of redistribution. This included representatives from the UCA and the Christian Democratic Party. Not surprisingly, in the intervening six years they had not changed their minds about the need for land reform, nor had they altered their disagreements with conservatives over the definition of modernization. The UCA, for example, continued to dispute the landowners' claim that redistribution would cause a sharp decline in production. Writing in favor of the 1976 reform, UCA representatives said that "the argument about productivity seems to ignore the fact that people who live and die cultivating soil know how to make it produce, particularly if they receive technical, credit and commercialization assistance." They expressed their support for the PCN plan by saying they "recognize and applaud" the government's attempt to "orient the existing factors of production toward . . . satisfying the dramatic needs of the oppressed minorities."[161] Similarly, the Christian Democrats explained that their deputies in the assembly voted in favor of the legislation, making the 1976 project possible because their party "always has and always will support profound, rapid and democratic changes to the unjust structures of our society."[162]

But much had changed in El Salvador between 1970 and 1976. Society was more polarized by radicals on both the left and the right. On the right, formal and informal security forces increased the repression against alleged communists and subversives. Death squads and paramilitaries were becoming more active and menacing. Meanwhile, the army had perpetrated multiple massacres of civilians in the name of repressing communism. For example, in 1974 security forces repressed peasants involved in a dispute with a landlord in the hamlet of La Cayetana. Six peasants were killed and thirteen "disappeared." In 1975 the National Guard attacked a student demonstration, killing at least thirty-seven.[163] On the left, four distinct guerrilla organizations had formed and were actively operating by 1976. Similarly, various mass front organizations had come into existence, counting tens of thousands of people as members. Some of the actions of the left terrified the upper classes, like the kidnapping and murder of prominent capitalists. This practice began with the case of Ernesto Regalado Dueñas, the young heir to two of the richest families in the country. He was abducted and subsequently killed in 1971. The kidnappings continued throughout the 1970s.[164] All remnants of the political opening of the Rivera administration and the early years of the Sánchez Hernández administration disappeared. By 1976 the PCN controlled all fifty-four deputies in the assembly and all 261 mayor's offices.

Back in 1970 the PCN's land reform initiative generated initial credibility with a broad array of progressives and leftists. But by 1976 almost all of these allies had abandoned support for the PCN. ANDES opposed the 1976 reform as a demagogic political stunt by the PCN to generate support for the 1977 presidential election.[165] Even the Christian Democrats worried that the 1976 reform was nothing more than a "smoke screen" for the PCN "to conceal its numerous acts of corruption."[166] The newer, radicalized organizations totally opposed the PCN. In its analysis of the 1976 reform, one of the front organizations, FAPU, called on its supporters to remember that the government had perpetrated "the massacres of 30 July, 'La Cayetana,' 'Tres Calles,' 'Santa Barbara,' etc., and that this same government had militarily occupied the University."[167] Another front, the BPR, identified the land reform as "counterrevolutionary" and encouraged its supporters to reject it entirely. The BPR even took fellow progressives and leftists to task for not taking a hard enough stance against the PCN. In response to the UCA's support for the reform, the BPR expressed its "total disagreement" because the UCA's "idealistic vision of class struggle aids the Military Tyranny."[168] When President Molina ultimately reversed his position and abandoned the reform, what little support the PCN had among leftists and progressives evaporated completely.

The presidential election in 1977 offered a repeat performance of 1972. UNO put forth a candidate only to witness the PCN remaining in power through widespread fraud, ensuring the victory of its candidate, Gen. Carlos Humberto Romero, the former minister of defense and the preferred choice of landowners.[169]

The reasons for the PCN's reversal and its decision to end the political reforms are multiple. The 1972 election showed that a core element of hardliners within the PCN were in control and had no intention of relinquishing power. Certainly the variety of polarizing events in preceding years helped them overwhelm more moderate voices. Those events included but were not limited to a surge in labor mobilization after 1967, the advance of liberation theology after the bishops' conference in Medellin in 1968, the war with Honduras in 1969, the emergence of the first guerrilla organization in 1970, and the polarization brought about by the debate over land reform in 1970. In hindsight, the 1972 election proved to be a watershed. When faced with the choice of relinquishing power and advancing its modernizing agenda, the PCN chose dictatorship and repression.[170]

Modernization theorists believed that economic development, social modernization, and political liberation were complementary and mutually reinforcing. Many of those theorists insisted that a local modernizing elite was necessary for any effort at modernization to succeed, and they even considered Latin American armies capable of fulfilling that role.

The early version of PCN reforms seemed to support the most optimistic vision of modernization theorists. President Rivera launched economic reforms in consultation with international development experts. He also began to open up the political system. Ironically, the resistance that Rivera and his successors incited with their modernizing schemes encouraged them to retract political liberalization.

Modernization projects had a central goal of stopping the advance of communism. PCN leaders made this goal explicit in their public pronouncements, particularly when they talked about land reform. In this regard modernization theory reinforced a strategy that was well established in the history of El Salvador's military regime—anticommunist reformism.

Initially PCN reformers received the benefit of the doubt from those who were likely to oppose them, including liberal intellectuals and members of the new opposition political parties. But as resistance to the PCN projects grew, the government's tendency was to stay the course, ignore objections, and label critics as enemies and threats to the nation. Deviations from government dictates were met with increasing levels of repression.

The two main projects launched in the 1970s, the Cerrón Grande Dam and land reform, followed a destabilizing and all-too-familiar pattern. First, governing elites conceived of the projects with the help of foreign advisors but without consulting members of local civil society. Then the projects provoked intra-right debates over the meaning of modernization and the appropriate role of government in achieving it. Once the government began putting its plans into action, it disregarded the opinions of the common citizens who were going to be most affected by the projects and who were facing increasing economic difficulties as the 1970s progressed. As the projects alienated more people, like teachers and the former inhabitants of the area flooded by Cerrón Grande, resistance to the government grew. The government interpreted that resistance as being inspired by obscure subversive forces and responded with repression. The people who resisted then faced two options: surrender and accept or persist and resist.

The two attempts at land reform in the 1970s barely got off the ground. The government learned that it could not impose land reform over the objections of conservative sectors in the same authoritarian manner as it had imposed other projects. Alienated landowners resisted the PCN with everything they had, including alliances with conservative elements in the army and the PCN and eventually by funding and promoting death squads. With each reform project and each presidential cycle, the varying stakeholders in El Salvador grew further apart as society became more polarized and violent.

CHAPTER 6

"The Most Thoroughly Studied
Educational Technology Project
in the World"

~≈℮

Educational television and the educational reform are controlled
by the imperialists to steer the thoughts of the Salvadoran youth to
fulfill their nefarious interests.
—ANDES 21 de Junio, 1971*

The Salvadoran experience points to a promising role for the mass
media in resolving the Third World's pressing educational problems.
—John K. Mayo, Robert C. Hornik, and
Emile G. McAnany, 1976**

✟ IN 1979 WILBUR SCHRAMM, SEVENTY-TWO YEARS OLD AND LIVING IN
semiretirement in Hawaii, sat down to write a document for UNESCO. It was
a reflection on his pathbreaking book *Mass Media and National Development.* The finished product proved to be an extraordinary essay, poignant for
its self-criticism. The title of the first section says it all: "The Passing of the
Old Paradigm." The first few sentences set the tone for the rest of the work:
"I have just had the humbling experience of rereading a book I wrote 17 years
ago." He continued: "I should've been more skeptical about the applicability
of the Western model of development. I should've paid more attention to the

problem of integrating mass media with local activity. Above all, I should've given more thought than I did to the social requirements and uncertainties of development, and in particular the cultural differences that make development almost necessarily different, culture to culture, country to country." Schramm acknowledged that "educational television did not work miracles," neither in American Samoa nor anywhere else.[1] He surmised that educational television failed because of the difficulty of adjusting to local variations in audience and national objectives.

Schramm did not include the Salvadoran "pilot project" in his analysis, even though he and his students had researched it thoroughly. So it is fair to ask if his critical reassessment applied to El Salvador as well. Did the results of the Béneke reforms justify the enormous investment of resources and the controversies and conflicts it generated? Lots of different stakeholders tried to answer that question, including international foreign aid professionals and academics, Salvadoran civil servants, union activists, intellectuals, and members of the education community. They arrived at vastly different answers, usually dictated by whether they assessed the reform in a political context or concentrated solely on its technical features. The implications of the different approaches—framing the evaluation in political or apolitical terms—were profound in late 1970s El Salvador. By that time the country was on a steady political decline, with the prior decade having produced two fraudulent presidential elections, the emergence of guerrilla groups, a surge in right-wing paramilitary murders, and a general increase in political polarization and violence. In the midst of all that, the education reform itself had become intensely politicized.

In this chapter we compare and contrast the various assessments of the education reform made during the 1970s. In doing so, we learn about educational outcomes as well as the profound debate over modernity that sat behind all discussions of the reform. We look at the assessments in chronological order, allowing us to situate them in their appropriate political context. The first section looks at assessments done in the early 1970s by international academics and aid agencies, mainly reports commissioned by USAID as part of its efforts to determine whether El Salvador's "pilot project" was replicable in other poor countries. Those reports were highly technical and narrowly focused on the classroom itself, avoiding the broader political context. The next two sections look at Salvadoran assessments from the late 1970s, which were highly attuned to domestic politics. Some of the assessors used the discussion of the education reform to criticize the ideological foundations of the PCN regime. The fourth section looks at Schramm's 1979 self-assessment, which, ironically, coincided with the Salvadorans' discussions. The fifth and sixth sections of the chapter show that as TVE was being abandoned in Salvadoran classrooms, it remained alive and well in U.S. reports and analyses that clung to the modernization narrative.

Assessments from International Agencies and U.S. Academics

At the end of the Sánchez Hernández administration in 1972 the Academy for Educational Development, serving as a subcontractor for USAID, hired Dr. Richard E. Speagle, associate professor of finance at Drexel University, to write a report on the costs of educational television.[2] The research and writing of the report were done during a particularly tense period in El Salvador. Speagle was collecting data at the time of the 1972 presidential election, when the PCN committed blatant fraud and had to fend off a violent coup by reformist officers to remain in power.[3]

Speagle's task was narrowly defined. As would be expected for that type of consulting assignment, his final report provided no indication that he conducted research in the midst of a profound crisis when the government's survival was uncertain. Instead, his report focused on the costs of the reform and revealed the hopes of the government and USAID that educational technology would provide a quality education to a large number of students at relatively low cost. He concluded that from 1966 to 1970 educational television consumed about one-half of the reform's total expenditures, US$3.1 million out of a total of US$6.2 million. Most of the non-television-related expenses were consumed by retraining junior high school teachers (US$2.7 million), expanding and reorganizing supervision at the primary and secondary levels, and printing and distributing new textbooks.[4]

Speagle claimed that in the future educational television would reduce the costs of instruction throughout the system. He estimated that television had increased the cost per student by about 15 percent, but he was optimistic that increasing enrollment would result in a net reduction in cost per student.[5] Television was also used in teacher training, with more than nine hundred secondary school teachers having received retraining through televised classes. This resulted in a significant savings compared to traditional methods. According to Speagle, the teachers' use of the new, pedagogically innovative workbooks and teaching guides in class made the act of teaching with television the functional equivalent of in-service training.

With cutting costs as his priority, Speagle made various recommendations to the Salvadoran government about educational television. First and foremost, he said it should increase the number of students in classrooms with television, ideally to about fifty in each class. In his words, "teaching by ITV [TVE] alone would be cheaper than ordinary classroom instruction when the audience goes above about 20,000 viewers per program annually at the junior-high level." He also pointed out that one option would be to do away with the teacher completely, at least in some circumstances. The teacher could be replaced by a "paraprofessional," who could receive a lower salary than a teacher. The proposal was troublesome because it was difficult to figure out who the paraprofessionals would be. "It's not very clear how this would work in El Salvador," Speagle admitted, "since at least in the primary schools many teachers themselves have only a primary school education." That observation led him to wonder if teachers could be eliminated entirely: "In the future there is also the possibility, in choosing a mix of media, of allowing the students to face the TV set alone." At the very least he believed that teachers did not need the same preparation when TV programs were available.[6]

The following year, 1973, another foreign report on the costs of instructional television appeared. It was authored by economists Dean Jamison and Steven Klees for the Institute for Communications Research at Stanford University.[7] The authors received significant help from Schramm in preparing their report. Their goal was to refine the methodology of cost analysis for educational television. They criticized Speagle's study but reinforced its main recommendations. The authors pointed out that Speagle had not used a social discount rate, and therefore the cost savings of using educational television were lower than he had estimated.[8] They figured the cost per student was US$19.72 as opposed to Speagle's US$16.00.[9] Their solution was to increase the number of students in each class to an even higher number than Speagle's recommendation of fifty.

By limiting the analysis of educational television to cost, the Speagle and Jamison-Klees studies led to very specific recommendations that if followed would have inflamed political opposition in El Salvador. The reports were not translated and did not enter into national discussion in El Salvador. However, the tone-deaf nature of their recommendations and their utter disregard for the local political context illustrate how a bureaucratic process imposed its own logic. It is understandable why donor agencies would commission studies to look solely at the issue of cost. But in doing so, the donor agency created a situation in which decision making would be devoid of awareness about the collateral damage that projects would create and thus about whether corrections would need to be carried out midcourse, to say nothing of whether implementation was even possible, given the two polarizing teacher strikes in 1968 and 1971.

The various studies produced by Stanford University's Institute of Communications Development provide the most elaborate demonstration of assessment from the perspective of a donor agency. The team from Stanford presented its results in diverse venues. In one document produced for UNESCO's Division of Methods, Materials, and Techniques, team members described the appropriate evaluation areas for assessing educational television. [10] They included cognitive achievement, teacher feedback, demographic data on teachers and students, data on social attitudes of teachers and students, classroom observation, school-community inventory, student follow-up, and parent aspiration for students. The document also acknowledged the difficulties of cost analysis mentioned by Jamison and Klees. In other words, their perspective was that of quantitative social scientists looking at a discrete problem and ignoring its political context.

The Stanford team published the full results of its study as a book with Stanford University Press. For the public at large, the study looked like a highly academic work that had gone through peer review at a leading university press. For USAID the book was the final product of contract AID/ta-G-1053 211(d). The agency filed a photocopy of the book as an official document in its archive. The cover page of the document file, often the only thing that people in the bureaucratic world read, includes a pithy summary that portrays the educational reform in El Salvador as successfully meeting some key objectives: "By 1972, four years after El Salvador's educational reform began, notable accomplishments were obvious: more students were enrolled, there was better learning, and there were equal or lower costs per student. Drawing upon data gathered and interpreted over a five-year period, this report demonstrates how El Salvador achieved such results where other countries failed. A unified program of reform and a strong, capable administrator are shown to be crucial. The publication concludes with a critical examination of television's role and with an analysis of how the El Salvador experience can be applied to other developing countries." [11] The book acknowledged that TVE's popularity was declining, probably because viewers thought its programming lacked imagination. But the authors insisted that focusing on this dip in popularity would be counterproductive because doing so "risks obscuring the system's significant impact on the quality of education in El Salvador." The book also reported a gradual flagging in teachers' support for reform but did not attribute it to educational television. Rather, it suggested that readers should ask "how legitimate one considers the teachers' grievances." The authors recognized that pay and working conditions promoted dissatisfaction among teachers but turned the criticisms back against the teachers to argue that the reform was working. They said that teacher criticism revealed the high-quality training they received at Ciudad Normal, where they became more analytical and had their consciousness raised "to the point that they were able to criticize."[12] As a typical example of their framework, the authors mentioned that television lowered costs when classes were sufficiently large but offered no comment on the extra burden that large class sizes placed on teachers.

The Stanford analysis rested on the premise that bureaucratic centralization is beneficial because it allows for quality control and the elimination of random variables. It described a main advantage of educational television as standardizing lessons and making instructional schedules uniform throughout the country. The authors made clear that the ultimate goal of education is to promote critical thinking among students, and therein they saw the Salvadoran reform and educational television as great leaps forward. The reform put an end to the pedagogy of rote memorization, challenged teachers as authorities, and "disrupted the authoritarian pattern of the traditional Salvadoran secondary school." The authors saw teachers relinquishing their monopoly on instruction to embrace their role as team members along with the teleteacher. In their opinion, teachers accepted "the role of television teachers as 'master teachers.'" Acknowledging the strong hand of the PCN regime and the active leadership of the Ministry of Education, the Stanford team concluded that the future of educational television and education reform seemed "more promising in El Salvador than in other countries that have launched television projects in the last fifteen years."[13] They found students to be enthusiastic about educational television, particularly those from rural or low-income backgrounds.

UNESCO had also been an important supporter of the reform. Its various experts and consultants produced myriad reports, all of which shared the same donor agency perspective as USAID. In a 1976 end-of-mission report UNESCO expert Giuseppe Anzaldi informed his superiors that El Salvador had "achieved part of its educational goals."[14] Its accomplishments included the 32 percent increase in total enrollment that had taken

Table 6.1

SCHOOL ENROLLMENT, 1967–1977

	1967	1977
Primary school enrollment (grade 1–6)	475,000	690,287
School-age population (age 7–12)	574,390	738,318
% of school-age population enrolled	82.70%	93.50%
Secondary school enrollment (grade 7–11)*	69,000	197,732
School-age population (age 13–18)	446,627	593,773
% of school-age population enrolled	15.0%	33.0%

Source: Enrollment figures for 1967 are from United States Agency for International Development, *Statistics for the Analysis of the Education Sector.* Those for 1977 are from Molina, "El sistema educativo," 593. All population figures are from El Salvador, Ministerio de Economía, *República de El Salvador, estimaciones y proyecciones*, 49.

*In 1977 grades seven to nine were considered part of primary school, while in 1967 they had been counted as part of secondary school. To make the figures comparable, the secondary school figures for 1977 include grades seven through nine, although technically they were primary school at that time.

place since 1971, a 35 percent increase in enrollment in the first years of school in rural areas, a 77 percent schooling rate for children age seven to fifteen, a 48 percent increase in the education budget since 1971, a 131 percent increase in education-related investments during the same period, and an educational television system that covered approximately 225,000 students. According to Anzaldi, educational television had achieved its first and most important goal—acceptance by teachers as a valid didactic aid. The next step was to fine-tune the system by revising the content of the teleclasses and considering new ways of delivering them (such as the newly available technology of videocassettes).

Consistent with Anzaldi's findings, the reform had indeed met many of the statistical goals that its designers had set. Included among them were expanded access to education, increases in the number of schools, and improvements to existing school buildings. They also included updates to curricula and textbooks and a vast overhaul of the teacher-training process. Statistics on enrollment provide a clear example of the reform's ability to meet one of its goals. Table 6.1 demonstrates that enrollment increased in both primary and secondary schools.

In 1967 almost 83 percent of the primary school–age population attended primary school; ten years later that had increased to 93.5 percent. In secondary schools enrollment rose from 15 percent of the population between the ages of thirteen and eighteen to 33 percent.

The controversy surrounding the "pilot project" of educational television obscured the reform's various accomplishments, such as school construction and the expansion of primary education in rural areas. One of the key individuals in the implementation of the reform suggested that Béneke's TVE-centered view of the reform may have hindered the government's ability to promote the reform's successes, because Béneke, in the words of one of his close associates, "didn't perceive the totality of the excellent components of the reform that he himself promoted; perhaps because of his inclination to favor educational television he didn't pay attention to other things."[15] The reform's achievements suggest how much more could have been done in areas like rural education, where the deficits were greatest, had the substantial resources devoted to television and to middle schools been used to expand educational opportunities for peasants. ANDES representatives frequently made this point in their critiques of the reform.[16] Aside from policymakers' ideological perspective, the successes of the reform reveal their serious effort to improve the content and delivery of education. Whether students learned more remained a matter of intense debate.

While donor agencies stuck to the technical aspects of the reform, higher-level decision makers in Washington focused on the broader issues of the Cold War and modernization, as revealed by a report presented to the U.S. Congress in 1976. The report was authored by John H. Clippinger of Harvard University's Program on Information Technologies and Public Policy. His study portrayed El Salvador's education reform as a Cold War victory, albeit one with a cautionary tale. Clippinger claimed that educational television in El Salvador had political and educational objectives. He saw the government as the primary beneficiary of the project, since communications technology "resulted in greater concentration of power within the government and reduction or diffusion of power for those outside the government." He argued that in the context of the Cuban Revolution and the perception that "Cuba may have set an example of revolution in Latin America," the educational television project "can be seen as an attempt to resolve these problems by establishing new linkages between various interest groups and reinforcing previous linkages," referring mainly to ties between the governing PCN, the Salvadoran state, economic elites, the U.S. government, and public opinion. In his view the reform had been politically beneficial for the government of El Salvador. TVE in particular had done wonders for the international image of the country "as being technologically innovative and reform minded." He even raised the possibility that the net effect of the 1971 teachers' strike had been a political bonus, since it had helped to "establish in the public eye the teachers' union as the principal impediment to reform."[17]

Yet Clippinger warned that the project neglected the rural sector and worried about "rising expectations" among the reform's beneficiaries. Consistent with modernization theory, Clippinger believed he was observing a society in transition, and so the beneficiaries of the reform could be the communists unless the masses' rising expectations were "realized in a healthy urban economy."[18] Although Clippinger's report put the reform in a wider sociopolitical perspective, it was still limited by official blinders and the prescriptive formula of modernization theory.

When the donor agency and U.S. government perspectives were removed from the assessment process, a far more complex picture of El Salvador's education reform emerged. Jorge Werthein, a doctoral student who went to El Salvador just one year after the publication of the Stanford study and Anzaldi's report, provided such a perspective. He was a student at Stanford's School of Education, which had a solid reputation for its independent stance. His advisor was Martin Carnoy, known for his work on education in Cuba. Emile McAnany, a member of the Stanford Communications Research Team in El Salvador, served on his doctoral committee.

To evaluate the reform, Werthein used the Stanford team's data along with more recent data collected by the Salvadoran Ministry of Education.[19] By the time he arrived in El Salvador in 1977, many signs indicated that neither the reform nor educational television were living up to the glowing reports of the Stanford team. At that time the country's political situation was in a visible downward spiral. The presidential election of February 1977 took place amid kidnappings and political assassinations. The results were even more fraudulent than the election in 1972, such that the new archbishop, Monsignor Oscar Arnulfo Romero, refused to attend the inauguration of the new president. Unlike his predecessors, Werthein described the profound problems caused by years of political turmoil in the country. The very premise of his research took into account wider political and economic contexts. Werthein set out to compare the use of educational television in El Salvador and Cuba. He said that in El Salvador it had been used "to hasten changes within the capitalist model of development," whereas in Cuba it had been used "to consolidate structural changes in a society that has redefined goals for development on a socialist basis."[20]

When he arrived in El Salvador, virtually all private schools had already abandoned educational television. Werthein reported that ministry officials withheld information from him. He described one official from the television unit refusing to release a report because "the Ministry" (referring to higher authorities) had "not seen this document, nor is it going to because if it saw the results, it would take away at least one of our four channels, if not close down the whole of educational television."[21] Werthein's account revealed that public officials were standing on rapidly shifting political ground, and they had created a system of self-censorship that buried unflattering reports. The television unit was no longer the darling of the new minister; it was now just one more unit that had to prove its value to leaders working under adverse conditions. Consequently, the only information that Werthein had available to him painted a favorable picture of both television and the other aspects of the reform. Nevertheless, Werthein found reason to question the effectiveness of the reform.

Werthein did find some data for the later years of the reform that indicated that television was not improving educational quality. On the contrary, there was "a statistically significant [school achievement] difference in favor of those students which do not [use television in class]." Werthein cited a World Bank mission report that concluded that television was encouraging a passive attitude among students and replacing the classroom teacher, who was transformed into a "subordinate of the teleteacher."[22] Instructors had even discarded the ten-minute introduction, a significant part of their role as member of a teaching "team." The small screen had transformed the classroom in a way that contradicted the reform's early claims that it would introduce more dynamic teaching methods. Class observation indicated that students and teachers in nontelevised classes were more active.[23] Teachers were reported to be passive and "inhibited" in the presence of the teleteacher.

Werthein's findings contradicted fundamentally the formula for economic development that the architects of the education reform had relied upon. He cited studies that questioned the relevance of an education reform in a country like El Salvador, where development problems were not the result "of a lack of skilled workers but rather of the internal economic structure and the international relations of the country." By 1977 nine years had passed since Béneke began his project, and Werthein argued that the reform had not delivered on the promises of economic and political modernization. The rampant inequality in wealth and power that characterized El Salvador had not

Table 6.2

Cost per Student, 1973

Cost per Student	Latin America (US$)	Ratio*	El Salvador (US$)	Ratio*
Primary school	82	1.0	40	1.0
Secondary school	135	1.6	166	4.1
Higher education	625	7.6	800	20.0

Source: Werthein, "Comparative Analysis."

*"Ratio" represents expenditures per student at each level compared to primary education.

improved; in fact, it had worsened. Instead of transforming society, schools continued to reproduce inequality and legitimize the existing social order.[24]

Werthein's study also challenged the reform's designers on the issue of cost savings. After all, costs were a big part of the preoccupation of Salvadoran authorities and USAID. Instead of asking whether the use of television lowered the cost of education in comparison to the traditional system, Werthein compared the ratio of cost per student at different levels of education in El Salvador with that of other Latin American countries. The results, summarized in table 6.2, place in perspective the choices made by Salvadoran authorities at the outset of the reform. Those authorities believed that upgrading middle school was the most important task to promote industrialization. Table 6.2 shows that by 1973 El Salvador spent less than half of the Latin American average on primary school and significantly more on secondary school and higher education. The column titled "ratio" shows the relation between expenditures per student at each level compared to primary education. The figures reveal clearly the distorting effect of El Salvador's reform relative to the rest of Latin America. Whereas secondary education was 1.6 times more expensive than primary education throughout Latin America, it was 4.1 times more expensive in El Salvador. Higher education received an even more disproportionate share of government expenditure—20.0 times higher than primary education. Werthein's study provided ample evidence for those who argued that the government's choice of educational expenditures was promoting inequality. He showed that the government was spending disproportionately high amounts of money on a select few, mostly urban students at the higher levels.

Salvadoran Perspectives

At about the same time that Werthein was doing research for his dissertation, the new government of General Romero was looking to boost its legitimacy in the wake of the blatant fraud that had brought it to power. In a surprise move the government decided to revisit the education reform by holding a national dialogue. In late 1977 the new minister of education, Carlos Herrera Rebollo, a former Christian Democratic mayor of San Salvador not identified with the conservative right, organized the Primer Seminario Nacional sobre la Reforma Educativa (First National Seminar on the Educational Reform). Either he was not satisfied with the studies that USAID had put on his desk or he saw political advantage in holding a nationwide consultation. Either way, he appointed as coordinator of the seminar Manuel Luis Escamilla, who had been a key player in every major educational reform since 1939 and who had written major policy documents for the 1968 reform.[25] The ministry went to great lengths to publicize the seminar and portray it as an exercise in openness.

The mere announcement of the seminar produced a flurry of commentary, demonstrating how seriously Salvadorans took the issue of education assessment as their society unraveled before them. One of the first and most profound commentaries appeared in the January/February 1978 issue of the journal published by the Jesuit-run UCA, *Estudios Centroamericanos*. The journal's editorial board included some of El Salvador's most prominent independent intellectuals: Father Ignacio Ellacuría, the brilliant Jesuit philosopher whose towering intellect made him the undisputed leader of Salvadoran academia; Segundo Montes, also a Jesuit and a distinguished anthropologist; Román Mayorga Quirós, who would become president of El Salvador in 1979; Salvador Samayoa, who would serve as minister of education in 1979 and as a leader in the FMLN during the civil war; Jon Sobrino, an internationally known Jesuit proponent of liberation theology; and two other respected Jesuits. The editorial was not signed, as was customary for the journal, and opened with a twist in terminology that summarized the authors' views. Instead of evaluating the "education reform," it set out to analyze "the education crisis." The editorial also expressed a belief in the urgency of the situation: "The permanent lack of solution to our problems and tensions," it warned, "shows that the social structure is approaching—if it has not already reached—a turning point where the only possible solution resides, justly, in the very transformation of the structure."[26]

The editorial began by questioning the sincerity of the minister to engage in a truly participatory exercise in light of the government's poor record on democracy. Readers were reminded of a failed public dialogue on land reform that President Molina's administration had organized in 1974. The editorial also pointed out that the individuals selected to participate in the seminar either worked for the government or belonged to powerful interest groups, while unions were excluded. In an apparent sign of openness the rules for the seminar mentioned that agrarian organizations would be allowed to participate but, as the editorial quickly pointed out, rural workers were prohibited by law from organizing and the organizations that they did have were persecuted by the government. Furthermore, the members of the seminar organization committee were people committed to the government's policies. The editorial suggested that the seminar might be a political stunt to obtain popular support by creating an image of consensus building. It also raised the concern that it could be used by nostalgic conservatives who wanted to return to the educational system of the 1950s.

The editorial conceded that at the time of its inception the reform was making progress and that some of its programs had value. But they judged it mostly as a colossal failure. Among the reform's many faults, the editorial identified a lack of preparation and the focus on middle school. The editorial questioned the credibility of the ministry to conduct an adequate review. "The question is, then, quite clear: will the Ministry of Education have the technical capacity, political freedom, and honesty necessary so that its action can become a real promotion of the people? History will judge."[27]

The teachers' union also responded to the ministry's announcement of the seminar. Its members found it hard to believe that the government was going to conduct a genuinely technical study of pedagogical problems. They issued a document that accused the government of having a flawed definition of development and therefore pursuing dubious objectives: "with the seminar or without it some of the most serious problems of education such as illiteracy will not be resolved, because they had an objective basis on the social and economic structure of the country. The position of the union is the same as it was in 1968: the rejection of the reform and denouncing the lack of interest that the ministry had given to the issue of illiteracy and the high degree of educational marginalization for thousands of Salvadorans mainly in the rural area."[28]

The union document went on to accuse the reform's designers of being willfully ignorant of the need to carry out radical and profound changes in El Salvador's economic and social structures. It said they did not care about mass education. Even more, it said they drew inspiration from North America, which increased dependency on foreign models. The aim of the reform, the union claimed, was to train people to participate in and defend the capitalist system: "The true objectives of the reform are to perfect the ideological machine to function in the interests of the local bourgeoisie, provide more investment for educational television, and strengthen the diversified high schools [to train] the technical people that foreign investors need."[29]

The union offered an alternative vision of education. The first goal was to "create a new man."[30] This new person had to learn not only about reality but also how to organize and fight to reorient the system toward total freedom. Education should train people to have a conscience and a critical political attitude. The strategy of the dominant class was manipulation, and people had to learn how to avoid it. The union declared it would not participate in the seminar. These critical reactions from the authors of the *Estudios Centroamericanos* editorial and the teachers' union illustrate that the national dialogue on education reform was going to be anything but easy.

Amid this environment of criticism, the seminar opened on schedule with activities taking place in provincial capitals—San Miguel, San Vicente, Santa Ana—as well as in the national capital, San Salvador. In Santa Ana participants included members of ANDES, even though the union had refused to participate. The last event was a national gathering in San Salvador in May 1978, with ninety participants attending from across the nation.[31] They included prominent individuals from every political persuasion, including the social democratic leader Guillermo Manuel Ungo, elected by his fellow members to serve as president of the seminar; the ANDES leader José Mario López; prominent Jesuits like Luis Achaerandio, former president of UCA, and anthropologist Segundo Montes; and members of the old guard of the teaching profession like former deputy education minister Carlos Lobato and prominent pedagogue Luis Aparicio.

Judging from the recommendations sent to the ministry, the debate ranged widely and reflected the political polarization of the country. It is hard to imagine that the meeting followed the organizers' plan, because critics clearly dominated the discussion. They disparaged the 1968 reform and the regime that sponsored it. They distinguished between training students "to learn how to learn" and "a political framework that tries to make students docile." Participants recommended that teachers and students be "critical agents and not passive subjects in the educational process." Not surprisingly they also discussed at great length the welfare of teachers and their professional activity, resulting in a recommendation that teachers' opinions be solicited and their human rights respected. Another recommendation called for "the immediate liberty of all the fellow teachers captured for political reasons or for other unproven accusations."[32]

When participants arrived at the topic of educational television their criticisms persisted, although they did not call for the complete demise of the system. They stated that television should be used "as a support unit and not as a substitute for the teacher in his/her interaction with students." But they also proposed that the coverage of educational television be broadened and that repeating stations be installed to improve reception.[33] One of the roundtables devoted its attention almost exclusively to educational television. Its members concluded that television had been extremely costly (36.8 million colones between 1968 and 1978). Seemingly unaware of the numerous evaluations by USAID and its consultants, they called for a full evaluation before investing any more money. But like the broader community of participants, the members of the roundtable did not condemn the system as a whole. Rather, they criticized the way it had been implemented. They recommended that the government "eliminate the teleclass as it is currently conceived" and reorient programming toward nonformal education, including cultural programs of interest to the general population.[34]

The topic of "doctrinal foundations of the reform" attracted the seminar's heavy hitters. In an appendix to the final report they criticized policymakers who implemented the 1968 reform for failing to consult stakeholders "before putting in practice a new technique, a new methodology for which teachers were not prepared, much less the people that it pretended to educate." They highlighted the high cost of the reform and its divorce from the reality of pervasive economic inequality. That issue surfaced frequently in the discussions. One roundtable, for example, concluded that the reform "deliberately ignored the education of the great marginalized sectors because they were not part of the economic interests of the dominant minority of the country."[35]

A standout issue at the seminar was how participants' priorities differed from those of foreign experts. A foremost concern for the seminar participants was what they perceived as undue foreign influence over the concept and design of the reform. "IT IS NOT SALVADORAN," they wrote in capital letters in one document.[36] Neither the content nor the direction of the seminar debate was informed by the Stanford team or the economists contracted by USAID. Comparing the proceedings of the seminar with documents produced by foreign sources is like reading about two entirely different education reforms.

The question of foreign influence over the reform struck a chord with conservative nationalists. One of the daily newspapers ran a story about the seminar titled, "Request that School Curriculum be Set by Nationals." The story reported that "participants of the Education Reform Seminar recommend that school curriculum be elaborated by Salvadoran teachers knowledgeable of the educational reality of the country in its economic, social, cultural and political aspects." The article gave a decidedly conservative twist to the story, contrary to participants' intentions, by saying that they favored a course in "morality, civics and civility," a common request of right-wing commentators.[37]

The seminar generated wide-ranging discussion in the national press. Newspapers variously labeled the seminar as the "reform of the reform" and even as a "counter-reform." By this time even the conservative press gave space in its editorial pages to the kind of criticism that teachers and other critics had raised back in 1968. An opinion piece in *La Prensa Gráfica* stated that "our educational system collapsed" because the authorities had not listened to teachers.[38] Another editorialist proposed that education transform individuals and "end social injustices." He said that the 1968 reform marginalized teachers and had been the product of a minister (Béneke) who was "lethal for education."[39] Various other editorials promoted ideas that seemed a far cry from the original capitalist vision of the reform. One op-ed piece called for cooperativism to be incorporated into the curriculum.[40]

Defenders of the reform tried to minimize the impact of the criticism. One newspaper published a biased description of the seminar that had been secretly provided to it by Manuel Luis Escamilla, the educator who had written some of the main documents of the 1968 reform. But the ruse was quickly discovered and the next day Guillermo Manuel Ungo, the seminar president and social democratic leader, sent a letter to the newspapers saying that Escamilla's statements reflected an attempt to "save the original philosophy and objectives" of the 1968 reform. In a separate letter the Jesuit Segundo Montes made another correction to Escamilla's description, saying that the seminar never considered the task of education "as a business enterprise, but as a social activity to form new citizens whose problems and difficulties are profoundly linked to the social structure of the country."[41]

At the conclusion of the seminar, participants made a final, overarching recommendation. They proposed the creation of a National Council of

Education to oversee the implementation of the seminar's recommendations. They stated explicitly that this recommendation emerged out of their distrust of the government: "there is some distrust among the Salvadoran people with regard to whether the reforms recommended by this seminar will be put into effect."[42] The council was to include representatives of the government, parents' associations, teachers' associations, and universities as well as other members of civil society. From the government's perspective, the recommendation amounted to surrendering education policy to the opposition. The council was never created.

UCA after the Seminar

By 1978 relations between UCA and the government had deteriorated significantly. From its foundation in 1965 as a conservative alternative to the radicalism of the public UES where rich families could safely send their children, the UCA had evolved into a rigorous research center defined by independent thinking and civic engagement. Its Jesuit leaders, young Spaniards when they first came to El Salvador in the early 1950s, had evolved into world-class intellectuals with high public visibility and progressive stances on politics and theology. Throughout the late 1960s and the 1970s they had repeatedly challenged the legitimacy of PCN development programs through highly technical, well-researched studies. Among others, their targets included the education reform when it was first conceived in 1968, the Cerrón Grande Dam project in 1972, and land reform throughout the 1970s. A recurrent theme in their studies was a warning about the consequences of failure on the part of government and elites to accept an alternative vision of national development. By the late 1970s, as the nation's social crisis was peaking, their warnings seemed all too prescient.

We already saw the UCA's journal, *Estudios Centroamericanos*, take a stand when the Romero administration proposed a national dialogue on education policy in 1978. After the subsequent seminar had concluded and its members had offered their critical recommendations to the government, the editorial board of *Estudios Centroamericanos* devoted an entire issue to the seminar in August 1978.[43] It was titled, "Where Is Education in El Salvador Going?"

The lead editorial, although authored anonymously, bears the distinct stylistic imprint of Father Ellacuría. It takes a philosophical perspective and counters the government's development paradigm by saying that education and the education system are not isolated from the rest of society. It says that people had lost faith in education as an instrument for change due to the government's failure to address the factors that affect social change, such as illiteracy, educational access, giving a popular orientation to education, and respecting teachers and their advancement. As things stood, education was an instrument for political domination.

The editorial speculated whether it was even worth talking about education reform under the prevailing political circumstances. It expressed doubt about whether those who held political and economic power were listening. On the other side, the left was engaging in new forms of militant popular action that weakened the influence of formal education over the country's youth. "It is no secret to anyone that the new ways of political struggle implemented by popular mass organizations in the last three years have tended to take possibilities away from the efficacy of traditional forms of struggle such as university work and changes in the formal educational system."[44]

Taking for granted that the 1968 reform was a failure, the various articles in the journal listed the causes. They criticized the way the reform was planned by a small group of individuals who did not consult anyone. The reform was designed to strengthen structures of domination and ideological control at the same time that it sought to introduce critical and positive elements. Many of the failures emerged not from its technical and administrative aspects but from the social and political conditions in the country.

According to the various authors, the reform was designed to keep El Salvador a capitalist, dependent country. Such a critique directly challenged the modernization theory premise that lay behind the Alliance for Progress. The authors said that modernizing the country to make it more urban and industrial reflected the interests of U.S. international policy. The education reform was born as part of a package of reforms sponsored by developed capitalism to modernize its periphery in places like El Salvador. It aimed to prepare a labor force for a certain type of development, which is why so much attention was given to middle school. The authors said the reform gave too much prominence to international advisors who viewed El Salvador through a homogenizing lens. In fact, they observed, the reform had many elements in common with other educational reforms that the United States had promoted throughout Latin America.

The authors claimed that the industrial development favored by the Salvadoran government was capital intensive and required less labor than the small businesses that it displaced. In addition, by the late 1970s the collapse of the Central American Common Market, the main Alliance for Progress tool to industrialize the region, rendered inadequate an education reform geared to training an industrial labor force. One article cited a World Bank report saying:

> The selected strategy, the emphasis on the third cycle [middle school], the diversified high schools, and the like, rests on an alleged economic efficiency. Nonetheless, the economic indicators show the development problem of El Salvador and the unemployment that goes with it are not based on the lack of skilled labor, but rather on the internal structures and international relations of the country. Given this, the emphasis on higher levels [of education] loses its economic meaning. Lacking any other justification, we think that [the strategy of the reform] is a rationalization of the continuation of an unjust situation being transmitted through the educational system.[45]

Moreover, as an Alliance for Progress program, the education reform was supposed to be part of a broader agenda that included modernizing the agricultural sector through an agrarian reform. But this never happened.

The issue concluded with a section of twenty questions about education in El Salvador. The questions reveal that the authors were concerned primarily with the social structure within which the education reform was being implemented. They asked about the relations between the educational system and the economic structure, the dependency of the country, the interference of elite economic associations, the interests of big business, the participation of the private sector in future planning, and the prevailing social injustice, political violence, dispossession of majorities, adult illiteracy, and high dropout rates. Only the last few questions had anything to do with pedagogical issues and the kinds of technical concerns that the ministry cared to discuss.

The analysis of the reform carried out by international donor agencies and their consultants stood in great contrast to what emerged from within El Salvador. Whereas the former concentrated almost entirely on internal aspects of the project, the latter concentrated most of their attention on the sociopolitical context. International agencies pointed to gains in enrollment while local observers emphasized that rural children were being ignored and that the beneficiaries of the reform were students trained for an industrial economy that had not materialized. An even greater discrepancy emerged over the vision of the country's future. International agencies wanted to move the country to a version of modernity inspired by the industrialized countries. They bolstered their arguments with figures that indicated the benefits of widespread use of modern educational technology. The Salvadoran critics of the reform saw education as a way to create free-thinking citizens who would help rectify the nation's social inequality and challenge its political structures that were intolerably authoritarian.

Wilbur Schramm in 1979: *Mass Media and National Development*

At about the same time that Salvadoran intellectuals were contemplating what they saw as the wreckage of the reform, the great promoter of educational television and mass media for development was having second thoughts as well. In his 1979 reassessment of *Mass Media and National Development* Wilbur Schramm admitted that two decades of modernizing policies had produced minimal improvement. The supposed gains of moving traditional societies into modernity were nowhere in evidence. Rural people in poor countries lived in the same conditions as before the United Nations declared the 1960s to be the Decade of Development. Schramm observed that the greatest lack of progress was in the poorest countries. He believed the failure was one of "strategy rather than tactics," that the fatal flaws lay in the reasoning behind development programs.[46] A key reason for failure, he said, was using Western nations as models for areas of the world with different histories. In fact, Schramm had to admit, contrary to the basic logic of modernization theory, Western development was a historical accident that could not be reproduced step by step elsewhere. Moreover, Western development had transpired over a long period of time, whereas modernization theory purported that the entire process could be accelerated under the wise guidance of technical experts. Schramm no longer agreed.

Schramm framed his reassessment of the transformative potential of mass media with that issue of wise leadership by experts. No longer believing that decisions by elites at the top trickled down in the form of development to people in villages and farms, Schramm challenged his earlier work. He now realized that mass media did not promote two-way communication or horizontal dialogue. Instead, by its very nature it was best suited for top-down communication. He now believed that for development to take place an open dialogue had to occur, and the way to do that was through interpersonal communications among local organizations and local media.

Schramm also directed his revisionism at his most cherished subject, educational television. Admitting that it too had failed, he pointed to its highly centralized design and delivery. The system was so centralized that it received little feedback from its recipients. The only choice for viewers was whether to turn off the television. The relentless rhythm imposed on the teacher left no room for innovation or initiative. If the children in the class learned at different speeds, the teacher did not have the flexibility to adapt. There was no possibility of stopping a teleclass midstream to clarify a point. It was not possible to repeat a program if necessary. Finally, cost-effectiveness never was realized, in American Samoa or anywhere else. So by 1979 the great advocate of modernization theory, educational television, and the use of mass communication for development had come to believe that his ideas had failed and that the cause was his former theoretical conceptualization.

USAID's 1979 Final Report on Educational Television in El Salvador

As Schramm was reassessing his previous views, USAID issued a new report insisting that the lessons of the Salvadoran experiment with television could be applied to other countries. There was little energy left in El Salvador for the "pilot project," but the USAID bureaucratic machine remained undeterred and sponsored a new study from the Academy for Educational Development. Whereas the seminar on education and *Estudios Centroamericanos* had devoted considerable energy to documenting the failure of the reform, or at least its limitations, the academy set out to explain its success. "Television," it said, "had been a key factor in the success of the educational reform in El Salvador." It noted that the system in El Salvador was "undoubtedly the most thoroughly studied educational technology project in the world."[47] But just as few Salvadoran critics seem to have read the USAID-sponsored documents, few international consultants demonstrated awareness of what had transpired in debates inside El Salvador.

The Academy for Educational Development study listed three reasons for undertaking the research: to evaluate the effects of television and the rest of the reform; to derive conclusions that might help other nations apply mass media to education; and to contribute data to develop future programs in El Salvador. The results of the research showed that the production of new programming for educational television was declining. The peak came in 1974 with 1,258 programs and then it declined sharply, to 1,000 in 1976 and 370 in 1977. Only 235 programs were budgeted for 1979.[48] The authors of the report did not interpret the decline as evidence that the entire system was drowning but rather argued that the necessary teleclasses were already available from previous years so new productions were not necessary. They cited the fact that the number of transmissions more than doubled between 1973 and 1976 (from 2,640 to 6,314), even though only 5,141 were planned for 1979.[49] This would seem a modest reduction, unless one realizes the changing content of the broadcasts. In 1976 two-thirds of the transmissions were teleclasses and only one-third was cultural programming. By 1979 the pattern was reversed. Just one-third of transmissions were going to the classroom. It was as if the government had actually accepted the recommendations of its critics in the 1978 seminar. Not surprisingly, the report complained that this change ran contrary to the original charter of educational television, which was to provide formal classes. The report claimed that educational television had been successful in achieving one of its goals, reducing educational costs. Adjusted for inflation, the operating cost of TVE divided by the number of student viewers dropped from sixty-five cents per student in 1970 to fourteen cents in 1973 and seven cents in 1979.[50] The report admitted that part of the decline in costs had to do with fewer resources being devoted to producing new programs.[51]

The report's final recommendations exhibit a lack of awareness of El Salvador's political context or the recent domestic debates over education. "The main challenges facing the current system," it asserted, "are in the areas of quality control and system maintenance." The recommendations addressed the operational aspects at length and took for granted that the original ideas from one decade ago would continue to be followed. The report made suggestions to improve cost accounting and observed some problems with facilities, like the doors in one studio being too small to permit the passage of stage scenery and heat and fumes from the cafeteria rising into the offices.[52]

Economists, 1983

By 1983 El Salvador was already in the midst of its brutal civil war, and few people in the country were in the mood to discuss the benefits or failures of educational television. Regardless, the reform and its most thoroughly studied project had achieved the disembodied and decontextualized status of analytical problems. Independent North American academic researchers decided to revisit the conclusions of some previous reports, and what

FIGURE 24. Television sets stacked in a trash heap outside a former school, now the Centro Arte Para la Paz, in Suchitoto. The nuns who ran the school fled at a moment's notice in 1980 in the face of death-squad threats. They left everything in the school behind, and here, nearly thirty years later, lay the remnants of TVE, symbolizing the broader legacy of losses incurred during the civil war. Photo taken by Erik Ching, June 2007.

they found validated Schramm's negative reassessment and Werthein's pessimism in 1977.

In 1983 economists Steven Klees and Stuart Wells published a methodological analysis of the major research projects that had assessed the Salvadoran reform and concluded that the benefits of educational television were ambiguous at best.[53] They analyzed data from various sources as part of their research, including the studies conducted by the Stanford team; the cost evaluation carried out by Speagle in 1972; comprehensive assessments of educational television published in 1975 by Martin Carnoy and Henry M. Levin, two professors in the Department of Education at Stanford University; and the Clippinger (1976) and Werthein (1977) reports discussed earlier.

The Klees-Wells cost analysis contrasted sharply with the sunny optimism of the work produced for USAID by Speagle and the Stanford team. Martin Carnoy, in his 1975 article on the costs and returns of educational television, had already found the average annual cost per student under the Salvadoran reform (including television and teaching retraining) to be 75 percent higher than Speagle had calculated. Part of the difference had to do with Carnoy's inclusion of the opportunity cost of capital expenditures, which Speagle had ignored. The more comprehensive analysis by Klees and Jamison in 1973 found small savings in the cost per student when educational television was included in the calculations. But the savings came only as the result of the dramatic rise in class size that increased teaching loads by 40 percent while keeping salary increases to only 20 percent. Moreover, Klees and Wells stressed that the comparison of different cost estimates revealed that "the [prior studies'] results are based on easily contestable judgmental assumptions and inadequate databases."[54]

Klees and Wells also said that even if the reform had resulted in significant cost savings, which it did not, it might still be bad policy because of its overall negative impact on society. As one example, they pointed to the terms of the loans for education that required El Salvador to acquire most of the corresponding goods and services from U.S. companies. They cited Werthein's dissertation to say that such an arrangement fostered "a relationship of dependence economically, politically, and culturally conditioned by the interests of the United States."[55]

Above all else, student learning was the most important issue. Aside from the money, the politics, and the debates over modernization, the question was simple: Were Salvadoran children learning better and more efficiently than before? Once again, Klees and Wells had sobering news. Even the Stanford research failed to show uniform or unambiguous benefits of educational television. Reading tests given to students in classes affected by the reform (with and without television) did not reveal significant improvement. General reading abilities improved a modest three to five points in classes with televisions compared to those without. The gains in math were significant, but in science classes the results were mixed. When Klees and Wells compared the economic costs of the reform to these modest gains in student achievement, they cited Carnoy, who found that "the cost effectiveness ratios argue for investing in the curriculum and teaching reforms and not installing ETV," and added that calculations based on more recent data reinforced this conclusion: "the cost per point gained is lower for the reformed classrooms without ETV than for those with ETV."[56]

Klees and Wells pointed out that it was also impossible to determine whether the modest gains were the result of the reform or whether they were the result of what has been called the Hawthorne Effect. Any educational innovation tends to produce positive results due to increased motivation inspired by novelty. The problem is that the effect wears off rather quickly. The improvements observed by the Stanford team may have been just the flashing of the Hawthorne Effect in the pan of Salvadoran schools. Klees and Wells also made another important point that Carnoy had raised initially. Even if the learning outcomes were positive, the population being studied, seventh graders in 1971, constituted a small percentage of the student population and possibly represented a select group. At that time only 25 percent of students of seventh-grade age throughout the country attended school. If a significantly higher percentage of that student population entered school, most of whom probably had low skill levels, it is likely the modest gains would disappear.[57]

The various assessment studies under evaluation here reveal that the results of the 1968 education reform were ambiguous at best. It did not make education more cost effective, even when televised classes are included in the calculations. Enrollment increased in seventh, eighth, and ninth grades thanks to the reform, but with disastrous results for teachers' morale and by ignoring the glaring educational needs in rural areas. The initial impression that learning had improved in junior high was not sustained over time. In fact, it seems that the uptick in performance was a typical case of the Hawthorne Effect. The results from every study either showed that the beneficial impact of televised teaching was unclear or that classes without television could perform better. Those who hoped televised classes would create a more interactive and dynamic classroom atmosphere had become disillusioned by the late 1970s. If anything, the all-knowing teleteachers seem to have inhibited their real-life classroom "partners." Moreover, technical difficulties undermined the project. Coverage was limited to 60 percent of the country, and poor maintenance meant that it was not uncommon to find that "one out of two" television sets were out of service.[58] In terms of the larger goals of development the failure was even more striking. Economic inequality increased. Industrialization floundered. Social conflict was exacerbated, and the appeal of radical alternatives grew steadily, especially when teachers began to join the revolutionary organizations.

But some aspects of the reform still generate positive memories, including teacher training innovations and the new textbooks. Although the diversified high school program was deemed a failure, the Bachillerato en Artes, the art school, represented a liberating experience for its students, many of whom went on to assume leadership positions throughout society. Moreover, the number of new schools that were built during the reform was unprecedented in the nation's history.

More than anything else, what this study of the varying assessments reveals is a chasm of difference between assessments conducted by the international development bureaucracy and those done by Salvadorans. For the international development experts working under contract for USAID, assessing the Salvadoran experiment was merely one piece of a much larger, global puzzle. The donor agency set parameters on how assessment was to proceed and the schedule under which it would operate. Naturally, the donor agencies had a strong incentive to portray themselves and their projects in a positive light. For North American researchers the wide-ranging reform was interpreted mostly through the narrow lens of its television component.

In a somewhat intermediate category we find the last report of Wilbur Schramm. At the time he wrote it he was in semiretirement in Hawaii. He had left Stanford University in the early 1970s to lead the East-West Center in Hawaii, where he was far removed from the bureaucratic pressures of specific projects. From this vantage he found himself in a position to see the flaws not only of the project in El Salvador but also in his overall ideas about communications and development.

The assessment of the educational reform was an entirely different story for people in El Salvador. For them, the reform was a lived experience, and they could not hide from social reality in an academic cocoon. Teachers who faced government repression, longer hours in the classroom, larger numbers of students, a state that seemed to devalue them as professionals, and day-to-day competition with an electronic box had a completely different perspective. The world around them was a world of intense political conflict. In no way could they limit their perspective to "indicators of quality control and system maintenance," as the international observers had done.

Conclusion

~~~e

If only the stubborn President Sánchez Hernández had gotten rid of his arrogant Minister Béneke and his unqualified undersecretary, the revolutionary movement would not have acquired the great force that it did years later.

—Jaime Roberto Serpas, 2006

✢ EARLY IN 1980 WALTER BÉNEKE WAS AGAIN APPOINTED AMBASSADOR to Japan. Almost twenty years had passed since he left Japan to become minister of education. He was looking forward to going back to the country that had inspired him to take up the cause of education reform and educational television. But he never made it there. On April 27, 1980, he arrived at his home on a tree-lined side street, half a block from the hotel favored by international journalists in San Salvador's exclusive Escalón neighborhood. As he got out of his car to open the gate to his house, the car door still open, "a gunman hiding behind a nearby tree walked up to Béneke, opened fire with a submachine gun and fled in a waiting car," wrote a United Press International (UPI) dispatch, citing a police report.[1] No one claimed responsibility at the time, but former guerrilla commander Eduardo Sancho told us in a 2007 interview that it was a guerrilla operation.[2]

By that time El Salvador was spinning out of control, with as many as one thousand people dying each month in politically related violence. Archbishop Romero had been assassinated by a right-wing death squad one month before Béneke. One year before that, in May 1979, Carlos Herrera Rebollo, the minister of education who had promoted the national dialogue on education in 1978, was shot down while driving to his office. The FPL guerrilla front claimed responsibility.[3] The same UPI dispatch that described Béneke's death mentioned the killing of his brother two months earlier, presumably by leftist guerrillas, in retaliation for an army raid on one of the Béneke family farms that had left twenty-five peasants dead after their families had occupied land on the property.

The murder of the ministers, Monsignor Romero, and former agriculture minister Enrique Álvarez in November 1980, together with the killing of countless peasants, teachers, office workers, intellectuals, politicians, and civilian bystanders as well as professional soldiers and guerrilla fighters marked El Salvador's decline into civil war and the beginning of the end of the military regime that had ruled the country throughout most of the twentieth century. At the time of Béneke's murder the civil war had not yet begun; that would happen nine months later, in January 1981, when the FMLN launched its so-called final offensive. But by April 1980 most Salvadorans felt that their society was unraveling and feared that a full-scale war was unavoidable.

What does the study of the 1968 education reform reveal about the PCN's modernizing agenda, about the nature of the Salvadoran state and the supposed alliance between the army and the oligarchy, about the role of foreign aid and the international development community, about Cold War politics in El Salvador, and about the country's descent into civil war? It is no coincidence that some of the most prominent victims of the carnage (some killed by left-wing guerrillas, most by the army and right-wing paramilitary groups) participated in the grand modernizing projects of the PCN regime. The modernizing ethos of the PCN had deep historical roots that helped define the confrontational fault lines in the second half of the twentieth century. Of those various modernization projects, the 1968 education reform was one of the most expensive, far-reaching, controversial, and deeply impactive.

Modernizing projects provided the main point of contact between the military and economic elites. A study of those projects reveals the complex nature of the relationship between the two groups. Almost everyone in El Salvador embraced *modernization* and *progress* as noble goals, but the meanings of those terms generated intense debate. Some members of the economic elite supported the modernization policies promoted by the military officers governing the country. Others automatically opposed what they saw as government interference with the only truly modernizing force—the marketplace.

Conservative elites promoted themselves as the front of modernization and progress, believing that since the late nineteenth century they had created

FIGURE 25. A portion of the mural in El Cenícero, the site settled by the former
residents of Copapayo Viejo after they returned from a United Nations refugee camp
in Honduras in 1987. Copapayo Viejo was one of the communities along the shores
of Lake Suchitlán, formerly along the Lempa River, before the building of the
Cerrón Grande Dam. The entire area around Lake Suchitlán was subjected to
intense army repression during the civil war, and the army massacred more than
150 of Copapayo Viejo's residents in 1983. The mural is a memory to that event,
with this portion of it depicting the helicopter that was part of the attack
and victims on the ground below. Photo taken by Erik Ching, March 2008.

the country's wealth through free markets, private enterprise, and entrepreneurial spirit. Most of them had made their fortunes from agriculture—coffee for the most part, but also sugar, cotton, and cattle. Many of them had diversified their investments, owning not only agricultural land but also banks, industry (particularly agro-industry), and various other commercial enterprises. They believed that any economic transformation should be done through the marketplace and as a consequence of private investment and entrepreneurial initiative, not through state bureaucratic activity. In conjunction with those views, they espoused an aggressive militarism to beat back challenges to the status quo, whether domestic or international in origin. They welcomed foreign investment but rejected foreign aid and advice. They accepted international alliances in the fight against communism but opposed foreigners monitoring how they waged their battle against communism at home.

For all their notoriety as a small, unified, insular collection of intermarried families, the elites of El Salvador were not a homogenous block. In fact, their economic diversification helps explain why they were not always on the same page. Some of them broke with the conservatism of their brethren, believing that long-term modernizing gain sometimes necessitated short-term pain. To that end they tolerated, even promoted, state-led reforms, and they believed that industrialization was essential, not optional. They reasoned that their country's future was bleak in the face of the status quo—an agricultural economy with a highly exclusive land tenure and a rapidly growing population of rural poor. These reform-oriented elites continued to be anticommunist, but they insisted that reform was the surest way to hinder communism's appeal. In general (and generalizations should always be taken with a grain of salt), the members of the elite more exclusively identified with landed interests had the tendency to be more inflexibly conservative than those who had an important stake in industry.[4]

After 1948 the military regime under the PRUD (1948–1960) and the PCN (1961–1979) advanced versions of modernization that received the support of reform-oriented elites. The various administrations that ruled during those three decades were not singular or uniform in their views, but they converged around some core principles. Those principles included the need for economic diversification and industrialization and leadership by an interventionist state to make that happen. The leaders of those governments reasoned that if the process was left solely to the marketplace and the whims of capitalists, change would occur too slowly, precipitating social ruin in advance of national progress. Many of those leaders distrusted the traditional oligarchy and presented themselves as champions of the common people.

An uncannily prescient example of the type of criticism that reformist military leaders directed against conservative landowners came from the emergent leaders of the PCN in 1961. It appeared in an article in *El Popular*, the controversial magazine that PCN leaders had founded to present themselves as social reformers who were not pawns of the landed oligarchy. The topic of the article was land reform and demographic trends in the Salvadoran countryside. Its basic purpose was to challenge elites to recognize the need for change, to tell them that if they did nothing but "bury their heads in the sand" and preserve the status quo, then they could expect social revolution. The authors told elites that they probably had one generation to change before "the hungry peasant masses in 1981 violently expropriate the coffee plantations." One is left to wonder if the authors of that article recalled their words when the civil war began, almost twenty years to the day from when they wrote them. The remark also reflects the belief that reform was the way to blunt the appeal of communism. In the hyperbolic rhetoric of the authors in *El Popular*, the solution lay in "readjusting our agrarian system . . . with a revolutionary process of humanizing wealth."[5]

Thus, the relationship between the military and the elites was complex, marked by an evolving series of convergent and divergent views that defy easy categorization. In general the military officers who governed the state shared some core values with conservative elites—namely, anticommunism and autocracy. And on various occasions the specific policies of those governments generated strong support in conservative circles. Just one example of their collaborative relationship comes from the education reform, when its designers allowed business leaders to more or less write the section of a new textbook covering industry and business practices. Perhaps it is for this reason that profoundly conservative members of the contemporary business class look back upon aspects of the 1968 education reform with nostalgia, such as Ricardo Paredes Osorio, who wrote a prologue to Ricardo Valdivieso Oriani's memoir. In that prologue, Paredes described El Salvador's development needs and said, "I have been greatly pleased with the efforts that some past administrations have put into education, such as the plan to build one school per day during the greater part of the Sánchez Hernández administration."[6]

But on many occasions the leaders of the military regime said or did things that caused consternation among conservative elites, such as proposing land reform, raising taxes on coffee exports, advocating for state intervention in the economy, accepting large amounts of foreign aid (both loans and grants), and welcoming international development experts to come to El Salvador and involve themselves in national affairs. One way conservatives responded was by promoting a highly polemical media voice that equated the military regime's modernizing reforms with communism. On other occasions, such as in response to land reform in the early and mid-1970s, they responded with legal action, political activism, and paramilitary violence.

The onset of the civil war after 1981 only confirmed for the conservative right the accuracy of their criticisms of reformism in the 1960s and 1970s. Take, for example, the writings of Mario Gómez Zimmerman, a conservative doctor who was kidnapped by guerrillas in the 1970s and then spent much of the 1980s in exile in the United States. An avid supporter of ARENA, he wrote a memoir/treatise on the situation in El Salvador in the mid-1980s, as the civil war was raging. It is no surprise that he looked back upon teacher activism in the 1960s and 1970s and accused teachers of being communists: "I remember Communist teachers preaching since my secondary school years. Their role was despicable because they took advantage of the imma- turity of youths to send them into the streets, where many met their deaths as cannon fodder." Perhaps more surprisingly, he looked back upon the PCN and left open the possibility that its military leaders were communists because of their reformist tendencies and their supposed willingness to hinder the operation of the free market in El Salvador. "The presidents who followed [Rivera], Sánchez Hernández (1967–1972) and Molina (1972–1977), are consid- ered by some to be Communists or in close contact with Communists. They are said to have been unable to act openly because the democratic structures were still intact, and to have attempted to dismantle them beginning with private enterprise."[7] While it may seem remarkable for a conservative spokes- person to accuse the stalwart anticommunist leaders of El Salvador's military governments of being communist, failure to appreciate the persistence of that view within conservative circles will hinder one's ability to understand the complex nature of the military-elite relationship in El Salvador, before, dur- ing, and after the civil war.

The response to the military regime by leftists and progressives was no less complex. Generally, they despised the regime's authoritarianism and anti- communism and viewed its leaders as stooges for U.S. imperialism. But they too embraced the concepts of modernization and progress, which included industrialization, agricultural diversification, and the creation of an inter- nal market by way of increasing the purchasing power of poor Salvadorans.

Thus, leftists and progressives found reason to support various aspects of the PRUD and PCN reform programs, including infrastructural development, land reform, income tax restructuring, and many others. And sometimes the military regime's reforms caught them off guard. For example, some rather doctrinaire leftist critics at the UES accused the PCN regime in 1971 of selling El Salvador out to Yankee imperialism by refusing to build a hydroelectric dam on the Lempa River. In a document opposing the 1968 education reform, they asked, "Why doesn't our government direct its efforts towards developing electrification from our rivers—abandoned since 1954—instead of experimenting in education reform?" It answered its question by saying that "this government is in league with the United States and it knows that because we do not have to buy the water in our rivers from anyone else, it would be a form of economic independence."[8] The next year, just days after coming to power, the new PCN president, Molina, announced the government's plan to move forward with the largest dam project in the nation's history—Cerrón Grande—to achieve exactly that economic independence that the UES critics had accused it of opposing.

But most leftists and progressives firmly opposed the military regime's approach to reform on two fronts—the manner in which the regime's policymakers implemented their programs (autocratic and top-down) and the way they defined development (economic growth rather than human development). As just one example of the latter, the research team assembled by the Jesuit-run UCA to investigate the Cerrón Grande Dam project in 1972 offered an alternative to the government's definition of development: "The fundamental objective of development, in our view, is to create living conditions that grant human dignity to all people; to eliminate those structures [in our society] that repress people and hinder their full and free self realization."[9] As the conflicts about modernity became more polarized, many people on the left came to believe that nothing short of a fundamental change in the economic structures of the country would be sufficient.

When the leaders of the military regime found themselves confronted by an increasingly vocal and well-organized center-left opposition in the early to mid-1970s, they retreated from reform and advanced toward militarism and repression. In other words, they increasingly found common cause with the traditional conservative elites who had never wavered in their belief that challenges to the status quo, especially by autonomous popular movements, had to be handled harshly. The teachers' union felt the state's heavy hand in response to its two strikes in 1968 and 1971, and so too did people displaced by the construction of the Cerrón Grande Dam between 1972 and 1976.

An early expression of the military regime's intolerance for progressives or leftists ever holding political office was made in the 1961 issue of *El Popular* mentioned above. Alongside their warning to intransigent elites about the pending social revolution, the editors informed their readers that their opponents "must never have access to Political Power!"[10] Only eleven years later that promise was tested, in the 1972 presidential election. In the face of a pending victory by the Christian Democratic leader José Napoleón Duarte, the PCN stole the election, repressed the opposition, and accelerated the polarizing descent into war.

Ultimately, the military-elite alliance was real. When put to the test, officers and landowners closed ranks and fought back tenaciously against their common enemy—whether real or perceived. But their alliance was characterized by a constant give-and-take over the definition of modernization and appropriate development programs. The debate was not between forward-looking modernizers and backward-looking reactionaries but rather between two visions of the future, sometimes complementary, sometimes in conflict. The standard characterization of the Salvadoran state as a tight alliance between soldiers and an oligarchy of retrograde landowners obscures the fact that the very modernization projects of the state, their disruptive consequences, and their inconsistency were as important, if not more important, in bringing about the demise of the military regime than their efforts to protect the traditional oligarchy. The relationship between the military and conservative elites was like the alliance between the United States and Israel or between Cuba and the former Soviet Union—full of friction, with each partner looking to advance its distinct agenda while remaining aware of their common enemies.

An analysis of the 1968 education reform provides a window into the day-to-day operation of the Salvadoran state when the PCN was at the height of its reformist drive. Other countries throughout the world initiated aggressive education reforms during the Cold War, and some of those reforms included educational television and sizeable quantities of foreign aid. In some places, such as American Samoa, Niger, or the Ivory Coast, the use of television was as ambitious as in El Salvador. Yet the failure of reform in those countries did not precipitate social immolation. What set El Salvador apart was its distinct concept of reform, the specific manner in which it was implemented, the unique societal setting that was subjected to it, and the peculiar response by the state to oppositional reaction. In this sense a study of the education reform reveals the characteristics of a regime that created the conditions for the war, nurtured the consolidation of its own enemies, and ultimately, in the words of Karl Marx, "created its own gravediggers."

A look at the 1972 education reform in Peru under the military government of President Juan Velasco Alvarado offers a valuable comparison for understanding the failure of military-led reformism in El Salvador. Despite ideological differences, the PCN and the Alvarado governments had in common a military-inspired tradition of authoritarianism and top-down rule. This commonality translated into similar approaches to education reform and produced similar outcomes. When the Alvarado government attempted to implement a far-reaching education reform in 1972, designed to modernize teaching and expand education to remote corners of the country, it faced a fervent oppositional backlash from both teachers and popular sectors. As in the Salvadoran case, they felt excluded from the process of design and implementation of the reform. According to a recent study by scholar Fiona Wilson, instead of modernizing the nation, as Alvarado and his functionaries dreamed, their plan backfired and fueled a radical insurgency under Sendero Luminoso.[11]

A counterfactual can help situate the repercussions of the authoritarian attitude of the modernizing technocrats in the Salvadoran state. What would have happened if the reform had been proposed in a political system that valued broad citizen participation? What if teachers, parents, and decision makers had engaged in prolonged dialogue as the education reform was in gestation? What if the voice of the powerful champions of industrialization had been just one more voice instead of the privileged one? Under these circumstances it is hard to see how the expenditures in education would have been so lopsided in favor of technology instead of teachers or so concentrated in the middle schools. Even if the project had retained its basic characteristics, the attitude of teachers would have been very different if they had felt integral to the discussion or if the adjustments that were made along the way had been sensitive to the affected stakeholders. The Jesuit Ignacio Ellacuría believed that this would have been the case. Writing in the midst of the 1971 teachers' strike, he said, "if only the Ministry [of education] had conducted itself in a way to keep alive the possibility of dialogue with guarantees, before and now, it could have prevented the strike."[12]

Similarly, what if the Alliance for Progress and U.S. financial and military aid had not been there to back the PCN? A project as large and intrusive

as the 1968 education reform, especially its educational television component, was possible only in a highly centralized state where decision making was concentrated in the hands of a few modernizing elites, or in the
words of Father Ellacuría, "a clique of technocrats or politicians."[13] Foreign
aid reinforced all the features of the state that made those types of intrusive
projects possible. The Alliance aid enabled and empowered the authoritarian tendencies of the Salvadoran regime. The Salvadoran state was a genuine "development dictatorship," the perfect centralized entity to implement
modernization theory–inspired projects.[14] In fact, from the point of view of
a modernization theory–based initiative like the Alliance for Progress, the
leaders of the Salvadoran PCN administrations were the ideal partners.

The main authors who have discussed the role of the Alliance in Central
America—Walter LaFeber, John Coatsworth, Michael Latham, and Greg
Grandin, among others—have mentioned how its projects strengthened the
existing elite by concentrating on infrastructural projects and pushing free-
market mechanisms and empowered the army through significant inputs of
military aid. In doing so, the argument goes, the Alliance helped precipitate the
type of left-wing insurgency that it was designed to keep at bay. Another argument about the failure of the Alliance for Progress is that it became an instrument of foreign policy, providing aid not to projects that were directly linked
to development but to projects that had political objectives.[15] These various
arguments all contribute to the "Alliance that lost its way" narrative, whereby
Kennedy's idealistic proposals were denatured by nameless bureaucrats.

Surprisingly, many aspects of the 1968 education reform and its educational television component challenge the lost Alliance perspective. The
reform and educational television could be classified as "good projects." Even
though they were implemented late in the Alliance calendar, when the insistence on free-market mechanisms was strongest and the idealism of the early
years was weakest, they stayed true to the original vision of the Alliance. The
education reform and educational television enjoyed tremendous political
and financial support, at both domestic and international levels. Various consultants and analysts devoted much time and effort to studying the programs,
evaluating their consequences, and making recommendations as to how best
to achieve the intended outcomes. Almost everyone involved in designing
and implementing the education reform was pursuing notable goals—making education in El Salvador more relevant to the real word, promoting young
Salvadorans' ability to be competitive in the marketplace, and expanding the
economy so that the material conditions of the poor majority would improve

and thus, hopefully, its members would be less inclined to support violent, destabilizing alternatives. The TVE project in particular embodied Kennedy's ideals in as pure a form as possible in a real-world setting. At the least, the TVE project in El Salvador exemplified the North American tradition of possessing deep faith in the capacity of technology to overcome social ills and to serve as a marker of modernity. As historian Michael Adas shows, a constant in recent U.S. foreign relations has been to measure progress, civilization, and modernity in technological terms.[16]

It must also be recognized that U.S. foreign aid funds were not the only ones at the disposal of Salvadoran authorities. The Alliance for Progress was rarely a solo act, neither in conception, financing, nor execution. Various other development agencies, in particular UNESCO, made explicit efforts to act in concert with the Alliance. For their part, Salvadoran government authorities took full advantage of the common goals of international aid agencies. They brought in Spanish art teachers, Japanese gym teachers, Japanese funds for the industrial high school, British money for a technology institute, and Italian support for television programs. In fact, studies of the impact of the Alliance fail to mention the extent to which U.S. foreign aid activities in the 1960s and 1970s were coordinated with resources from other countries and other development organizations.

Even the very conception of the TVE project, with its prominent support from President Johnson, was hardly an exclusive product of USAID. The idea that television would be a mechanism to achieve development in El Salvador, or anywhere else for that matter, required that many divergent variables converge. In the Salvadoran case those variables included, but were hardly limited to, the emergence of "development" as a field of study and as a policy objective in the 1960s; Béneke's tenure in Japan as a diplomatic officer, and his positive encounter with the Japanese educational television system; the emergence of the belief among development economists that education could promote economic growth; the emergence of modernization theory and its application to practical development projects; the belief in the role of mass media as a key instrument of modernization; UNESCO's embrace of the link between modernization and mass media; the vision among policymakers in El Salvador that the nation's prosperity lay in rapid industrialization; the identification of the lack of middle managers as a hindrance to industrialization; the belief that the peculiarities of the Salvadoran educational system were the cause of the missing middle managers; the singling out of middle school as the weak link in the Salvadoran education system; and the willingness of the PCN administrations under Presidents Rivera and Sánchez Hernández to open up the system and promote reform as an antidote to communism.

The final version of the TVE project was the product of a remarkable collaboration among universities (MIT, Stanford), nongovernmental organizations (Academy for Educational Development), international organizations (UNESCO, the World Bank, the Inter-American Development Bank), and U.S. agencies (USAID, the Peace Corps) as well as bilateral aid agreements (Japan, Great Britain, Italy, Spain). In a parallel fashion the coordinated activities of international organizations helped create an institutional apparatus within El Salvador that came to collaborate with the international community in implementing development projects. The new planning agencies that came to exist at the national and ministerial level in El Salvador—partly due to pressure from the United States and international development agencies— became the vehicle for a power shift in El Salvador, away from experienced educators and toward technocrats staffing planning agencies. The new planning agencies empowered an influential, hands-on modernizing elite. That elite, in turn, became the preferred interlocutor of international agencies. The good press that Béneke received in all the published reports on the TVE experiment had much to do with glorifying the modernizing elite that he supposedly represented. The flaws of his assertive approach, so keenly perceived by teachers in El Salvador, scarcely register in the accounts provided by international development experts. Quite the contrary, those experts portrayed his ability to steamroll over obstacles as a virtue.

The modernizing impulses of the military regime and of government functionaries like Béneke had deep historical roots in El Salvador. Foreign development specialists did not go to El Salvador to impose something that was not wanted. Moreover, not all their ideas prevailed with the Salvadorans, who were discriminating consumers of foreign ideas and advice. Béneke's famous assertiveness was directed at high-level U.S. and UNESCO representatives as well as rank-and-file members of the teachers' union. But the manner in which educational problems were conceived in El Salvador, even the institutional structures that were set up to address those problems, had been deeply influenced by the international development community. The practice of educational planning had been advocated by foreign advisors, and it became a key entrée for new ideas. Projects became viable not necessarily because experience had shown them to be effective but because the international development community had a series of mechanisms in place to inform poor countries of its legitimacy and the wisdom of its ideas.

The United States succeeded in globalizing one of the key concepts of modernization theory when the United Nations declared the 1960s to be the Decade of Development. The assumption that ten years could make a huge difference in the development status of poor countries throughout the world drew directly upon Rostow's idea that the process of advancing through the stages of economic growth could be accelerated by technical and financial inputs. Rostow himself was involved in the maneuvers to persuade the members of the UN General Assembly to adopt the concept of the Decade of Development. The United States also persuaded UNESCO to make it an official policy to support the Alliance for Progress. Over the decades UNESCO reports helped manufacture consensus about the nature of educational problems in El Salvador. Widely distributed UNESCO publications, such as Wilbur Schramm's *The New Media: Memo to Educational Planners* and the *UNESCO Courier*, along with various U.S. publications, such as *Facetas*, constantly reinforced modernization theory and the benefits of educational television. Salvadoran officials were barraged with ideas from the development community through high-level UN meetings on communications, meetings of education and planning ministers, the presence of international consultants, specialized courses for government officials, and lower-level meetings carried out in local countries. Accepting educational television as a valid and effective tool of development became part of the repertoire of "acceptable statements and utterances," as James Ferguson would say.[17] In the specific case of educational television, the work of Wilbur Schramm provided a template that UNESCO experts replicated in their reports and then delivered as policy suggestions to governing officials in poor countries throughout the globe. International donors offered mutually reinforcing advice and financial aid to support policy suggestions.

What made the TVE project attractive to Alliance for Progress officers was its core proposition that mass communication could promote development in poor countries. That belief was rooted in modernization theory, and mass communication was seen as an inspired tool to stop the advance of communism. With the 1968 educational reform, Schramm's grand Cold War scheme found its way into Salvadoran classrooms, thereby altering the quotidian experience of thousands of teachers and students. When students went to school during the education reform, they had new and surprising experiences. Many of them enjoyed the novelty of learning with television. The new curriculum challenged them, and the system told them that they were the font of national development. Yet the government's version of development and modernization could be subverted by teachers who opposed it. Students experienced the conflict that emerged from the reform, such as their teachers going on strike, sometimes returning angry and politicized, sometimes disappearing or returning after a stint in jail. During the teachers' strikes, tensions arose between parents and teachers. After seeing what happened to their teachers, some students concluded that the nation's power relations were out of balance, and many of them joined student organizations that quickly became radicalized. Teachers felt threatened by the possibility of being replaced by a machine; the daily routine for many of them was one of competition with an imperturbable electronic box that presided over their classrooms and commanded the attention of students. They saw the government giving great attention to education while simultaneously downplaying the importance of teachers; expenditures on educational technology went up, while teachers' workloads increased without a proportional change in salary. Interviews with former teachers show that they questioned the system and took the opportunity to tell students about the inequalities of their country and direct them to visit poor communities.

The most blatant intrusion of the Cold War in the school experience was the reaction of the state to opposition. The military regime saw teacher grievances through the lens of the Cold War and reacted ruthlessly. Schools were shaken by the strikes. The increasing activism of teachers and students became part of the school routine, as did their conversations about the consequences of challenging the state. Government officials accused politically active teachers and students of participating in international communist conspiracies, and they directed countless acts of repression against them as a consequence.

It can be argued that this late blossoming of the Alliance in its purest form did as much or more to create the brew that produced the Salvadoran insurgency as the "bad projects" that gave weapons to repressive armies and distributed loans that benefited big landowners. Step by step the ambitious project to improve education ended up alienating teachers, the largest group of civil servants in the country. The scale of the reform, possible only because of foreign funding, meant that the alienation it caused would also be large-scale. The government's failure to understand teachers' plight created conditions that pushed the teachers into increasingly activist stances. The response by the state turned the reform into a petri dish with the ideal conditions to incubate opposition. The example of the education reform ran parallel to other modernizing programs, like the promotion of commercial agriculture and the building of the Cerrón Grande Dam. Like the education reform, they too were ambitious projects imposed from above that sent destabilizing ripples into society. The ripples from each project built on the others, and soon the government found itself confronted with a wave of oppositional mobilization, exactly what it had been trying to avoid by pursuing modernizing reform. The way in which the PCN regime attempted to modernize the country is a classic example of the "structures and practices [that] actively form or 'construct' revolutionary movements as effectively as the best professional revolutionaries, by channeling and organizing political dissent along radical lines."[18]

El Salvador's Ministry of Education slowly abandoned educational television in the late 1970s and early 1980s. No one thought of replacing the TV monitors when they fell into disrepair. Guerrillas bombed the transmission towers. The government's political communication officers who took over the broadcasting station during the war destroyed the taped lessons.[19] The teachers' union joined the mass revolutionary movement that challenged the military regime. Death squads announced in 1975 that they would eliminate union leaders and identified teachers as one of their main targets.[20] Former education ministers Carlos Herrera Rebollo and Walter Béneke were assassinated a few months before the civil war started in earnest. Former ANDES leader Mélida Anaya Montes was murdered in April 1983, stabbed dozens of times by a rival guerrilla as part of an internal power dispute within the guerrilla front she had joined.[21] Ignacio Ellacuría and Segundo Montes, two of the most insightful Jesuit critics of the reform at the UCA, were murdered by the army in November 1989. Perhaps the most telling metaphor for the fate of the TVE-led educational reform was the closing down of the teacher training school to turn it into a garrison for the infamous U.S.-trained Atlacatl battalion, a military unit responsible for some of the worst human rights violations during the civil war.

The tragic outcome of the reform may have been a surprise to those who witnessed the planning stages. When the project was announced, there was a great sense of optimism in official circles. The minister of education had surrounded himself with some of the best and brightest people that El Salvador had to offer. In fact, many of the people who were working in the ministry at that time remain to this day important leaders. Besides, the project had the full support of the army and financing promised by the United States. There was every expectation that this combination of talent, economic resources, and political will would bring to a successful completion a project that was so clearly striving to create a better future for the country. Yet it was this type of collaboration between the modernizing impulses of the army and the Salvadoran elites, facilitated by substantial amounts of foreign aid, that helped unleash the very forces that challenged the system and pushed the nation into war.

Since the Salvadoran civil war ended in 1992, some of its main protagonists have taken a retrospective look at their lives and their nation's tumultuous history. Common points of reference for many of them are the 1968 education reform and the teachers' strikes in 1968 and 1971. For example, in 2004, at an event commemorating the twentieth-fifth anniversary of the 1979 coup d'etat that marked the end of the PCN's reign, one of the coup organizers, Gen. Jaime Abdul Gutiérrez, singled out the education reform as a decisive antecedent to the civil war. "The reform," said Gutiérrez during a public address, "did not persuade the main actors, the teachers; they launched strikes and felt repressed because their salaries were held down; all of this pushed the profession to the left, and it included high school students, who contributed to the formation of mass organizations."[22]

As a guerrilla commander in 1979, Eduardo Sancho was on the opposite side of the political spectrum from General Gutiérrez, but he too believed the 1968 education reform was a major contributing factor to El Salvador's descent into war. When we asked him in 2007 to look back at the causes of polarization in the 1960s and 1970s, he immediately turned to the education reform, saying that, "without the [1968] reform, a lot of things could have been avoided in this country."[23] One of his counterparts, commander Joaquín Villalobos of the People's Revolutionary Army (ERP), made a similar reference to the education reform in a 2000 book review: "In El Salvador, the conflict was basically generated by the struggle between agroindustrialists and landowners. This brought about the division of the Catholic Church, the army and the intellectual class, the emergence of the Christian Democratic Party, the realisation of an educational reform at the end of the sixties, and electoral frauds and coups d'etat that included military battles for power, all taking place before the development of the guerrilla."[24]

Our study suggests that General Gutiérrez, Sancho, and Villalobos are right: the education reform advanced the polarization of Salvadoran society. It is quite possible that the civil war would have happened without the education reform, but as an expression of the way in which the Salvadoran state operated, the reform certainly contributed to the conditions that caused the war. The Salvadoran author Jaime Roberto Serpas stated it this way in his 2006 chronicle of the war years: "If only the stubborn President Sánchez Hernández had gotten rid of his arrogant Minister Béneke and his unqualified Undersecretary, the revolutionary movement would not have acquired the great force that it did years later."[25]

Serpas's comment points to one of the central arguments of our study, that of the responsibility of the Salvadoran state and the officials who ran it for creating the conditions that culminated in war. Indeed, the particular policies that the PCN administrations attempted to implement generated great controversy and debate. But as important as the actual policies, if not more so, was the manner in which the PCN implemented them—top-down and authoritarian. Enlightened technocrats who believed that they knew what was best for everyone had no need to solicit anyone else's opinion.

A North American political science graduate student observed this first-hand in the early 1970s. George Browder went to El Salvador to conduct research for his dissertation analyzing Salvadoran electoral voting patterns. He arrived in El Salvador at a propitious moment, when the conflict between teachers and the state was at its apogee, the effects of the education reform were beginning to be felt in earnest, the economy was struggling to reorient itself in the aftermath of the collapse of the Central American Common Market following the 1969 war with Honduras, the first guerrilla front (the FPL) was being founded, and the competition around the soon-to-be-notorious 1972 presidential election was intensifying. Who knows whether Browder found these conditions beneficial to his research, but one thing is certain—he could hardly have chosen a more turbulent laboratory for the study of politics. After returning safe and sound to South Carolina to write up his results, Browder chose to conclude his eventual dissertation with a comment about El Salvador's future prospects that in hindsight proves highly prescient and insightful: "However, if the process of urbanization, communication, education, and modernization continue and governmental repression is held at a minimum or discouraged, democratizing forces could continue to grow in El Salvador providing at the least, more progressive social benefits for the masses than exist at present. A policy of increased repression on the contrary, running counter to the modernizing forces could mean another revolt and massacre of 1932 or worse. From this vantage point, the outcome could go either way."[26] Browder recognized the aggressively modernizing ethos of the Salvadoran state, and he believed that it had the potential to help resolve some of El Salvador's serious problems. But Browder also believed that the state possessed the capacity to derail its own prospects for success. It was up to the state's managers to determine which direction they were going to go. Unfortunately, we all know the tragic choice they made.

Notes

Throughout the notes, page numbers are listed in the order in which quotations appear in the text.

Introduction

* Fidel Sánchez Hernández, public speech of September 20, 1971, reprinted in Universidad Centroamericana, *Análisis de una experiencia nacional*, 238.

** Kalijarvi, *Central America*, 119.

1. Our description is based on the account in the *Pittsburgh Post-Gazette*, July 8, 1968. For an academic analysis of Johnson's visit, see Leonard, "Meeting in San Salvador."

2. Lyndon B. Johnson, "Remarks at the Alberto Masferrer Normal School, San Andres, El Salvador," July 7, 1968, in Woolley and Peters, *American Presidency Project*, http://www.presidency.ucsb.edu/ws/?pid=28994.

3. "Minutes of Cabinet Meeting," July 10, 1968, in United States, Department of State, *Foreign Relations of the United States, 1964–1968*, vol. 31, doc. 112, http://history.state.gov/historicaldocuments/frus1964-68v31/d112.

4. *Boletín del Ejército*, January 14, 1949, 1.

5. Consejo de Gobierno Revolucionario, Decreto #1, *Diario Oficial*, December 16, 1948, 4273. For overviews of the Partido Revolucionario de Unificación Democrática (PRUD) years, see Cáceres Prendes, "Discourses of Reformism"; Guevara, "Military Justice and Social Control," chap. 3; Turcios, *Autoritarismo y modernización*; Castellanos, *El Salvador, 1930–1960*; Williams and Walter, *Militarization and Demilitarization*; and Stanley, *Protection Racket State*.

6. For just a few examples, see United Nations, Economic Commission for Latin America, *El desarrollo económico*; Choussy, *Economía agrícola salvadoreña*; and Márquez and Montealegre, *Informe sobre la estructura bancaria*. A report created by University of Chicago economist Bert Hoselitz under the auspices of the United Nations was first provided to the Salvadoran government in 1952 as a secret report. It was then published in 1954 as *Industrial Development in El Salvador*. Hoselitz also mentions a mimeographed 1950 report on the economy of El Salvador by the Economic Commission for Latin

America entitled "Hechos y tendencias recientes de la economía salvadoreña" (p. 14). For population figures, the leaders had the 1930 census and the classic demographic study by Rodolofo Barón Castro from 1942, *La población de El Salvador*.

7. Cáceres Prendes, "Discourses of Reformism," 78–79.

8. For the 1961 census, see El Salvador, Asamblea Legislativa, *Memoria del Primer Congreso Nacional*, 121–37. A delegation at the congress from the National University of El Salvador (UES) disputed the figure of 3.4 million acres of arable land, insisting it was closer to 2.5 million, which, if accurate, would have exacerbated the degree of concentration. The original amounts were recorded in manzanas, which we converted to acres at a scale of 1.7 acres per manzana.

9. See Colindres's analysis of the 1971 agricultural census in "La tenencia de la tierra."

10. For the 1961 to 1971 figures, see Almeida, *Waves of Protest*, 99, which cites Pelupessy, *Limits of Economic Reform*, 38. For the 1975 figure, see Kirby, "Agrarian Politics," 112, which cites Pearce, *Under the Eagle*, 209.

11. United Nations, Economic Commission for Latin America, "Crisis in Central America," 61–62, also cited in Wood, *Insurgent Collective Action*, 24.

12. Ellacuría, *Escritos politicos*, 543.

13. Turits's analysis of the Trujillo era in the Dominican Republic is comparable to what we are arguing here. The Trujillo regime has long been recognized for its tyrannical and esoteric qualities, and one scholar describes it as a classic case of a "sultanistic" regime. Turits shows the complexities of Trujillo's rule and explains how he garnered widespread support among the rural poor through a series of complex policies that combined modernization and tradition. See Turits, *Foundations of Despotism*, esp. 4, for reference to the historiography of sultanism.

14. "El Salvador. The Full Enchilada," *Time*, March 9, 1959.

15. Grenier, *Emergence of Insurgency*, uses the term *dominant paradigm* in reference to the insurgency originating in the fight against that ruling alliance.

16. Rosenberg, *Children of Cain*, 242.

17. Even though El Salvador was the smallest country in Central America, it routinely exported the most coffee per year; only Guatemala came close, and only twice between 1940 and 1970 did it edge out El Salvador in annual production. See Williams, *States and Social Evolution*, 269–73. Accordingly, Salvadoran coffee growers were some of the region's most efficient, typically getting twice as much coffee per acre as their counterparts, even though, or perhaps because, El Salvador's coffee plantations (*fincas*) were much smaller than plantations in larger countries with abundant land, like Brazil. See Bulmer-Thomas, *Political Economy of Central America*, 154. Paige describes the Salvadoran coffee growers as being the most efficient in the entire world by the 1970s. See Paige, *Coffee and Power*, 10.

18. The figure is for 1971. See Programa Regional del Empleo para América Latina y el Caribe, *Situación y perspectivas*, table 31.

19. For good summaries of elite self-conceptualization, see Paige, *Coffee and Power*; and Grenier, *Emergence of Insurgency*, 40–41. For more contemporary accounts, see Valdivieso Oriani, *Cruzando El Imposible*, by a founding member of the ARENA party,

and Gómez Zimmerman, *El Salvador*, by a conservative doctor who took up exile in the United States.

20. Paige, *Coffee and Power*, 12–13.

21. Wood, *Insurgent Collective Action*, 21.

22. Johnson, "Between Revolution and Democracy."

23. Baloyra, *El Salvador in Transition*, 18, 54 (citing the López Vallecillos phrase); Montgomery, *Revolution in El Salvador*; Goodwin, *No Other Way Out*; and Stanley, *Protection Racket State*.

24. Another example of this interpretive framework is Chávez, "Pedagogy of Revolution." See the rest of the introduction for more extensive analysis of that work.

25. Stanley, *Protection Racket State*, 8; and Wood, *Insurgent Collective Action*, 21.

26. Stanley, *Protection Racket State*, 7.

27. Ibid., 3.

28. Cáceres Prendes, "Discourses of Reformism," 86.

29. Ibid., 87, 86, 90. Another scholar who describes the complex divisions within the Salvadoran military between reformers and conservatives is Chávez, in "Pedagogy of Revolution," 332–33. An example of the curious syncretisms that have emerged around this argument of complexity within the Salvadoran ruling sectors is provided by Brian Bosch, the U.S. military attaché to El Salvador between 1980 and 1981. He advances an argument similar to that of Jorge Cáceres Prendes, who was a politically active leftist in the early 1970s before becoming an academic in Costa Rica. In Bosch's words, "the relationship between landowners and officers was far more complicated [than most studies presume]." Bosch, *Salvadoran Officer Corps*, 8.

30. Paige provides a sound executive summary of the historiographic discussion of the supposed intra-elite split between "agro-financial" and "agro-industrial-financial," with the latter supposedly being more open to reform than the former. See Paige, *Coffee and Power*, 7.

31. Generational differences provide a possible explanation for ideological divergences within the Salvadoran army. Younger officers might have been willing to embrace reform not only on its own merits but also because it allowed them to distinguish themselves from senior officers who may have been blocking their ascent. For a brief overview of the generational (*tanda*) system in the Salvadoran army and its potential impact on the political aspirations of younger officers, see Bosch, *Salvadoran Officer Corps*, chap. 1.

32. El Salvador, Public Administration Service, Ministerio de Economía, *Vivienda en El Salvador*; and Masís, *Proyectos de viviendas económicas*.

33. For analyses of modernization theory, its origin, and its impact on U.S. development policies, see Gilman, *Mandarins of the Future*; Latham, *Modernization as Ideology* and *Right Kind of Revolution*; Simpson, *Universities and Empire*; and Engerman et al., *Staging Growth*.

34. Rostow, *Stages of Economic Growth*; Simpson, *Economists with Guns*.

35. Kalijarvi, *Central America*, 15, 119. Guevara provides examples of diplomatic correspondence in which Kalijarvi makes the same sorts of claims while still serving as ambassador to El Salvador. See Guevara, "Military Justice and Social Control," 154.

36. See Scheman, *Alliance for Progress*. Some of the chapters in this edited volume are by members of Kennedy's original Alliance team.

37. Frei Montalva, "Alliance That Lost Its Way."

38. Levinson and de Onís, *Alliance That Lost Its Way*.

39. Smith, "Alliance for Progress," 86.

40. Rabe, *Most Dangerous Area in the World*, 157; and Schoultz, *Beneath the United States*, 384.

41. Taffet, *Foreign Aid as Foreign Policy*, 6. One of the most consistent criticisms directed against the Alliance is its failure to genuinely promote democracy. Adherents of this view commonly portray U.S. policymakers' short-term concerns with social and political stability as having gotten in the way. See, for example, Levinson and de Onís, *Alliance That Lost Its Way*, 13; Coatsworth, *Central America and the United States*, 116. Raymont, *Troubled Neighbors*, 174; Smith, "Alliance for Progress," 78; Rabe, *Most Dangerous Area in the World*, 161; O'Brien, *Making the Americas*, 223–27; Grandin, *Empire's Workshop*, 49; and Schoultz, *Beneath the United States*, 358.

42. Levinson and de Onís, *Alliance That Lost Its Way*, 14; Kryzanek, *U.S.-Latin American Relations*, 60; Smith, "Alliance for Progress," 84; Schoultz, *Beneath the United States*, 384; and Coatsworth, *Central America and the United States*, 116. The argument about U.S. domestic pressures is made by Gambone, *Capturing the Revolution*, 117.

43. Grandin, *Empire's Workshop*, 49; Rabe, *Most Dangerous Area in the World*, 154; Niess, *Hemisphere to Itself*, 176; and Kryzanek, *U.S.-Latin American Relations*, 61.

44. The bureaucratic problems are discussed in Rabe, *Most Dangerous Area in the World*, 150.

45. Levinson and de Onís, *Alliance That Lost Its Way*, 14; and Rabe, *Most Dangerous Area in the World*, 164, 168.

46. LaFeber, *Inevitable Revolutions*, 176, 178; and Coatsworth, *Central America and the United States*, 117.

47. Examples of authors making such an argument include Ferguson, *Anti-Politics Machine* and *Expectations of Modernity*; Escobar, *Encountering Development*; Cooper and Packard, *International Development*; Saldaña-Portillo, *Revolutionary Imagination*; Gilman, *Mandarins of the Future*; and Krieckhal, *Dictating Development*.

48. The phrase is used extensively by Escobar in *Encountering Development*.

49. Ibid., 41.

50. Ferguson, *Anti-Politics Machine*.

51. Scott, *Seeing Like a State*, 5.

52. Joseph and Spenser, *In from the Cold*, 11, 29. See also Brands, *Latin America's Cold War*; and Grandin and Joseph, *Century of Revolution*.

53. Brands, *Latin America's Cold War*, 7.

54. Ibid., 26. For good examples of the conservative explanatory narrative, see Valdivieso Oriani, *Cruzando El Imposible*; and Gómez Zimmerman, *El Salvador*.

55. Brands, *Latin America's Cold War*, 29.

56. For a comparable example of education policy in the United States during the Cold War, see Hartman, *Education and the Cold War*.

57. For just a few examples of studies focused exclusively on El Salvador, see Chávez, "Pedagogy of Revolution"; Gordon Rapoport, *Crisis política*; Grenier, *Emergence of Insurgency*; Pirker, "La redefinición de la possible"; Wood, *Insurgent Collective Action*; Montgomery, *Revolution in El Salvador*; and Cabarrús, *Génesis de una revolución*; Baloyra, *El Salvador in Transition*. For a few works incorporating El Salvador into a comparative analysis, see Goodwin, *No Other Way Out*; Wickham Crowley, *Guerrillas and Revolution*; Mason, *Caught in the Crossfire*; and McClintock, *Revolutionary Movements*.

58. Goodwin, *No Other Way Out*, 24–25.

59. Wolf, *Peasant Wars*; and Paige, *Agrarian Revolution*. See also the debate among Diskin, Paige, and Seligson on the "agrarian question" in El Salvador in *Latin American Research Review* 31, no. 2 (1996): 111–57.

60. Cabarrús, *Génesis de una revolución*. The early work of Enrique Baloyra is a notable exception in that it pays significant attention to the state. See Baloyra, *El Salvador in Transition*. For a good analysis of this historiographic debate, see Chávez, "Pedagogy of Revolution," 25, 222.

61. Grenier, *Emergence of Insurgency*, 157.

62. See Goodwin, *No Other Way Out*, 16–23, for a good description of the Marxist vs. capitalist-modernization debate. See also Durham, *Scarcity and Survival*. For good historiographic discussions of this debate, see Stanley, *Protection Racket State*; Williams and Walter, *Militarization and Demilitarization*; Brockett, *Political Movements*; and Wood, *Insurgent Collective Action*. For the classics in this historiographic vein, see Paige, *Agrarian Revolution*; Wolf, *Peasant Wars*; Moore, *Social Origins*; and Gurr's "relative deprivation theory" in *Why Men Rebel*.

63. Prosterman, "IRI." See also Prosterman, Riedinger, and Temple, "Land Reform." For further discussion of Prosterman in the context of El Salvador, see the debate among Diskin, Paige, and Seligson in *Latin American Research Review* 31, no. 2 (1996): 111–57.

64. Grenier offers a main case for the determinant role of the guerrilla leadership in *Emergence of Insurgency*, as does Wickham Crowley, in *Guerrillas and Revolution*. For an interesting critique of Grenier, see Stanley, Review of *Emergence of Insurgency*. As for analyses that give more autonomy to the peasantry, see Chávez, "Pedagogy of Revolution"; and Cabarrús's study of peasants around Aguilares in the 1970s, in *Génesis de una revolución*; see also Williams's study of how cattle and cotton displaced peasants in the 1970s, making them ready to rebel, in *Export Agriculture*. On peasants in Chalatenango, see Pearce, *Promised Land*; and Todd, *Beyond Displacement*. In Morazán, see Binford's various works, including "Grassroots Development," "Hegemony in the Interior," and "Peasants, Catechists and Revolutionaries." For general studies across time and space, see Mason's argument about the "rational peasant" in *Caught in the Crossfire*; and Kincaid, "Peasants into Rebels." For the impact of liberation theology and its role in creating the incentive to participate in the rebellion, see Wood, *Insurgent Collective Action*; Whitfield, *Paying the Price*; and Alas, *Iglesia, tierra y lucha campesina*. All of those works reveal the importance of educated priests but also the highly autonomous actions of peasants once the seed of liberation theology was planted. Harnecker's interviews with former Fuerzas Populares de Liberación Farabundo Martí (FPL)

commanders in *Con la mirada el alto* reveal the strong influence of liberation theology in sparking their politicization.

65. See Goodwin, *No Other Way Out*; see also Wickham Crowley, *Guerrillas and Revolution*; and Williams, *States and Social Evolution*. Williams's view is more long term, going back to the nineteenth century, and he focuses on politics and state policy-making decisions. Goodwin offers an interesting critique of Wickham Crowley's assumption about the origins of peasant radicalism in "Review: Towards a New Sociology."

66. Wood, *Insurgent Collective Action*, 195.

67. Ibid., 231–35.

68. Chávez, "Pedagogy of Revolution," 25.

69. Goodwin, *No Other Way Out*; and Almeida, *Waves of Protest*.

70. Goodwin, *No Other Way Out*, 23.

71. See also Brockett, *Political Movements*; Stanley, *Protection Racket State*; and Williams and Walter, *Militarization and Demilitarization*.

72. Schramm, "Mass media and National Development," 4.

Chapter 1

* José René Tobar, from Armenia, "El voto popular: Una distracción efímera," *El Diario de Hoy*, March 4, 1968, 13.

** From U.S. journalist Tina Rosenberg's interview with an anonymous member of the Salvadoran elite in the late 1980s, in Rosenberg, *Children of Cain*, 221.

1. *El Popular*, June 30, 1961, 1, in DOS-IAES, 1960–1963, 716.00/7–1061, Sowash, U.S. Embassy, San Salvador, to U.S. Department of State, Washington, D.C., July 10, 1961.

2. Grenier, *Emergence of Insurgency*, 40–41. For a contemporary account by a founding member of the Alianza Republicana Nationalista (ARENA) party, see Valdivieso Oriani, *Cruzando El Imposible*.

3. See Lindo-Fuentes, *Weak Foundations*; Lauria, *Agrarian Republic*; Alvarenga, *Cultura y ética*; Colindres, *Fundamentos económicos*; and López Bernal, *Tradiciones inventadas*.

4. "Ley de extinción de ejidos y otras disposiciones relativas a la material," *Diario Oficial*, March 14, 1882.

5. For the emergence of the coffee economy, see Lindo-Fuentes, *Weak Foundations*; and Lauria, *Agrarian Republic*.

6. It should be noted that scholarship on nineteenth-century Latin America, and especially nineteenth-century El Salvador, tends to downplay the differences between liberals and conservatives, saying that they shared more in common than not. See Gudmundson and Lindo-Fuentes, *Central America, 1821–1871*.

7. "Ley de extinción de ejidos y otras disposiciones relativas a la material," *Diario Oficial*, March 14, 1882.

8. Lindo-Fuentes, *Weak Foundations*, chap. 6.

9. Lindo-Fuentes, *Weak Foundations*; and Lauria, *Agrarian Republic*.

10. See Yarrington, *Coffee Frontier*; and Gudmundson, *Costa Rica before Coffee*.

11. Colindres, *Fundamentos económicos*; and Lindo-Fuentes, *Weak Foundations*.

12. The reference to slavery is found in the lead editorial of *La República*, January 24, 1885, 1.

13. A reference to Enlightenment and Romantic philosophers is found in *La República*, December 20, 1883, 1. The reference to the United States and England is found in the lead editorial of *La Libertad*, January 8, 1887, 1.

14. One of many references to "democratic systems" can be found in *La República*, November 19, 1883, 1. The term "altos finos de la democracia" is found in *La República*, January 25, 1883, 1.

15. *La República*, June 21, 1883, 1.

16. *La República*, November 8, 1883, 1.

17. *La Libertad*, January 8, 1887, 1.

18. Dionisio González, in *La República*, January 21, 1885, 1; see also January 14, 1885, 1.

19. Galindo, *Cartilla del ciudadano*, xxii.

20. Ibid., viii.

21. Ibid.

22. El Salvador, *Memoria que el Ministro del Estado*.

23. Heater, *History of Education for Citizenship*.

24. See the twenty-six-page document *Catecismo político para instrucción del pueblo español*, which was reprinted in Guatemala in 1811, and the more elaborate, ninety-six-page variation that was printed in Guatemala in 1813, *Catecismo político arreglado a la constitución de la monarquía española*. The Museo del Libro in Antigua, Guatemala, has a copy of this text.

25. Herrera, "Primary Education," 23. Herrera's chapter is the best work to date on Bourbon education in San Salvador.

26. Pedro Molina followed the Spanish tradition with his *Cartilla del ciudadano* in 1825, in which he set forth the principles that were to guide education in the new republic. According to him, "Un gobierno como el que se ha establecido en Centro-América, fundado en la razón y los derechos del hombre, no necesita para consolidarse otra cosa que hacer estensivas las luces." Molina, *Cartilla del ciudadano*. The federal decree that exempted individuals from military service stated that "la instrucción pública es el cimiento de las buenas instituciones sociales" and that education was "esencial el desarroyo [*sic*] y fomento de las luces." Decreto Federal del 7 de octubre de 1829, AGN, Impresos I #136.

27. Molina's *Cartilla del ciudadano* or a variation of it was used in civics lessons in primary schools. In 1853 a teacher in Sonsonate said that he taught the Constitution in accordance with a text prepared "por el infrascrito en forma de catecismo." Cuadro enviado por Lorenzo López a la Junta de Instrucción Pública, 11 de Agosto 1853, Archivo Municipal de Sonsonate.

28. Cárdenal, *El poder eclesiástico*, 118.

29. Galindo, *Cartilla del ciudadano*, 1. (¿Qué cosa es el pueblo? Es una reunión de hombres que tiene por objeto la conservación y felicidad de los asociados y que se gobierna por instituciones políticas emanadas de ella misma. En este sentido, pueblo es

lo mismo que sociedad, a diferencia de la acepción vulgar de la palabra, en que, pueblo significa populacho. Así la proposición "el pueblo es el soberano" equivale a esta, menos peligrosa: "la sociedad es la soberana.")

30. El Salvador, *Memoria que el Ministro del Estado.*

31. Munro, *Five Republics of Central America*, 110.

32. Lindo-Fuentes, "Schooling in El Salvador," 184.

33. Ibid. See also Tilley, *Seeing Indians.*

34. Lindo-Fuentes, "Schooling in El Salvador."

35. The reference to ignorant masses and bad faith is found in *La República*, June 6, 1883, 1.

36. For discussions of politics and rebellions in the late nineteenth and early twentieth centuries, see Lauria, *Agrarian Republic*; Ching, "From Clientelism to Militarism"; Holden, *Armies without Nations*; López Bernal, *Tradiciones inventadas*; and Alvarenga, *Cultura y ética.*

37. Cárdenal, *El poder eclesiástico*, 118.

38. López Bernal, *Tradiciones inventadas*, 88–90; and Burns, "Intellectual Infra-structure of Modernization." As just one example of the extensive work on Rodo and his essay "Ariel," see Miller, *In the Shadow of the State.*

39. Ching, "Patronage and Politics"; Gould and Lauria, *To Rise in Darkness*, chap. 5; Grieb, "The U.S. and the Rise of Maximiliano"; and Alvarenga, *Cultura y ética.*

40. Hernández Martínez went by his maternal name, and so from this point forward we will refer to him as Martínez.

41. "Mensaje del Señor Presidente de la República, General Maximiliano Hernández Martínez, leído ante la Asamblea Nacional, en el acto de la apertura de su período de sesiones ordinarias, el día 4 de febrero de 1932," *Diario Oficial*, February 4, 1932, 183.

42. Salisbury, *Anti-Imperialism.*

43. Cáceres Prendes, "Discourses of Reformism," 26.

44. Lindo-Fuentes, Ching, and Lara-Martínez, *Remembering a Massacre*; and Gould and Lauria, *To Rise in Darkness.*

45. A specific case from the municipality of Nahuizalco is contained in the reports from Enrique Uribe, sub-comandante local, Nahuizalco, to comandante of Sonsonate Department, March 4, 1932, AGN, MG, Sección Sonsonate, box 3. See also Ching, "From Clientelism to Militarism," 468.

46. "Mensaje del Señor Presidente," February 4, 1932. See also Ching and Tilley, "Indians, the Military," 144.

47. El Salvador, Instituto de Vivienda Urbana, *Memoria 1959–1960*. On the housing deficit, see El Salvador, Public Administration Service, Ministerio de Economía, *Vivienda en El Salvador.*

48. Report from "Comrade R" to the committee assembled by the Caribbean Bureau to investigate the Salvadoran Communist Party's activities during the 1932 uprising in El Salvador, p. 15, fond 495, opis 119, inventory 1, Russian State Archive of Social and Political History, Moscow, Russia. For more on Mejoramiento Social, see Ching, "From Clientelism to Militarism," chap. 8.

49. For descriptions of these and other eccentric behaviors on the part of Martínez, see Krehm, *Democracies and Tyrannies.*

50. The documents relating to the 1939–1940 campaign against plantation-owned stores are in AGN, MG, 1940, unclassified paquete, folder "Tiendas en fincas." For further elaboration on this campaign, see Ching, "From Clientelism to Militarism," 478–85.

51. Minister of government to departmental governor of Usulután, September 19, 1939, AGN, MG, 1940, folder "Tiendas en fincas."

52. Arturo Sánchez, secretary of the Cámara de Comerciantes en Pequeño, to minister of government, December 5, 1939, AGN, MG, 1940, folder "Tiendas en fincas."

53. Arturo Sánchez, secretary of the Cámara de Comerciantes en Pequeño, to minister of government, December 24, 1940, AGN, MG, 1940, folder "Tiendas en fincas."

54. See a critique of the 1940 reform in "La reforma educativa en El Salvador—1939–1967," *La Prensa Gráfica*, October 9, 1968, 7. See also the critique by Carlos Sandoval in "Dos reformas educativas salvadoreñas," *El Diario de Hoy*, October 27, 1973, 8, about the issue of rote memorization remaining the standard pedagogy.

55. Ebaugh, *Education in El Salvador*, 39. See also Lindo-Fuentes, "Schooling in El Salvador," 187.

56. Escamilla, *Reformas educativas*, 52.

57. The interview was between Jorge Cáceres Prendes and Manuel Luis Escamilla in San José, Costa Rica, 1994. See Cáceres Prendes, "Discourses of Reformism," 28.

58. Escamilla, *Reformas educativas*; and Lindo-Fuentes, "Schooling in El Salvador." See also Cáceres Prendes's description of the 1940 education reform in "Discourses of Reformism," 28.

59. Luna, "Análisis de una dictadura"; Almeida, *Waves of Protest*, chap. 2; Ching, "Patronage and Politics"; and Parada, *Maximiliano Hernández Martínez.*

60. McCafferty, San Salvador, to U.S. secretary of state, January 4, 1934, USNA, Records Group 59, 816.00/934, box 5506, folder #3.

61. See Rock, *Latin America in the 1940s*; and Bethel and Roxborough, Latin America 1944–1948.

62. Parkman, *Nonviolent Insurrection*; Parada, *Maximiliano Hernández Martínez.*

63. Salvador Vitelli, interview by Robert J. Alexander, San Salvador, August 7, 1948, Papers of Robert J. Alexander, reel 7. Vitelli was manager of the Cámara de Comercio e Industria.

64. Cáceres Prendes, "Discourses of Reformism"; Guevara, "Military Justice and Social Control"; Turcios, *Autoritarismo y modernización*; Stanley, *Protection Racket State*; Williams and Walter, *Militarization and Demilitarization*; and Castellanos, *El Salvador, 1930–1960.*

65. For a description of the fall of Martínez that includes many previously unpublished images of Romero, see Parada, *Maximiliano Hernández Martínez.*

66. On the Castaneda era, see Cáceres Prendes, "Discourses of Reformism"; Guevara, "Military Justice and Social Control"; and Castellanos, *El Salvador, 1930–1960.*

67. See the reprint of *El Diario de Hoy* in *Boletín del Ejército*, June 10, 1949, 3.

68. Lemus interview with Jorge Cáceres Prendes in 1992, as described in Cáceres Prendes, "Discourses of Reformism," 47–48.

69. For overviews of this period see Cáceres Prendes, "Discourses of Reformism"; Turcios, *Autoritarismo y modernización*; Guevara, "Military Justice and Social Control; Castellanos, *El Salvador, 1930–1960*; Stanley, *Protection Racket State*; and Williams and Walter, *Militarization and Demilitarization*.

70. Turcios, *Autoritarismo y modernización*, 61.

71. Benjamin Mejía Martínez, interview by Robert J. Alexander, Havana, September 10, 1949, Papers of Robert J. Alexander, reel 7. Mejía Martínez was president of the Railroad Workers Union.

72. For this comparison of El Salvador to Mexico under Osorio, see Cáceres Prendes, "Discourses of Reformism," 83–85. Another interesting comparison to El Salvador is made by Turits in regard to the Dominican Republic during the reign of Trujillo (1930–1961). Turits claims that Trujillo did not face such a powerful landed elite because the elite had never been consolidated in the Dominican Republic. Furthermore, the military was more independent in the Dominican Republic than in El Salvador because it had been created directly under the auspices of the United States and so owed fewer domestic allegiances. See Turits, *Foundations of Despotism*, 21–23.

73. Article 135 of the 1950 Constitution, *Diario Oficial*, September 8, 1950. This article was literally lifted from the Bolivian Constitution of 1945 (art. 107), but it had antecedents in the Mexican Constitution of 1917 and the Cuban Constitution of 1940.

74. For a list of Osorio's cabinet, see Cáceres Prendes, "Discourses of Reformism," 81; and Castellanos, *El Salvador, 1930–1960*, 258. For Alvarez's service in 1948, see Cáceres Prendes, "Discourses of Reformism," 53, 71.

75. *Boletín del Ejército*, June 21 and June 25, 1954. See also Castellanos, *El Salvador, 1930–1960*, 192–93.

76. Hoselitz, *Industrial Development*, 75, 83, 88; interview with Jorge Cáceres Prendes as described in Cáceres Prendes, "Discourses of Reformism," 79. See also p. 79 for Cáceres Prendes's description of the Hoselitz visit.

77. Castellanos, *El Salvador, 1930–1960*, 193.

78. Hoselitz, *Industrial Development*, 9, 23.

79. Lindo-Fuentes, "Schooling in El Salvador," 190; Aguilar Avilés, "El camino hacia la modernización," 456; Osorio, "Mensaje Presidencial al Pueblo Salvadoreño," 8.

80. *Boletín del Ejército*, April 14, 1950, 1.

81. *Boletín del Ejército*, January 14, 1949, 5; April 14, 1950, 1; and February 26, 1951, 1.

82. *Boletín del Ejército*, February 18, 1949, 3.

83. Jorge Sol Castellanos as cited in Turcios, *Autoritarismo y modernización*, 30.

84. *Boletín del Ejército*, February 16, 1951, 1.

85. The speech was reprinted in *Boletín del Ejército*, March 13, 1951, 6.

86. *Boletín del Ejército*, April 6, 1951, 1.

87. *Boletín del Ejército*, April 20, 1951, 4. This article also referred to the 1932 massacre as a blemish on national history.

88. For a concise summary of the absence of electoral competition during this era, see the tables contained in the report on elections from DOS-IAES, 1960–1963, 716.00/1–362, Sowash, U.S. Embassy, San Salvador, to U.S. State Department, Washington, D.C., January 3, 1962.

89. See El Salvador, Secretaria de Información, *Maquinaciones contra el estado*. See also Castellanos, *El Salvador, 1930–1960*, 259.

90. Cited in Turcios, *Autoritarismo y modernización*, 48.

91. Cáceres Prendes, "Discourses of Reformism," 8.

92. One of the complex aspects of modern Salvadoran history is the absence of coordinated and purposeful public expressions by the economic elites. Not until the 1970s, and then only in direct opposition to land reform programs, did business and landowners' organizations emerge with an explicit public presence to defend their version of liberalism and development. As a consequence, historical sources relating to the Salvadoran elites and their ideological views have been lacking, as have scholarly studies about them. One exception is Ramírez, "El discurso anticomunista," which is based partly on research that Ramírez did under our auspices for this project. Another exception is the Jesuit Ignacio Martín Baró's master's thesis at the University of Chicago in 1977, "Group Attitudes and Social Conflict in El Salvador."

93. For just one reference to Sarmiento, see "La ley social y la ley de la selva," *El Diario de Hoy*, August 8, 1949, 3. See also López Vallecillos, *El periodismo*, 400–402.

94. For a description of Viera Altamirano, his work habits, and the founding of *El Diario de Hoy*, see Carlos Sandoval's prologue in Viera Altamirano, *Obras escogidas*.

95. "Economía dirigida y leyes del trabajo," *El Diario de Hoy*, March 18, 1950, 5.

96. "La CEL y la opinión en la prensa," *El Diario de Hoy*, August 10, 1949, 5.

97. See the initial editorial by Benjamín Guzmán, *El Diario de Hoy*, February 28, 1949, 9; and "¿Dinero para electrificar?" *El Diario de Hoy*, March 29, 1949, 3.

98. "El pueblo salvadoreño quiere trabajar," *El Diario de Hoy*, May 30, 1950, n.p.

99. "La electrificación y las sanas diversiones del pueblo," *El Diario de Hoy*, December 20, 1949, 5.

100. "Defendamos nuestra industria textil," *El Diario de Hoy*, July 28, 1949, 5; and "El problema lechero y la economía nacional," *El Diario de Hoy*, July 30, 1949, 5.

101. "Una cooperación económica de alcance mayor," *El Diario de Hoy*, September 10, 1949, 5.

102. *El Diario de Hoy*, March 8, 1950, 5.

103. Summarized in Viera Altamirano, *Integración económica de Centro-América*, illustrating that he had been consistent in his views on this subject for many years.

104. Hal Brands contends that the Cold War really began in earnest in Latin America only after the Cuban Revolution. See Brands, *Latin America's Cold War*.

105. Gilman, *Mandarins of the Future*; Taffet, *Foreign Aid as Foreign Policy*; Levinson and de Onís, *Alliance That Lost Its Way*; and Rabe, *Most Dangerous Area in the World*.

106. Eisenhower, *Wine Is Bitter*, 219–20.

107. See Holden, *Armies without Nations*, 169. Holden draws on U.S. State Department sources, USNA, Records Group 59, Hemba, U.S. Embassy, San Salvador, to U.S. State Department, Washington D.C., August 24, 1956.

108. "Salvadoran Loan Weighed," *New York Times*, July 30, 1958. Cáceres Prendes also describes this in "Discourses of Reformism." On MAP, see Holden, *Armies without Nations*, 168–69.

109. "El Salvador Head Is Greeted Here," *New York Times*, March 14, 1959; and "Americas' Unity Urged by Visitor," *New York Times*, March 12, 1959. *Time* reported that communism was not an urgent matter in El Salvador: "The planter-army oligarchy that runs El Salvador makes certain that no leftist ideologies flourish." See "El Salvador. The Full Enchilada," *Time*, March 9, 1959. See also Castellanos, *El Salvador 1930–1960*, 274–75.

110. DOS-IAES, 1960–1963, 716.5-MSP/1–2060, Kalijarvi, U.S. Embassy, San Salvador, to U.S. Department of State, Washington, D.C., October 14, 1960. See also memo with subject line "Development Program to Help Combat Communism in El Salvador," DOS-IAES, 1960–1963, 716.5-MSP/10–14160.

111. The army occupied the National University and even arrested its main administrators, despite the university's legal autonomy, which disallowed government intervention. See DOS-IAES, 1960–1963, reel 1, for extensive coverage, including copies of the university's student newspaper, *Opinión Estudiantil*. See also Castellanos, *El Salvador, 1930–1960*.

112. Castellanos, *El Salvador, 1930–1960*, 283.

113. For a good description of Lemus's attack on the university and his eventual fall, see Chávez, "Pedagogy of Revolution," 41–52.

114. DOS-IAES, 1960–1963, 716.00/11–2860, HBS p. 4, Sowash, U.S. Embassy, San Salvador, to U.S. Department of State, Washington, D.C., November 28, 1960.

115. For a good description of the junta from October 1960 to January 1961, see Chávez, "Pedagogy of Revolution," 52–73.

116. At least one academic study makes the claim that the U.S. Embassy orchestrated the coup. Montgomery, *Revolution in El Salvador*, 53.

117. DOS-IAES, 1960–1963, 716.001/6–1961 CS, Sowash, U.S. Embassy, San Salvador, to U.S. Department of State, Washington, D.C., June 19, 1961.

118. Nevertheless, the Communist Party had issued a rare public statement expressing its support for the October coup: "Manifesto del Partido Comunista Salvadoreño," San Salvador, November, 1960, in DOS-IAES, 1960–1963, 716.001/1–1261, Downs, U.S. Embassy, San Salvador, to U.S. Department of State, Washington, D.C., January 12, 1961. See also DOS-IAES, 1960–1963, 716.00/10–1362, "Manifesto del Partido Comunista de El Salvador," September 1962, in Downs, U.S. Embassy, San Salvador, to U.S. Department of State, Washington, D.C., October 13, 1962.

119. DOS-IAES, 1960–1963, 716.5-MSP/2–1161 HBS, Williams, U.S. Embassy, San Salvador, to U.S. Department of State, February 11, 1961, p. 1.

120. DOS-IAES, 1960–1963, 720.5/8–1562, secret cable from U.S. Embassy, San Salvador, to U.S. Department of State, Washington, D.C., August 15, 1962.

121. "Action Program for El Salvador; Act of Bogota Main points," Joint Embassy USOM USIS dispatch, DOS-IAES, 1960–1963, 716.5-MSP/2–1161 HBS, Williams, U.S. Embassy, San Salvador, to U.S. Department of State, Washington, D.C., February 11, 1961.

122. DOS-IAES, 1960–1963, 716.00/6–961, Memorandum of Conversation with Ambassador Francisco Lima, U.S. Department of State, June 9, 1961.

123. "Directorio combatirá comunismo con trabajo," *El Diario de Hoy*, February 4, 1961, 6.

124. DOS-IAES, 1960–1963, 716.00/7–1061, Sowash, U.S. Embassy, San Salvador, to U.S. Department of State, Washington, D.C., July 10, 1961. Rodríguez Porth's broadside, "Parentesis necesario," *El Diario de Hoy*, February 13, 1968, 17, mentions another, similar magazine created by the Directorate, called *Combate*.

125. As just one example, see "Población y reforma agraria," *El Popular*, June 23, 1961, 4, in DOS-IAES, 1960–1963, 716.00/7–1061, Sowash, U.S. Embassy, San Salvador, to U.S. Department of State, Washington, D.C., July 10, 1961.

126. *El Popular*, June 15, 1961, 3, in DOS-IAES, 1960–1963, 716.00/7–1061, Sowash, U.S. Embassy, San Salvador, to U.S. Department of State, Washington, D.C., July 10, 1961.

127. *El Popular*, June 8, 1961, 2; see also "Las nefastas luchas de clases no existen," *El Popular*, June 1, 1961, 6; and *El Popular*, June 7, 1961, 4. All three articles are in DOS-IAES, 1960–1963, 716.00/7–1061, Sowash, U.S. Embassy, San Salvador, to U.S. Department of State, Washington, D.C., July 10, 1961.

128. "Población y reforma agraria," *El Popular*, June 23, 1961, 4, in DOS-IAES, 1960–1963, 716.00/7–1061, Sowash, U.S. Embassy, San Salvador, to U.S. Department of State, Washington, D.C., July 10, 1961.

129. DOS-IAES, 1960–1963, 716.00/7–1061, Sowash, U.S. Embassy, San Salvador, to Department of State, Washington, D.C., July 10, 1961.

130. *El Diario de Hoy*, December 8, 1961. See also the broadside by Rodríguez Porth, "Parentesis necesario," *El Diario de Hoy*, February 13, 1968, 17.

131. DOS-IAES, 1960–1963, 716.00/7–3161, Williams, U.S. Embassy, San Salvador, to U.S. Department of State, Washington, D.C., July 31, 1961.

132. DOS-IAES, 1960–1963, 716.00/10–1761, Sowash, U.S. Embassy, San Salvador, to U.S. Department of State, Washington, D.C., October 17, 1961. See also the enclosure of a manifesto from the Confederación General de Sindicatos (CGS) responding to the conservative critiques in defense of the government—"Manifesto de la CGS . . . al Pueblo Salvadoreño."

133. As an early example of this, see the opposition mounted to the government's program in 1939 to ban the payment of workers on plantations in coupons (fichas) instead of legal currency, in Ching, "From Clientalism to Militarism," chap. 8.

134. For the perspective of the Communist Party, see DOS-IAES, 1960–1963, 716.00/10–1362, Downs, U.S. Embassy, San Salvador, to U.S. Department of State, Washington, D.C., October 13, 1962. For the perspective of the Association of University Students at the National University (AGEUS) and various other labor organizations, see the broadsides and copies of the student newspaper *Opinión Estudiantil* in DOS-IAES,

1960–1963, 716.001/3–1661, Sowash, U.S. Embassy, San Salvador, to U.S. Department of State, Washington, D.C., March 16, 1961.

135. FUAR manifesto, March 1961, in DOS-IAES, 1960–1963, 716.001/3–1661, Sowash, U.S. Embassy, San Salvador, to U.S. Department of State, Washington, D.C., March 16, 1961. See also Menjívar, *Tiempos de locura*, 27–29. Roque Dalton celebrates the FUAR in *El Salvador: Monografía*. For the CIA's assessment of the FUAR, see its declassified report United States, Central Intelligence Agency, "Survey of Communism," K-7.

136. DOS-IAES, 1960–1963, 716.5/11–662, Williams, U.S. Embassy, San Salvador, to U.S. Department of State, Washington, D.C., November 6, 1962. For the CIA's assessment of communism, see United States, Central Intelligence Agency, "Survey of Communism."

137. For the latest and most well-documented discussion of the rise and fall of the FUAR, see Chávez, "Pedagogy of Revolution," 74–80. For a summary of the left's internal debates, see Lindo-Fuentes, Ching, and Lara-Martínez, *Remembering a Massacre*, chap. 5. For the emergence of the PDC, see Webre, *José Napoleón Duarte*; and Rey Prendes, *De la dictadura militar*.

138. "Hacia el caos de reformismo social," *El Diario de Hoy*, April 15, 1961, 7.

139. "El programa económico y social en la Carta de Bogotá," and "La cuestión agraria en primer término," *El Diario de Hoy*, January 18, 1961, 7.

140. "Fomento de capitales e inversiones," *El Diario de Hoy*, April 7, 1961, 7.

141. "Día a día," *El Diario de Hoy*, April 5, 1961, 7.

142. "El consejo consultivo pre-electoral," *El Diario de Hoy*, January 31, 1961, 7.

143. "Factores que limitan el desarrollo algodonero," *El Diario de Hoy*, February 2, 1961, 7.

144. "Día a día," *El Diario de Hoy*, April 5, 1961, 7.

145. "Aportes de justicia social," *El Diario de Hoy*, February 17, 1961, 7.

146. Viera Altamirano, *Obras escogidas*, 545, 605. Originally appearing in Viera Altamirano, *Ingenieros sociales*.

147. "Día a día," *El Diario de Hoy*, February 7, 1961, 7. The quote is actually drawn from a "Día a día" editorial from *El Diario de Hoy*, February 5, 1973, 9, demonstrating the consistency in Viera Altamirano's thinking throughout the years.

148. For just two examples, see "Día a día," *El Diario de Hoy*, January 30, 1961, 7; and "El continente pobre y analfabeta," *El Diario de Hoy*, February 15, 1961, 7.

149. "Día a día," *El Diario de Hoy*, April 15, 1961, 7. See also "Pero también la civilización es la civilización," *El Diario de Hoy*, March 12, 1961, 7, which refers to Japan leaving the middle ages.

150. Viera Altamirano, *Obras escogidas*, 547, 551–52. Originally appearing in Viera Altamirano, *Ingenieros sociales*.

151. "Otra vez el reformador deconocido," *El Diario de Hoy*, January 31, 1961, 7.

152. "Una misión sin bienvenida: Alimentos para la paz," *El Diario de Hoy*, March 5, 1961, 7. See also Jaume Miravitiles, "Alimentos para la paz," *El Diario de Hoy*, February 4, 1961, 6.

153. "La hora de América Latina" and "Día a día," *El Diario de Hoy*, February 6, 1961, 7; and "Día a día," *El Diario de Hoy*, February 20, 1961, 7.

154. Viera Altamirano, *Obras escogidas*, 622–23. Originally appearing in Viera Altamirano, *Instituciones y revoluciones.*

155. The quote is from "Desde arriba se ve mejor nuestra montaña de la pobreza," *El Diario de Hoy*, February 8, 1961, 7. Another Sarmiento reference is found in "Pero también la civilización es la civilización," *El Diario de Hoy*, March 12, 1961, 7, 18. The need for foreigners and foreign investment can be found in "Actitud de bienvenida al inversionista extranjero," *El Diario de Hoy*, January 10, 1961, 7; "Desde arriba se ve mejor nuestra montaña de la pobreza," February, 8, 1961, 7; and "Día a día," February 17, 1961, 7.

156. Valdivieso Oriani, *Cruzando El Imposible*, 89. In addition to his written memoir, Valdivieso Oriani has posted video monologues on YouTube: http://youtu.be/6so6vQNkxX8 and http://youtube/JJ2-NjI7rWA.

157. Valdivieso Oriani, *Cruzando El Imposible*, 299.

158. Ibid., 152.

Chapter 2

* Rivera, *Mensaje del Teniente Coronel Julio A. Rivera*, 8. The full text reads, "Contra el comunismo vamos a luchar con las armas de la reforma socio-económica, dignificando al hombre como ciudadano y trabajador, y a la familia como sustento de la nacionalidad."

1. The text of the speech can found in *El Diario de Hoy*, June 29, 1966; June 30, 1966; and July 1, 1966.

2. *El Diario de Hoy*, July 1, 1966, 44.

3. *El Diario de Hoy*, June 30, 1966, 52.

4. Domínguez, *Datos para una biografía*, 31.

5. For a profile of Rivera, see Kennedy, *Middle Beat*, 183. On the CIA's positive reception toward him in 1965, see a declassified CIA report that describes him as a model U.S. ally, United States, Central Intelligence Agency, "Survey of Communism," K-1. See also the biography of Rivera by Carlos Armando Domínguez, who served as secretary general of the cabinet during his presidency, *Datos para una biografía*, including p. 24 for reference to Rivera's participation in the 1944 coup.

6. For U.S. foreign aid figures the best source is USAID, *U.S. Overseas Loans and Grants* (the *Greenbook*), http://gbk.eads.usaidallnet.gov. For a list of projects during the first five years of the Alliance in El Salvador, see "La Alianza cumple 5 años de progreso en El Salvador," *El Diario de Hoy*, August 17, 1966.

7. The debate over the tax reform attempts in 1962 can be found in DOS-IAES, 1960–1963, 816.112/12–1562, Downs, U.S. Embassy, San Salvador, to U.S. Department of State, Washington, D.C., December 15, 1962. See also Henry Lepidus, "Factional Strife Divides El Salvador," *New York Times*, January 10, 1962, 66.

8. See the pamphlet published by the Partido Demócrata Cristiano, *Historia de una farsa*, 1962, in DOS-IAES, 1960–1963, 716.00/3–2762; U.S. Embassy, San Salvador, to U.S. Department of State, Washington, D.C., March 27, 1962.

9. See Domínguez, *La representación proporcional*; and Domínguez, *Datos para una biografía*.

10. "La Tragedia Comunista de 1932," *El Diario de Hoy*, various dates in January and February 1967. See Lindo-Fuentes, Ching, and Lara-Martínez, *Remembering a Massacre*, chap. 6 for analysis of the 1967 presidential election and the accompanying use of fear-based rhetoric; see also Webre, *José Napoleón Duarte*.

11. Rey Prendes, *De la dictadura militar*, 172.

12. Vaquerano interview.

13. United States, Central Intelligence Agency, "Survey of Communism," K-1.

14. U.S. State Department records report that CGS leaders were given positions in the PCN and elected to serve in the assembly during the 1961 elections. DOS-IAES, 1960–1963, 716.00/1–362, Sowash, U.S. Embassy, San Salvador, to U.S. Department of State, Washington, D.C., January 3, 1962, p. 2.

15. For overviews of the these various unions, their formation, and their respective orientations, see Molina Arévalo, "La repuesta sindical"; Menjívar, *Formación y lucha*; Larín, "Historia del movimiento sindical"; Richter, "Social Classes," 118; Castellanos, *El Salvador 1930–1960*, 260–61; and Almeida, *Waves of Protest*. For the CIA's overview of these various unions, see United States, Central Intelligence Agency, "Survey of Communism," K-6.

16. "Salario mínimo de la industria desde el 12," *El Diario de Hoy*, November 7, 1967, 3, 36.

17. World Bank/FUSADES, *El Salvador Rural Development Study*, 82.

18. "Medrano señala peligro comunista," *El Diario de Hoy*, November 7, 1968, 2, 43. The reference to "father of the death squads" comes from José Napoleón Duarte, as cited in Nairn, "Behind the Death Squads," 21.

19. "¿Por qué los comunistas y sus aliados vergonzantes atacan a ORDEN?" *El Diario de Hoy*, June 2, 1971, 31.

20. Héctor David Martínez Arguera, "Campaña armada contra el comunismo," *La Prensa Gráfica*, November 26, 1968, 6.

21. Chávez Velasco, *Lo que no conté*, 87.

22. For more on the history of ORDEN and its activities, see Cárdenal, *Historia de una esperanza*; Cabarrús, *Génesis de una revolución*; Nairn, "Behind the Death Squads"; and the various citations compiled by Ralph McGehee on the website CIA Support of Death Squads, http://www.serendipity.li/cia/death_squads1.htm#El.

23. Chávez Velasco, *Lo que no conté*, 87.

24. Murat W. Williams, "Still More U.S. Arms Won't Aid Salvador," *New York Times*, April 17, 1980.

25. Once again, the U.S. historian Bradley Simpson captured the essence of this paradox with the title to his study of U.S. policy in Indonesia in the 1960s, *Economists with Guns*. See also Gilman, *Mandarins of the Future*.

26. See Gilman, *Mandarins of the Future*; Latham, *Modernization as Ideology* and *Right Kind of Revolution*; Simpson, *Universities and Empire*; and Engerman et al., *Staging Growth*.

27. Gilman, *Mandarins of the Future*, 156.

28. Rostow, *Stages of Economic Growth*. See Gilman, *Mandarins of the Future*, chap. 5, for more on the organization and intellectual foundations of CIS. On Rostow, see Milne,

America's Rasputin; Rostow's 1972 memoir, *Diffusion of Power*; and Taffet, *Foreign Aid as Foreign Policy*, chap. 1.

29. Rostow, *Stages of Economic Growth*, 5.

30. Lerner, "Modernization," 387.

31. Rostow, *Stages of Economic Growth*, 7.

32. Ibid., 162.

33. Ibid., 163.

34. Cited in Gilman, *Mandarins of the Future*, 190.

35. John F. Kennedy, "Address on the First Anniversary of the Alliance for Progress," March 13, 1962, in Woolley and Peters, *American Presidency Project*, http://www.presidency.ucsb.edu/ws/?pid=9100.

36. Lerner, "Modernization," 391.

37. In Spanish these titles were, "El impulso hacia la modernización," "Desarrollo, productividad y talento," and "Tres modelos de naciones en desarrollo."

38. DOS-IAES, 1960–1963, 716.0012–162, Downs, U.S. Embassy, San Salvador, to U.S. Department of State, Washington, D.C., January 31, 1962, "Memorandum of Conversation."

39. Quoted in DOS-IAES, 1960–1963, 716.11/7–762, Sowash, U.S. Embassy, San Salvador, to U.S. Department of State, Washington, D.C., July 7, 1962. Although CONAPLAN was a direct response to the Alliance, it had antecedents. Since 1958 the Salvadoran government had been taking steps to institutionalize coordinated governmental planning. A reprint of the law that created CONAPLAN can be found in *La Prensa Gráfica*, April 25, 1962, 3.

40. "Planificación elogia Moscoso," *La Prensa Gráfica*, June 11, 1962, 2.

41. Comité Pro Defensa de la Dignidad Nacional, in *El Diario de Hoy*, February, 27, 1968, 15.

42. "Ideas, leyendas y prejuicios en torno al desarrollo," *El Diario de Hoy*, January 10, 1961, 7.

43. "Día a día," *El Diario de Hoy*, March 27, 1961, 7. For two other examples of critiques of the Act of Bogota, see "El programa económica y social en la Carta de Bogotá," *El Diario de Hoy*, January 18, 1961, 7, and "La Carta de Bogotá y el problema agraria," January 19, 1961, 7.

44. As just a few examples, see the front page of *El Diario de Hoy* on March 21, 1961, and of *La Prensa Gráfica* on April 26, 1962, and May 23, 1962.

45. DOS-IAES, 1960–1963, 716.00/6–1262, Sowash, U.S. Embassy, San Salvador, to U.S. Department of State, Washington, D.C., June 12, 1962.

46. "La empresa privada y la 'Alianza para el Progreso,'" *La Prensa Gráfica*, June 14, 1962, 7.

47. In Spanish the last two terms are *desarrollistas* and *tercermundistas*.

48. "La Alianza para el Progreso y el socialismo," *El Diario de Hoy*, April 14, 1966, 38.

49. "Internacionalismo o nacionalismo," *El Diario de Hoy*, February 21, 1968, 6, 39.

50. "Reformas sociales disparatadas, pero profundas," *El Diario de Hoy*, March 4, 1968, 13.

51. "Día a día," *El Diario de Hoy*, February 3, 1968, 9.

52. "Día a día," *El Diario de Hoy*, February 17, 1968, 9.

53. *El Diario de Hoy*, February 27, 1968, 15. See also *El Diario de Hoy*, February 9, 1968, 13; *El Diario de Hoy*, February 13, 1968, 13; and *La Prensa Gráfica*, February 23, 1968, 32. It is not clear whether, or to what extent, the committee's use of the term *mafia* originated with the specific case of the so-called Berkeley Mafia in 1960s Indonesia. For descriptions of the Indonesian case, see Klein, *Shock Doctrine*, 83; Shuman, *Miracle*, 154; and Simpson, *Economists with Guns*.

54. "Internacionalismo o nacionalismo," *El Diario de Hoy*, February 21, 1968, 6.

55. "Día a día," *El Diario de Hoy*, February 13, 1973, 7.

56. "No hace falta alguna el Banco de Obrero de la Alianza," *El Diario de Hoy*, March 1, 1968, 7.

57. See broadside in *La Prensa Gráfica*, February 27, 1968, 32. See the announcement about joining ANEP in *El Diario de Hoy*, May 24, 1973, 15. For a corresponding broadside from the Coffee Growers' Association, see *El Diario de Hoy*, August 10, 1973, 33.

58. "¿Es socialista la Alianza para el progreso?" *La Prensa Gráfica*, March 14, 1966, 7.

59. "Hacia una nueva 'Operación Manos a la Obra,'" *El Diario de Hoy*, February 8, 1968, 6. In 1970 Rodríguez Porth would serve as the main voice for landowners at the land reform congress—see chap. 5.

60. "Hacia una nueva 'Operación Manos a la Obra,'" *El Diario de Hoy*, February 8, 1968, 6.

61. "La línea comunista: Exaltación dirigida del nacionalismo," *La Prensa Gráfica*, February 12, 1968, 37. See "La cooperación técnica norteamericana," *La Prensa Gráfica*, February 14, 1968, 23, for another editorial in which Salcedo criticizes both Rodríguez Porth and Viera Altamirano by name. Rodríguez Porth resigned in April 1961 and explained his decision to do so in *El Diario de Hoy* on December 8, 1961. For more by Rodríguez Porth and his explanation, see his response to Salcedo in "Parentesis necesario," *El Diario de Hoy*, February 13, 1968, 17. See "La supuesta 'inocencia' de Cáceres Prendes en el caso Regalado," *El Diario de Hoy*, August 13, 1973, 15, for Rodríguez Porth and Manuel Castro Ramírez offering their views on the issue of Jorge Cáceres Prendes's incarceration for his supposed involvement in the assassination of Neto Dueñas.

62. See the FUAR platform in Valle, *Siembra de vientos*, 205.

63. Universidad Centroamericana, Facultad de Ciencias del Hombre y de la Naturaleza, "Informe sobre el 'Anteproyecto de Ley General de Educación,'" in Valle, *Siembra de vientos*, 270.

64. Menjívar, "Educación y desarrollo," 9.

65. Melgar interview.

66. Acosta (padre) interview.

67. Valle, *Siembra de vientos*, 96.

68. *Informaciones de El Salvador*, June 14, 1954, 10.

69. One exception is Almeida, *Waves of Protest*.

70. Flores Cienfuegos collection, MUPI.

71. Vaquerano interview.

72. Vaquerano interview.

73. For valuable insight from Castillo years later about this decisive moment, see Fabio Castillo Figueroa, "Los problemas de democratización y de educación siempre presentes: Hace 36 años los dos proyectos de la junta de gobierno," *Diario Co-Latino*, October 26, 1996.

74. Arnoldo Vaquerano used the term *oficialista* in our interview with him, and the term *gobiernista* appears in a speech delivered by Mélida Anaya Montes before the Primero Congreso of ANDES in December 1965, p. 1 of "Discurso y breve informe de las actividades realizadas por el comité central pro-derechos de maestro," in Flores Cienfuegos collection, caja #3, folder "1965 Primer Congreso Nacional de Educadores Salvadoreños," MUPI.

75. Chávez, "Pedagogy of Revolution," 191.

76. Acosta (padre) interview.

77. "PCN al Magisterio Nacional," in DOS-IAES, 1960–1963, 716.00/12–861, U.S. Embassy, San Salvador, to U.S. Department of State, Washington, D.C., December 8, 1961.

78. Frente Magisterio Nacional, "Manifesto al Magisterio Nacional," December 12, 1961, in DOS-IAES, 1960–1963, 716.00/1–362, U.S. Embassy, San Salvador, to Department of State, Washington, D.C., January 3, 1962.

79. Vaquerano interview. See also Almeida, *Waves of Protest*, 61. Historian Joaquín Chávez was told in an interview with Domingo Santacruz that teachers formed one of the eight columns in the nascent militant wing of the Communist Party (the FUAR) in 1961. See Chávez, "Pedagogy of Revolution," 75n137.

80. Vaquerano interview. See also Almeida, *Waves of Protest*, 83 and chap. 3, note 25.

81. Chávez, "Pedagogy of Revolution," 192.

82. Flores interview. For one additional portrayal of Mélida Anaya, see Alegría, *They Won't Take Me Alive*, chap. 8.

83. Mélida Anaya Montes before the Primer Congreso of ANDES in December 1965, p. 1 of "Discurso y breve informe de las actividades realizadas por el comité central pro-derechos de maestro," in Flores Cienfuegos collection, caja #3, folder "1965 Primer Congreso Nacional de Educadores Salvadoreños," MUPI.

84. Aldo Guevara documents examples of debates at the local level between military officials and civilians in which the former illustrate through their appeals to the national level that the norm was for the military officials to assume predominance. See Guevara, "Military Justice and Social Control," end of chap. 2.

85. Flores interview.

86. Gómez interview.

87. Portillo interview.

88. Sánchez Cerén, *Con sueños se escribe la vida*, 76.

89. For other good analyses of teacher organizing during this period, see Almeida, *Waves of Protest*; and Chávez, "Pedagogy of Revolution," esp. 180–213.

90. Vaquerano interview; see also Sánchez Cerén, *Con sueños se escribe la vida*, 76–77; and Valle, *Siembra de vientos*, 96–97.

91. "Maestros respaldan ley que les dará protección," *La Prensa Gráfica*, September 14, 1964, photo caption, found in press clippings in the Flores Cienfuegos collection, caja #3, folder "Recortes de periódicos," MUPI.

92. "A los maestros," *El Diario de Hoy*, September 15, 1964, found in press clippings in the Flores Cienfuegos collection, caja #3, folder "Recortes de periódicos," MUPI.

93. See, for example, "Más respaldo a ley en favor de maestros," *La Prensa Gráfica*, September 28, 1964, found in press clippings in the Flores Cienfuegos collection, caja #2, MUPI.

94. Letter to teachers signed by the National Coordinating Committee, San Salvador, October 30, 1964, Flores Cienfuegos collection, caja #1, folder "Comité Pro-Ley de Protección Social 1964," MUPI.

95. Vaquerano interview. See also Almeida, *Waves of Protest*, 83 and chap. 3, note 26.

96. "Indicaciones del Comité Coordinador Pro-Derechos del Maestro Para la Manifestación del 21 de junio de 1965," Flores Cienfuegos collection, caja #1, folder "Comité Pro-Ley de Protección Social, 1964," MUPI.

97. Vaquerano interview. See also Almedia, *Waves of Protest*, 84.

98. Vaquerano interview. See also Almedia, *Waves of Protest*, 83–85. Vaquerano may have altered the chronology to give greater dramatic impact to his narrative. In July 1966 the Executive Committee of ANDES sent a letter to *El Diario de Hoy* stating that their movement started September 8, 1964. "Magisterio no tiene compromiso político," *El Diario de Hoy*, September 22, 1966, 13.

99. Webre, *José Napoleón Duarte*, 102.

100. Acosta (padre) interview; and Acosta (hijo) interview.

101. Webre, *José Napoleón Duarte*; and Rey Prendes, *De la dictadura militar*. See also *El Popular*, as discussed in chapter 1. A weekly magazine founded in 1961 under the auspices of the Directorate, which took power in January 1961, *El Popular* is filled with criticisms of the Christian Democrats. The reference to the PDC as "fascist" is found in the June 23, 1961, edition, p. 2; see also June 15, 1961, 2. The copies of *El Popular* are found in DOS-IAES, 1960–1963, 716.00/7–1061, U.S. Embassy, San Salvador, to U.S. Department of State, Washington, D.C., July 10, 1961.

102. Flores interview. For more on the PCN attacks on the PDC, see Webre, *José Napoleón Duarte*; and the memoir by PDC founder Julio Adolfo Rey Prendes, *De la dictadura militar*. For studies of ORDEN, see Cárdenal, *Historia de una esperanza*; Cabarrús, *Génesis de una revolución*; and Nairn, "Behind the Death Squads."

103. Flores interview.

104. Mélida Anaya Montes before the Primero Congreso of ANDES in December 1965, pp. 1, 5 of "Discurso y breve informe de las actividades realizadas por el comité central pro-derechos de maestro," in Flores Cienfuegos collection, caja #3, folder "1965 Primer Congreso Nacional de Educadores Salvadoreños," MUPI.

105. Carlos Samayoa Martínez, "Impactos" (editorial), July 10, 1965, undetermined newspaper, found in press clippings in the Flores Cienfuegos collection, caja #3, folder "1965 Primer Congreso Nacional de Educadores Salvadoreños," MUPI.

106. "Los Maestros del Departamento de San Miguel Presentan al Primero Congreso," Flores Cienfuegos collection, caja #1, folder "Comité Pro-Ley de Protección Social, 1964," MUPI.

107. "A los maestros," *El Diario de Hoy*, September 15, 1964, found in press clippings in the Flores Cienfuegos collection, caja #3, folder "Recortes de periódicos," MUPI.

108. Such as the large march that occurred in Usulután in May 1967; see "Gran mitin magisterial en Usulután," *El Diario de Hoy*, May 15, 1967, 13, 48.

109. Vaquerano interview.

Chapter 3

* Siepmann, *Television and Education*, p. 122.

** *El Popular*, June 23, 1961, 2, in DOS-IAES, 1960–1963, 716.00/7–1061, Sowash, U.S. Embassy, San Salvador, to U.S. Department of State, Washington, D.C., July 10, 1961.

1. The fieldwork was carried out by Yolanda Ingle. The results of her work are in Ingle et al., "Television and Educational Reform: Report on the Fourth Year," 68–81.

2. Mayo, Hornik, and McAnany, "Educational Reform with Television," 23. A similar list had appeared in Mayo, Hornik, and McAnany, "Instructional Television," 120.

3. Hornik et al., "Television and Educational Reform: Summary Report of the First Year," 3.

4. Ibid., 122.

5. Academy for Educational Development, "Educational Reform," 3.

6. Clippinger, "Who Gains," 125. All dollar figures mentioned throughout the book are in historical dollars.

7. Cited in El Salvador, Ministerio de Educación, "Estado de la educación media," 7.

8. "Número de ciudadanos y número de votantes," *La Prensa Gráfica*, May 7, 1962, 7.

9. See, for example, "Maestra habla de los problemas de educación," *La Prensa Gráfica*, March 19, 1962, 3. There were numerous articles like this, with teachers being interviewed about the problems in the education system.

10. "Miserias de la enseñanza," *El Popular*, June 15, 1961, in DOS-IAES, 1960–1963, 716.00/7–1061, Sowash, U.S. Embassy, San Salvador, to U.S. Department of State, Washington, D.C., July 10, 1961.

11. For a fascinating analysis of the impact of the educational initiatives of the Catholic Church in the countryside, see Chávez, "Pedagogy of Revolution," chap. 3.

12. Walter Béneke, "Algo sobre la educación en el Japón," *El Diario de Hoy*, April 24, 1961, 6.

13. Walter Béneke, "Algo sobre la educación industrial en El Salvador," *El Diario de Hoy*, April 25, 1961, 6.

14. El Salvador, Ministerio de Educación, "Estado de la educación media," 20.

15. "Reforma educativa anuncia Ministro," *La Prensa Gráfica*, March 31, 1962, 2.

16. "Inician reunión de UNESCO en Chile," *La Prensa Gráfica*, March 6, 1962, 5.

17. Quoted in DOS-IAES, 1960–1963, 716.11/7–762, William B. Sowash, San Salvador, to U.S. Department of State, Washington, D.C., July 7, 1962. CONAPLAN was created in April 1962. See "Ley crea Consejo de Planificación," *La Prensa Gráfica*, April 25, 1962, 3.

18. "Convenio cultural de El Salvador y EEUU," *La Prensa Gráfica*, May 4, 1962, 2. It was a loan of 5.25 million colones (US$2.1 million in 1962 dollars) for primary school construction, teacher training, and curriculum development.

19. Rivera, *Mensaje del Teniente Coronel Julio A. Rivera*, 10.

20. Rivera, *Informe presidencial*, 46.

21. El Salvador, Consejo Nacional de Planificación y Coordinación Económica, *Primer plan*, 590–95.

22. Vera, *Educational Television in Japan*, 33. Béneke became ambassador in 1963 but had been consul general in Tokyo prior to that. See Gardiner, "Japanese and Central America," 30.

23. Vera, *Educational Television in Japan*, 121.

24. Ibid., 122.

25. Ibid., 25.

26. Ibid., 68.

27. "Civilizadores y máquinas de civilizar," *El Diario de Hoy*, February 16, 1961, 7.

28. Aguilar Avilés interview.

29. "Programa para el período 1963–1964, petición de El Salvador," UNESCO Archive Reg. X07.21(728.4), AMS Aid to Member States Programme—Salvador.

30. UNESCO director general, A.I., letter to minister of education, April 12, 1963, UNESCO Archive Reg. X07.21(728.4), AMS Aid to Member States Programme—Salvador.

31. Acuerdo Ejecutivo no. 6643, October 18, 1963, *Diario Oficial*, October 31, 1963, p. 10261.

32. Borja Nathan to Orvis Schmidt, director of operations, World Bank, June 25, 1964, and Borja Nathan to Maheu, September 1, 1964. UNESCO Archive Reg. X07.21(728.4), Relations w. El Salvador—Official.

33. Roberto Posso E., regional chief, A.I., of UNESCO's mission in Central America, to Juan Díaz Lewis, UNESCO Latin America division chief, 7 September 1964, UNESCO Archive Reg. X07.21(728.4), TA "63/64" El Salvador—TA/ CP 1963–64.

34. The commission that revised the curriculum had nine members, including representatives from UNESCO, CONAPLAN, the industrial association, and the public university, as well as members of the Ministry of Education. Escamilla, *Reformas educativas*, 124.

35. Emerson et al., "Educational Priority Projects."

36. Ibid., 4, 25, 28.

37. Ibid., 39.

38. "Un ahorro ilusorio en televisión educativa," *El Diario de Hoy*, May 17, 1967, 7.

39. Prof. Sergio Ovidio Garcia, "Algo sobre la televisión educativa," *El Diario de Hoy*, May 23, 1967, 7.

40. Alfonso Reyes, "El mito de la educación por televisión," *El Diario de Hoy*, May 30, 1967, 7.

41. Prof. Dr. Martín Barraza, "En torno a la televisión educativa," *La Prensa Gráfica*, June 5, 1967, 6.

42. "Congreso rechaza plan de Instituto de Educación por TV," *La Prensa Gráfica*, June 20, 1967, 2.

43. McGinn et al., "Educational Planning as Political Process," 224. The authors of the article do not provide the name of the interviewee.

44. Ross, "Educational planning," 6.

45. As just one example, see Park, *Latin American Underdevelopment*.

46. For insights on the importance of the Lancasterian system in Latin America, see Caruso and Roldán Vera, "Pluralizing Meanings." For an example of the internationalization of education policy in the Mexican case, see Lacy, "Autonomy versus Foreign Influence."

47. Rodolfo Baron Castro, delegate of El Salvador, to D. G. of UNESCO Jaime Torres Bodet, July 3, 1950, UNESCO Archive Reg. X07.21(728.4), TA Relations w. El Salvador—TA Part I.

48. "Request for Technical Assistance," Reference SaL-4, November 2, 1950, UNESCO Archive Reg. X07.21(728.4), TA Relations w. El Salvador—TA Part I.

49. "El Salvador's 'Point Four,'" *New York Times*, March 14, 1951.

50. Roberto Masferrer, subsecretario de cultura, to director general, March 19, 1951, UNESCO Archive Reg. X07.21(728.4), TA Relations w. El Salvador—TA Part I.

51. See Memo from J. Ingersool to Rowena Rommel, TA memo 2582, May 30, 1952, UNESCO Archive Reg. X07.21(728.4), TA Relations w. El Salvador—TA Part I.

52. "Suggestions for the Further Development of El Salvador," General Report of the Mission (preliminary draft), 1952, p. 35, UNESCO Archive Reg. X07.21(728.4), TA Relations w. El Salvador—TA Part II.

53. All these quotations are from DOS-IAES, 1960–1963, 716.5-MSP/2–1161, "Action Program for El Salvador: Act of Bogota Main points," Joint Embassy USOM USIS, February 11, 1961.

54. For U.S. foreign aid figures the best source is USAID, *U.S. Overseas Loans and Grants* (the *Greenbook*), http://gbk.eads.usaidallnet.gov. For a list of projects during the first five years of the Alliance in El Salvador, see "La Alianza cumple 5 años de progreso en El Salvador," *El Diario de Hoy*, August 17, 1966, 23–26.

55. DOS-IAES, 1960–1963, 716.5-MSP/6–2061, U.S. Embassy, San Salvador, to U.S. Department of State, Washington, D.C., June 20, 1961.

56. Levinson and de Onís, *Alliance That Lost Its Way*, 181. See also Taffet, *Foreign Aid as Foreign Policy*; and Leonard, "Meeting in San Salvador."

57. Lyndon B. Johnson, "Remarks upon Arrival at Tafuna International Airport, Pago Pago, American Samoa,": October 18, 1966, in Woolley and Peters, *American Presidency Project*, http://www.presidency.ucsb.edu/ws/?pid=27945.

58. Lyndon B. Johnson, "Memorandum on Appointing a Task Force to Study the Role of Educational Television in the Less-Developed Countries," November 26, 1966, in Woolley and Peters, *American Presidency Project*, http://www.presidency.ucsb.edu/ws/?pid=28048.

59. Lyndon B. Johnson, White House Diary, April 14, 1967, p. 4a, Lyndon Baines Johnson Library and Museum, http://www.lbjlibrary.org/collections/daily-diary.html.

60. Marks, "White House Task Force," 3.

61. Lyndon B. Johnson. "Remarks in Punta del Este at the Public Session of the Meeting of American Chiefs of State," April 13, 1967, in Woolley and Peters, *American Presidency Project*, http://www.presidency.ucsb.edu/ws/?pid=28201.

62. United States Agency for International Development, "El Salvador: Educational Reform Program," 54.

63. United States Agency for International Development, "El Salvador: Educational Reform Program."

64. Lyndon B. Johnson, "Remarks at the Alberto Masferrer Normal School, San Andres, El Salvador," July 7, 1968, in Woolley and Peters, *American Presidency Project*, http://www.presidency.ucsb.edu/ws/?pid=28994.

65. Lerner and Schramm, *Communication and Change*. Johnson's foreword is dated December 1964.

66. "Movies," *Time*, May 28, 1923.

67. Saettler, *Evolution of American Educational Technology*, 197.

68. "N.E.A. at Columbus," *Time*, July 14, 1930.

69. "Dedication of RCA Seen on Television," *New York Times*, April 21, 1939.

70. "Imagery for Profit: Television Goes into the Entertainment Field as a New Merchandising Medium," *New York Times*, July 16, 1941.

71. Cuban, *Teachers and Machines*, 64–67.

72. Christopher Simpson provides a fascinating account of the origins of this network in *Science of Coercion*.

73. Simpson, *Science of Coercion*, 22, 23, 10.

74. Schramm, *Beginnings of Communication Study*, 130, 133.

75. Ibid., 134–35; Simpson, *Science of Coercion*, 26.

76. Clausen, "Research on the American Soldier," 210.

77. Cited in ibid., 211.

78. Schramm, *Beginnings of Communication Study*, 133, 134.

79. Riley and Schramm, *Reds Take a City*.

80. Riley, Schramm, and Williams, "Flight from Communism," 274.

81. Riley and Schramm, *Reds Take a City*, 5, 33, 122.

82. See Riley, Schramm, and Williams, "Flight from Communism"; Schramm, Review of *How the Soviet System Works*; and Schramm, Review of *The Weapon on the Wall*.

83. Schramm, Review of *The Weapon on the Wall*, 151.

84. Cited in Schramm, *Beginnings of Communication Study*, 147.

85. Schramm, *Mass Media and National Development*.

86. Millikan and Rostow, *A Proposal*; and Millikan and Blackmer, *Emerging Nations*.

87. Haefele, "Walt Rostow's Stages of Economic Growth."

88. Schramm, *Mass Media and National Development*, 19.

89. Ibid., p. 26; and Millikan and Blackmer, *Emerging Nations*, 23.

90. Schramm, *Mass Media and National Development*, 31, 114.

91. Ibid., 110, 140.

92. Ibid., 141. The evidence that he cites is explained in greater detail in Schramm, "What We Know."

93. Schramm, *Mass Media and National Development*, 144, 164.

94. Ibid., 37.

95. "Havana Conference Resolutions Reflect Regional Support for UNESCO's Programme," *UNESCO Courier* 4, no. 1 (1951): 10.

96. Lynn Poole, "Television Explains Science to 15,000,000 Americans," *UNESCO Courier* 4, no. 6 (1951): 3.

97. UNESCO, "Report of a Committee of Experts in Television," Paris, 7–12 April, 1952, UNESCO/MC/16, Paris, 14 May 1952.

98. See Henry Cassirer's remarks in UNESCO, "Final Results," 10.

99. Siepmann, *Television and Education*.

100. *UNESCO Courier* 4, no. 3 (1953).

101. Henry Cassirer, "1955: Big Year of Decision for TV," *UNESCO Courier* 4, no. 3 (1955): 29.

102. Cassirer, *Seeds in the Winds of Change*, 235.

103. UNESCO, "UNESCO Contribution," 1.

104. Memo from Pio Carlo Terenzio, director, Bureau of Relations with Member States, to Resident Representatives, December 17, 1963, UNESCO Archive Reg. X07.21(728.4), TA "65/66" El Salvador—TA Programme for 1965–66, Records of the General Conference, Eleventh Session, Paris, 1960.

105. Archives of UNESCO, *Report of the Director General, 1961*, XIX, 109.

106. UNESCO, Executive Board, 60th session, 60 EX/Decisions, Paris, December 22, 1961, p. 9.

107. UNESCO, Executive Board, 60th session, 60 EX/Decisions, Paris, December 22, 1961.

108. "Memorandum of Conversation," February 16, 1962, in United States, Department of State, *Foreign Relations of the United States, 1961–1963*, vol. 12, doc. 41, http://history.state.gov/historicaldocuments/frus1961–63v12/d41.

109. "Educación tendrá la ayuda de Estados Unidos," *La Prensa Gráfica*, February 4, 1962, 3.

110. "Señalan importancia de conferencia en educación," *La Prensa Gráfica*, January 24, 1962, 2; "Preparan documentos de junta sobre educación," *La Prensa Gráfica*, February 3, 1962, 3; and Gilberto Aguilar Avilés, "Lo que esperamos de la conferencia en Chile," *La Prensa Gráfica*, February 16, 1962, 7. Other articles relating to the conference in Chile included opinion pieces such as Coronado Delgado, "Algunos delegados a la conferencia de Chile," *La Prensa Gráfica*, February 28, 1962, 6.

111. "Inauguran reunion de UNESCO en Chile," *La Prensa Gráfica*, March 6, 1962, 1; and "Conferencia sobre educación," *La Prensa Gráfica*, March 6, 1962, 7.

112. "Exponen necesidad socioeconómica de El Salvador," *La Prensa Gráfica*, March 25, 1962, 3.

113. "Doce millones para ayuda a educación," *La Prensa Gráfica*, March 27, 1962, 3.

114. Junta de Ministros de Educación de Centroamérica," *La Prensa Gráfica*, March 30, 1962, 2; and "Los factores humanos en el desenvolvimiento de las naciones," *La Prensa Gráfica*, March 8, 1962, 37.

115. "Reforma educativa anuncia Ministro," *La Prensa Gráfica*, March 31, 1962, 2.

116. Thapar, "Visual Aids," 32.

117. Brunswick interview.

118. "Oral Report by the Director General on the Period from January 1, 1967, to the Opening of the 76th Session," UNESCO House, April 28, 1967, UNESCO Archive 76 EX/INF/42.

119. "Oral Report by the Director General on the Activities of the Organization since the Close of the Executive Board 76th Session," UNESCO House, October 9, 1967, UNESCO Archive 77 EX/INF.2.

120. *UNESCO Courier* 18, no. 2 (1964): 26.

121. Schramm, *Mass Media and National Development*, vii.

122. Ibid., viii.

123. See Wilbur Schramm, "A Programme of Research for Mass Media Development," Paris, November 16, 1960, mimeo document for the Meeting of Experts on Development of Information Media in Latin America, Santiago, Chile, February 1–14, 1961, UNESCO/MC/DEVLA/4 (the document is stamped for limited distribution). For a summary of the discussions at the Santiago meeting, see Report by the Director General of UNESCO, "Meeting on Development of Information Media in Latin America," United Nations Economic and Social Council, UNESCO Archive E/3437/Add.1, E/CN.4/814/Add.1, February 16, 1961.

124. Schramm et al., *New Media*. The research for these volumes was carried out with USAID funds.

125. Power, "International Collaboration."

126. See, for example, Yaseen, "Mass Communication."

127. UNESCO, "Radio and Television," 18.

128. Caty, Charconnet, and Waniewicz, "Côte-d'Ivoire."

129. Assistant Director General for Communications A. Obligado to Rene Maheu, director general, January 27, 1971, UNESCO Archive 307 A 54/022.

130. "Proposals for an International Programme of Communications Research," p. 4, UNESCO Archive 307 A 54/022.

131. UNESCO, "Radio and Television." 23.

132. Cited in Haefele, "Walt Rostow's *Stages of Economic Growth*," 86–87.

133. Gilman, "Modernization Theory," 52.

134. UNESCO, "Radio and Television," 14.

135. "République de Côte d'Ivoire, Ministère de l'Éducation Nationale, *Programme d'éducation télévisuelle*.

136. "Misión Africana llegará al País para conocer la TV educativa," *El Diario de Hoy*, February 23, 1971, 3.

137. A. Okkenhaug and G. F. Rowland, "Thailand. Educational Radio and Television," January 1968, UNESCO 424/BMS.RD/MC/ED; B. Ouldah and R. Zumstag, "Télévision

éducative en Haute-Volta," June 1967, UNESCO 88/BMS.RD/MC; Bekaddour Ouldali et al., "Educational Television in the United Arab Emirates—(mission) 14–24 April 1976," UNESCO FMR/CC/DCS/76/257(FIT), FIT/9348/Technical report; Daniel P.E.G. Martin, "Educational Television: Syrian Arab Republic—(mission) April–May 1972," UNESCO 2723/RMO.RD/MC; and Daniel P.E.G. Martin, "Educational Television: Iraq—(mission) February–April 1972," UNESCO 2705/RMO.RD/MC.

138. Leonard, "Meeting in San Salvador," 135.

139. Hornik et al., "Television and Educational Reform: Summary Report of the First Year," 7.

Chapter 4

* Sánchez Hernández, "Informe anual," 149.

1. "Educación: Principal objetivo de Sánchez H.," *El Diario de Hoy*, October 25, 1966, 2.

2. United States, Central Intelligence Agency, "President's Trip," 4.

3. Ross, "Educational planning."

4. The idea of education as a tool to form citizens had prevailed in El Salvador since independence from Spain in 1821. It is an idea that has a long tradition in the West. See Heater, *History of Education for Citizenship*.

5. Aguilar Avilés interview.

6. "Será reorganizado el ramo de educación," *El Diario de Hoy*, July 27, 1967, 3.

7. "Educación por TV no desplazará maestros," *El Diario de Hoy*, August 24, 1967, 3.

8. McAnany, Mayo, and Hornik, "Television and Educational Reform," 13.

9. Aguilar Avilés interview. Among the members were two of the most prominent captains of industry, Francisco de Sola and Ricardo Sagrera. Aguilar Avilés was also a member.

10. Comisión Nacional de Educación por T.V., "La televisión educativa en El Salvador," *El Diario de Hoy*, August 28, 1967, 12; September 1, 1967, 6; September 5, 1967, 6; September 12, 1967, 6; and September 14, 1967, 6.

11. "Sánchez Hernández inaugura Televisión Educativa," *El Diario de Hoy*, February 18, 1969, 2.

12. Bruno E. M. Stiglitz, "El Salvador: Reforma educativa, Julio de 1967–Marzo de 1973," Paris, June 1973, p. 10, UNESCO Archive, 2920/RMO.RD/ESM.

13. Ibid.

14. Ibid., 11.

15. Cited in McGinn, Schieflebein, and Warwick, "Educational Planning as Political Process," 224.

16. El Salvador, Ministerio de Educación, *Documentos de la reforma educativa #2*. A chart with the main elements of the plans had been published in the main newspapers on February 21, 1970.

17. Aguilar Avilés interview.

18. UNESCO Archive Reg. X07.21(728.4), AR Relations w. El Salvador—Annual Reports, "El Salvador. Informe sobre la educación."

19. A famous example of a work that privileges elites is Bell, *Coming of Post-Industrial Society.*

20. Lerner, *Passing of Traditional Society*, 407.

21. Johnson, *Military and Society*. For a discussion on the role of civilian and military elites in modernization theory, see Gilman, *Mandarins of the Future*, 111–12, 186–87.

22. "Excerpts from a Report by Nelson A. Rockefeller, Chairman of the United States Presidential Mission for the Western Hemisphere, on the Quality of Life in the Americas," in Schlesinger, *Dynamics of World Power*, 748.

23. Schramm, *Big Media, Little Media*, 166.

24. Departamento de Relaciones Públicas de Casa Presidencial, *El Salvador 1971*, 111, 115.

25. Victor Valle, a student activist and member of the political opposition in the 1960s, described in his memoir how Béneke's personality was a key variable in the implementation of the education reform and the emerging teacher-state conflict. See Valle, *Siembra de vientos*, 97.

26. Imberton interview.

27. Aguilar Avilés interview.

28. Imberton interview.

29. Galicia interview.

30. Valle, *Siembra de vientos*, 97.

31. Alfredo Picasso, regional chief of mission in Central America and Panama, to Pio Carlo Terenzio, March 15, 1968, UNESCO Archive Reg. X07.21(728.4), TA "67/68" El Salvador-1967–78 TA Programme.

32. *La Prensa Gráfica*, February 20, 1968, 1; *El Diario de Hoy*, February 21, 1968, 2.

33. Aguilar Avilés interview.

34. Ramón Cárcamo Callejas, "Retorna 'al cementerio de los políticos fracasados,'" *La Prensa Gráfica*, August 1, 1972, 8; and "'Bowling Push' en educación comercial," *La Prensa Gráfica*, September 19, 1972, 7.

35. Valle, *Siembra de Vientos*, 95–96.

36. Ross, "Educational Planning," 6.

37. Aguilar Avilés interview.

38. McGinn, Schieflebein, and Warwick, "Educational Planning as Political Process," 239.

39. "Mensaje al magisterio nacional dirigido por el Señor Presidente de la República, Coronel Fidel Sánchez Hernández," *El Diario de Hoy*, September 21, 1967, 15.

40. "Mensaje al magisterio nacional dirigido por el Señor Presidente de la República, Coronel Fidel Sánchez Hernández," *El Diario de Hoy*, September 21, 1967, 15.

41. "Maestros deciden paro de actividades," *El Diario de Hoy*, September 25, 1967, 21.

42. Portillo interview; also described in his unpublished memoir, "El Salvador," 6.

43. Comité de Emergencia Magisterial a señor director y compañeros maestros, October 1, 1967, Flores Cienfuegos collection, caja #2, folder "1966–1967," MUPI.

44. "Comunicado urgente del Ministro de Educación," *El Diario de Hoy*, October 3, 1967, 37.

45. "Millares de maestros en debates en Congreso," *La Prensa Gráfica*, October 10, 1967, 2, 21.

46. "En enero abrirán de nuevo escuelas," *El Diario de Hoy*, October 17, 1967, 3.

47. For first-person accounts of the mutually reinforcing relationship between the ACERO strike and teacher mobilization, see Sánchez Cerén, *Con sueños se escribe la vida*, 78–79; and Valle, *Siembra de vientos*, 94–95. On the history of labor mobilization leading into 1967–1968, see Carpio, *La huelga general*; Griffith and Gates, "Colonels and Industrial Workers"; Molina Arévalo, "La repuesta sindical"; Menjívar, *Formación y lucha*; Larín, "Historia del movimiento sindical"; Richter, "Social Classes"; and Almeida, *Waves of Protest*.

48. Carpio, *La huelga general*; Valle, *Siembra de vientos*, 92–94; Almeida, *Waves of Protest*, chap. 3.

49. "Salario mínimo de la industria desde el 12," *El Diario de Hoy*, November 7, 1967, 3, 32.

50. "Amenazan extender huelga de buses," *El Diario de Hoy*, October 11, 1967, 2; "Queda solucionada problema de buses," *El Diario de Hoy*, October 24, 1967, 2.

51. Vaquerano, Flores, and Acosta (hijo) interviews.

52. Portillo interview; also described in his unpublished memoir, "El Salvador," 6.

53. Vaquerano interview. It must be remembered that Vaquerano was a member of the Communist Party at the time. See Issawi, *Issawi's Laws*, for more on political factionalism.

54. "Palabras de inauguración . . . por Prof. José Mario López," Flores Cienfuegos collection, caja #2, folder "1966–1967," MUPI.

55. As outlined in its accusations against the government in broadsides in the newspapers: "Que el pueblo juzgue," *La Prensa Gráfica*, January 29, 1968, 21; "Que el pueblo juzgue," *La Prensa Gráfica*, January 31, 1968, 21; and "Exposición presentada al Señor Presidente de la República," *La Prensa Gráfica*, February 2, 1968, 48.

56. "Que el pueblo juzgue," *El Diario de Hoy*, February 21, 1968, 10.

57. Vaquerano interview.

58. Portillo interview.

59. Portillo, "El Salvador," chap. 3, p. 4; also described in his interview.

60. Vaquerano interview.

61. Portillo interview; also described in his unpublished memoir, "El Salvador," chap. 3, p. 4.

62. "Exposición presentada al Señor Presidente de la República," *La Prensa Gráfica*, February 2, 1968, 48.

63. "Llamamiento del Pdte. Sánchez H. a maestros," *La Prensa Gráfica*, February 23, 1968, 18.

64. "Huelga de comunistas pero no de maestros," *El Diario de Hoy*, February 25, 1968, 3.

65. "El Partido de Conciliación Nacional denuncia," *El Diario de Hoy*, February 23, 1968, 29; *La Prensa Gráfica*, February 23, 1968, 23.

66. "Informe del Ministro de Educación," *La Prensa Gráfica*, February 28, 1968, 19, 20.

67. Descriptions of Béneke's personality came from interviews with people who worked with him or knew him personally, including Madeleine Imberton, Eduardo Sancho, and Roberto Galicia. Victor Valle specifically referred to Béneke's personality as an independent variable in the events. See *Siembra de vientos*, 97.

68. "Emplazamiento del Señor Ministro de Educación a los lideres maestros," *La Prensa Gráfica*, February 23, 1968, 43.

69. *La Prensa Gráfica*, February 15, 1968, 22.

70. "ANDES se reúne con el Presidente," *La Prensa Gráfica*, February 18, 1968, 19.

71. *El Diario de Hoy*, February 24, 1968, 1, 4.

72. "Comunicado oficial sobre el desarrollo de la huelga general progresiva," *La Prensa Gráfica*, February 27, 1968, 30.

73. *El Diario de Hoy*, February 22, 1968, 1.

74. Sánchez Céren, *Con sueños se escribe la vida*, 78; Valle, *Siembra de vientos*, 98; and Vaquerano interview.

75. Flores interview.

76. Acosta (hijo) interview.

77. Portillo interview.

78. *El Diario de Hoy*, February 28, 1968, 9.

79. "Comunistas empujan a estudiantes: Medrano," *La Prensa Gráfica*, March 1, 1968, 2, 20.

80. "Alerta a la comunidad universitaria," *La Prensa Gráfica*, March 1, 1968, 28.

81. Portillo interview.

82. ANDES 21 de Junio, "Memoria de labores, 1968," pp. 5–6, in Flores Cienfuegos collection, caja #1, folder "Comité Pro-Ley de Protección Social, 1964," MUPI.

83. Ibid., 5.

84. Vaquerano interview.

85. Almeida, *Waves of Protest*, 92. This is a widely accepted view; see also Lungo, *La lucha de las masas*, 62.

86. Gómez interview.

87. Comisión Nacional de Educación por T.V., "La televisión educativa en El Salvador II," *El Diario de Hoy*, September 1, 1967, 6.

88. Comisión Nacional de Educación por T.V., "La televisión educativa en El Salvador III," *El Diario de Hoy*, September 5, 1967, 6; and Hornik et al. "Television and Educational Reform: Report on the Third Year," 100.

89. United States Agency for International Development, *Statistics*, 5.

90. United States Agency for International Development, Mission to El Salvador, "El Salvador," 1969, 7–8, and annex B, 12; and El Salvador, Ministerio de Educación, *Documentos de la reforma educativa*. There are minor discrepancies in the figures in these two documents.

91. Bruno E. M. Stiglitz, "El Salvador: Reforma educativa, Julio de 1967–Marzo de 1973," Paris, June 1973, p. 6, UNESCO Archive, 2920/RMO.RD/ESM.

92. Aguilar Avilés interview.

93. Ibid.

94. The "canning" metaphor was attributed to Béneke by one of his main aides, Gilberto Aguilar Avilés, in his interview.

95. "Completada cuota de Televisión Educativa," *El Diario de Hoy*, May 25, 1968, 5; "En septiembre inician educación televisada," *El Diario de Hoy*, June 7, 1968, 2; and McAnany, Mayo, and Hornik, "Television and Educational Reform," 13.

96. "Johnson inaugura la Televisión Educativa," *El Diario de Hoy*, July 8, 1968, 1.

97. Lyndon B. Johnson, "Remarks at the Alberto Masferrer Normal School, San Andres, El Salvador," July 7, 1968, in Woolley and Peters, *American Presidency Project*, http://www.presidency.ucsb.edu/ws/?pid=28994.

98. "Béneke inaugurara hoy TV Educativa," *El Diario de Hoy*, August 30, 1968, 3.

99. "Sánchez H. inaugura Televisión Educativa," *El Diario de Hoy*, February 18, 1969, 2.

100. "Más de mil alumnos para TVE Educativa," *El Diario de Hoy*, February 9, 1969, 3.

101. Schramm et al., "Television and Educational Reform: Report on the Second Year," 14.

102. Thirteen percent of the 9,401 seventh graders in the TVE system in 1970 were in private schools. Ibid.

103. The description of the reform in eleven elements comes from Mayo, Hornik, and McAnany, "Instructional Television," 120. See also Bruno E. M. Stiglitz, "El Salvador: Reforma educativa, Julio de 1967–Marzo de 1973," Paris, June 1973, p. 6, UNESCO Archive, 2920/RMO.RD/ESM.

104. McAnany, Mayo, and Hornik, "Television and Educational Reform," 5, 6.

105. Bruno E. M. Stiglitz, "El Salvador: Reforma educativa, Julio de 1967–Marzo de 1973," Paris, June 1973, p. 8, UNESCO Archive, 2920/RMO.RD/ESM.

106. Ruiz Paniagua, "La educación normal," 3; and Aguilar Avilés interview.

107. "Posible cierre de normales en 1969," *El Diario de Hoy*, October 12, 1968, 5; and Aguilar Avilés interview.

108. Aguilar Avilés interview.

109. Bracamonte interview. Bracamonte was the last principal of Ciudad Normal.

110. McAnany, Mayo, and Hornik, "Television and Educational Reform," 21.

111. "Explican razones de reorganización escolar," *El Diario de Hoy*, December 12, 1968, 5.

112. Aguilar Avilés interview.

113. Ibid.

114. "Total reorganización en sistema de educación," *La Prensa Gráfica*, September 8, 1968, 3.

115. McAnany, Mayo, and Hornik, "Television and Educational Reform"; and "Reorganizan oficinas de M. de Educación," *El Diario de Hoy*, December 22, 1968, 3.

116. The organizational charts before and after the reform appear in El Salvador, Ministerio de Educación, *Documentos de la reforma educativa #2*, 33.

117. McAnany, Mayo, and Hornik, "Television and Educational Reform," 23.

118. Mayo, "Teacher Observation," 2, 9–10.

119. Hornik et al. "Television and Educational Reform: Report on the Third Year," 6.

120. Schramm et al., "Television and Educational Reform: Report on the Second Year," 19–20.

121. Hornik et al. "Television and Educational Reform: Report on the Third Year," 6.

122. Ibid., 4; and Schramm et al., "Television and Educational Reform: Report on the Second Year," 20.

123. Hornik et al., "Television and Educational Reform: Report on the Third Year," 5.

124. A summary of school construction plans appears in *El Diario de Hoy*, February 21, 1970.

125. Bruno E. M. Stiglitz, "El Salvador: Reforma educativa, Julio de 1967–Marzo de 1973," Paris, June 1973, p. 7, UNESCO Archive, 2920/RMO.RD/ESM.

126. Ibid., 6, 10.

127. Galicia interview.

128. Roberto Salomón, interview by Jessica P. Alpert, "Oral History of the Jewish Community of El Salvador," private collection, 2005–2006; the interview can be found at *The StoryListener*, http://storylistener.blogspot.com/2006_06_01_archive.html, under "Creating Theater. (literally)," June 8, 2006 (Salomón is referred to as "Roby").

129. For an account of the theater school, see Salomón and Velis, "El desarrollo de la educación teatral."

130. The experiences of the music Peace Corps volunteers in El Salvador are told in fascinating detail in Reedy, "Music Education."

131. Galicia interview.

132. Imberton interview.

133. Vom Hau, "Unpacking the Schools," 129.

134. El Salvador, Ministerio de Educación, *Documentos básicos*, 71.

135. Ibid., 73, 77, 97, 116.

136. El Salvador, Ministerio de Educación, Dirección de Televisión Educativa, *Estudios sociales, 8° grado*, 166.

137. Ibid., 189.

138. El Salvador, Ministerio de Educación, Dirección de Televisión Educativa, *Estudios sociales, 7° grado*, 167.

139. El Salvador, Ministerio de Educación, Dirección de Televisión Educativa, *Estudios sociales, 9° grado*, 223.

140. El Salvador, Ministerio de Educación, Dirección de Televisión Educativa, *Estudios sociales, 8° grado*, 195, 196.

141. El Salvador, Ministerio de Educación, Dirección de Televisión Educativa, *Estudios sociales, 7° grado*, 21–22.

142. El Salvador, Ministerio de Educación, *Documentos básicos*, 114, 118.

143. El Salvador, Ministerio de Educación, Dirección de Televisión Educativa, *Estudios sociales, 7° grado*, 169–70, 173.

144. Ibid., 166.

145. See McAnany, Mayo, and Hornik, "Television and Educational Reform," 31; and Ovares Ramírez, *Educación como integración ideológica*.

146. Davison, *International Political Communication*, 151 (emphasis in the original).

Chapter 5

* Walter Béneke, "Que el pueblo salvadoreño juzgue," *El Diario de Hoy*, February 21, 1968, 10.

* Arturo Armando Molina in Chávez Velasco, *Lo que no conté*, p. 179.

1. "Construcción masiva de escuelas este año," *El Diario de Hoy*, February 13, 3.

2. "Sánchez H. inaugura Televisión Educativa," *El Diario de Hoy*, February 18, 1969, 2; and "Más de mil alumnos para TV Educativa," *El Diario de Hoy*, February 9, 1969, 3.

3. "Sánchez H. inaugura Televisión Educativa," *El Diario de Hoy*, February 18, 1969, 2.

4. Ingle et al., "Television and Educational Reform: Report on the Fourth Year," i.

5. López Bernal and Erroa interviews.

6. Najarro and Ortiz interviews.

7. López Bernal and Acosta (hijo) interviews.

8. Najarro interview.

9. Cañas Dinarte interview.

10. Najarro interview.

11. López Bernal interview.

12. Ibid.

13. Acosta (hijo) interview.

14. Erroa and López Bernal interviews.

15. Ingle et al., "Television and Educational Reform: Report on the Fourth Year," 33.

16. Interview with anonymous Co-ANDES activist who asked that his/her name be withheld.

17. Ibid.

18. Ibid; and Contreras de Santamaría and Erroa interviews.

19. López Bernal interview.

20. Najarro interview.

21. Ibid.

22. Contreras de Santamaría interview.

23. Portillo interview.

24. Najarro interview.

25. Mayo et al., "Television and Educational Reform: Report on the Fourth Year," 100–102.

26. Wolff, "Educational Reform."

27. Hornik et al., "Television and Educational Reform: Summary Report of the First Year," 156, 158.

28. Ortíz interview.

29. Contreras de Santamaría interview.

30. López de García interview.

31. Ibid.

32. Najarro interview.

33. Gómez and Contreras de Santamaría interviews.

34. Contreras de Santamaría interview.

35. Ibid.; and López de García interview.

36. López de García interview.

37. Portillo interview.

38. Gómez interview.

39. Contreras de Santamaría interview.

40. Acosta (hijo) interview.

41. Werthein, "Comparative Analysis," 272.

42. Cañas Dinarte interview.

43. Mantilla, "Los Hechos," 393.

44. Cited in Anderson, *War of the Dispossessed*, 92. A photocopy of the letter is reproduced in El Salvador, Ministerio de Defensa, *La barbarie hondureña*, 18.

45. "Unidad nacional ante Honduras," *La Prensa Gráfica*, June 24, 1969, 3. On the National Unity Front, see also Rey Prendes, *De la dictadura militar*, 194. Napoleón Duarte claims in his memoirs that the formation of the National Unity Front was his idea. Duarte, *Duarte*, 62.

46. For useful discussions of the war, see Durham, *Scarcity and Survival*; and Anderson, *War of the Dispossessed*.

47. Duarte, *Duarte*, 65.

48. See Chávez Velasco, *Lo que no conté*, 102.

49. Conferencia Episcopal de El Salvador, "Llamamiento del episcopado salvadoreño," 531.

50. "Plan democrático reforma agraria," *La Prensa Gráfica*, August 15, 1969, 43.

51. "ANDES 21 de Junio: Los bonos de dignidad," *La Prensa Gráfica*, August 20, 1969, 24.

52. Sánchez Hernández, *Cruzada por la dignidad*, 90.

53. For a pair of contemporary analyses on Chilean land reform, see Feder, "Land Reform"; and "Notes and Comments: Chilean Land Reform." Feder was affiliated with the United Nations and ECLA and was serving as an advisor for the Inter-American Committee for Agricultural Development.

54. Declaration of Punta del Este, August 17, 1961, in "The Inter-American System: Agreements, Conventions, and Other Documents," *The Avalon Project: Documents in Law, History and Diplomacy*, Yale Law School, http://avalon.law.yale.edu/20th_century/intam15.asp.

55. For the case of Mexico being referenced by participants of the 1970 Congress on Agrarian Reform in El Salvador, see the transcripts of the presentation by the delegation from the Catholic Church, in El Salvador, Asamblea Legislativa, *Memoria del Primer Congreso Nacional*, 199. For President Molina citing his admiration for Mexico and its land reforms as a model, see his brief memoir in Chávez Velasco, *Lo que no conté*, 183. For just two examples of the extensive historiography on land reform in Chile, see Strasma, "Economic Aspects"; and Steenland, *Agrarian Reform*.

56. Lamperti, *Enrique Alvarez Cordova*, 99–100. Lamperti based this claim about Alvarez's demands on interviews with Lino Osegueda, Alvarez's friend and professional associate.

57. Ibid., 103; See also the report in *La Prensa Gráfica*, October 16, 1969, 23.

58. See Rey Prendes, *De la dictadura militar*, 197–98. The most detailed account of the leadership change is in Webre, *José Napoleón Duarte*. Webre's book is an excellent guide to the political history of this period.

59. El Salvador, Asamblea Legislativa, *Memoria del Primer Congreso Nacional*; Webre, *José Napoleón Duarte*, 122–30; and Kirby, "Agrarian Politics," 115–20.

60. On Shafik Handal, see El Salvador, Asamblea Legislativa, *Memoria del Primer Congreso Nacional*, 375–76. For Molina identifying FECCAS as a "guerrilla organization," see Chávez Velasco, *Lo que no conté*, 184.

61. El Salvador, Asamblea Legislativa, *Memoria del Primer Congreso Nacional*, 29.

62. See ibid., 325, for UCS representatives describing their presence.

63. Ibid. The presentations were also published in the UES's main journal, *La Universidad*, January/February 1970.

64. Or "virulence," as José Inocencio Alas later described it. The government quickly lost control of the agenda. Alas, *Iglesia, tierra y lucha campesina*, 109.

65. The speaker was Dr. Abelardo Torres. El Salvador, Asamblea Legislativa, *Memoria del Primer Congreso Nacional*, 59.

66. Ibid., 28–29.

67. Ibid.

68. In his memoir, Alas describes his mother telling him about the conservative radio programs speaking out against the congress; see Alas, *Iglesia, tierra y lucha campesina*, 113.

69. El Salvador, Asamblea Legislativa, *Memoria del Primer Congreso Nacional*, 166.

70. Ibid., 360.

71. Ibid., 341.

72. Ibid., 351.

73. For the church's position, see ibid., 125, 338.

74. Ibid., 393.

75. Alas, *Iglesia, tierra y lucha campesina*, chap. 6. For protest by members of the congress, see El Salvador, Asamblea Legislativa, *Memoria del Primer Congreso Nacional*, 404.

76. Cited by Webre, *José Napoleón Duarte*, 134.

77. See Duarte, *Duarte*; and Rey Prendes, *De la dictadura militar*.

78. Lamperti, *Enrique Alvarez Cordova*, 108–9.

79. Anaya Montes, *Segunda gran batalla*, 32.

80. Sánchez Cerén, *Con sueños se escribe la vida*, 80–81.

81. Vaquerano interview.

82. Valle, *Siembra de vientos*, 97.

83. Anaya Montes, *Segunda gran batalla*, 11.

84. "Análisis de la situación actual . . . San Salvador, 14 de diciembre, 1969," Flores Cienfuegos collection, caja #1, folder "Sindicato trabajadores de educación, 1969," MUPI

85. White, "Social Structure," 195. White's data comes from an Instituto de Vivienda Urbana survey taken in San Salvador early in 1966.

86. Ramón Cárcamo Callejas, "Justa negativa de los maestros," *La Prensa Gráfica*, March 23, 1971, 6.

87. Anaya Montes, *Segunda gran batalla*, 11–14.

88. "Nuevo y definitivo emplazamiento al Consejo Ejecutivo de ANDES," *El Diario de Hoy*, April 24, 1971, 20.

89. Anaya Montes, *Segunda gran batalla*, 31.

90. "Debates en Asamblea por Ley de Educación," *La Prensa Gráfica*, July 9, 1971, 30. The total number of deputies was fifty-two. For the composition of the Legislative Assembly, see Webre, *José Napoleón Duarte*, 136.

91. "Partidos de oposición piden solución a problema magisterial," *La Prensa Gráfica*, July 29, 1971, 11.

92. Universidad Centroamericana, *Análisis*, 118, 150, 151.

93. "ANDES contra aprobación de proyecto de Ley Educación," *La Prensa Gráfica*, July 8, 1971, 3, 22; "Partidos de oposición piden solución a problema magisterial," *La Prensa Gráfica*, July 29, 1971, 11.

94. Hornik et al., "Television and Educational Reform: Report on the Third Year," 2.

95. Contreras de Santamaría interview.

96. López de García interview.

97. Hornik et al., "Television and Educational Reform: Report on the Third Year," 10.

98. "El Ministro de Educación define su posición . . . ," *La Prensa Gráfica*, August 1, 1971, 11.

99. For a complete description of the minister's law, see *El Diario de Hoy*, July 21, 1971, 3, 21, 22, 24. See also Béneke in *La Prensa Gráfica*, August 31, 1971, 3, 36.

100. "¡Atención maestros!," *La Prensa Gráfica*, July 8, 1971, 36.

101. Portillo and López de García interviews. Portillo also described this in his unpublished memoir, "El Salvador," 16–17.

102. Vaquerano interview.

103. Anaya Montes, *Segunda gran batalla*, 48–49, 104, 106. See also Sánchez Cerén, *Con sueños se escribe la vida*, 81–83, for descriptions of government repression and the conflicts between ANDES and ORDEN at the local level.

104. "Partidos de oposición piden solución a problema magisterial," *La Prensa Gráfica*, July 29, 1971, 11.

105. "Profesores se concentran en el Palacio Nacional y alrededores," *El Diario de Hoy*, July 17, 1971, 5; "Pagan sus sueldos a los maestros que no están en huelga en el pais," *El Diario de Hoy*, July 27, 1971, 3; and "Nuevo descuento para maestros en huelga a partir del 1° de agosto," *El Diario de Hoy*, July 31, 1971, 5.

106. "Manifestantes causan daños en desfile de apoyo a ANDES," *La Prensa Gráfica*, August 25, 1971, 2, 26, 50; "Turba disuelta causa destrozos," *La Prensa Gráfica*, August 27, 1971, 48; "Fuertes pérdidas ataques de las turbas," *La Prensa Gráfica*, August 28, 1971, 15.

107. As described by Salvador Sánchez Céren, who was involved in the occupation of the Escuela República de Nicaragua in Quezaltepeque in La Libertad Department. See *Con sueños se escribe la vida*, 80. See also Anaya Montes, *Segunda gran batalla*.

108. "Estamos en disposición de buscar soluciones dice ANDES," *La Prensa Gráfica*, August 3, 1971, 4.

109. Almeida, *Waves of Protest*, 93.

110. United States Agency for International Development, *Statistics*, 46.

111. Lungo, *La lucha de las masas*, 62.

112. "Resoluciones y Acuerdos . . . diciembre, 1971, Comisión no. 2, Asuntos Varios," p. 4, Flores Cienfuegos collection, caja #1, folder "Sindicato Trabajadores de Educación, 1969," MUPI.

113. "Comisión no. 1, Posición de ANDES . . . ante la Reforma Educativa," p. 2, Flores Cienfuegos collection, caja #1, folder "Sindicato Trabajadores de Educación, 1969," MUPI.

114. Juan Ulloa, "Plan comunista que fracasó en El Salvador," *La Prensa Gráfica*, September 13, 1971, 7, 66.

115. For that particular quote being attributed to Duarte, see "Hace 40 años los comunistas . . . ," *El Diario de Hoy*, February 11, 1972, 48. The series went on for multiple days, starting with that first installment on February 11.

116. For a lively description of how the army cooperated in the fraud, see Mena Sandoval, *Del ejército nacional*. Even conservative historians like Mariano Castro Morán agree that the election was fraudulent. See Castro Morán, *Función política*, 234.

117. Hernández Pico, *El Salvador*; Almeida, *Waves of Protest*; Montgomery, *Revolution in El Salvador*; Rey Prendes, *De la dictadura militar*; and Webre, *José Napoleón Duarte*. See also Molina's brief memoir, "El Presidente Osorio visto por el Presidente Molina," in Chávez Velasco, *Lo que no conté*, 217–28.

118. Durán de Duarte, *Mi destino*, 44.

119. For the occupation of the UES, see Webre, *José Napoleón Duarte*, 185; and Castro Morán, *Función política*, 237. *La Prensa Gráfica* had extensive coverage of the event in its July 20 issue.

120. Molina in Chávez Velasco, *Lo que no conté*, 187.

121. Ibid. 185.

122. Ibid. 190.

123. See Molina's "Confesiones" and "El Presidente Osorio Visto por el Presidente Molina," in Chávez Velasco, *Lo que no conté*, 179–206, 217–28.

124. For descriptions of Cerrón Grande, see Lamperti, *Enrique Alvarez Cordova*, 113–16; Alas, *Iglesia, tierra y lucha campesina*, chap. 10, 12; Chávez Velasco, *Lo que no conté*, 127–42; Universidad Centroamericana, "Estudio de proyecto"; and Goodland, "Cerrón Grande Hydroelectric Project."

125. Chávez Velasco, *Lo que no conté*, 227.

126. Goodland, "Cerrón Grande Hydroelectric Project."

127. For a comprehensive look at displacement caused by development projects, especially dams, (a.k.a. "development-forced displacement and resettlement," or DFDR), see Oliver-Smith, *Defying Displacement*. For a parallel case to Cerrón Grande, see Nick Cullather's study of the consequences of a U.S.-backed dam-building and development project in the Helmand Valley of Afghanistan in the 1940s and 1950s, "Damming Afghanistan."

128. See Goodland, "Cerrón Grande Hydroelectric Project," 83–84, for a description of the Orellanas and the Commission of Landowners and Affected Populations (Comisión de Propietarios y Poblaciones Afectadas). For the patron-client networks and landowners mobilizing workers in their defense, see Universidad Centroamericana, "Estudio de proyecto," 598–99; see also 565 for reference to the anti-CEL organization and the citation to it in *Diario Latino*, March 6, 1972, 16–17. The report by the Orellana brothers is Orellana and Orellana, "Análisis del estudio del proyecto"; a copy is in UCA's library.

129. Chávez Velasco, *Lo que no conté*, 138.

130. Goodland, "Cerrón Grande Hydroelectric Project," 79.

131. Universidad Centroamericana, "Estudio de proyecto."

132. The UCA's study would be followed up three years later by a socioeconomic study from the Ministry of Education, Recinos Escobar, "El proyecto hidroeléctrico de Cerrón Grande."

133. Universidad Centroamericana, "Estudio de proyecto," 599.

134. Goodland, "Cerrón Grande Hydroelectric Project," 85.

135. Ibid., 61, 79–80.

136. Ibid., 59, 86.

137. Ibid., 79.

138. Universidad Centroamericana, "Estudio de proyecto," 617. A noteworthy contrast to UCA's criticism was provided by the U.S.-based Committee for Economic Development (CED), which wrote in a 1966 report that "social and political objectives must be reconciled and balanced against the basic goal of economic growth." The committee went on to say that it believed that development was more likely when the emphasis was placed on growth. See Committee for Economic Development, *How Low Income Countries*, 18.

139. Universidad Centroamericana, "Estudio de proyecto," 623.

140. Ibid., 618.

141. Cited in Alas, *Iglesia, tierra y lucha campesina*, 173.

142. For the main report from Osegueda's commission, see El Salvador, Comisión de Reubicación y Desarrollo Integral de Cerrón Grande, "Documento oficial." For an example of the work being done by Osegueda's architectural firm, see the advertised design for affordable housing in *El Diario de Hoy*, January 4, 1973, 32.

143. Alas, *Iglesia, tierra y lucha campesina*, 181–85.

144. Ibid., 185–89.

145. Altschul interview.

146. Ibid. Altschul mentioned the example of Común de Yanco, which has survived to this day, despite the war. Altschul's description of the opposition by the peasantry was reiterated in an interview with Fidel Recinos.

147. Ibid. Altschul said that a noteworthy exception to this was Victor de Sola, who was the president of CEL and a member of one El Salvador's wealthiest families but also someone with a more expansive vision than many of his wealthy counterparts. But even his openness to the relocation program could not undermine the stout resistance from other CEL managers, described in the rest of this chapter.

148. El Salvador, Asamblea Legislativa, *Memoria del Primer Congreso Nacional*, 20.

149. Menjívar de Rivas interview.

150. Anaya Montes, *Segunda gran batalla*, 133; and Alas, *Iglesia, tierra y lucha campesina*, chap. 8.

151. Alas, *Iglesia, tierra y lucha campesina*, 80.

152. Recinos interview. For more on the peasants' organization, Frente de Acción Popular Unificada (Unified Popular Action Front, FAPU), and its factional divisions, see Kirby, "Agrarian Politics," 200–206; and Montgomery, *Revolution in El Salvador*, 125–26.

153. Recinos interview. Recinos also provided a similar, summary perspective a few years earlier in an interview with Carlos Eduardo Rico Mira. See Rico Mira, *En silencio,* chap. 2, esp. 256.

154. Alas, *Iglesia, tierra y lucha campesina,* chap. 10.

155. Ibid., 220–21; see also chap. 12.

156. Charles Issawi called this the Law of Political Fission, i.e., factional splintering due to ideological and personal disputes. See Issawi, *Issawi's Laws of Social Motion.*

157. Joaquín Chávez's 2010 dissertation is a well-developed and well-documented study of the formation of the insurgency in the region around Lake Suchitlán; in particular, he focuses on the link between rural and urban organizers. Chávez, "Pedagogy of Revolution."

158. Chávez Velasco, *Lo que no conté,* 175.

159. For a concise overview of the reaction, see Montes, *El agro salvadoreño,* chap. 4.

160. See Molina's speech in *El Diario de Hoy,* July 10, 1976, 25.

161. Ellacuría, *Escritos políticos,* 564; originally published in *Estudios Centroamericanos* 335/336 (1976).

162. "Pronunciamiento de Partido Demócrata Cristiana," 627.

163. Montgomery, *Revolution in El Salvador,* 89.

164. Webre, *José Napoleón Duarte,* 148.

165. "Pronunciamiento de Asociación Nacional de Educadores Salvadoreños," 633.

166. "Pronunciamiento de Partido Demócrata Cristiana," 627.

167. "Pronunciamiento de Frente Acción Popular Unificada," 632.

168. "Pronunciamiento del Bloque Popular Revolucionario," 629. For more on the position of the BPR, see Cárdenal, *Historia de una esperanza,* 511–14.

169. For an insider account of the pressures from the right to impose the candidacy of General Romero, see Chávez Velasco, *Lo que no conté,* 205.

170. For good summaries of the polarizing events in the roughly five years leading up to the 1972 election, see Richter, "Social Classes"; Valle, *Siembra de vientos*; Rey Prendes, *De la dictadura militar*; and Webre, *José Napoleón Duarte.*

Chapter 6

* "Análisis sobre la T.V.E. de El Salvador por el Consejo Ejecutivo de ANDES y el Departamento de Extensión Cultural de la Universidad de El Salvador," in Anaya Montes, *La segunda gran batalla,* 250.

** Mayo, Hornik, and McAnany, *Educational Reform with Television,* 169.

1. Schramm, "Mass Media and National Development, 1979," 1.

2. Speagle, "Educational Reform."

3. Webre, *José Napoleón Duarte*; Mena Sandoval, *Del ejército nacional*; and Hernández Pico, *El Salvador: Año político.*

4. Speagle, "Educational Reform," 3, 5.

5. Ibid., 13.

6. Ibid., 14.

7. Jamison and Klees, "Cost of Instructional Radio."

8. A social discount rate is the interest rate used for social projects, which assumes that consumption today means sacrificing greater consumption tomorrow.

9. Jamison and Klees, "Cost of Instructional Radio," 27.

10. McAnany, Hornik, and Mayo, "Studying Instructional Television."

11. Mayo, Hornik, and McAnany, "Educational Reform with Television," document cover page.

12. Ibid., 164, 141.

13. Ibid., 163, 167.

14. Anzaldi, "Informe de fin de misión."

15. Aguilar Avilés interview.

16. As just one example, see Anaya Montes, *La segunda gran batalla.*

17. Clippinger, "Who Gains by Communications Development?," 70, 128, 126.

18. Ibid., 71.

19. The ministry's data covered three additional school years. Werthein, "Comparative Analysis of Educational Television."

20. Ibid., 14.

21. Ibid., 309, 303.

22. Ibid., 306. We could not find the original World Bank report in U.S. or Salvadoran libraries.

23. Ibid., 309.

24. Ibid., 198, 201, 203.

25. Lindo-Fuentes, "Schooling in El Salvador."

26. "Crisis educativa," 3, 5.

27. Ibid., 5.

28. ANDES 21 de Junio, "ANDES 21 de Junio y el 1er Seminario."

29. Ibid., 678.

30. Ibid., 679.

31. "Empieza última etapa de Reforma Educativa," *La Prensa Gráfica,* May 15, 1978; and El Salvador, Ministerio de Educación, *Informe Final.*

32. El Salvador, Ministerio de Educación, *Informe Final,* 10, 43, 69.

33. Ibid., 28, 31.

34. "Que se suprima la teleclase tal y como está concebida actualmente." El Salvador, Ministerio de Educación, *Seminario nacional,* 153.

35. Ibid., 71, 125.

36. "NO ES SALVADOREÑA." Ibid., 72.

37. "Programas de estudio por nacionales, pídase," *La Prensa Gráfica,* May 25, 1978.

38. Angela del Carmen Platero de Henríquez, "Contrareforma educativa," *La Prensa Gráfica,* May 8, 1978.

39. Régulo Pastor Murcia, "Comentando la participación del maestro en la educación," *La Prensa Gráfica,* May 10, 1978.

40. Alonso Mira, "El cooperativismo en la reforma educativa," *La Prensa Gráfica,* May 3, 1978.

41. "Exponen realidad del seminario a Reforma," *La Prensa Gráfica*, May 27, 1978.

42. El Salvador, Ministerio de Educación, *Seminario nacional*, 219.

43. *Estudios Centroamericanos* 33, no. 358 (August 1978).

44. "Educación: ¿Palabra extraviada?," 564, 565.

45. Ungo and Valero Iglesias, "Fundamentos sociopolíticos," 572.

46. Schramm, "Mass media and national development, 1979," 1.

47. Cabrera et al., "Educational Television: Final Report," 45.

48. Ibid., table 4, p. 53.

49. Ibid., table 5, p. 54.

50. Ibid., table 3, p. 52.

51. Ibid., 55.

52. Ibid., 65, 80.

53. Klees and Wells, "Economic Evaluation of Education."

54. Ibid., 330, 331.

55. Jorge Werthein, quoted in ibid., 332.

56. Klees and Wells, "Economic Evaluation of Education," 333.

57. Ibid., 335.

58. Werthein, "Comparative Analysis," 264, 270.

Conclusion

* Serpas, *La lucha por un sueño*, 72.

1. "Ex-Salvadoran Official Assassinated at Home," *Eugene (Oregon) Register-Guard*, April 28, 1980.

2. Sancho interview.

3. "Salvadoran Officer Is Assassinated and Leader Orders State of Siege," *New York Times*, May 24, 1979. See also Chávez, "Pedagogy of Revolution," 310.

4. Sociologist Jeffery Paige offers an insightful analysis of the differences between the agrarian and agro-industrial factions of the Salvadoran elite in *Coffee and Power*, chap. 6.

5. *El Popular*, June 23, 1961, 4, 2, in DOS-IAES, 1960–1963, 716.00/7–1061, Sowash, U.S. Embassy, San Salvador, to U.S. Department of State, Washington, D.C., July 10, 1961.

6. Valdivieso Oriani, *Cruzando El Imposible*, iii, iv.

7. Gómez Zimmerman, *El Salvador*, 116, 56.

8. "Opinión de las autoridades centrales de la Universidad de El Salvador sobre el proyecto de 'Ley General de Educación,'" July 1971, in Anaya Montes, *La segunda gran batalla*, 277.

9. Universidad Centroamericana, "Estudio de proyecto"; "Estudio de proyecto," 618.

10. *El Popular*, June 23, 1961, 4, in DOS-IAES, 1960–1963, 716.00/7–1061, Sowash, U.S. Embassy, San Salvador, to U.S. Department of State, Washington, D.C., July 10, 1961.

11. See Wilson, "In the Name of the State?"

12. Ellacuría, *Escritos políticos*, 537.

13. Ibid., 554.

14. Gilman, *Mandarins of the Future*, 11.

15. See LaFeber, *Inevitable Revolutions*; Coatsworth, *Central America and the United States*; Latham, *The Right Kind of Revolution*; and Grandin, *Last Colonial Massacre* and *Empire's Workshop*. See also Taffet, *Foreign Aid as Foreign Policy*.

16. Adas, *Dominance by Design*.

17. Ferguson, *Anti-Politics Machine*, 18.

18. Goodwin, *No Other Way Out*, 24–25.

19. Suvillaga interview.

20. "Political Violence Increases," *Facts on File World News Digest*, November 29, 1975, 893 D1; and Dunkerley, *Long War*, 69.

21. Christopher Dickey, "Salvadoran Rebel Intrigue; Dispute Leads to Deaths of Two Guerrilla Leaders," *Washington Post*, June 27, 1983.

22. Gen. Jaime Abdul Gutiérrez, remarks at the conference El Golpe del '79: 25 años después, San Salvador, Casa Presidencial, November 15, 2004, handwritten transcription by the authors.

23. Sancho interview.

24. Villalobos, Review of *Revolutionary Movements in Latin America*, 587.

25. Serpas, *La lucha por un sueño*, 72.

26. Browder, "Political Participation in El Salvador," 158–59.

Bibliography

Adas, Michael. *Dominance by Design: Technological Imperatives and America's Civilizing Mission*. Cambridge, MA: Belknap Press of Harvard University Press, 2009.

Aguilar Avilés, Gilberto. "El camino hacia la modernización 1948–1960." In *El Salvador: La República 1924–1999*, by Alvaro Magaña et al., 2: 444–65. San Salvador: Fomento Cultural Banco Agrícola, 2000.

Alas, José Inocencio. *Iglesia, tierra y lucha campesina: Suchitoto, El Salvador, 1968–1977*. El Salvador: Asociación de Frailes Franciscanos, 2003.

Alegría, Claribel. *They Won't Take Me Alive: Salvadoran Women in Struggle for National Liberation*. London: Women's Press, 1987.

Almeida. Paul. *Waves of Protest: Popular Struggle in El Salvador, 1925–2005*. Minneapolis: University of Minnesota Press, 2008.

Alvarenga, Patricia. *Cultura y ética de la violencia: El Salvador 1880–1932*. San José, Costa Rica: EDUCA, 1996.

Anaya Montes, Mélida. *La segunda gran batalla de ANDES*. San Salvador: Editorial Universitaria, 1972.

Anderson, Thomas P. *The War of the Dispossessed: Honduras and El Salvador, 1969*. Lincoln: University of Nebraska Press, 1981.

ANDES 21 de Junio. "ANDES 21 de Junio y el 1er Seminario Sobre la Reforma Educativa." *Estudios Centroamericanos* 33, no. 358 (August 1978): 677–79.

———. *Las luchas magisteriales en El Salvador*. Mexico: Ediciones y Impresiones Pedagógicas, 1980.

Baloyra, Enrique. *El Salvador in Transition*. Chapel Hill: University of North Carolina Press, 1982.

Baró, Ignacio Martín. "Group Attitudes and Social Conflict in El Salvador." Master's thesis, University of Chicago, 1977.

Barón Castro, Rodolfo. *La población de El Salvador*. Madrid: Inst. Gonzalo Fernández de Oviedo, 1942.

Bell, Daniel. *The Coming of Post-Industrial Society*. New York: Basic Books, 1973.

Bethel, Leslie, and Ian Roxborough. *Latin America between the Second World War and the Cold War, 1944–1948*. New York: Cambridge University Press, 1992.

Binford, Leigh. "Grassroots Development in Conflict Zones of Northeastern El Salvador." *Latin American Perspectives* 24, no. 2 (March 1997): 56–79.

————. "Hegemony in the Interior of the Revolution: The ERP in Northern Morazán, El Salvador." *Journal of Latin American Anthropology* 4, no. 1 (1999): 2–45.

————. "Peasants, Catechists and Revolutionaries: Organic Intellectuals in the Salvadoran Revolution, 1980–1992." In *Landscapes of Struggle: Politics, Society and Community in El Salvador*, edited by Aldo Lauria and Leigh Binford, 105–25. Pittsburgh, PA: University of Pittsburgh Press, 2004.

Bosch, Brian. *The Salvadoran Officer Corps and the Final Offensive of 1981*. Jefferson, NC: McFarland, 1999.

Brands, Hal. *Latin America's Cold War*. Cambridge, MA: Harvard University Press, 2010.

Brockett, Charles. *Political Movements and Violence in Central America*. New York: Cambridge University Press, 2005.

Browder, George. "Political Participation in El Salvador: A Statistical Analysis of Spatial, Historico-Temporal and Socio-Economic Relationships to Voter Registration and Total Votes Cast, 1964–1974." PhD diss., University of South Carolina, 1974.

Bulmer-Thomas, Victor. *The Political Economy of Central America since 1920*. New York: Cambridge University Press, 1987.

Burns, E. Bradford. "The Intellectual Infrastructure of Modernization in El Salvador, 1870–1900." *The Americas* 51, no. 3 (January 1985): 57–82.

Cabarrús, Carlos Rafael. *Génesis de una revolución*. Mexico City: CIESAS, 1983.

Cáceres Prendes, Jorge. "Discourses of Reformism: El Salvador, 1944–1960." PhD diss., University of Texas, Austin, 1995.

Cárdenal, Rodolfo. *Historia de una esperanza: Vida de Rutilio Grande*. 3rd ed. San Salvador: UCA Editores, 2002.

————. *El poder eclesiástico en El Salvador*. San Salvador: UCA Editores, 1980.

Carnoy, Martin. "The Economic Costs and Returns to Educational Television." *Economic Development and Cultural Change* 23 (January 1975): 207–48.

Carnoy, Martin, and Henry M. Levin. "Evaluation of Educational Media: Some Issues." *Instructional Science* 4 (1975): 385–406.

Carpio, Cayetano. *La huelga general obrera de abril: El Salvador*. San Salvador: Editorial Farabundo Martí, 1967.

Caruso, Marcelo, and Eugenia Roldán Vera. "Pluralizing Meanings: The Monitorial System of Education in Latin America in the Early Nineteenth Century." *Paedagogica Historica: International Journal of the History of Education* 41, no. 6 (2005): 645–54.

Cassirer, Henry R. *Seeds in the Winds of Change*. Dereham, Norfolk: Peter Francis Publishers, 1989.

Castellanos, Juan Mario. *El Salvador, 1930–1960: Antecendentes históricos de la guerra civil*. San Salvador: Dirección de Publicaciones, 2001.

Castro Morán, Mariano. *Función política del Ejército Salvadoreño*. San Salvador: UCA Editores, 1984.

Chávez, Joaquín, "Pedagogy of Revolution: Popular Intellectuals and the Origins of the Salvadoran Insurgency, 1960–1980." PhD diss., New York University, 2010.

Chávez Velasco, Waldo. *Lo que no conté sobre los presidentes militares*. San Salvador: Indole Editores, 2006.

Ching, Erik. "From Clientalism to Militarism: The State, Politics and Authoritarianism in El Salvador, 1840–1940." PhD diss., University of California, Santa Barbara, 1997.

———. "Patronage and Politics under General Maximiliano Hernández Martínez, 1931–1939: The Local Roots of Military Authoritarianism in El Salvador." In *Landscapes of Struggle: Politics, Society and Community in El Salvador*, edited by Aldo Lauria and Leigh Binford, 50–70. Pittsburgh, PA: University of Pittsburgh Press, 2005.

Ching, Erik, and Virginia Tilley. "Indians, the Military and the Rebellion of 1932 in El Salvador." *Journal of Latin American Studies* 30 (1998): 121–56.

Choussy, Felix. *Economía agrícola salvadoreña*. San Salvador: Ahora, 1950.

Clausen, John A. "Research on the American Soldier as a Career Contingency." *Social Psychology Quarterly* 47, no. 2 (1984): 207–13.

Coatsworth, John, H. *Central America and the United States: The Clients and the Colossus*. New York: Twayne, 1994.

Colindres, Eduardo. *Fundamentos económicos de la burguesía salvadoreña*. San Salvador: UCA Editores.

———. "La tenencia de la tierra en El Salvador." *Estudios Centroamericanos* 31, no. 335–36 (September–October 1976): 463–72.

Committee for Economic Development. *How Low Income Countries Can Advance Their Own Growth*. New York: Committee for Economic Development, 1966.

Conferencia Episcopal de El Salvador. "Llamamiento del episcopado salvadoreño en nombre de la paz (15 Agosto 1969)." *Estudios Centroamericanos*, no. 254–55 (November–December 1969): 531.

Cooper, Frederick, and Randall Packard. *International Development and the Social Sciences: Essays on the History and Politics of Knowledge*. Berkeley: University of California Press, 1997.

"Crisis educativa y responsabilidad del estado en El Salvador." *Estudios Centroamericanos* 33, no. 351–52 (January–February 1978): 3–5.

Cuban, Larry. *Teachers and Machines: The Classroom Use of Technology since 1920*. New York: Teacher's College, 1986.

Cullather, Nick. "Damming Afghanistan: Modernization in a Buffer State." *Journal of American History* 89, no. 2 (September 2002): 512–37.

———. "Modernization Theory." In *Explaining the History of American Foreign Relations*, 2nd ed., edited by Michael Hogan and Thomas Patterson, 212–20. Cambridge, UK: Cambridge University Press, 2004.

Dalton, Roque. *El Salvador: Monografía*. Havana: Enciclopedia Popular, 1963.

Davison, W. Phillips. *International Political Communication*. New York: Praeger, 1965.

Departamento de Relaciones Públicas de Casa Presidencial. *El Salvador 1971*. San Salvador: Departamento de Relaciones Publicas de Casa Presidencial, 1971.

———. *El Salvador 1973*. San Salvador: Departamento de Relaciones Publicas de Casa Presidencial, 1973.

Domínguez, Carlos Armando. *Datos para una biografía del ex presidente de la república: Julio Adalberto Rivera*. San Salvador: Talleres Gráficos, UCA, 1998.

——. *La representación proporcional y la apertura política en el periodo del Presidente Rivera, 1962–1967*. San Salvador: Tribunal Supremo Electoral, 1997.

Duarte, José Napoleón, with Diana Paige. *Duarte: My Story*. New York: G.P. Putnam's Sons, 1986.

Dunkerley, James. *The Long War: Dictatorship and Revolution in El Salvador*. London: Verso, 1982.

Durán de Duarte, María Inés. *Mi destino, mi vida*. San Salvador: Tecnoimpresos, 2005.

Durham, William. *Scarcity and Survival in Central America: Ecological Origins of the Soccer War*. Stanford, CA: Stanford University Press, 1979.

Ebaugh, Cameron. *Education in El Salvador*. Washington, D.C.: United States Office of Education, 1947.

"Educación: ¿Palabra extraviada en El Salvador?" *Estudios Centroamericanos* 33, no. 358 (August 1978): 563–68.

Eisenhower, Milton S. *The Wine Is Bitter*. Garden City, NY: Doubleday, 1963.

Ellacuría, Ignacio. *Escritos políticos: Veinte años de historia en El Salvador, 1969–1989*. Vol. 1. San Salvador: UCA Editores, 2005.

El Salvador. *Memoria que el Ministro de Estado en el Departamento de Justicia, Instrucción Pública y Negocios Eclesiásticos presenta al cuerpo legislativo en el año de 1872*. San Salvador: Imprenta del Gobierno, 1872.

El Salvador, Asamblea Legislativa. *Memoria del Primer Congreso Nacional de Reforma Agraria*. San Salvador: Publicaciones de la Asamblea Legislativa, 1970.

El Salvador, Consejo Nacional de Planificación y Coordinación Económica. *Primer plan de desarrollo económico y social, 1965–1969*. San Salvador: CONAPLAN, 1964.

El Salvador, Instituto de Vivienda Urbana. *Memoria 1959–1960*. San Salvador: IVU, 1960.

El Salvador, Ministerio de Defensa. *La barbarie hondureña y los derechos humanos*. San Salvador: Ministerio de Defensa, 1969.

El Salvador, Ministerio de Economía. *República de El Salvador, estimaciones y proyecciones de la población 1950–2050*. San Salvador: Ministerio de Economía, 2009.

El Salvador, Ministerio de Educación. *Documentos básicos de la reforma educativa 10: Programas de estudio del séptimo grado de educación básica*. San Salvador: Ministerio de Educación, 1971.

——. *Documentos de la reforma educativa #2: Plan quinquenal de educación (julio 1967–junio 1972)*. San Salvador: Dirección de Publicaciones, 1970.

——. *Informe final: Seminario nacional sobre la reforma educativa*. Vol. 16. San Salvador: Ministerio de Educación, 1978.

——. *Seminario nacional sobre reforma educativa: Etapa nacional. Catálogo de documentos*. San Salvador: Dirección de Publicaciones, 1979.

El Salvador, Ministerio de Educación, Dirección de Televisión Educativa. *Estudios sociales, libro de trabajo 7º grado*. San Salvador: Ministerio de Educación, 1972.

——. *Estudios sociales, libro de trabajo 8º grado*. San Salvador: Ministerio de Educación, 1972.

————. *Estudios sociales, libro de trabajo 9° grado*. San Salvador: Ministerio de Educación, 1972.

El Salvador, Public Administration Service, Ministerio de Economía. *Vivienda en El Salvador: Análisis del problema y recomendaciones para un programa nacional de la vivienda*. San Salvador: Publicaciones del Ministerio de Economía, 1949.

El Salvador, Secretaria de Información. *Maquinaciones contra el estado: Comunismo y reacción pretendieron subvertir el orden en el país*. San Salvador: Imprenta Nacional, 1951.

Engerman, David C., Nils Gilman, Mark H. Haefele, and Michael E. Latham, eds. *Staging Growth: Modernization, Development, and the Cold War*. Amherst: University of Massachusetts Press, 2003.

Escamilla, Manuel Luis. *Reformas educativas. Historia contemporánea de la educación formal en El Salvador*. San Salvador: Dirección de Publicaciones, 1981.

Escobar, Arturo. *Encountering Development: The Making and Unmaking of the Third World*. Princeton, NJ: Princeton University Press, 1995.

Feder, Ernest. "Land Reform under the Alliance for Progress." *Journal of Farm Economics* 47, no. 3 (1965): 652–68.

Ferguson, James. *The Anti-Politics Machine: "Development," Depoliticization and Bureaucratic Power in Lesotho*. New York: Cambridge University Press, 1990.

————. *Expectations of Modernity: Myths and Meaning on Urban Life on the Zambian Copperbelt*. Berkeley: University of California Press, 1999.

Frei Montalva, Eduardo. "The Alliance That Lost Its Way." *Foreign Affairs* 45, no. 3 (April 1967): 437–48.

Galindo, Francisco E. *Cartilla del ciudadano.1874*. 4th ed. San Salvador: Imprenta Nacional, 1904.

Gambone, Michael D. *Capturing the Revolution: The United States, Central America, and Nicaragua, 1961–1972*. Westport, CT: Praeger, 2001.

Gardiner, C. Harvey. "The Japanese and Central America." *Journal of Interamerican Studies and World Affairs* 14, no. 1 (February 1972): 15–47.

Gilman, Nils. *Mandarins of the Future: Modernization Theory in Cold-War America*. Baltimore, MD: Johns Hopkins University Press, 2003.

————. "Modernization Theory: The Highest Stage of American Intellectual History." In *Staging Growth: Modernization, Development, and the Global Cold War*, edited by David C. Engerman et al., 47–80. Amherst: University of Massachusetts Press, 2003.

Gómez Zimmerman, Mario. *El Salvador: Who Speaks for the People?* Miami, FL: Editorial SIBI, 1989.

González Ruiz, Ricardo, ed. *El Salvador de Hoy 1952*. San Salvador, 1952.

Goodwin, Jeff. *No Other Way Out: States and Revolutionary Movements, 1945–1991*. New York: Cambridge University Press, 2001.

————. "Review: Towards a New Sociology of Revolutions." *Theory and Society* 23, no. 6 (December 1994): 731–66.

Gordon Rapoport, Sara. *Crisis política y guerra en El Salvador*. Mexico City: Siglo Veintiuno Editores, 1989.

Gould, Jeffrey, and Aldo Lauria. *To Rise in Darkness*. Durham, NC: Duke University Press, 2008.

Grandin, Greg. *Empire's Workshop: Latin America, the United States, and the Rise of the New Imperialism*. New York: Metropolitan Books, 2006.

———. *The Last Colonial Massacre: Latin America in the Cold War*. Chicago: University of Chicago Press, 2004.

Grandin, Greg, and Gilbert Joseph, eds. *A Century of Revolution: Insurgent and Counterinsurgent Violence during Latin America's Long Cold War*. Durham, NC: Duke University Press, 2010.

Grenier, Yvon. *Emergence of Insurgency in El Salvador: Ideology and Political Will*. Pittsburgh, PA: University of Pittsburgh Press, 1999

Grieb, Kenneth. "The U.S. and the Rise of Maximiliano Hernández Martínez." *Journal of Latin American Studies* 3, no. 2 (1970): 151–72.

Griffith, Katie, and Leslie Gates. "Colonels and Industrial Workers in El Salvador, 1944–1972: Seeking Societal Reform through Gendered Labor Reforms." In *Landscapes of Struggle: Politics, Society and Community in El Salvador*, edited by Aldo Lauria and Leigh Binford, 71–84. Pittsburgh, PA: University of Pittsburgh Press, 2005.

Gudmundson, Lowell. *Costa Rica before Coffee: Society and Economy on the Eve of the Export Boom*. Baton Rouge: Louisiana State University Press, 1986.

Gudmundson, Lowell, and Héctor Lindo-Fuentes. *Central America, 1821–1871: Liberalism before Liberal Reform*. Tuscaloosa: University of Alabama Press, 1995.

Guevara, Aldo. "Military Justice and Social Control: El Salvador, 1931–1960." PhD diss., University of Texas, Austin, 2007.

Gurr, Ted Robert. *Why Men Rebel*. Princeton, NJ: Princeton University Press, 1970.

Haefele, Mark H. "Walt Rostow's *Stages of Economic Growth*: Ideas and Action." In *Staging Growth: Modernization, Development, and the Global Cold War*, edited by David C. Engerman et al., 81–106. Amherst: University of Massachusetts Press, 2003.

Harnecker, Marta. *Con la mirada el alto: Historia de las Fuerzas Populares de Liberación Farabundo Martí a través de entrevistas con sus dirigentes*. San Salvador: UCA Editores, 1993.

Hartman, Andrew. *Education and the Cold War: The Battle for the American School*. New York: Palgrave Macmillan, 2008.

Heater, Derek. *A History of Education for Citizenship*. London: Routledge, 2003.

Hernández Pico, Juan. *El Salvador: Año político, 1971–72*. San Salvador: UCA Editores, 1973.

Herrera, Sajid Alfredo. "Primary Education in Bourbon San Salvador and Sonsonate, 1750–1808." In *Politics, Economy and Society in Bourbon Central America*, edited by Jordana Dym and Christophe Belaubre. Boulder: University Press of Colorado, 2007.

Holden, Robert. *Armies without Nations: Public Violence and State Formation in Central America, 1821–1960*. New York: Oxford University Press, 2004.

Hoselitz, Bert. *Industrial Development in El Salvador.* New York: United Nations, 1954.

Issawi, Charles. *Issawi's Laws of Social Motion.* New York: Hawthorn Books, 1973.

Johnson, John J. *The Military and Society in Latin America.* Stanford, CA: Stanford University Press, 1964.

Johnson, Kenneth Lance. "Between Revolution and Democracy: Business Elites and the State in El Salvador during the 1980s." PhD diss., Tulane University, 1993.

Joseph, Gilbert, and Daniela Spenser, eds. *In from the Cold: Latin America's New Encounter with the Cold War.* Durham, NC: Duke University Press, 2008.

Kalijarvi, Thorsten. *Central America: Land of Lords and Lizards.* Princeton, NJ: Van Nostrand, 1962.

Kennedy, Paul P. *The Middle Beat.* New York: Teachers College Press, 1971.

Kincaid, Douglas. "Peasants into Rebels: Community and Class in Rural El Salvador." *Comparative Studies in Society and History* 29, no. 3 (1987): 466–94.

Kirby, Robert. "Agrarian Politics in El Salvador, 1950–1984." PhD diss., University of Pennsylvania, 1992.

Klees, Steven J., and Stuart J. Wells. "Economic Evaluation of Education: A Critical Analysis in the Context of Applications to Educational Reform in El Salvador." *Educational Evaluation and Policy Analysis* 3 (1983): 327–45.

Klein, Naomi. *Shock Doctrine: The Rise of Disaster Capitalism.* New York: Picador, 2008.

Krehm, William. *Democracies and Tyrannies in the Caribbean.* Westport, CT: Lawrence Hill, 1984.

Krieckhal, Jonathan. *Dictating Development: How Europe Shaped the Global Periphery.* Pittsburgh, PA: University of Pittsburgh Press, 2006.

Kryzanek, Michael J. *U.S.-Latin American Relations.* New York: Praeger, 1985.

Lacy, Elaine C. "Autonomy versus Foreign Influence: Mexican Education Policy and UNESCO." In *Molding the Hearts and Minds,* by John A. Britton, 233–40. Wilmington, DE: Scholarly Resources, 1994.

LaFeber, Walter. *Inevitable Revolutions: The United States in Central America.* 2nd ed. New York: W.W. Norton, 1993.

Lamperti, John. *Enrique Alvarez Cordova: Life of a Salvadoran Revolutionary and Gentleman.* Jefferson, NC: McFarland, 2006.

Larín, Arístedes Augusto. "Historia del movimiento sindical de El Salvador." *La Universidad* (San Salvador) 96, no. 4 (1971): 135–79.

Latham, Michael. *Modernization as Ideology: American Social Science and "Nation Building" in the Kennedy Era.* Chapel Hill: University of North Carolina Press, 2000.

———. *The Right Kind of Revolution: Modernization, Development, and U.S. Foreign Policy from the Cold War to the Present.* Ithaca, NY: Cornell University Press, 2011.

Lauria, Aldo. *An Agrarian Republic: Commercial Agriculture and the Politics of Peasant Communities in El Salvador, 1823–1914.* Pittsburgh, PA: University of Pittsburgh Press, 1999.

Leonard, Thomas M. "Meeting in San Salvador: President Lyndon B. Johnson and the 1968 Central American Summit Conference." *Journal of Third World Studies* 23, no. 2 (Fall 2006): 119–46.

Lerner, Daniel. "Modernization." In *International Encyclopedia of the Social Sciences*, edited by David L. Sills, 10:386–95. New York: Macmillan, 1968.

———. *The Passing of Traditional Society: Modernizing the Middle East.* Glencoe, IL: Free Press, 1958.

Lerner, Daniel, and Wilbur Schramm, eds. *Communication and Change in Developing Countries.* Honolulu, HI: East-West Center Press, 1967.

Levinson, Jerome, and Juan de Onís. *The Alliance That Lost Its Way: A Critical Report on the Alliance for Progress.* Chicago: Quadrangle Books, 1970.

Lindo-Fuentes, Héctor. "Schooling in El Salvador." In *Going to School in Latin America*, edited by Silvina Gvirtz and Jason Beech, 179–201. Westport, CT: Greenwood, 2008.

———. *Weak Foundations: The Economy of El Salvador in the Nineteenth Century, 1821–1898.* Berkeley: University of California Press, 1990.

Lindo-Fuentes, Héctor, Erik Ching, and Rafael Lara-Martínez. *Remembering a Massacre in El Salvador: The Insurrection of 1932, Roque Dalton and the Politics of Historical Memory.* Albuquerque: University of New Mexico Press, 2007.

Lipset, Seymour Martin, and Aldo Solari. *Elites in Latin America.* New York: Oxford University Press, 1967.

López Bernal, Carlos Gregorio. *Tradiciones inventadas y discursos nacionalistas: El imaginario nacional de la época liberal en El Salvador, 1876–1932.* San Salvador: Imprenta Universitaria, 2007.

López Vallecillos, Italo. *El periodismo en El Salvador.* San Salvador: UCA Editores, 1987.

Luna, David. "Análisis de una dictadura fascista latinoamericano: Maximiliano Hernández Martínez, 1931–1944." *La Universidad* (San Salvador) 94, no. 5 (1969).

Lungo, Mario. *La lucha de las masas en El Salvador.* San Salvador: UCA Editores, 1987.

Mantilla, Sebastián. "Los Hechos." *Estudios Centroamericanos*, no. 254–55 (November–December 1969): 393–98.

Márquez, Javier, and Educardo Montealegre. *Informe sobre la estructura bancaria y la política monetario de El Salvador.* Washington, D.C.: Publicaciones del Ministerio de Economía, 1952.

Masís, Rodrigo. *Proyectos de viviendas económicas para San Salvador.* Washington, D.C.: Unión Panamericana, 1950.

Mason, T. David. *Caught in the Crossfire: Revolutions, Repression and the Rational Peasant.* Lanham, MD: Rowman and Littlefield, 2004.

Mayo, John K., Robert C. Hornik, and Emile G. McAnany. "Instructional Television in El Salvador's Educational Reform." *Prospects: Quarterly Review of Education* 5, no. 1 (Spring 1975): 120–26.

———. *Educational Reform with Television: The El Salvador Experience.* Stanford, CA: Stanford University Press, 1976.

McClintock, Cynthia. *Revolutionary Movements in Latin America: El Salvador's FMLN and Peru's Shining Path.* Washington, D.C.: United States Institute of Peace, 1998.

McGinn, Noel. *The Evolution of Education Planning in El Salvador: A Case Study.* Cambridge, MA: Harvard Institute for International Development, 1979.

McGinn, Noel, Ernesto Schieflebein, and Donald P. Warwick. "Educational Planning as Political Process: Two Case Studies from Latin America." *Comparative Education Review* 23, no. 2 (June 1979): 218–39.

Medrano Guzmán, Juan Ramón (Comandante Balta). *Memorias de un guerrillero.* San Salvador: New Graphic S.A. de C.V., 2006.

Mena Sandoval, Francisco. *Del ejército nacional al ejército guerrillero.* San Salvador: Ediciones Arcoiris, 1990.

Menjívar, Rafael. *Formación y lucha del proletariado industrial salvadoreño.* San Salvador: UCA Editores, 1979.

———. "Educación y desarrollo económico en El Salvador." *La Universidad* (San Salvador) 95, no. 4 (July–August 1970): 5–32.

———. *Tiempos de locura: El Salvador, 1979–1981.* San Salvador: FLACSO, 2006.

Miller, Nicola. *In the Shadow of the State: Intellectuals and the Quest for National Identity in Twentieth-Century Latin America.* London: Verso, 1999.

Millikan, Max F., and Donald L. M. Blackmer, eds. *The Emerging Nations: Their Growth and United States Policy.* Boston: Little Brown, 1961.

Millikan, Max F., and Walt Whitman Rostow. *A Proposal: Key to an Effective Foreign Policy.* New York: Harper and Bros., 1957.

Milne, David. *America's Rasputin: Walt Rostow and the Vietnam War.* New York: Hill and Wang, 2008.

Molina, Hugo. "El sistema educativo y estructuras socioeconómicas." *Estudios Centroamericanos* 33 (August 1978).

Molina, Pedro. *Cartilla del ciudadano reimpresa en San Salvador de orden suprema para uso de las escuelas de la república.* 1825. San Salvador: Imprenta del Gobierno, 1861.

Molina Arévalo, José Ernesto. "La repuesta sindical ante la crisis en El Salvador, 1944–1987." Maestría en Ciencias Sociales, Mexico City, Facultad Latinoamericano de Ciencias Sociales (FLACSO), 1988.

Montes, Segundo. *El agro salvadoreño, 1973–1980.* San Salvador: UCA Editores, 1980.

Montgomery, Tommie Sue. *Revolution in El Salvador: From Civil Strife to Civil Peace.* 2nd ed. Boulder, CO: Westview, 1995.

Moore, Barrington. *Social Origins of Dictatorship and Democracy: Lord and Peasant in the Making of the Modern World.* Boston: Beacon, 1966.

Munro, Dana G. *The Five Republics of Central America.* New York: Oxford University Press, 1918.

Nairn, Allan. "Behind the Death Squads." *The Progressive* (May 1984): 20–28.

Niess, Frank. *A Hemisphere to Itself: A History of US-Latin American Relations.* London: Zed Books, 1990.

"Notes and Comments: The Chilean Land Reform: A Laboratory for Alliance-for-Progress Techniques." *Yale Law Journal* 73, no. 2 (December 1963): 310–33.

O'Brien, Thomas F. *Making the Americas: The United States and Latin America from the Age of Revolutions to the Era of Globalization.* Albuquerque: University of New Mexico Press, 2007.

Oliver-Smith, Anthony. *Defying Displacement: Grassroots Resistance and the Critique of Development*. Austin: University of Texas Press, 2010.

Osorio, Oscar. "Mensaje presidencial al Pueblo Salvadoreño." *Informaciones de El Salvador*, October 14, 1952, 2–19.

Ovares Ramírez, Flora Eugenia. *Educación como integración ideológica: Lectura crítica de los textos ODECA-ROCAP*. San José, Costa Rica: Territorio, 1977.

Paige, Jeffrey. *Agrarian Revolution: Social Movements and Export Agriculture in the Underdeveloped World*. New York: Free Press, 1975.

———. "Coffee and Power in El Salvador." *Latin American Research Review* 28, no. 3 (1993): 7–40.

———. *Coffee and Power: Revolution and the Rise of Democracy in Central America*. Cambridge, MA: Harvard University Press, 1997.

Parada, Alfredo. *Maximiliano Hernández Martínez: Ascenso y caído del General*. San Salvador: Editorial Universidad Francisco Gavidia, 2007.

Park, James William. *Latin American Underdevelopment: A History of Perspectives in the United States, 1870–1965*. Baton Rouge: Louisiana State University Press, 1995.

Parkman, Patricia. *Nonviolent Insurrection in El Salvador: The Fall of Maximiliano Hernández Martínez*. Tucson: University of Arizona Press, 1988.

Pearce, Jenny. *Promised Land: Peasant Rebellion in Chalatenango, El Salvador*. London: Latin American Bureau, 1986.

———. *Under the Eagle: U.S. Intervention in Central America and the Caribbean*. Boston: South End Press, 1982.

Pelupessy, Wim. *The Limits of Economic Reform in El Salvador*. New York: St. Martin's Press, 1997.

Pirker, Kristina. "'La redefinición de la posible': Militancia política y movilización social en El Salvador, 1970–2004." Tesis doctorado, UNAM, Mexico, 2007.

Programa Regional del Empleo para América Latina y el Caribe. *Situación y perspectivas del empleo en El Salvador*. Santiago, Chile: OIT, 1977.

Prosterman, Roy L. "'IRI': A Simplified Predictive Index of Rural Instability." In special issue on Peasants and Revolution, *Comparative Politics* 8, no. 3 (April 1976): 339–53.

Prosterman, Roy L., Jeffrey M. Riedinger, and Mary N. Temple. "Land Reform and the El Salvador Crisis." *International Security* 6, no. 1 (Summer 1981): 53–74.

Rabe, Stephen. *The Most Dangerous Area in the World: John F. Kennedy Confronts Communist Revolution in Latin America*. Chapel Hill: University of North Carolina Press, 1999.

Ramírez, Alfredo. "El discurso anticomunista en El Salvador de las derechas y el estado como antecedente de la guerra civil en El Salvador, 1967–1972." Tesis de Licenciatura, Universidad Nacional de El Salvador, 2008.

Raymont, Henry. *Troubled Neighbors: The Story of U.S.-Latin American Relations, from FDR to the Present*. Cambridge, MA: Westview, 2005.

Recinos Escobar, Edith, et al. *El proyecto hidroeléctrico de Cerrón Grande y su impacto en las unidades agrícolas y la población desplazada*. San Salvador: Escuela de Trabajo Social, Ministerio de Educación, 1975.

Reedy, Frances S. "Music Education Joins the Peace Corps." Pts. 1 and 2. *Music Educators Journal* 61, no. 5 (January 1975): 44–49, 99, 101, 103–4; 61, no. 6 (February 1975): 40–45, 95–97.

Rey Prendes, Julio Adolfo. *De la dictadura militar: Memorias de un político salvadoreño, 1931–1994*. San Salvador: Inverprint, 2008.

Richter, Ernesto, "Social Classes, Accumulation and the Crisis of 'Overpopulation' in El Salvador." *Latin American Perspectives* 7, no. 2/3 (Spring–Summer 1980): 114–39.

Rico Mira, Carlos Eduardo. *En silencio tenía que ser: Testimonio del conflicto armado en El Salvador, 1967–2000*. San Salvador: Editorial Universidad Francisco Gavidia, 2003.

Riley, John W., Jr., and Wilbur Schramm. *The Reds Take a City*. New Brunswick, NJ: Rutgers University Press, 1951.

Riley, John W., Jr., Wilbur Schramm, and Frederick W. Williams. "Flight from Communism: A Report on Korean Refugees." *Public Opinion Quarterly* 15, no. 2 (1951): 274–86.

Rivera, Julio. *Mensaje del Teniente Coronel Julio A. Rivera al pueblo salvadoreño al tomar posesión de la presidencia de la república*. San Salvador: Secretaría de Información, 1962.

Rock, David. *Latin America in the 1940s: War and Postwar Transitions*. Berkeley: University of California Press, 1994.

Rosenberg, Tina. *Children of Cain: Violence and the Violent in Latin America*. New York: William Morrow, 1991.

Rostow, Walt Whitman. *The Diffusion of Power: An Essay in Recent History*. New York: Macmillan, 1972.

———. *The Stages of Economic Growth: A Non-Communist Manifesto*. Cambridge, UK: Cambridge University Press, 1960.

Ruiz Paniagua, Javier. "La educación normal en El Salvador." Mimeograph. Guatemala City: Instituto de Investigaciones y Mejoramiento Educativo, 1965.

Saettler, Paul. *Evolution of American Educational Technology*. Englewood, CO: Libraries Unlimited, 1990.

Saldaña-Portillo, María Josefina. *The Revolutionary Imagination in the Americas and the Age of Development*. Durham, NC: Duke University Press, 2003.

Salisbury, Richard. *Anti-Imperialism and International Competition in Central America, 1920–1929*. Wilmington, DE: Scholarly Resources, 1989.

Salomón, Roberto, and Carlos Velis. "El desarrollo de la educación teatral en El Salvador." *Latin American Theater Review* 27, no. 1 (Fall 1993): 75–82.

Sánchez Cerén, Salvador. *Con sueños se escribe la vida: Autobiografía de un revolucionario salvadoreño*. Mexico: Ocean Sur, 2008.

Sánchez Hernández, Fidel. *Cruzada por la dignidad*. San Salvador: Publicaciones del CNI, 1971.

———. *Discursos del Señor Presidente de la República*. Vol. 1. San Salvador: Imprenta Nacional, 1968.

———. "Informe anual a la Asamblea Legislativa 1° de Julio de 1971." In *El Salvador 1971*. San Salvador: Departamento de Relaciones Publicas de Casa Presidencia, 1971.

Scheman, L. Ronald, ed. *The Alliance for Progress: A Retrospective.* New York: Praeger, 1988.

Schlesinger, Arthur M., Jr., ed. *The Dynamics of World Power: A Documentary History of United States Foreign Policy, 1945–1973.* Vol. 2. New York: McGraw Hill, 1973.

Schoultz, Lars. *Beneath the United States: A History of U.S. Policy towards Latin America.* Cambridge, MA: Harvard University Press, 1998.

Schramm, Wilbur. *The Beginnings of Communication Study in America: A Personal Memoir.* Thousand Oaks, CA: Sage, 1997.

——. *Big Media, Little Media: A Report to the Agency for International Development.* Stanford, CA: Institute for Communication Research, Stanford University, 1973.

——. *Mass Media and National Development: The Role of Information in Developing Countries.* Stanford, CA: Stanford University Press, 1964.

——. Review of *How the Soviet System Works: Cultural, Psychological, and Social Themes,* by Raymond Bauer et al. *Public Opinion Quarterly* 21, no. 4 (1957): 558–60.

——. Review of *The Weapon on the Wall: Rethinking Psychological Warfare,* by Murray Dyer. *Annals of the American Academy of Political and Social Science* 331 (September 1960): 151–52.

——. "What We Know about Learning from Instructional Television." In *Educational Television: The Next Ten Years,* by Lester Asheim et al., 52–76. Stanford, CA: Institute for Communication Research, 1962.

Schramm, Wilbur, Philip H. Coombs, Friedrich Kahnert, and Jack Lyle. *The New Media: Memo to Educational Planners.* Paris: UNESCO, International Institute for Educational Planning, 1967.

Scott, James. *Seeing Like a State: How Certain Schemes to Improve the Human Condition Have Failed.* New Haven, CT: Yale University Press, 1998.

Serpas, Jaime Roberto. *La lucha por un sueño: Antecedentes y crónicas completas de la guerra civil de El Salvador.* San Salvador: Impresos Soriano, 2006.

Shuman, Michael. *The Miracle: The Epic Story of Asia's Quest for Wealth.* New York: Harper Business, 2009.

Siepmann, Charles. *Television and Education in the United States.* Paris: UNESCO, 1952.

Simpson, Bradley. *Economists with Guns: Authoritarian Development and US-Indonesian Relations, 1960–1968.* Stanford, CA: Stanford University Press, 2008.

Simpson, Christopher. *Science of Coercion: Communication Research and Psychological Warfare, 1945–1960.* New York: Oxford University Press, 1994.

——, ed. *Universities and Empire: Money and Politics in the Social Sciences during the Cold War.* New York: New Press, 1998.

Smith, Tony. "The Alliance for Progress: The 1960s." In *Exporting Democracy: The United States and Latin America, Themes and Issues,* by Abraham F. Lowenthal, 71–89. Baltimore, MD: Johns Hopkins University Press, 1991.

Stanley, Bill. *The Protection Racket State: Elite Politics, Military Extortion and Civil War in El Salvador.* Philadelphia, PA: Temple University Press, 1996.

——. Review of *Emergence of Insurgency in El Salvador: Ideology and Political Will,* by Yvon Grenier. *Comparative Politics* 94, no. 1 (March 2000): 214–15.

Steenland, Kyle. *Agrarian Reform under Allende*. Albuquerque: University of New Mexico Press, 1977.

Strasma, John. "Economic Aspects of Chile's Land Use." *American Journal of Economics and Sociology* 59, no. 5 (December 2000): 85–96.

Taffet, Jeffrey F. *Foreign Aid as Foreign Policy: The Alliance for Progress in Latin America*. New York: Routledge, 2007.

Tilley, Virginia. *Seeing Indians: A Study of Race, Nation and Power in El Salvador*. Albuquerque: University of New Mexico Press, 2005.

Todd, Molly. *Beyond Displacement: Campesinos, Refugees, and Collective Action in the Salvadoran Civil War*. Madison: University of Wisconsin Press, 2010.

Turcios, Roberto. *Autoritarismo y modernización: El Salvador, 1950–1960*. San Salvador: Ediciones Tendencias, 1993. Reprint, San Salvador: Concultura, 2003.

Turits, Richard Lee. *Foundations of Despotism: Peasants, the Trujillo Regime and Modernity in Dominican History*. Stanford, CA: Stanford University Press, 2003.

Ungo, Guillermo, and Luis Fernando Valero Iglesias. "Fundamentos sociopolíticos y fines de la reforma educativa." *Estudios Centroamericanos* 33, no. 358 (August 1978): 569–78.

United Nations, Economic Commission for Latin America. "The Crisis in Central America: Its Origin, Scope and Consequences." *CEPAL Review* 22 (April 1984): 53–80.

———. *El desarrollo económico de El Salvador*. Mexico City: Naciones Unidas, 1959.

United States, Agency for International Development. *Statistics for the Analysis of the Education Sector. El Salvador*. Washington, D.C.: Agency for International Development, 1973.

United States, Department of State. *Foreign Relations of the United States, 1961–1963*. Vol. 12, *American Republics*. Washington, D.C.: GPO. Available at http://history.state.gov/historicaldocuments/.

———. *Foreign Relations of the United States, 1964–1968*. Vol. 31, *South and Central America; Mexico*. Washington, D.C.: GPO. Available at http://history.state.gov/historicaldocuments/.

Universidad Centroamericana. *Análisis de una experiencia nacional*. San Salvador: UCA Editores, 1971.

———. "Estudio de proyecto 'Cerrón Grande.'" *Estudios Centroamericanos*, no. 286–87 (August–September 1972): 511–633.

Valdivieso Oriani, Ricardo Orlando. *Cruzando El Imposible: Una saga*. 2nd ed. San Salvador: Imprenta Wilbot, 2008.

Valle, Victor. *Siembra de vientos: El Salvador 1960–1969*. San Salvador: CINAS, 1993.

Vera, Jose Maria de. *Educational Television in Japan*. Tokyo: Sophia University, 1967.

Viera Altamirano, Napoleón. *Ingenieros sociales para América Latina*. San Salvador: El Diario de Hoy, 1961.

———. *Instituciones y revoluciones*. San Salvador: El Diario de Hoy, 1963.

———. *Integración económica de Centro-América*. San Salvador: n.p., 1957.

————. *Obras escogidas*. San Salvador: Dirección de Publicaciones, 1998.

Villalobos, Joaquín. Review of *Revolutionary Movements in Latin America: El Salvador's FMLN and Peru's Shining Path*, by Cynthia McClintock. *Journal of Latin American Studies* 32 (2000): 586–88.

vom Hau, Matthias. "Unpacking the School: Textbooks, Teachers and the Construction of Nationhood in Mexico, Argentina and Peru." *Latin American Research Review* 44, no. 3 (2009): 127–54.

Webre, Stephen. *José Napoleón Duarte and the Christian Democratic Party in Salvadoran Politics, 1960–1972*. Baton Rouge: Louisiana State University Press, 1979.

Werthein, Jorge Ricardo. "A Comparative Analysis of Educational Television in El Salvador and Cuba." PhD diss., Stanford University, 1977.

White, Alastair T. "The Social Structure of the Lower Classes in San Salvador, Central America." PhD diss., Cambridge University, 1969.

Whitfield, Theresa. *Paying the Price: Ignacio Ellacuría and the Murdered Jesuits of El Salvador*. Philadelphia, PA: Temple University Press, 1994.

Wickham Crowley, Timothy. *Guerrillas and Revolution in Latin America: A Comparative Study of Insurgents and Regimes since 1956*. Princeton, NJ: Princeton University Press, 1991.

Williams, Philip, and Knut Walter. *Militarization and Demilitarization in El Salvador's Transition to Democracy*. Pittsburgh, PA: University of Pittsburgh Press, 1997.

Williams, Robert. *Export Agriculture and the Crisis in Central America*. Chapel Hill: University of North Carolina Press, 1986.

————. *States and Social Evolution: Coffee and the Rise of National Governments in Central America*. Chapel Hill: University of North Carolina Press, 1994.

Wilson, Fiona. "In the Name of the State? Schools and Teachers in an Andean Province." In *States of Imagination: Ethnographic Explorations of the Postcolonial State*, edited by Thomas Blom Hansen and Finn Stepputat, 313–44. Durham, NC: Duke University Press, 2001.

Wolf, Eric. *Peasant Wars of the Twentieth Century*. New York: Harper and Row, 1969.

Wood, Elizabeth Jean. *Insurgent Collective Action and Civil War in El Salvador*. Cambridge, UK: Cambridge University Press, 2003.

Yarrington, Doug. *A Coffee Frontier: Land, Society and Politics in Duaca, Venezuela, 1830–1936*. Pittsburgh, PA: University of Pittsburgh Press, 1997.

Yaseen, Juma Abdullah. "Mass Communication in the Arab World: The Implications of Applying the UNESCO-Schramm Strategy of Mass Media." PhD diss., United States International University, 1979.

Archives and Published Archival Collections

Alexander, Robert J., Papers. Interview Collection, 1947–1994. Box 7. 15 microfilm reels. Leiden, Netherlands: IDC, 2002.

Archivo General de la Nación (AGN), San Salvador, El Salvador.

Archivo Municipal de Sonsonate, Sonsonate, El Salvador.

Russian State Archive of Social and Political History, Moscow, Russia.

Museo de la Palabra y la Imagen (MUPI), San Salvador, El Salvador.

Adolfo Flores Cienfuegos Collection.

UNESCO Archives, Paris, France.

United States National Archives (USNA), Washington, D.C., United States.

United States Department of State. *Records of the U.S. Department of State Relating to the Internal Affairs of El Salvador, 1960–1963.* (DOS-IAES 1960–1963.) 6 microfilm reels. Wilmington, DE: Scholarly Resources, 2003.

Records Group 59. U.S. Department of State.

Interviews

Acosta, Salvador (padre). Suchitoto, El Salvador, July 13, 2007.

Acosta, Salvador (hijo). Suchitoto, El Salvador, June 3, 2005, and July 13, 2007.

Aguilar Avilés, Gilberto. San Salvador, August 22, 2002.

Altschul, Francisco. Washington, D.C., June 11, 2009. Telephone interview.

Anonymous, former teacher and member of Co-ANDES. San Salvador, El Salvador, June 8, 2005.

Bracamonte, Ricardo (the last principal of Ciudad Normal). February 3, 2003. Electronic communication.

Brunswick, Ettiene (vice president, AAFU [Association of Ex-functionaries of UNESCO]). Paris, September 14, 2004.

Cáceres, Jorge. San José, Costa Rica, August 18, 2008. Electronic communication.

Cañas Dinarte, Carlos. San Salvador, El Salvador, July 12, 2007.

Contreras de Santamaría, Susana. San Salvador, El Salvador, June 18, 2005.

Erroa, Wilmer. San Salvador, El Salvador, May 15, 2005.

Flores, Julio. San Salvador, El Salvador, July 17 and 18, 2007.

Galicia, Roberto. San Salvador, El Salvador, July 19, 2007.

Gómez, Julio Alberto. San Salvador, El Salvador, June 25, 2005.

Imberton, Madeleine. Suchitoto, El Salvador, July 14, 2007.

López Bernal, Carlos Gregorio. San Salvador, El Salvador, July 9, 2007.

López de García, Rosa Margarita. San Salvador, El Salvador, June 28, 2005.

Melgar, Rutilio. Suchitoto, April 11, 2008.

Menjívar de Rivas, Mercedes. Viejo Copapayo, El Salvador, April 10, 2008.

Najarro, Juilio César. San Salvador, El Salvador, June 16, 2009.

Orellano López, Ricardo. San Salvador, El Salvador, July 17, 2007.

Ortiz, Osmín. San Salvador, El Salvador, June 16, 2009.

Portillo, Julio César. San Salvador, El Salvador, June 28, 2005.

Recinos, Fidel. San Salvador, El Salvador, June 19, 2009.

Sancho, Eduardo. San Salvador, El Salvador, July 20, 2007, April 8, 2008, and October 23, 2008.

Suvillaga, Eduardo. Santa Tecla, November 23, 2004.

Vaquerano, Arnoldo. San Salvador, El Salvador, July 18, 2007, and April 8, 2008.

Newspapers and Magazines

Boletín del Ejército
Diario Co-Latino
Diario Oficial
El Diario de Hoy
El Popular
Facetas
La Libertad (IHNCA)
La Prensa Gráfica
La República (IHNCA)
New York Times
Opinión Estudiantil
Time
UNESCO Courier
Voz de la Fuerza Armada
Washington Post

Official Reports

Academy for Educational Development. "Educational Reform and Instructional Television in El Salvador: Costs, Benefits and Payoffs. A Summary of Richard E. Speagle's Report." Information Center on Instructional Technology, Information Bulletin no. 2. Academy for Instructional Development, October 1972.

Anzaldi, Giuseppe. "Informe de fin de misión: Desarrollo educativo." UNESCO, Paris, 1976.

Cabrera, Rodrigo, et al. "Educational Television in El Salvador; Final Report." Academy for Educational Development, 1979.

Caty, R. A. Charconnet, and I. Waniewicz. "Côte-d'Ivoire. La Télévision éducative et le développement économique et social." May–June 1967. 192/BMS.RD/COM. UNESCO Archives, Paris, France.

Clippinger, John H. "Who Gains by Communications Development?" Harvard University, Program on Information Technologies and Public Policy, 1976. In United States Senate, *Hearings before the Subcommittee on International Operations of the Committee on Foreign Relations.* 95th Cong., 1st sess., June 8–10, 1977. Washington, D.C.: Government Printing Office, 1977.

El Salvador, Comisión de Reubicación y Desarrollo Integral de Cerrón Grande. "Documento oficial para el plan organizativo y proyecto de reubicación de Cerrón Grande." June 19, 1973.

El Salvador, Ministerio de Educación. "Estado de la educación media en América Latina. Informes nacionales. El Salvador." June 1965.

Emerson, L.H.S., Guilhermo Dutra da Fonseca, J. A. Laing, and Maya J. Paez. "Educational Priority Projects for Development: El Salvador—Mission." Foreword by Director General R. Maheu. UNESCO, 1965.

Goodland, Robert. "Cerrón Grande Hydroelectric Project: Environmental Impact Reconnaissance." Washington, D.C.: World Bank, April 1973.

Hornik, Robert C., et al. "Television and Educational Reform in El Salvador: Report on the Third Year of Research." Academy for Educational Development, 1972.

———. "Television and Educational Reform in El Salvador: Summary Report of the First Year of Research (02/01/69–11/01/69)." Stanford University. Institute for Communications Research, 1970.

Ingle, Henry T., et al. "Television and Educational Reform in El Salvador: Report on the Fourth Year of Research." Academy for Educational Development, 1973.

Jamison, Dean, with Steven Klees. "The Cost of Instructional Radio and Television in Developing Countries." Academy for Educational Development, 1973.

Marks, Leonard H. "White House Task Force on Educational Television in Less-Developed Countries: Summary and Recommendations." USAID Development Information Center. Recommendation No. 2. June 27, 1967.

Mayo, John K., Robert C. Hornik, and Emile G. McAnany. "Educational Reform with Television: The El Salvador Experience." Stanford University, 1976.

Mayo, John K., et al. "Television and Educational Reform in El Salvador: Report on the Fourth Year of Research." Stanford University, Institute for Communication Research, 1973.

Mayo, Judith E. "Teacher Observation in El Salvador." Research Report Number Five. Stanford University, Institute for Communication Research, January 1971.

McAnany, Emile G., Robert C. Hornik, and John K. Mayo. "Studying Instructional Television: What Should Be Evaluated." ED-74/WS/40. August 1974. UNESCO Archives, Paris, France.

McAnany, Emile G., John K. Mayo, and Robert C. Hornik. "Television and Educational Reform in El Salvador: Complete Report on the First Year of Research." Academy for Educational Development, 1970.

McGinn, Noel, et al. "Educational Planning as Political Process: Two Case Studies from Latin America." *Comparative Education Review* 23, no. 2 (June 1979): 218–39.

Orellana, Francisco, and Roberto Orellana. "Análisis del estudio del proyecto de Cerrón Grande elaborado por Harza Engineering Co." June 2, 1972.

République de Côte d'Ivoire, Ministère de l'Éducation Nationale. *Programme d'éducation télévisuelle, 1968–1980.* Vol. 3, *Rapport des missions d'évaluation de la télévision éducative au Niger, au Salvador et aux Samoa américaines.*

Ross, John G. "Educational Planning: El Salvador" (mission). 924/BMS.RD/EP; FR/AT/ELSALED 9. August 1967–August 1968. UNESCO Archives, Paris, France.

Schramm, Wilbur. "Mass Media and National Development, 1979." International Commission for the Study of Communication Problems series, vol. 42. UNESCO, 1979.

Schramm, Wilbur, et al. "Television and Educational Reform in El Salvador: Report on the Second Year of Research." Academy for Educational Development, 1971.

———. "Television and Educational Reform in El Salvador: Summary Report of the First Year of Research." Project report series, no. 10. USAID Supported Study/Document, Academy for Educational Development, 1970.

Speagle, Richard E. "Educational Reform and Instructional Television in El Salvador: Costs, Benefits and Payoffs (summary)." Academy for Educational Development, 1972.

Thapar, Romesh. "Visual Aids in Fundamental Education and Community Development." Report on the UNESCO Regional Seminar in South and South-East Asia, New Delhi, India, September 8–27, 1958.

UNESCO. "Final Results of the Study Course for Producers and Directors of Educational and Cultural Television Programmes." London, July 5–24, 1954.

———. "Radio and Television in the Service of Education and Development in Asia." Reports and Papers on Mass Communication, no. 49. Paris, 1967.

———. "The UNESCO Contribution to the United Nations Development Decade." General Conference 12C/34, Annex II. UNESCO Archives, Paris, France.

United States Agency for International Development. "El Salvador: Educational Reform Program Including ITV." AID-DLC/P-738. June 1968.

United States Agency for International Development, Mission to El Salvador. "El Salvador: Educational Reform Program, Instructional Television Expansion Stage Loan." 1969.

United States, Central Intelligence Agency. "The President's Trip to Central America: Security Conditions." SNIE 82/83–68. 3 July 1968. Available at http://www.foia.cia.gov/docs/DOC_0000863059/DOC_0000863059.pdf.

———. "A Survey of Communism in Latin America." November 1, 1965. Available at http://www.foia.cia.gov/docs/DOC_0001462211/DOC_0001462211.pdf .

Wolff, Laurence. "Educational Reform and Instructional Television in El Salvador: A Summary of Research Findings." Academy for Educational Development, 1973.

World Bank/FUSADES. El Salvador Rural Development Study. Washington, D.C.: World Bank, 1988.

Pamphlets, Speeches, and Ephemera

Abdul Gutiérrez, General Jaime. Remarks at the conference El Golpe del '79: 25 Años Después. San Salvador, Casa Presidencial, November 15, 2004. Handwritten transcription by the authors.

Catecismo político para instrucción del pueblo español. Guatemala, 1811. Reprinted in a more elaborate, ninety-six-page variation as Catecismo político arreglado a la constitución de la monarquía española: Para ilustración del pueblo, instrucción de la juventud, y uso de las escuelas de primeras letras. Guatemala: Reimpreso en la Imprenta de Arévalo, 1813.

Portillo, Julio César. "El Salvador: Historias del movimiento popular." Unpublished memoir provided to the authors by Portillo.

Power, Colin N. "International Collaboration and Facilitation of Learning Environment Technology." An address to LETA 94 Conference (Learning Environment Technology Australia), Adelaide, Australia, September 25–30, 1994.

"Pronunciamiento de Asociación Nacional de Educadores Salvadoreños." *Estudios Centroamericanos* 31, no. 335–36 (September–October 1976): 632–34.

"Pronunciamiento de Frente Acción Popular Unificada." *Estudios Centroamericanos* 31, no. 335–36 (September–October 1976): 630–32.

"Pronunciamiento del Bloque Popular Revolucionario." *Estudios Centroamericanos* 31, no. 335–36 (September–October 1976): 628–30.

"Pronunciamiento de Partido Demócrata Cristiana, Frente a la Transformación Agraria." *Estudios Centroamericanos* 31, no. 335–36 (September–October 1976): 626–28.

Rivera, Julio A. *Informe presidencial, primer año de gobierno.* San Salvador, 1963.

Websites

Alpert, Jessica P. "Oral History of the Jewish Community of El Salvador." Private Collection: 2005–2006. Selections available at Jessica Alpert-Reich, *The Story-Listener,* http://storylistener.blogspot.com/2006_06_01_archive.html.

"The Inter-American System: Agreements, Conventions, and Other Documents." *The Avalon Project: Documents in Law, History, and Diplomacy.* Yale Law School. http://avalon.law.yale.edu.

Johnson, Lyndon B. White House Diary. Lyndon Baines Johnson Library and Museum. http://www.lbjlibrary.org/collections/daily-diary.html.

McGehee, Ralph. CIA Support of Death Squads. Compilations of references to studies of death squads and paramilitary organizations in El Salvador. http://www.serendipity.li/cia/death_squads1.htm#El.

Valdivieso Oriani, Ricardo. YouTube video monologues. http://youtu.be/6so6vQNkxX8 and http://youtu.be/JJ2-NjI7rWA.

United States Agency for International Development. *U.S. Overseas Loans and Grants* (the *Greenbook*). http://gbk.eads.usaidallnet.gov.

Woolley, John, and Gerhard Peters. *The American Presidency Project.* Santa Barbara, CA: University of California (hosted), Gerhard Peters (database). http://www.presidency.ucsb.edu/.

Index

Academy for Educational Development, 229, 247

ACERO metal factory strike, 147–49, 151, 155, 299n47

Achaerandio, Luis, 240

Act of Bogota, 57, 61, 67, 84, 116, 124

Agencia Nacional de Seguridad de El Salvador (National Security Agency, ANSESAL), 77

Aguilar, Magda, 172

Aguilar Avilés, Gilberto, 141–43, 166

Alas, Father José Inocencio "Chencho," 197, 199–200, 218

Alianza Republicana Nacionalista (Nationalist Republican Alliance, ARENA), 69, 174, 258

Alliance for Progress, 56, 262–63; during the administration of President Julio Rivera, 72–74, 108–9; appeals to land reform, 194; conservative opposition to, 86, 101; cooperation with UNESCO, 129; early efforts to obtain support of, 60–61; impact on El Salvador, 261–65; interpreted by progressives in El Salvador, 88–89; and PCN approach to education, 106, 181, 184; planning in disbursing aid, 83; in school curriculum, 174–76; support to educational reform, 116–19, 131, 170

Altschul, Francisco, 218–19

Alvarez, Enrique, 195, 197, 219

American Samoa, 118–19, 132, 134, 228, 247, 260

Anaya Montes, Mélida, 92–93; attitude to land reform project, 224; death, 267; and 1971 teachers' strike, 201–9; and 1968 teachers' strike, 149–52; opposition to the closing of teachers' school, 166; and peasant mobilization, 221–22

ANDES 21 de Junio. *See* Asociación Nacional de Educadores Salvadoreños

Anzaldi, Giuseppe, 232–33, 235

Aparicio, Luis, 240

Araujo, Arturo, 8, 39

army: alliance with elite, 7–10; conservative wing, 11; generational (*tanda*) system, 273n31; as modernizing force, 45–51, 72; reaction to teacher strikes, 156, 207; relations with teachers, 90; repression, 224

Asociación de Profesores Normalistas de Secundaria (Association of Secondary School Teachers, APNES), 92, 95

Asociación General de Estudiantes Universitarios Salvadoreños (Association of University Students at the National University, AGEUS), 156

Asociación Nacional de Educadores Salvadoreños (National Association of Salvadoran Teachers, ANDES 21 de Junio): attitude to land reform project, 224; founding of, 94–102; participation in education reform seminar, 239–40;

333

and peasant mobilization, 221–22; reaction to 1969 war with Honduras, 193; strike of 1971, 201–9; strike of 1968, 146–58. *See also* teachers

Asociación Nacional de la Empresa Privada (National Association of Private Enterprise, ANEP), 86, 156, 223–26

Asociación Salvadoreña de Industriales (Salvadoran Industrial Association, ASI), 175

Barrios, Gerardo, 8

Béneke, Walter: advocacy of educational TV, 107, 109–11, 114–15; and arts high school, 172–74; assassination of, 253–54; and educational reform, 138–41, 162–64; personality of, 141–45; reaction to the 1971 teachers' strike, 201–9; reaction to the 1968 teachers' strike, 147–53

Bloque Popular Revolucionario (Revolutionary Popular Block, BPR), 224

Boletín del Ejército, 51

Borja Nathan, Guillermo, 111

business community, 111, 139, 180. *See also* Asociación Nacional de la Empresa Privada

Canessa, Roberto, 48, 59

Carpio, Cayetano, 149

Cassirer, Henry, 127, 129

Castañeda, Carlos, 29–30

Castaneda Castro, Salvador, 3, 46

Castro, Fidel, 13, 57, 78, 124

Cartilla del Ciudadano, 34–35

Catholic Church, 20, 268, 291n11; in land reform seminar, 197, 199; liberationist wing, 11, 88; and nineteenth century liberalism, 35, 37; radio schools, 107; social doctrine, 20; traditional wing, 10

Center for International Studies (CIS), 78–79

Central American Common Market: as modernizing project, 74; and relationship to 1969 war with Honduras, 191–92; in textbooks, 176

Central American University (UCA). *See* Universidad Centroamericana José Simeón Cañas

Central Intelligence Agency (CIA), 66, 76, 137

Centre for Educational Television Overseas (CETO), 142

Cerrón Grande, 10, 27, 211–22, 243

Chávez Velasco, Waldo, 77, 213

Chávez y González, Luis, 157

Choussy, Salvador, 143, 173

Christian Democratic Party. *See* Partido Demócrata Cristiano

Ciudad Normal Alberto Masferrer, 142, 160, 166–67, 232

Clapp and Mayne, Inc., 167

Clippinger, John H., 234–35, 249

coffee: and the economy, 3, 7, 32–33, 38, 48, 55, 272n17; and elites, 5, 8, 31–32, 256

Coffee Growers Association, 42, 64, 74, 87, 287n39

Columbia Teachers College, 120

Comisión de Defensa de la Economía Nacional (Commission for the Defense of the National Economy), 64, 85

Comisión Ejecutiva Hidroeléctrica del Río Lempa (Hydroelectric Executive Committee of the Lempa River, CEL), 211–22

Comisión Nacional de Educación por T.V. (National Commission of Education through Television), 139

Comité de Información Cívica (Committee of Civic Information), 64

Comité Pro-Defensa de la Dignidad Nacional (Committee in Defense of National Dignity), 86

Commission on Relocation and Integral Development of Cerrón Grande, 218–20

communism. *See* Partido Comunista Salvadoreño

Confederación General de Trabajadores Salvadoreños (General Confederation of Salvadoran Workers, CGTS), 76

Confederación General Salvadoreña (General Confederation of Salvadoran Unions, CGS), 76, 148

Consejo Nacional de Planificación (National Planning Council, CONAPLAN): and Cerrón Grande Dam project, 219; and educational planning, 108, 114; and educational TV, 111; founding of, in 1961, 83

conservatives, definitions of development, 255–58; interpretations of PCN and U.S., 84–87; views at the 1970 Land Reform Congress, 197–205. See also *El Diario de Hoy*; elites; Viera Altamirano, Napoleón

Constitution: of 1880, 35; of 1939, 42; of 1950, 48, 51, 70, 280n73; of 1962, 106, 169

Contreras, Saúl Santiago, 156–57

Cordón, Eusebio, 83, 107–8

Corporation for Public Broadcasting, 118

Cuban Revolution, 148, 234; and impact on U.S. foreign policy, 56–57, 80, 116; as stimulus for reform, 5, 13

curricula: in colonial period, 34; criticism of, 208, 242; and educational TV, 125, 163, 165, 188; and modernization theory, 174–79; in 1968 reform, 105, 140, 158, 162, 171, 180, 185; in nineteenth century, 35; and textbooks, 186

Cuscatlán Park, 97, 150

death squads: attacks on Catholic priests, 199; attacks on teachers, 156, 207, 267; and land reform, 223, 226; in rural areas, 224

Decade of Development, 13–14, 246, 265

Department of Student Welfare, 141

de Sola, Carlos, 173

de Sola, Victor, 211–13

development: and debates at the 1970 Land Reform Congress, 197–210; and debates due to Cerrón Grande Dam project, 211–22; and debates during the 1971 teachers' strike, 204–10; and debates over definition of, 88–89, 254–60

developmentalism, 16

development community: defined, 16; emergence of, 11; and modernization theory, 12, 82; and promotion of educational TV, 14, 180, 264–65; and UNESCO, 129

Directorate of Bellas Artes, 143

Directorio Cívico Militar (the Directorate), 60–68; cracking down on teachers' organizations, 92; formation of, 60; relations with U.S., 61

Division of Secondary Education, 168

dropout rate, 109, 138, 170, 245

Duarte, José Napoleón, 210–11

East-West Center, 252

Education for Citizenship, 34, 44

Eisenhower, Dwight, 57, 124

Ejército Revolucionario del Pueblo (People's Revolutionary Army, ERP), 265

El Diario de Hoy, 66–68; as the voice of an emergent conservatism in the 1950s, 53–56

elections: general, 46, 52, 74; municipal and legislative, 151, 196, 200; presidential, of 1926, 39; presidential, of 1931, 39; presidential, of 1950, 47–48; presidential, of 1962, 60, 92, 106; presidential, of 1967, 74–76, 137, 153; presidential, of 1972, 98, 209–11, 225, 229; presidential, of 1977, 224–25

elites: and relations with the Directorate in 1961, 61–66; and relations with the military regime, 7–10, 51, 53, 253–58; and self-image, 30–31, 69–70

Ellacuría, Father Ignacio, 261–62; analysis of educational reform, 238, 243; murder of, 267; on PCN regime, 6; views at the 1970 Land Reform Congress, 199

El Popular, 29–30, 61–64, 257, 260

enrollments: as argument for educational television, 111; in assessment of reform, 245, 251; and costs per pupil, 229; expansion of, 158, 232; middle school, 163, 169, 205; in 1967, 162; in 1967–1977, 233; primary, 109; and school construction, 170

Escamilla, Manuel Luis, 238, 242

Escuela Normal Superior, 51, 166

Estudios Centroamericanos, 238, 240, 243, 247

Facetas, 82

family planning, 176

Federación Cristiana de Campesinos Salvadoreños (Christian Federation of Salvadoran Peasants, FECCAS), 196
Federación Magisterial Salvadoreña (Salvadoran Teachers' Federation, FMS), 91–92
Federación Sindical de Trabajadores de la Industria de Alimentos, Vestidos, y Similares de El Salvador (Federation of Workers in Food, Clothing, Textiles, and Related Industries, FESTIAVTCES), 208
Federación Unitaria Sindical de El Salvador (Unitary Federation of Salvadoran Workers, FUSS), 76; and 1967 labor mobilizations, 148–49; and 1968 teachers' strike, 151, 155–57; and 1971 teachers' strike, 208
First Regional Conference of National Commissions of the Western Hemisphere, 126
Food and Agriculture Organization of the United Nations (FAO), 116, 130
foreign advisors: influence of, 181, 226, 204; initial involvement in El Salvador, 12; and Minister Béneke, 145, 163; opposition to, 55
foreign aid. See UNESCO; USAID; World Bank
"fourteen families," 31, 62. See also elites
Frei Montalva, President Eduardo, 14, 194
Frente Agrario (Agrarian Front of the Eastern Region, FARO), 223–26
Frente de Acción Popular Unificada (Unified Popular Action Front, FAPU), 222–24
Frente Magisterial Revolucionario (Teachers Revolutionary Front, FMR), 90
Frente Unido de Acción Revolucionaria (United Revolutionary Action Front, FUAR), 66, 88
Fuentes Castellanos, Ricardo, 54, 86
Fuerzas Populares de Liberación Farabundo Martí (Farabundo Martí Popular Liberation Forces, FPL), 149, 222, 254, 269

Galindo, Francisco, 34–35
Ghana, 134
Goodland, Robert, 215–16, 221
Guevara, Ernesto "Che," 138

Hagerstown County, Maryland, 121
Harza Engineering, 212–20
Hawthorne Effect, 251
Hernández Martínez, General Maximilano: biographical information, 39; economic policy, 44–45; education policies, 43–44, 105; first regime of, 1931–1944, 39–46; and the 1939 campaign against plantation-owned stores and payment of workers in *fichas*, 41–43
Herrera Rebollo, Carlos, 238, 253, 267
high school: arts (*bachillerato en artes*), 172, 251; diversified (*bachilleratos diversificados*) 171–72, 204
Hoselitz, Bert, 49–51

Imberton, Madeleine, 142, 173
Index of Rural Instability (IRI), 21–22
industrialization: Alliance for Progress and, 15; as argument to reform education, 51, 104–5, 107–9, 111, 138, 179–80, 263; Cerrón Grande Dam project and, 211; conservative views on, 55, 68; foreign advise to pursue, 50, 55; in modernization theory, 134; military views on, 5, 10, 48, 72, 256; and 1969 war, 191–92; progressive views on, 244–45, 258; in textbooks, 175–77, 257; UNESCO views on, 113, 116, 133
inequality: as argument for land reform, 198–99; as causal variable for civil war, 6, 21; conservative views on, 67; and school system, 236–37, 241, 246, 251
Institute for Communications Research, Stanford University, 119, 230
Instituto de Educación por TV, 113
Instituto de Educación Técnica, 107
Instituto Magisterial de Prestaciones Sociales (Teachers' Institute for Social Welfare, IMPRESS), 100–101, 146–47, 158, 203

Instituto Nacional Agrario, Honduras
    (National Agrarian Institute, INA), 192
Inter-American Committee of the Alliance
    for Progress, 119
Inter-American Development Bank, 12, 73,
    115, 212, 264
International Labor Organization (ILO),
    116, 130
International Monetary Fund (IMF), 12
Ivory Coast, 133–34, 260

Japan: as inspiration for educational
    reform, 107, 109–10, 121, 134–35; support
    for reform, 173, 263
Japanese Broadcasting Corporation
    (Nippon Hōsō Kyōkai, NHK), 110, 121
Jiménez, Flavio, *hijo*, 146
Johns Hopkins University, 126
Johnson, President Lyndon B.: and Alli-
    ance for Progress, 14; and educational
    TV, 118–19, 134; visit to El Salvador in
    1968, 1–2, 163–64, 191–92

Kalijarvi, Ambassador Thorsten, 13, 57–59
Kennedy, President John F.: and Alliance
    for Progress, 12–15, 56, 61, 73, 263; and
    modernization theory, 13, 79–80; 123–24;
    Salvadoran opposition to, 68, 85–86
kindergarten, 110
Korea, 122, 123

Lancaster, Joseph, 115
land, and privatization of communal
    holdings in 1880s, 32, 199
land reform: as debated in the wake of 1969
    war with Honduras, 193–95; failed effort
    in 1976, 223–26; and 1970 Land Reform
    Congress, 196–201; and opposition by
    conservative spokespersons in early
    1960s, 67–68; and proposed need due
    to Cerrón Grande, 216–21
Lanza Diego, José, 130
La Prensa Gráfica, 77, 106, 203, 242
Lee, Rex, 142
Lemus, President José María, 50, 57–59,
    90–91

Lerner, Daniel, 79–80, 124, 141
Ley de Escalafón del Magisterio Nacional
    (Teachers' Salary Scale Law), 203–10
Ley de Protección Social para el Magisterio
    Nacional (Social Protection Law for
    National Teachers), 95
Ley General de Educación, 203–4
liberalism, 33–38
literacy, campaigns, 51, 108, 117; and the 1948
    junta, 12; and television, 125, 127, 130
Lobato, Carlos, 240
López, José Mario, 149, 150–51, 207, 240

Maheu, René, 129, 131
Mann, Thomas, 14
Manzinni, Sidney, 153
Martínez, Oscar Hilberto, 156
Masferrer, Alberto, 20
Matanza. *See* rebellion of 1932
Mayorga Quirós, Román, 114, 238
McAnany, Emile, 235
Medrano, General José Alberto "Chele,"
    77, 209
Mejoramiento Social (Social Betterment), 41
middle school: assessment of, 234, 237, 239,
    244–45; classroom construction, 170;
    as cornerstone of the reform, 162–63,
    181, 263; and educational TV, 140–41,
    159, 165; enrollments, 169, 205; in Japan,
    110; reclassified as primary school, 169;
    supervision of, 168; teachers, 166–67,
    201; teleclasses in, 185
Military Assistance Program, United States
    (MAP), 57
modernization. *See* development
modernization theory: and agenda of
    military regime, 135, 181, 225, 262;
    description of, 12, 78–83; and develop-
    ment community, 16, 181, 194, 265; as
    ideological foundation of Alliance for
    Progress, 13, 56; Salvadoran critiques
    of, 85, 244; in textbooks, 174; and
    UNESCO, 131, 133–34. *See also* Rostow,
    Walt Whitman; Schramm, Wilbur
Molina, President Arturo Armando,
    210–11, 211–22, 223–26

Montes, Segundo, 238, 240, 242, 267
Moscoso, Teodoro, 83
Murray Meza, Roberto, 173

National Arts Center, 172
National Association of Educational
    Broadcasters, 139, 159
National Conciliation Party. *See* Partido de
    Conciliación Nacional
National Directorate for Education, 167
National Guard, 77, 156, 199, 224
National Library, 143, 151, 174
National Palace, 97, 147, 150, 199, 207
Nippon Hōsō Kyōkai. *See* Japanese
    Broadcasting Corporation
normal schools, 37, 90, 141, 189. *See also*
    teacher training schools

Office of Facts and Figures, 122
Office of War Information, United States
    (OWI), 122
oligarchy. *See* elites
Orellana family, 212–14
Organización de Estados Centroameri-
    canos (Organization of Central Amer-
    ican States, ODECA), 178
Organización Democrática Nacionalista
    (National Democratic Organization,
    ORDEN), 77–78, 99, 156
Organization of American States (OAS),
    57, 130
Osegueda, Felix, 218
Osorio, President Oscar, 47–48

Pan American Union, 11
parents, 105, 170, 189, 243, 261, 266
Partido Comunista Salvadoreño
    (Communist Party of El Salvador,
    PCS), 66, 193
Partido de Acción Renovadora (Party of
    Renovating Action, PAR), 196
Partido de Conciliación Nacional
    (National Conciliation Party, PCN):
    critique of Christian Democratic Party,
    99–100; defending reforms against
    conservative attacks, 87–89; during the
era of President Rivera, 73–78; early
    attention to education, 106–7, 138;
    formation of, in 1961–1962, 60,
    72; and teachers' demands, 147. *See
    also* elections
Partido Demócrata Cristiano (Christian
    Democratic Party, PDC), 74; formation
    of, in 1960, 59; and IMPRESS, 147; as
    initial outlet for teachers' opposition
    to PCN, 93, 98; and the 1976 land
    reform, 223–24; during 1968 teachers'
    strike, 151–53, 156; reaction to the 1969
    war with Honduras, 192–93. *See also*
    elections
Partido Popular Salvadoreño (Salvadoran
    Popular Party, PPS), 196, 209
Partido Revolucionario de Unificación
    Democrática (Revolutionary Party
    of Democratic Unification, PRUD),
    47–53; reaction by conservative
    spokespersons, 53–56
Partido Revolucionario Institucional,
    Mexico (Institutional Revolutionary
    Party, PRI), 47
peace accords, 7, 22, 174
Peace Corps, 173, 264
pedagogy, and curricular innovations,
    179, 181, 232; deficiencies in, 138; in
    nineteenth century, 34–35; television
    and, 110, 114
plan básico. See middle school
Plan Quinquenal de Educación (Five-Year
    Plan for Education), 140
Plaza Libertad, 150–51
Point Four Program, 115
Portillo, Julio César, 132
Power, Colin N., 132
presidential elections. *See* elections
Presidential House, 98–99, 150
primary school: classroom construction,
    170; costs of, 237; discussion of educa-
    tional TV in, 161–63, 165; enrollments,
    36, 44, 161, 233; in Japan, 110; middle
    school reclassified as, 141; in nineteenth
    century, 37; supervision of, 168;
    textbooks, 178

Primer Seminario Nacional sobre la
Reforma Educativa, 238–43
private schools, 35–36, 162, 165–66, 236
Program on Information Technologies and
Public Policy, Harvard University, 234
psychological warfare, 121–23
Public Administration Service, 11
Punta del Este, 89, 118, 12–30, 134, 194

radio, 81, 107, 120–21, 125–26, 131
rebellion of 1932, 75, 210
Resistencia Nacional (National Resistance,
RN), 222
Revelo Borja, Ernesto, 110
revolution of 1948, 3, 10, 25, 46–53
Rey Prendes, Julio Adolfo, 75–76
Rivera, President Julio Adalberto,
antecedents of educational reform
under, 106–10, 113, 138, 140; election
of, 92, 106; meeting teachers during
1965 march, 98–99; as modernizer,
71–78, 102, 196, 225, 264; problems with
Honduras, 192; role in 1961 coup, 160;
on the role of planning in development
projects, 83; and teacher demands, 97,
100–101, 114
Rockefeller, Nelson A., 141
Rockefeller Foundation, 121–22, 175
Rodo, José Enrique, 38
Rodríguez Porth, José Antonio, 54, 64,
209; and role at 1970 Land Reform
Congress, 197–201; as propaganda
target of PCN, 87–88
Romero, Archbishop Oscar Arnulfo, 235,
253–54
Romero, Arturo, 46
Romero, President Carlos Humberto, 225,
238, 243
Romero Bosque, President Pío, and
democratization, 39
Ross, John, 138
Rostow, Walt Whitman, 12–13, 79–85,
123–24, 132, 134, 265

Salcedo, José Luís, 87
Salomón, Roberto, 172, 174

Samayoa, Salvador, 238
Sánchez Hernández, President Fidel: and
1969 war with Honduras, 193–98; and
1972 presidential election, 209–11; and
planning educational reform, 137–41;
and President Johnson's visit, 1–2;
remarks on educational television, 164,
183; response to teachers' demands,
145–47, 150, 154
Santiago, Chile, 129–32
Sarmiento, Domingo Faustino, 34, 53
Sarnoff, David, 120
school, administration, 37, 110, 158, 181;
construction, 73, 117, 130, 160–61, 167–68,
185, 229; supervision, 104, 111, 158–61,
167–68, 185, 229. *See also* high school;
middle school; primary school; private
schools; teacher training schools
Schramm, Wilbur, 80; and development
community, 265; ideas, 119–26;
influence on UNESCO, 121–33; revision
of his theories, 227–28, 246–47
Schultz, Theodore, 124
Seoul, 122
service sector, 111, 113
Siepmann, Charles, 127
Sistema Nacional de Retiros (National
Retirement System), 94, 97
Sobrino, Jon, 238
Sol Castellanos, Jorge, 48, 51, 53, 199
Soviet Union, 19, 153, 156, 260
Speagle, Richard E., 229–30, 249–50
*Stages of Economic Growth: A Non-
Communist Manifesto, The. See* Rostow,
Walt Whitman
Stiglitz, Bruno, 139–40, 162–63, 171
strikes: in the context of education reform
assessments, 235; effect on students,
266; 1971 teachers' strike, 201–9; 1968
teachers' strike, 143–44, 146–47, 149–58;
and peasant mobilization, 221. *See also*
ACERO metal factory strike

Taylor, Francis Henry, 120–21
teacher benefits, 26, 91, 100, 114, 146, 202
teacher manuals, 159, 177

teacher training schools, 1, 51, 92, 95, 119, 141, 143, 160, 166, 267. *See also* Ciudad Normal Alberto Masferrer; Escuela Normal Superior; normal schools

technical education, 107–8, 119

teleclasses, 233, 248; described, 165; problems with, 187–88, 190–91, 241, 247; and teacher manuals, 159; and textbooks, 186

teleclubs, 121

Telescuola, 121, 134, 159

teleteachers, 103–4, 159; interaction with classroom teachers, 165, 167, 188–89, 191, 201, 232, 236, 251; and students, 186–87, 190

textbooks, 104; and anticommunism, 117; business community input in, 257; as component of educational reform, 159, 174, 233, 251; costs of, 229; mass media and, 123, 125; modernization theory in, 175–80; student appreciation of, 186, 190

Third World, 12, 19, 115

traditional society, in El Salvador, 13, 84, 181; mass communications and, 120, 123–24, 133, 246; modernization theory and, 12, 79–80; in textbooks, 177

tuition, 104, 169, 205

UN Economic Commission for Latin America (ECLA), 150

UNESCO (United Nations Education, Scientific, and Cultural Organization), advisors, 111, 113–16, 145, 162, 171, 181, 232; cooperation with Alliance for Progress, 129; director general, 113, 126, 129, 132; and educational TV, 126–41, 231–32; General Conference, 110, 126, 129; and mass media, 110, 126, 263; and modernization theory, 16, 105; as part of development community, 16, 165, 264–65

UNESCO Courier, 82, 126–27, 131, 265

UNESCO International Institute for Educational Planning, 132

UN General Assembly, 131, 265

Ungo, Guillermo Manuel, 197, 240, 242

Unión Comunal Salvadoreña (Communal Union of El Salvador, UCS), 197

Unión Democrática Salvadoreña (Salvadoran Democratic Union), 65

Unión Magisterial Salvadoreña (Salvadoran Teachers' Union, UMS), 92, 95

Unión Nacional Opositora (National Opposition Union, UNO), 210–11, 225

United States: changes in policy toward Latin America due to the Cuban Revolution, 56–57; role in founding ORDEN, 78; role in promoting modernization theory, 82; views of the January 1961 coup, 60

United States Congress, 57, 117–18, 163, 234

United States Information Agency (USIA), 2, 82

United States Information Service (USIS), 61

United States Operations Mission (USOM), 61

Universidad Centroamericana "José Simeón Cañas" (Central American University, UCA), 6; assessment of educational reform, 238, 240, 243; participation in agrarian reform congress, 196–99; reaction to educational reform, 238–39, 243–46; report on 1968 education reform, 204; report on Cerrón Grande project, 214–17, 259; response to 1976 land reform, 223–26; response to PCN modernization, 88

Universidad Nacional de El Salvador (National University of El Salvador, UES), 88, 90, 196–97, 210, 218, 243, 259

USAID (United States Agency for International Development): advisors, 140, 165, 181; assessment of educational reform, 229–32, 237–38, 241, 247–49; and development community, 16, 130; and educational reform in general, 167, 178, 228; origins of, 115; support for educational TV, 2, 114, 117, 119, 134, 139; support for land reform, 223

USAID Regional Office for Central America and Panama (ROCAP), 178

Valdivieso Oriani, Ricardo, 69–70
Valiente, José Francisco, 64
Valle, Victor, 144, 202
Vaquerano, Arnoldo, 90, 98, 202; and 1971 teachers' strike, 201; and 1968 teachers' strike, 150–51, 158; opinion of President Rivera's political reforms, 76; on origins of ANDES, 90–91, 95, 98
Viera Altamirano, Napoleón, 25, 53–56, 66–68, 84–88

War Communications Division, 122
war with Honduras, in 1969, 191–96
Werthein, Jorge, 235–38, 249

White House Task Force on Educational Television in Less-Developed Countries, 118
World Bank, 74, 140; assessment of educational reform, 236, 245; El Salvador's requests to, 4, 111; and environmental impact report on Cerrón Grande, 215–16; loans for educational reform, 105, 143, 145, 163, 171; origins of, 115; in textbooks, 175
World Health Organization (WHO), 116
World War II, 45, 105, 115, 120–22, 194

Zapotitán Valley, 200–201

DIÁLOGOS

OTHER TITLES IN THE DIÁLOGOS SERIES AVAILABLE
FROM THE UNIVERSITY OF NEW MEXICO PRESS:

*Independence in Spanish America: Civil Wars, Revolutions,
and Underdevelopment* (revised edition)
—Jay Kinsbruner

Heroes on Horseback: A Life and Times of the Last Gaucho Caudillos
—John Charles Chasteen

The Life and Death of Carolina Maria de Jesus
—Robert M. Levine and José Carlos Sebe Bom Meihy

¡Que vivan los tamales! Food and the Making of Mexican Identity
—Jeffrey M. Pilcher

The Faces of Honor: Sex, Shame, and Violence in Colonial Latin America
—Edited by Lyman L. Johnson and Sonya Lipsett-Rivera

The Century of U.S. Capitalism in Latin America
—Thomas F. O'Brien

Tangled Destinies: Latin America and the United States
—Don Coerver and Linda Hall

Everyday Life and Politics in Nineteenth Century Mexico: Men, Women, and War
—Mark Wasserman

Lives of the Bigamists: Marriage, Family, and Community in Colonial Mexico
—Richard Boyer

*Andean Worlds: Indigenous History, Culture, and Consciousness
Under Spanish Rule, 1532–1825*
—Kenneth J. Andrien

The Mexican Revolution, 1910–1940
—Michael J. Gonzales

Quito 1599: City and Colony in Transition
—Kris Lane

A Pest in the Land: New World Epidemics in a Global Perspective
—Suzanne Austin Alchon

The Silver King: The Remarkable Life of the Count of Regla in Colonial Mexico
—Edith Boorstein Couturier

National Rhythms, African Roots: The Deep History of Latin American Popular Dance
—John Charles Chasteen

The Great Festivals of Colonial Mexico City: Performing Power and Identity
—Linda A. Curcio-Nagy

*The Souls of Purgatory: The Spiritual Diary of a
Seventeenth-Century Afro-Peruvian Mystic, Ursula de Jesús*
—Nancy E. van Deusen

Dutra's World: Wealth and Family in Nineteenth-Century Rio de Janeiro
—Zephyr L. Frank

Death, Dismemberment, and Memory: Body Politics in Latin America
—Edited by Lyman L. Johnson

Plaza of Sacrifices: Gender, Power, and Terror in 1968 Mexico
—Elaine Carey

*Women in the Crucible of Conquest: The Gendered Genesis of
Spanish American Society, 1500–1600*
—Karen Vieira Powers

Beyond Black and Red: African-Native Relations in Colonial Latin America
—Edited by Matthew Restall

Mexico OtherWise: Modern Mexico in the Eyes of Foreign Observers
—Edited and translated by Jürgen Buchenau

Local Religion in Colonial Mexico
—Edited by Martin Austin Nesvig

Malintzin's Choices: An Indian Woman in the Conquest of Mexico
—Camilla Townsend

From Slavery to Freedom in Brazil: Bahia, 1835–1900
—Dale Torston Graden

Slaves, Subjects, and Subversives: Blacks in Colonial Latin America
—Edited by Jane G. Landers and Barry M. Robinson

Private Passions and Public Sins: Men and Women in Seventeenth-Century Lima
—María Emma Mannarelli

*Making the Americas: The United States and Latin America
from the Age of Revolutions to the Era of Globalization*
—Thomas F. O'Brien

*Remembering a Massacre in El Salvador: The Insurrection of 1932,
Roque Dalton, and the Politics of Historical Memory*
—Héctor Lindo-Fuentes, Erik Ching, and Rafael A. Lara-Martínez

Raising an Empire: Children in Early Modern Iberia and Colonial Latin America
—Ondina E. González and Bianca Premo

*Christians, Blasphemers, and Witches: Afro-Mexican Rituals
in the Seventeenth Century*
—Joan Cameron Bristol

Art and Architecture of Viceregal Latin America, 1521–1821
—Kelly Donahue-Wallace

Rethinking Jewish-Latin Americans
—Edited by Jeffrey Lesser and Raanan Rein

True Stories of Crime in Modern Mexico
—Edited by Robert Buffington and Pablo Piccato

Aftershocks: Earthquakes and Popular Politics in Latin America
—Edited by Jürgen Buchenau and Lyman L. Johnson

Black Mexico: Race and Society from Colonial to Modern Times
—Edited by Ben Vinson III and Matthew Restall

The War for Mexico's West: Indians and Spaniards in New Galicia, 1524–1550
—Ida Altman

Damned Notions of Liberty: Slavery, Culture, and Power in Colonial Mexico, 1640–1769
—Frank Proctor

*Irresistible Forces: Latin American Migration to
the United States and its Effects on the South*
—Gregory B. Weeks and John R. Weeks

Cuauhtémoc's Bones: Forging National Identity in Modern Mexico
—Paul Gillingham

Slavery, Freedom, and Abolition in Latin America and the Atlantic World
—Christopher Schmidt-Nowara

SERIES ADVISORY EDITOR:
**Lyman L. Johnson,
University of North Carolina at Charlotte**